# THE FATHERS OF THE CHURCH

A NEW TRANSLATION

VOLUME 17

# THE FATHERS OF THE CHURCH

A NEW TRANSLATION

# SAINT PETER CHRYSOLOGUS
## SELECTED SERMONS

AND

# SAINT VALERIAN
## HOMILIES

*Translated by*

GEORGE E. GANSS, S.J.

THE CATHOLIC UNIVERSITY OF AMERICA PRESS
Washington, D. C.

IMPRIMI POTEST:

DANIEL H. CONWAY, S.J.
*Provincial, Missouri Province,*
*Society of Jesus*

NIHIL OBSTAT:

JOHN M. A. FEARNS, S.T.D.
*Censor Librorum*

IMPRIMATUR:

✠ FRANCIS CARDINAL SPELLMAN
*Archbishop of New York*

*January 12, 1953*

*The Nihil obstat and Imprimatur are official declarations that a book or pamphlet is free of doctrinal or moral error. No implication is contained therein that those who have granted the Nihil obstat and Imprimatur agree with the contents, opinions or statements expressed.*

Library of Congress Catalog Card No.: 65-27500


Reprinted, 1965, 1984

First Paperback Reprint 2004
ISBN 0-8132-1389-4 (pbk)

## CONTENTS

ST. PETER CHRYSOLOGUS

ST. VALERIAN

# SAINT PETER CHRYSOLOGUS

## SELECTED SERMONS AND LETTER TO EUTYCHES

*Translated by*

GEORGE E. GANSS, S.J., S.T.L., Ph.D.

*Marquette University*

## INTRODUCTION

IN MOST OF THE VOLUMES of this series, we chiefly see the Fathers as early champions of the faith philosophizing on the contents of the deposit of faith. They are restating in their contemporary terminology what God revealed, thrashing out what is obscure, showing the consistency of one revealed truth with another and with right reason, and little by little reducing the revealed truths of Scripture and tradition to an ordered system.

The present volume is somewhat different. In it we see two of the Fathers chiefly as preachers endeavoring to impart the life-giving message of Christianity to the people at large. St. Peter Chrysologus (*c.* 406-450), Archbishop of Ravenna and Doctor of the Church, and St. Valerian (fl. 439-460), Bishop of Cimiez near Nice in southern Gaul, were organs of tradition who were addressing their message not to the learned partisans of this or that school, but to the ordinary men and women of northern Italy or southern Gaul whose lives and manners were those of the fifth century.

In the Western Church, the terms sermon (*sermo*) and homily (*homilia*) were often interchangeable.[1] They seem to be so used in the titles of the printed collections which have come down to us: 'Sermons of St. Peter Chrysologus' and 'Homilies of St. Valerian.'

However, since the time of Origen (186-254 or 255), a distinction has been current between lógos (*sermo,* discourse, sermon) and homília (*homilia,* homily). The term sermon is generally used to designate an artistic production, and homily

1 *Catholic Encyclopedia* 7.488, *s.v.* Homily; *Oxford English Dictionary, s.v.* Homily; *Lexikon für Theologie und Kirche* 5, *s.v.* Homilitek.

to denote an informal discourse. A sermon generally develops some definite theme; a homily explains or comments on a passage of Scripture. The sermon usually deals with a doctrinal or moral subject, and is more likely to contain a structural form of introduction, body, and conclusion such as textbooks of rhetoric advocate. The homily is more likely to lack structural form, and move or even digress wherever the text leads the preacher. Generally, its purpose is to explain the literal meaning of the Scriptural passage, point out moral or ascetical applications, and perhaps develop accommodated or allegorical meanings. If we should follow this terminology, we could well reverse the titles which appear on our current Latin editions. Most of St. Peter's discourses are homilies giving a running commentary on a passage (*lectio*) of Scripture. St. Valerian's discourses usually take their departure from one verse of such a passage, but their nature is far more that of sermons treating a definite theme.

The oldest biography[2] we have of St. Peter Chrysologus was written about 830 by Abbot Andrew Agnellus, the ecclesiastical historian of Ravenna, and deserves limited credence. Manifestly written to edify as well as to recount history according to ninth-century skill in historical writing, it contains a substratum of fact which was enlarged by legend.

From this biography and the sermons of St. Peter does emerge the portrait of an able administrator and a faithful, zealous, holy bishop who effectively and regularly preached God's word to his flock and won their admiration of his ability as a sacred orator. Modern scientific historians,[3] by

2 Cf. *PL* 52.13-20; 106.554-559.

3 O. Bardenhewer, *Patrology* (1908) 526-527; G. Bardy, *Dictionnaire de théologie catholique* 12, 2e, cols. 1916-1917; G. Böhmer, *Bibliothek der Kirchenväter* 43 1-14; F. Cayré, *Handbook of Patrology* (1940) 2 154-155; H. Leclercq, *Dictionaire d'archaeologie chrétienne et de liturgie* 14, 2e, col. 2081, *s.v.* Ravenna; M. Schanz, *Gesch. der Röm. Litteratur* (1920) 4 538-540; *LTK s.v.* Chrysologus.

sifting Agnellus' account and seeking evidence from archaeology as well as St. Peter's sermons, have gathered the following details of his life.

He was born *c.* 406 at Forum Cornelii, present day Imola, in Aemilia. Under Pope Sixtus III (432-440) he was appointed Archbishop of Ravenna, probably *c.* 433, and perhaps while he was still only a deacon. Agnellus' story that St. Peter the Apostle and St. Appolinaris instructed the Pope in a vision to consecrate Peter rather than the candidate whom the Ravennese had chosen is quite certainly merely a legend. St. Peter preached his inaugural sermon in the presence of the daughter of Theodosius the Great, Galla Placidia,[4] who was regent of the Western Empire during the minority of her son Valentinian III. Peter was much interested in constructing and decorating ecclesiastical buildings and received help from her. Sometime before 439, Peter consecrated the Church of St. John the Evangelist, which was constructed in fulfillment of a vow made during a storm. In its apse, Peter was portrayed with a long beard, celebrating Mass in a ship, and with the empress present.[5]

St. Peter's chief importance was not as an outstanding theologian like Athanasius or Augustine, but as a shepherd who ruled his flock and preached well to its members. Loyally orthodox, he urged them to practice the Christian virtues. He explained to them the doctrines of the Church, especially the Incarnation, Virgin birth, and grace, and he vigorously attacked erroneous and dangerous doctrines. He faithfully supported the authority of the Roman See, too, and enjoyed the close friendship of St. Leo the Great (Pope, 440-461). In 448, Eutyches, the author of Monophysitism, was condemned by Bishop Flavian of Constantinople and his

4 Cf. Sermon 130 ( *PL* 52.556-557) ; Leclercq, *loc. cit.*
5 Cf. *DACL,* fasc. 145, cols. 2081, 2112; 6, col. 257, fig. 4850, *s.v.* Galla Placidia.

standing council. Eutyches refused to accept the sentence. He wrote for protection to Pope St. Leo and to St. Peter Chrysologus. St. Peter wrote a prudent, moderate and kindly reply[6] which is a model of Catholic spirit. He refused to express a judgment before the case was fully clear, and with tact and kindness admonished Eutyches to obey the Bishop of Rome: 'We give you this exhortation in regard to everything, honorable brother: obediently heed these matters which the most blessed Pope of the city of Rome has written; because blessed Peter who lives and presides in his own see proffers the truth of faith to those who seek it. For, in accordance with our pursuit of peace and of faith, we cannot decide upon cases of faith without the harmonious agreement of the Bishop of Rome.' This letter to Eutyches is the only piece of St. Peter's correspondence we possess.

Shortly after writing this letter he left his See of Ravenna for some unknown reason, and returned to Imola. He died there in about 450 and was buried in the Basilica of St. Cassian.

We first find his epithet Chrysologus, 'The Golden Orator,' in the *Life* written by Agnellus. Probably enough, someone invented it to give the Western Church a counterpart to St. John of Antioch, called Chrysostom, 'The Golden Mouthed.' St. Peter was declared a Doctor of the Church by Pope Benedict XIII in 1729. His feast is celebrated on December 4.

St. Peter and St. Valerian lived during the political and social changes brought on by the migration of nations and the crumbling of the Roman Empire in the West. During their lifetime, Ravenna, not Rome, was the political capital of the Roman Empire in the West, although Rome remained the religious capital.

The death of the Emperor Theodosius the Great in 395 resulted in the division of the Empire. His son Arcadius ruled

6 Cf. below p. 283.

at Constantinople and Honorius assumed power in the West. Pressure from the Huns who came from the interior of Russia forced such Germanic tribes as the Visigoths, Vandals, Alans, and Sueves to infiltrate into the Roman Empire in Gaul, Italy, Spain, and even Africa. Honorius deemed Rome too indefensible and therefore moved his residence to Ravenna, quite impregnable amid its network of canals. In 410, the Visigoths captured Rome, and plundered it for three days.

Honorius died in 423. In 425, Theodosius II, Emperor of the East, put Valentinian III upon the Western throne, which he held until 455. He was the five-year-old son of Galla Placidia and Constantius III. During his minority, his mother Galla Placidia was regent with the title of Augusta. From 429 until 454, except for a while in 432, the true director of imperial policy in the West was Valentinian's supporter Aetius, the Master of the Soldiers. His chief effort was to preserve central and southeastern Gaul for the Empire. While he was winning success in this, Africa, Britain, and most of Spain were lost. Attila led his Huns into Italy in 451 (perhaps the year of St. Peter's death), but a combination of circumstances led him to heed the appeal of Pope St. Leo I to withdraw without seizing Rome.

The gradual infiltration of the Germanic tribes grew to such proportions that when Romulus Augustulus, the puppet emperor crowned in 475, surrendered to Odovacar in 476, the point was reached which we today commonly regard as the end of the Roman Empire in the West. During the kingship of Odovacar (476-493), the last remnants of Roman authority vanished in Gaul and Spain, while Raetia and Noricum were abandoned to the Alemanni, Thuringi, and Rugii. Odovacar was blockaded in Ravenna by Theodoric, King of the Ostrogoths, in 490, and eventually surrendered. He was assasinated in 493.

During the fourth century, Christianity gradually triumphed over paganism as the official religion of the Roman

Empire. This left to the fifth century the work of consolidating the gains.

The last great persecution of the Christians stretched from 302 to 311 under Diocletian. In 313, at Milan, almost a century before St. Peter's birth, Constantine and Licinius published the edict of toleration which gave Christianity equal standing with paganism in the Empire. From that time on, Christianity gained one official victory after another. In 341, Constantius and Constans prohibited public performance of pagan sacrifices. They also permitted public confiscation of pagan temples and their conversion into Christian churches. Julian (Emperor, 360-363) attempted to make paganism once more the chief religion of the Empire, but the pagan cults had ceased to have enough appeal for the masses, and he failed. Gratian (Emperor, 375-383) deprived paganism of its status as an official religion of Rome. In 382, he withdrew the support of the pagan priesthoods and removed from the Senate House the altar and the statue of Victory—a symbol for many senators of Rome's devotion to her gods. Their spokesman Symmachus pleaded eloquently for its restoration, but Gratian, encouraged by Ambrose, remained firm. In 380, Theodosius I (Emperor, 378-395) issued an edict requiring all his subjects to embrace Christianity.

While this series of legal enactments eliminated paganism as one of Rome's official religions, it nevertheless lived on in many individuals. This was especially true of the rural districts, so that the very word for rural or rustic, *paganus,* came to designate a devotee of one of the old religions. The Oriental cults, the Orphic mysteries of Eleusis, the Graeco-Roman Olympic divinities, Neo-Platonism, and Stoicism still had a powerful hold on many votaries. The whole literature of Rome was pagan in origin and spirit, and it was all that was available for the rhetorical studies which were almost the only higher education of the times. Hence, it is small wonder that in the first half of the fifth century pagan practices and superstitions still clung to many Christians, especially the converts. The deeply ingrained outlook, morals, and mores of heathenism could not be removed from a society in one or two generations. In the fifth century we see the Christian writers—among them St. Peter Chrysologus and St. Valerian of Cimiez—hard at work trying to replace these relics of paganism with a truly Christian outlook and practice. Noteworthy examples are St. Peter's Sermon 155 on the pagan profanation of New Year's Day, and St. Valerian's castigation of parasites and other abuses at banquets in his Homily 10.

Their sermons and homilies quite naturally reflect the social conditions of the times. Their hearers lived in a society which, still full of the customs of paganism, took delight in the public games, with bleeding beasts and even men, riotous banquetings, the coarse theater, and other amusements which rather horrify us today. Sometimes we may be shocked so badly at the vices revealed in the discourses as to wonder if the hearers were as yet truly Christians at heart. But we should remember that in the discourses we also see the ideals of virtue which the preachers and their hearers recognized. The men of any generation should be judged more by the ideals they were striving to formulate and attain than by their shortcomings through human weakness.

The fourth and fifth centuries were days of theological controversies, which re-echo in the sermons. Hence, a brief review of several of the burning issues of that age will aid the general reader towards a better understanding of the sermons of St. Peter or St. Valerian. We today can express the fundamental Catholic beliefs about the Trinity, Incarnation, and grace with a clear and time-tested terminology. The theologians of those earlier centuries were hard at work evolving a suitable terminology to explain or defend them.

The Catholic doctrine of the Trinity, briefly put, is this: The Father, and the Son or 'Word,' and the Holy Spirit are three distinct and equal divine Persons who possess the numerically one divine nature, and operate by it. The Word or Son, the second Person of the Trinity, eternally proceeds from the Father by generation from His intellect. Likewise, He eternally possesses the divine nature and by it performs all the activities of God. At the time of the Incarnation He took to Himself also a human nature, was born of Mary and named Jesus. By that human nature He performed the activities natural to men. Thus, we have a second great mystery: one divine Person possesses two complete natures, one human and one divine, and He operates by them. He received the human nature from the Virgin Mary. She conceived Him miraculously without the intervention of any human father, and miraculously retained even bodily virginity after His birth. In human speech we say that a mother is the mother of the person of her son, or, more simply still, that she is the mother of him who is her son; we do not pedantically say that she is the mother of the body of her son. We say that Monica was the mother of Augustine; we do not take pains to say that she was the mother of Augustine's body. Now, in the case of Mary, she was the mother of Him who is named Jesus. But, He is a divine Person, He is God, God become also a man. Hence, we rightly say either that Mary was the mother of Jesus, or that she was the mother of God, or of Him who is God become a man. This Catholic doctrine is a restatement in philosophical terms of data revealed by God, especially in Scripture. Naturally enough, some of the earlier efforts to restate Scripture miscarried. Many errors were made in good faith. But some theologians became tenacious in error.

Arianism, inaugurated by Bishop Arius (*c.* 250-336), regarded the Word or Son of God not as God, but as a creature greater than other creatures. He was not a person possessing the same nature or substance as the Father (consubstantial, homooúsios), but only a person like the Father (*homoi*-oúsios). He was unlike the Father in that He had a beginning, but like Him in possesssing the other divine perfections. The doctrine of Arianism was condemned at the Council of Nicaea (325), but adherents continued to multiply. In the first half of the fifth century almost half of the Christians were Arians, especially in the East. St. Peter Chrysologus often opposes Arianism in his sermons.

While opposing Arianism, Nestorius (Patriarch of Constantinople, 428-431; died, *c.* 451) came to conceive the two natures possessed by Christ as being possessed by two persons, one divine and one human. In the case of Christ, these two persons were united, like men forming a society, into one *moral* person. Consequently, Nestorius denied that Mary was *theótokos,* mother of God (a term already long in use at Constantinople). He would admit only that she was *Christótokos,* mother of Christ, that is, of the human person and nature of Christ.[7] His doctrine was condemned at the Council of Ephesus (431) about the time when St. Peter became Archbishop of Ravenna, and again at Chalcedon (451). St. Peter frequently insists that Mary is the Mother of Him who is God.

Eutyches (*c.* 378-451) went so far in combatting Nestorianism that he fell into an opposite error: after the union of the two natures there is but one nature in Christ. This doctrine, called Monophysitism, was condemned by the General Council of Chalcedon in 451. The words of the Council are: 'Wherefore all of us, following the holy Fathers, have learned to confess with one voice one and the same Jesus Christ our Lord, and that He is perfect in His divinity and perfect in His humanity, truly God and truly man, and that He has a rational soul and a body; that He is consubstantial with

7 St. Peter combats this opinion in Sermon 145; cf. below, pp. 235, 236.

the Father according to His divinity, and consubstantial with us according to His humanity, like to us in all things except sin; begotten from the Father before time according to His divinity, but in these last days, for us and for our salvation, born according to His humanity from Mary the Virgin, the Mother of God.'[8]

A third important doctrine filled with mysteries is that of grace. Every human person has a nature composed of a body and soul. Man, having a body, can walk and eat; having a soul, he can reason, love and freely decide. The power to think and reason is called the intellect. The power to love and freely decide is named the will. By these powers which belong to his nature man has the physical abilities to obey the natural law and achieve a natural everlasting happiness which would satisfy all his capacities of intellect and will. He would know God, the infinite Truth, by means of indirect or mirrorlike concepts; this would satisfy his capacities of intellect. He would know God as being the infinite Good; consequently, he would love Him; this would satisfy his capacities of loving. By this knowing and loving He would have joy.

But God chose to elevate man to the supernatural order. He gave man the wonderful destiny of knowing God directly, 'face to face,' of loving God, and of enjoying Him. Man does not, from his nature, have the means to attain the end God set for him. But, because of His overflowing love, God gave man such a means: a new quality which God infuses into the soul. It is called grace, or supernatural life. It is of two kinds. The permanent grace, called sanctifying, makes the soul a source or principle capable of performing here below supernaturalized acts meritorious of the direct vision of God. The transient grace, called actual, is a supernaturalized light sent by God into man's intellect, or an impulse sent into his will

8 From the Greek in Denzinger, *Enchiridion symbolorum*, n. 148.

which enables these powers to perform their acts as supernaturalized acts, meritorious of the supernatural happiness, direct vision of God.

Without these supernaturalized lights and impulses, man could perform some acts of virtue; for example, of justice or fortitude. But he would not have the physical power to perform these as supernaturalized acts, that is, as acts furthering him to the supernaturalized destiny. Actual grace also exerts a strengthening or healing effect on the human will, so that the person develops the strength to carry through with his virtuous acts.

Without this interior influence of grace on his soul, the 'unjustified' adult (he who has not yet received sanctifying grace) cannot begin or complete any supernaturalized act positively leading him to God's free gift of sanctifying grace or to the actual vision of God. Christ said: 'Without me you can do nothing.'[9] 'No one can come to me unless the Father . . . draw him.'[10] And St. Paul stated: 'work out your salvation with fear and trembling. For it is God who of his good pleasure works in you both the will and the performance.'[11]

Pelagianism, inaugurated by the monk Pelagius at Rome about 405, flourished especially in Italy, Africa, and Gaul. It maintained at first that man can by his own strength of will avoid sin and merit heaven or supernatural happiness; that, consequently, man does not need an interior grace to perform virtuous acts. What, then, is grace? Merely God's gift of free will itself; or (in Semi-Pelagianism later on), having the Gospel preached to one. After a time, Pelagius admitted grace as something interior in the will but distinct from it. Nevertheless, he held that its function was not to begin virtuous acts but to complete them, and that it is not

9 John 15.5.
10 John 6.44.
11 Phil. 2.12,13.

necessary for the attainment of the beatific vision, but only makes it easier for man to do what he could otherwise do by himself. St. Augustine was the vigorous opponent of Pelagianism. It was condemned at the Council of Carthage in 318 and again at the Council of Orange in 529.

A modified form of Pelagianism lived on as Semi-Pelagianism, which arose largely from some teachings of the holy and sincere abbot Cassian (*c*.360-*c*.435). Trying to strike a position midway between Augustine and the Pelagians, it maintained that man can 'of himself' (*de se*) do some good works conducive to supernatural salvation. Man can of himself produce the 'beginning of faith' by good resolutions, holy aspirations and desires—though, assuredly, God can also produce them. Thus, grace merely follows the movement of the intellect or will.

Many propositions of Semi-Pelagianism were condemned at the Council of Orange in 529. The reader will find in St. Peter and St. Valerian,[12] many passages in similar vein to the following statements of the Council of Orange which the two saints antedate.[13]

*Canon 4.* 'If anyone says that, for us to be cleansed from sin, God ought to await our will, but he does not admit that it happens through the infusion of the Holy Spirit into us and His operating upon us that we even desire to be cleansed, he resists the Holy Spirit, who spoke through Solomon: "The will is prepared by God"; and he also resists Paul who preaches: "It is God who of His good pleasure works in you both the will and the performance." '

*Canon 18.* 'A reward is due because of good works, if they are performed; but grace, which is not due, comes beforehand in order that they may be performed.'

---

12 E.g., St. Peter, Sermons 2 (below, p. 32); 47 (below, p. 101); 114 (below, p. 187); St. Valerian, Homily 11 (below, pp. 369-376).

13 Denzinger, *op. cit.*, n. 177, which quotes Prov. 8.35 (Itala) and Prov. 2.13; also, n. 191.

A collection of 176 discourses has come down to us under the title, 'Sermons of St. Peter Chrysologus.' He referred to them by the words,[14] often used as synonyms in close proximity, *sermo* (discourse, discussion, sermon) and *tractatus* (treatise, homily, sermon). No doubt, he understood the term *tractatus* as St. Augustine did: 'treatises to the people which are called homilies in Greek.'[15] Felix, Archbishop of Ravenna from about 707 to 717, first gathered the sermons from some private library.[16] They were first printed by Agapitus Vincentinus in 1534 at Bologna. Schoenemann[17] lists forty-four printings of the collection between 1534 and 1761—a fact which attests their popularity in this era. In 1643, the parish priest of the diocese of Imola, Dominic Mita, published an annotated edition, and composed the titles which are printed above the single sermons in Migne.[18] Perhaps the best edition of the text is that published by Sebastian Pauli at Venice in 1750. Our translation is chiefly based on it. It was reprinted in Migne, *PL* 52, where it is somewhat marred by troublesome misprints. The text of the collection has come down to us in very poor condition, and no critical edition has yet been produced. Some of the sermons in this collection are not genuine; among these are Sermons 107, 135, 138, 149.[19] Possibly, too, some other sermons of St. Peter have been published under the names of other authors. The best means as yet available to distinguish the genuine from the spurious sermons are the style and language, especially the handling

---

14 Cf. Sermons 5 (below, p. 51); 40 (below, p. 86, n. 2); 82 (*PL* 52.432C); 122 (below, p. 209).

15 Cited in *Harper's Latin Dictionary, s.v. tractatus: tractatus populares, quos Graece homilias vocant,* Aug. Haeres. 4 praef. Cf. also, Souter, *Glossary of Later Latin.*

16 *PL* 52.13,14. Cf. also, F. J. Peters, *Petrus Chrysologus als Homilet* (Köln 1918) 3-4.

17 *PL* 52.79-90.

18 *PL* 52.13; 46.

19 Böhmer, *op. cit.* 3; Peters, *op. cit.* 45-46.

of the rhythms of the *cursus*. But this means is highly unsatisfactory because of the poor condition of the text.

Most of the sermons are moral in character. Their chief purpose is to bring the hearers to lead a more intensively Christian life and to avoid the vices then prevalent in society. Instruction in matters of doctrine is abundantly present, but for the most part it is brought in incidentally and as a means to the moral end.

Some of the sermons, however, are doctrinal. In these the favorite subjects are the Incarnation and the Blessed Virgin, and they are directed against the Arians and Nestorians. Sermons 56-62 form a series of explanations of the Apostle's Creed, and Sermons 67-72 a series of commentaries on the Lord's Prayer. The two series were given to the catechumens to prepare them for baptism.

The sermons indicate that St. Peter preached on almost all Sundays, on the feasts of saints and martyrs, and on such special occasions as the consecration of bishops. He was a firm believer in short sermons. Most of those we have require approximately fifteen minutes to deliver, and the rest are much shorter. He frequently stated[20] that he did not want to weary his hearers by speaking too long. When his theme or the passage of Scripture required long treatment, he extended it through several discourses. Thus, his treatment of the Parable of the Prodigal Son runs through five complete sermons. His opinion on the value of short sermons can be gathered from Sermons 32, 122, 132. Sometimes he preached from the altar steps; sometimes, from his episcopal chair (Sermon 173).[21]

Most of the sermons were evidently connected with the divine service of the Mass or Office.[22] In the liturgy of the

20 E.g., in the conclusions of Sermons 1-4.
21 Böhmer, *op. cit.* 4; cf. Sermon 173 (*PL* 52.651A).
22 Böhmer, *op. cit.* 4.

fourth and fifth centuries,[23] the Mass of the Catechumens included the singing of psalms and the reading aloud of passages or pericopes from Scripture. After the Kyrie came one reading (*lectio*: reading, passage, pericope) from the Old Testament, then a chanting of psalms usually in the form of responses, then a reading from the Epistles of the New Testament. Shortly later was a reading from the Gospel to the people, usually by a deacon. These passages were not yet fully fixed or assembled in the liturgical books called lectionaries, but often were selected by the bishop. A commentary followed the reading from the Gospel. This is the moment at which most of the homilies of the Fathers were delivered. Immediately afterwards, the catechumens were dismissed. Abundant evidence within the sermons reveals their connection with these liturgical chantings and readings. For example, Sermon 44 contains 'The psalm which we sang today';[24] Sermon 114 has 'Let us hear what the Apostle has said today';[25] Sermon 98, on Luke 13.18,19, begins with, 'Today, brethren, you have heard.'[26]

St. Peter almost always began with an introduction of a paragraph or two. Then he would generally repeat the phrases of the passage (*lectio*) one by one and make his comments upon them, though sometimes, as in Sermon 40, he merely used the passage or a phrase from it to launch into a sermon on a theme of his own. No set or customary order is found in the body of his homilies. He went where his text or his own thought took him. He made applications to the daily lives of his hearers as he went along, and especially in his conclusions. Often, he added a short doxology.

23 Poulet-Raemers, *A History of the Catholic Church* I 260.

24 Cf. below, p. 95.

25 Cf. below, p. 185, and similar remarks near the beginnings of Sermons 108-120.

26 Cf. below, p. 156.

Sometimes he spoke in the colloquial language of his hearers, as he says in Sermon 43,[27] but generally his language reflects the rhetorical training and tastes of his age,[28] and his sermons can be arranged in sense lines with ease. He takes a Roman rhetorician's manifest delight in the clever turning of words, phrases, and thoughts. In fact, without this deference to the tastes of his age, he would scarcely have pleased his hearers who had been educated in the schools of rhetoric. His thought moves quickly.[29] Sermon 108, for example, is in a beautiful, terse and rapid style. Its unusually short sentences form a series of staccato blows, and it must have produced a strong emotional effect on the hearers both by its form and its solid, beautiful content. Much the same is true of Sermon 132. At times, he heaps up synonyms or similar phrases in a manner which perhaps wearies a modern reader,[30] and occasionally he loses the importance of his point in a display of rhetoric.[31] Now and then there are abrupt changes of thought or of tense, statements, or citations from Scripture which seem to have little or nothing to do with the context. No doubt, many of these cases arise from the poor condition of the text from which some sentences have disappeared. While there are some obscure passages,[32] the general tenor of his thought is almost always clear.

His deep sincerity shines through the sermons in a delightful manner. Undoubtedly, he loved God, Christ, Mary, the saints, the martyrs, and his fellow men very deeply. In many

27 Cf. below, p. 90; also, Sermon 112 (below, p. 180).

28 E.g., Sermons 4 (below, pp. 39-40); 40 (below, pp. 85-89); 152 (below, p. 258). J. H. Baxter, in *Journal of Theological Studies* 22 (1921) 250-258, is excellent on the rhetoric of St. Peter Chrysologus.

29 E.g., in Sermons 40, 43, 44, 108.

30 E.g., in Sermons 4 (below, pp. 39-43) and 38 (below, pp. 81-85).

31 Sermon 57 (below, p. 108 n. 13).

32 Sermons 1 (below, p. 26 n. 3); 5 (below, pp. 43-46); 40 (below, p. 87 n. 6).

passages, if the reader proceeds slowly while relishing each thought, he will discover that he is not so much reading a sermon as making mental prayer of contemplation.[33]

Saint Peter's sermons, being exegetical homilies, are heavily weighted with quotations from Scripture. According to Sebastian Pauli,[34] there are 357 citations from the Old Testament and 234 from the New. This shows that he was thoroughly acquainted with the Bible and could readily draw from memory an apt text to reinforce his moral teaching and edify the faithful.

His interpretations are, on the whole, in harmony with the other Fathers. But sometimes they are ingenious rather than profound.[35] He was acting not so much as a scholarly exegete as a writer of homilies seeking to edify his hearers, and also to please them. Hence, his interpretation occasionally sprang more from the Roman rhetorician's instinct to play on words than from scholarly investigation,[36] as in Sermon 3: 'The stout calf is evidence that the father's charity is stout.' Quite naturally, he had a love of the allegorical or mystical interpretation so much used by many of the Fathers, even Augustine, in their homilies. This, too, was something in which a Roman audience, trained in rhetoric, would take delight. St. Peter's views on exegesis found clear expression in Sermons 36 and 146. 'The historical narrative should always be raised to a higher meaning, and mysteries of the future should become known through figures of the present.'[37] 'Neither the tips of the letters, nor the letters themselves, nor the syllables, nor any word, nor the names, nor

---

33 E.g., the first half of Sermon 6 or the last half of 40.

34 Cited by Böhmer, *op. cit.* 10.

35 As S. Pauli pointed out already in 1758 (*PL* 52.9,10). Cf. also, Böhmer, *op. cit.* 10-11.

36 E.g., Sermon 44 (below, p. 97 n. 5).

37 Cf. below, p. 78.

the persons in the Gospel are free from divine allegorical meanings.'[38]

The allegorical interpretation of Scripture is a useful means for a preacher to illustrate and clarify the point he is making for the edification of his audience. But it has disadvantages and a danger, too. It often leads him to make a minor point into a major one, to give explanations which are strained, to digress, or to substitute an allegorical interpretation for an explanation of a difficult passage. The danger is that the hearers may mistake the allegorical interpretation of the preacher as one of the meanings intended by God when He inspired the Scriptural writer to pen the passage. To know what to make of St. Peter's methods, the modern reader will do well to recall the chief principles of the interpretation of Scripture commonly accepted by Catholic interpreters today.

Catholic interpreters,[39] speak of three 'senses' or meanings which a passage of Scripture may have: (1) the literal sense; (2) the typical sense; (3) the accomodated sense.

The *literal* sense (also called the historical or grammatical sense) is the meaning which the inspired writer directly intended to express by his words. For example, we readily see the literal sense of Luke 1.5: 'In the days of Herod, ... there was a certain priest named Zachary.' The literal sense may be expressed by a figure, for example, a metaphor; then it is called the improper literal sense. Thus, in Ps. 76.16, by '*With thy arm* thou hast redeemed thy people,' the Psalmist meant: '*By thy power* Thou has redeemed thy people.' Every passage in the Bible has one literal sense.

The *typical* sense (also called spiritual, mystical) is an additional meaning *added by God* (through an inspired writer) to some thing, event, or person designated by the lit-

38 Cf. below, p. 240.

39 Cf., for example, J. E. Steinmueller, *A Companion to Scripture Studies* (New York 1941) I 226-265.

eral sense of some passage. Thus, we readily see that by the literal sense of Gen. 2.7, 'The Lord God formed man out of the dust of the ground,' God through the inspired writer is telling us about Adam, the father of all men; and in Rom. 5.14, 'Adam, who is a figure of him who was to come,' *God* is telling us, through St. Paul, that Adam is a type foreshadowing Christ. The typical sense presupposes the literal sense and is built upon it. Only God can put a typical sense upon the thing, event, or person signified by the literal sense. A mere man may discover similarities in the persons, events, or things which made them suitable for God to give them the additional typical meaning had He wished to do so. But, if the man says on his own authority alone that they actually have such a typical meaning, he is unwarrantedly reading something into God's text. The man may, of course, notice the similarities, use them as the occasions of his own meditations, and draw much edification and profit for his own or his neighbor's spiritual life. But he should not say on his own authority alone that God intended to prefigure.

The *accomodated* sense is a meaning read into a Scriptural text by an interpreter. It is not a means of theological proof, because, unlike the literal and the typical senses, it was not intended by the sacred writer as a meaning of the passage. The interpreter finds words of Scripture which out of their context fit another situation, and uses them. He may do this for purposes of edification. The writers of the New Testament, the Fathers, and the Church herself in her liturgy have thus 'accomodated' texts. An accomodated sense should not be given as the true meaning of a passage.

Naturally enough, in the third, fourth, and fifth centuries these precise principles, definitions, and terms were not yet worked out fully, or universally accepted. Two outstanding schools of interpretation of Scripture were still debating each other. The school of Alexandria promoted the allegorical interpretation of Scripture; its chief scholar was Origen (186-254 or 255). The school of Antioch insisted on the literal or historical meaning, and opposed the allegorical interpretation. Its brilliant star was St. John Chrysostom (344-407).

Origen distinguished three senses in Scripture.[40] (1) The *corporal* or obvious sense—roughly equivalent to our present-day literal sense—is the lowest. It is expressed without figures, and is meant for beginners who cannot grasp the higher senses. (2) The *psychic* sense is a kind of moral sense: Scripture was intended to teach men what they should do. Origen gives this sense almost no attention. (2) The *spiritual* sense (which may also be called the anagogical, allegorical, mystical, or metaphorical sense) is the highest sense, intelligible only to the most learned. It included everything under what we call the improper literal sense, the typical sense, and the accommodated sense. Thus, for Origen, historical facts could be taken as symbols for other things; and metaphors, especially the highly developed metaphors called allegories, could supplement or even replace the literal sense. Origen also held this theory which all modern exegetes reject: everything in Scripture has a higher or allegorical meaning, but many passages do not have a corporal or literal sense; for if they did, there would be scandals and absurdities in the Bible.

This allegorical method of interpreting Scripture won wide acceptance among the Greek and Latin Fathers, but, because it obviously opens the way to abuses and far-fetched interpretations, it soon met strong and continued opposition, especially from the school of Antioch. This school insisted on the grammatical and historical meaning of Scripture, our modern literal sense. St. John Chrysostom of Antioch explained most of the Scriptures in his homilies. He prudently rejected the allegorical interpretation of Origen, and held,[41]

40 *Ibid.* 254; Cayré, *op. cit.* I 208
41 Steinmuller. *op. cit.* I 258.

(1) the literal sense, (2) the allegorical sense, which is what we term the improper literal or the figurative sense, (3) the anagogical sense (which is what we term the typical sense).

Among the Latin Fathers,[42] large use of Origen's principles was made by St. Hilary of Poitier (315-367) and St. Ambrose (340-397). St. Jerome, steering a middle course between the historical and allegorical senses, preferred the allegorical meaning when he found the historical sense difficult. In his later works he insisted more on the literal sense.

St. Augustine (354-430) adhered to the literal sense in his theological works, but in his homilies he indulged in allegories, moral applications, and mystical interpretation of numbers.

Hence, it is clear that St. Peter Chrysologus was following a practice common in his times when he so frequently used allegorical interpretation, as did Origen and Ambrose, and mystical interpretation of numbers,[43] as did Augustine. But, to his credit, St. Peter did not follow Origen in the opinion that some passages of Scripture lack a literal sense.[44]

The Scriptural texts as cited by St. Peter and St. Valerian often but not always differ slightly from the wording of our Latin Vulgate, either because they were using the Latin translation of the Greek Septuagint known as the Itala, or because they were quoting from memory. I have translated the Latin wording used by the saints, but tried to use, as far as possible, the English of the Confraternity Edition of the New Testament and of Genesis, and that of the Challoner-Rheims-Douay version for the rest of the Old Testament.

---

42 *Ibid.* I 261.

43 E.g., in Sermons 5, 11, 36, 170 (*PL* 52.198A; 221A; 303; 645).

44 Cf. S. Pauli's observation in *PL* 52.9D.

## SELECT BIBLIOGRAPHY

*Texts*:

J. P. Migne, *S. Petri Chrysologi Archiepiscopi Ravennatis Opera Omnia*, et *S. Valeriani Episcopi Cemeliensis Scripta Universa*, *PL* 52 (Paris 1894).

Margarino de La Bigne, in *Maxima Bibliotheca Veterum Patrum* (Lyons 1677). Vol. 7, S. Petri Chrysologi, *Sermones in evangelia;* Vol 8, S. Valeriani Episcopi Cemeliensis, *Homiliae XX*.

Seb. Pauli, *S. Petri Chrysologi Sermones, Editio omnium certe castigatissima* (Augsburg 1758).

J. Sirmond, *Sancti Valeriani Episcopi Cemeliensis Homiliae XX* (Augsburg 1758).

*Translations*:

M. Held, *Ausgewählte Reden des hl. Petrus Chrysologus, in Bibliothek der Kirchenväter* 67 (Kempten 1874).

G. Böhmer, *Des hl. Petrus Chrysologus... ausgewählte Predigten*, in *Bibliothek der Kirchenväter* 43 (München und Kempten 1923).

There are no translations of St. Valerian.

*Secondary Works*:

J. H. Baxter, 'The Homilies of St. Peter Chrysologus,' *Journal of Theological Studies* 22 (1921) 250-258.

G. Böhmer, *Petrus Chrysologus, Erzbischof von Ravenna, als Prediger. Ein Beitrag zur Geschichte der altchristl. Predigt.* (Paderborn 1919).

G. Bardy, 'Pierre Chrysologue,' *Dictionnaire de Théologie Catholique*, XII, 2e, cols. 1916-1917 (Paris 1935).

G. Bardy, 'Valerian de Cimelium', *DTC*, fascicules 144-145. Ulfila-Vatican, cols. 2520-2522 (Paris 1948).

F. Cayré, *Manual of Patrology and History of Theology*, tr. H. Howitt, 2 vols. (Rome 1936, 1940).

D. De Bruyne, O.S.B., 'Nouveaux Sermons de St. Pierre Chrysologue,' *Journal of Theological Studies* 29 (1928) 362-368.

S. Dill, *Roman Society in the Last Century of the Western Empire* (London 1898).

C. Jenkins, 'Aspects of the Theology of St. Peter Chrysologus,' *Church Quarterly Review* 103 (1927) 233-259.

H. Leclercq, 'Ravenne', *Dictionnaire d'archéologié chretienne et de liturgie*, fascicules 160-161, cols. 2079-2146 (Paris 1947).

C. Poulet, *A History of the Catholic Church*, tr. S. Raemers, Vol. I, (St. Louis 1934).

M. Schanz, C. Hosius, G. Krüger, *Geschichte der römischen Litteratur*, Vierter Teil,... bis zum Gesetzgebungswerk Justinians (München 1920).

A. Souter, *A Glossary of Later Latin to 600 A.D.* (Oxford 1949).

# SERMON 1

## *The Prodigal Son and His Brother: The Prodigal's Departure*

(On Luke 15.11-16)

Today, the Lord has summoned a father with his two sons and made them the center of our attention.[1] By this beautiful figure He has desired to open up for us an unfathomable revelation of His own love, the fierce jealousy of the Jewish race, and the penitent return of the Christian people.[2]

'A certain man had two sons. And the younger of them said to his father, Father, give me the share of the property that falls to me. And,' the text goes on, 'he divided his means between them.' The son is as impatient as the father was kind. He is weary of his father's being alive. Since he cannot shorten his father's life, he strives to get possession of his property. He was not content to possess his father's wealth

1 Luke 15.11-32, the entire account of the Prodigal Son, formed the *lectio* or passage read aloud to the congregation during the liturgical service. Then St. Peter began his homily on the passage. In Sermon 1 he treated verses 11-16. In Sermons 2, 3, 4 he treated the remaining verses. Finally, in Sermon 5, he gave an allegorical interpretation of the entire passage.

Throughout the rest of St. Peter's sermons no further references will be given to citations of Scripture which formed part of the *lectio*.

2 This introductory paragraph gives the theme of the entire series and foreshadows the allegorical interpretation given in Sermon 5. St. Irenaeus, St. Jerome, St. Augustine, Pseudo-Dionysius, and many other Fathers also regarded the Prodigal Son as a symbol of the Gentiles and his elder brother as a symbol of the Jews. Cf. *PL* 52.190.

in company with his father; and he deserved to lose the privileges of a son.

But let us make some inquiries. What reason brought the son to such attempts? What bold prospect raised his spirits to make so startling a request? What reason? Clearly, the fact that the Father in heaven cannot be bounded by any limit, or shut in by any time, or destroyed by any power of death.[3] The son could not await his father's death to get his wealth. So he conceived the desire to get his pleasure from the generosity[4] of his father still alive. That was the insult which lay in his request, as the father's very bounty proved.

'And he divided his means between them,' the text states. At the request of the one son he soon divided all his means between the two. He wanted both sons to know the fact that up till then he had been holding on to his property because of love, not miserliness; that foresight, not jealousy, was the reason he had not given it away. He retained control of his property to preserve it for his sons, not to refuse it to them. He did not want his fortune to perish, but to remain intact for his sons.

Oh, happy are the sons whose entire property rests in the love of their father! Happy are the sons whose whole wealth consists in showing allegiance and honor to a father! Material riches, by contrast, tear unity apart, break the bond of brotherly love, disrupt family relationships, and violently sunder the ties of love between the members of a family. All this grows perfectly clear from the words which follow. 'Father, give me the share of the property that falls to me. And,' the text

3 This sentence, shifting the thought so suddenly from the earthly to the heavenly Father, is obscure at this point. Its meaning becomes clear only in the light of the entire series, which expounds the limitless goodness of God.

4 *viventis liberalitate* with Böhmer, B K V 43, 200, not *videndi libertate* or *vivendi libertate*.

continues, 'he divided his means between them. And not many days later the younger son gathered up all his wealth, and took his journey into a far country; there he squandered his fortune in loose living. And after he had spent all, there came a grievous famine over that country, and he began himself to suffer want. And he went and joined one of the citizens of that country who sent him to his farm to feed swine. And he longed to fill his belly with the pods which the swine were eating, but no one offered to give them to him.'

See what covetousness works in its headlong pursuit of wealth. See how, without the father, this wealth did not enrich the son; it stripped him. It took him away from his father's bosom, expelled him from his house, withdrew him from his country, despoiled him of his reputation, and robbed him of his chastity. Whatever there is of life, good morals, filial reverence, liberty, glory—of all these it left him nothing. Indeed, it changed a citizen into a wanderer, a son into a hired servant, a rich man into a beggar, a free man into a slave. It separated him from a devoted father, and made him the companion of the swine. Consequently, he who spurned obedience to his father's sacred love became the servant of the muddy herd.

'The younger son gathered up all his wealth,' the text goes on. Clearly, it was because of his mentality rather than his age that he was the younger. It was in mind rather than in regard to place that he gathered up his father's goods and went far away. And it was by paying a price rather than by receiving one that he wretchedly sold himself into slavery. That is the type of contract this trader came to—he who did not know how to pay his debt to his parents, or make a fit return to his father. In his father's house is agreeable order, free service, perfect care, pleasant reverence, kindly correction, rich poverty, unworried possession. The work is done for the father, but the fruit redounds to the sons.

'He squandered his fortune,' it says. The spendthrift son dissipates the goods accumulated under the father's control; all too late does he realize that his father has been the manager of his wealth, not its miserly possessor. 'In loose living.' Such a life is destined to death, because its virtues are dying. If a man lives for vices, his reputation gets buried, his glory perishes. If he tarries for debauchery, his infamy grows.

'And after he had spent all, there came a grievous famine over that country.' Like a torturer, famine becomes the inseparable companion to debauched living, and to the stomach, and to gluttony, in order that avenging pain may be fierce where punishable guilt once flamed up. 'There came a grievous famine over that country.' Ravenous living always tends to an end like that; extravagance of pleasure which ought to be avoided always comes to just such an end.

'And he began himself to suffer want.' The wealth which was given to the son brought him to suffer want. If it had been refused to him, it would have kept him rich. Consequently, he who in his father's house had abounded in wealth while not controlling it fell into want out on his own because he did control it.

'And he went and joined one of the citizens of that country, who sent him to his farm to feed swine.' This is the experience which comes to one who refuses to entrust himself to his father, but consigns himself to a stranger: he flees from a most indulgent provider and endures a severe judge. A deserter from affection, a refugee from fatherly love, he is assigned to the swine, sentenced to them, and given over to their service. He stirs about in their muddy fodder. He is bruised and soiled by the rush of the restless herd, so that he perceives how wretched and bitter it is to have lost the happiness of peaceful life in his father's house.

'And he longed to fill his body with the pods which the swine were eating, but no one offered to give them to him.'

What a thankless task is his! He who is living for the swine does not even eat with them! O wretched man, who yearns and hungers for the fattening fodder of the dirty herd! O wretched man, who desires even such sordid food and fails to get even that!

Taught by these matters, and instructed by others like them, let us stay in the house of our Father; let us remain in the bosom of our Mother;[5] and may we be held fast in our relatives' embraces. May our Father's affection hold us back, to keep that pitiful recklessness of youth from drawing us into the evils mentioned above. May our Father's love surround us like a hedge, and may our Mother's affection put us at ease, and may our relatives' esteem to be a protection for ourselves. Under the eyes of these dear ones we cannot easily sin; their eyes are just so many lanterns. The glance of our Mother is the day; the sun is aglow in the countenance of our Father. Consequently, the darkness of crimes cannot draw nigh to one living amid so many lights of virtues. On the contrary, our Father's table nourishes us with the food of virtue, with the banquet of salvation, with the delights of uprightness and of glory.

The great length of the passage read compels us to say more about this parable. Who is the father so ready to forgive, and readier still to welcome back his son? Who is the brother grieving over his brother's return? Who is the younger brother, foolish in his departure but most wise in his return? As you all desire, we shall investigate these matters in a later sermon.

---

5 The Church.

## SERMON 2

### *The Son's Return to His Father*

### (On Luke 15.17-19)

In the preceding sermon, to the best of our ability we censured the extravagant son—that son who deserted his deeply devoted father. We recalled what evils beset him to such an extent that, reduced by hunger, he gave himself to the service of the swine. Now, with more joyful words, we take up something more in line with our desires: his return and repentance.

'When he came to himself,' the text reads, 'he said, How many hired men in my father's house have bread in abundance!' Previously, when he departed from his father, he had ceased to be himself; now, he came to himself. He first returned to himself that he might return to his father. The man who is unminful of his father's devotion, and forgetful of his parent's love, departs from himself, and changes his whole self from man to beast.

'How many hired men in my father's house have bread in abundance, while I am perishing here with hunger!' Hunger calls back him whom abundance had exiled. Hunger enabled the son to understand his father, whereas abundance had caused him to recognize only a sire.

If even involuntary hunger did all this, try by experiment how beneficial a voluntary fast can be. A burdened stomach drags down the heart toward vices, and depresses the mind to keep it unable to experience heavenly piety. Scripture tells us: 'The corruptible body is a load upon the soul, and the earthly habitation presseth down the mind that museth upon many things.'[1] Hence, the Lord said, too: 'Take heed lest your hearts be overburdened with self-indulgence and drunk-

1 Wisd. 9.15.

enness.'[2] Wherefore, the stomach should be relieved by the tempering influence of a fast, that the mind can be unburdened and attend to higher things, rise to virtues, and like a winged bird fly in its entirety to the very Author of piety. The case of Elias proves this. Relieved of bodily weight by continuing that fast which the Lord arranged, he flew to heaven[3] as victor over death.

'I will get up and go to my father.' He who said 'I will arise' was lying down. He had understood his fall, he was aware of his ruin, and gazed upon himself lying in the mire of disgraceful prodigality. That is why he cried out: 'I will get up and go to my father.' With what hope? With what confidence? With what assurance?

With what hope? With that by which [he reflects]: He is a father. I have squandered the marks of a son; he has not lost the characteristics of a father. It is not a stranger who intercedes with a father; rather, it is that affection inside his own breast which intervenes and pleads. The father's heart is moved to beget his son again through forgiveness. I shall go as a culprit to a father. But a father, on seeing his son, soon covers up the guilt. He conceals his role of judge, and is more eager to fulfil that of father. He wants his son to return, not to perish, and soon changes his condemnation into forgiveness.

'I will get up and go to my father, and will say to him, Father I have sinned against heaven and before thee.' His confession touches his father; his repentence addresses his sire. 'I have sinned against heaven and before thee.' He in heaven against whom he sinned is not merely an earthly father, but indeed a heavenly Father. That is why the son added: 'before thee.' All things which are done in heaven and on earth are before the eyes of God.

2 Luke 21.34.
3 3 Kings 19.9; 4 Kings 2.11.

'I have sinned against heaven and before thee. I am no longer worthy to be called thy son.' The son set out abroad and fled into a far country; but he did not escape from those accusing witnesses, the eyes of the heavenly Father. David explains this more clearly by his words: 'Whither shall I go from thy spirit? or whither shall I flee from thy face? If I ascend into heaven thou art there; if I descend into hell thou art present. If I take my wings early in the morning, and dwell in the uttermost parts of the sea: Even there shall thy hand lead me: and thy right hand shall hold me.'[4] David sees that throughout the world all transgressions stand exposed to the eyes of God. Neither the sky, nor the earth, nor the seas, nor a deep cavern, nor night itself can hide sins from Him. The Psalmist perceives how criminal and evil it is to sin in the sight of God. Therefore, he cries out: 'To thee only have I sinned, and have done evil before thee.'[5]

In similar manner, therefore, the younger son, too, cries aloud, and exclaims: 'I have sinned against heaven and before thee. I am no longer worthy to be called thy son.' He does not say: 'I am not worthy to be thy son,' but: 'I am not worthy to be called thy son.' The reason is that to be called pertains to grace; to be pertains to nature. Listen to the Apostle saying: 'from him who called you to the grace of Christ.'[6] Therefore, since this younger son had lost the characteristic of his nature as a son, he judged himself not to deserve that which pertains to grace.

'Make me as one of thy hired men.' Look! To what point of his power has the son come? Look! To what have wanton pleasure and youthful license promoted him? 'Make me as one of thy hired men,' he cries. He desires his servitude to be renewed by his leasing out his services every year. He desires to pay off the obligations of his contract gradually by

4 Ps. 138.7-10.
5 Ps. 50.6.
6 Gal. 1.6.

his unceasing labor. He desires to be as one of the slaves born in his father's house, to sigh the whole day in work which brings but little pay, and never to be able to get out of his state of dependence. There is a reason why he asks for this. Under a foreign master he had experienced a freedom which was really slavery; and he believes that under his father he will have a slavery which is really freedom.

Brethren, at this point I would already be willing to explain the mystery[7] in this passage,[8] but greater profit can be gained from doing this later on, and this restrains me. I observe that as you listen you are not experiencing fitting compassion, nor deeming these matters our concern; rather, you are passing over them quickly with fleeting attention.

But, messages which Christ speaks are indeed our concern; they will always be profitable to every one of us. Moreover, for our instruction the Lord often uses symbolic[9] examples.

---

7 *Mysterium:* type, symbol. This is a reference to the allegorical interpretation which is given in Sermon 5. *Mysterium* in St. Peter's sermons often mean symbolic mystery, i.e., something both profound and difficult to understand, and reminding us of something else. From the second century on, this word was used in the sense of symbol, figure, prophetic figure. In the early third century, the author of *De Pascha computus* (*PL* 4.955-960) uses *sacramentum, typus, mysterium, imago,* and *similitudo* as synonyms. See J. De Ghellinck *et al., Pour l'histoire du mot 'sacramentum'* (Louvain, 1924) 54, 175, 177, 186; Sr. Mary Magdaleine Mueller, *The Vocabulary of Pope St. Leo the Great* (Washington, D. C. 1943) 126; Souter, *Glossary, s.v. sacramentum.* These same meanings are often carried by these words in St. Peter Chrysologus. For example, in a rhetorical display he rounds out a double chiasmus with four synonyms in Sermon 96 (below, p. 152): Christus doctrinam suam *parabolis* velat, tegit *figuris, sacramentis* operit, reddit obscuram *mysteriis* (Christ veils His doctrine by parables, covers it with figures, hides it under symbols, makes it obscure by mysteries).

8 From here on the Latin text is very difficult, and may be partially corrupt.

9 *Mysticus* often means symbolic or figurative in St. Peter, and is practically an adjectival form of *mysterium.* Cf., e.g., Sermon 96, as interpreted by the synonymous expressions in *PL* 52-469D, 146 (below, p. 242), 166 (below, pp. 272, 273), and *Letter to Eutyches* (below, p. 285).

He has always desired to be the Father of His servants, and to be loved more than feared. He gave Himself as the Bread of life, and poured His Blood into the cup of salvation. By these comparisons of the past He improves the men of the present and the future, to keep us from deserting our good and loving Father and going off to the remote and utterly foreign parts of the world. He does not want us to live riotously there and squander the whole substance of our welfare and life. He does not want us to use up everything we have, suffer an extreme hunger for hope, and through it to surrender ourselves soon to the ruler of that region—that is, to the Devil, the author of despair. Our Father does not want him to send us to his own farm, that is, to the seductive valleys of this world; nor to send us to give food to the swine, namely, those creatures who are always prone to grovel on the earth, who live for their stomach, temper their hot passions in a wallowing-place of mud, depress themselves in the mire, and cool themselves in a whirpool of vices.

The Devil's insatiable cruelty is what causes him to send his hirelings to the swine. Not content that men become criminal, he also makes them leaders in vice and teachers of crime. And once he has made them such, he does not let them get satisfied even with the food and fodder of the swine. Wanton men cannot find satiety; their passion cannot be satisfied; consequently, in their hunger they commit more vices still.

Therefore, let us be with our good Father; let us remain with this devoted Parent. In this way we can avoid the Devil's snares and always enjoy our Father's goods. We shall scrutinize the deeper matters later, because we have greater obligation to our congregation and our customs.[10]

10 Of preaching only short sermons.

# SERMON 3

## *The Father's Welcome to the Son*

## (On Luke 15.20-24)

In two sermons so far, we have run through the prodigal son's departure, return, guilt, and repentance. Now let us proceed to treat the father's meeting his son, his goodness, and his indescribable mercy. The text tells us: 'He arose and went to his father. But while he was yet a long way off, his father saw him and was moved with compassion, and ran and fell upon his neck and kissed him.'

'He arose and went to his father.' He arose from the wreckage of his conscience and body alike. He arose from the depths of hell and touched the heights of heaven. Before the heavenly Father, a child rises higher because of pardon than he fell low because of guilt.[1]

'He arose and went to his father.' He went not by the motion of his feet, but by the progress of his thought. Being afar off, he had no need of an earthly journey, because he had found short cuts along the way of salvation. He who seeks the divine Father by faith soon finds Him present to Himself, and has no need to seek Him by traversing roads.

'He arose and went to his father. But when he was yet a long way off.' How is he who is coming a long way off? Because he has not yet arrived. He who is coming is coming to do penance, but he has not yet arrived at grace. He is coming to his Father's house, but he has not yet reached the glory of his former condition, appearance, and honor.

'But when he was yet a long way off, his father saw him.'

1 'Because in reformation through repentance grace ordinarily rises higher,' Mita appropriately remarks (*PL* 52.191). He gives numerous references to other Fathers who express this same idea.

That Father saw, He 'who dwelleth on high; and looketh down on the low things,'[2] 'and the high he knoweth afar off.'[3] 'His father saw him.' The father saw him, in such a way that the son could also behold his father. The father's countenance illumined the face of the approaching son in such a way that all the dark aspect was dispelled which his guilt had previously cast about it. The darkness of the night is not such as that which comes from shame over sins. Hear the Prophet's words: 'My iniquities have overtaken me, and I was not able to see.'[4] Elsewhere, he says: 'My iniquities are become heavy upon me,' and afterwards: 'And the light of my eyes is not with me.'[5] Night overwhelms the light of the day just past; sins ruin our power of perception; our members encumber our soul. Clearly, if the heavenly Father had not cast His rays upon the returning son's face, if He had not lifted the mist of his shame by the light streaming from His own glance, that son would never have seen God's brilliant face.

'He saw him from afar and was moved with compassion.' He who cannot be removed from his location is moved with compassion. He runs forward, not by a movement of his body, but by his affectionate devotion. 'He fell upon his neck,' not because his muscles failed, but because of his compassion. 'He fell upon his neck' that he might raise up the son who lay upon the earth. 'He fell upon his neck' to remove the burden of sins by a burden of love. 'Come to me,' Scripture says, 'all you who labor and are burdened. Take my burden upon you because it is light.'[6] You see that the son is helped, not weighed down, by the burden of that father.

'He fell upon his neck and kissed him.' This is how the father judges and corrects his wayward son, and gives him

2 Ps. 112.5,6.
3 Ps. 137.6.
4 Ps. 39.13.
5 Ps. 37.5,11.
6 Matt. 11.28-30.

not floggings but kisses. The power of love overlooked the transgressions. Therefore, the father redeemed the sins of his son by his kiss, and covered them by his embrace, in order not to expose the crimes or debase the son. The father so healed the son's wounds as not to leave a scar or blemish upon him. 'Blessed are they', says Scripture 'whose iniquities are forgiven, and whose sins are covered.'[7]

If the deed of this young son displeases us, and his departure horrifies us, then let us by no means depart from such a Father. A father's glance puts sins to flight, banishes crime, and drives away all malice and temptations. Certainly, if we have gone away, if by living riotously we have squandered the whole substance of our Father, if we have committed any crime or transgression anywhere, if we have come to the whole rocky coast of impurity and to complete ruin, let us now at last get up. An example like that of the son is an invitation to us. Let us return to such a Father.

'But when his father saw him, he was moved with compassion, and ran and fell upon his neck and kissed him.' What place for despair, I ask, is here? What occasion to make excuses? What false display of fear? None—unless perhaps the father's meeting is feared, and his kiss strikes up terror, and his embrace is disturbing, and he is believed to be seizing the son for punishment rather than receiving him with forgiveness when he leads him by the hand, draws him into his bosom, and winds his arms about him.

But the words which follow completely sweep away such a thought which is destructive of life and opposed to salvation. 'But the father said to his servants, fetch quickly the best robe and put it on him, and give a ring of gold for his finger and sandals for his feet; and bring out the fattened calf and kill it, and let us eat and make merry; because this

7 Ps. 31.1.

my son was dead, and has come to life again; he was lost, and is found.' After hearing this do we yet delay? Do we still fail to return to the Father?

'Fetch quickly the best robe and put it on him.' He put up with his son's transgressions, but not his nakedness. Consequently, he wanted his servants to clothe the son before he was seen, that his nakedness might be known to his father alone. It was only a father who could not bear to see the nakedness of a son.

'Fetch quickly the best robe.' Here the father who did not suffer the sinner to be poorly clothed wants to derive his joy from pardon rather than justice. 'Fetch quickly the best robe.' He did not ask: 'Where are you coming from? Where have you been? Where are the goods you carried off? Why did you exchange such great honor for such disgrace?' No, his words were: 'Fetch quickly the best robe and put it on him.' You see that the power of love overlooks transgressions. The mercy which a father knows is not a tardy kind. He who discusses sins publicizes them.

'Give him a ring for his finger.' The father's devotion is not content to restore his innocence alone; it also brings back his former honor. 'And give him sandals for his feet.' He was rich when he departed; how poor he has returned! Of all his substance he brings back not even shoes on his feet! 'Give him sandals for his feet'—that nakedness may disgrace not even a foot, and surely that he may have shoes when he returns to his former course of life.

'And bring out the fattened calf.' An ordinary calf is not good enough; it must be one sleek and fattened. The stout calf is evidence that the father's charity is stout. 'And bring out the fattened calf and kill it, and let us eat and make merry; because this my son was dead, and has come to life again; he was lost, and is found.' We are still recounting the narrative,[8] and we are already planning to explain the hidden symbolic mystery[9] in it. Through the death of a calf a dead son is resuscitated, and one calf is sacrificed for the feasting of the entire family.[10] However, we must postpone this mystery, to set forth in proper order the elder brother's deep rooted grief and even deeper rooted envy.

## SERMON 4

### *The Elder Brother's Jealousy*

(On Luke 15.25-32)

We have rejoiced over the younger son's return and safety; with tearful grief we now take up the elder son's envy. Through his excessive sin of envious jealousy he spoiled the great virtue of his thriftiness.

The text reads: 'Now his elder son was in the field; and as he came and drew near the house, he heard music and dancing. And calling one of the servants he inquired what this meant. And he said to him, Thy brother has come, and thy father has killed the fattened calf, because he has got him back safe. But he was angered and would not go in.'

'His elder son was in the field.' He was in the field, cultivating the earth but leaving himself uncared for. He breaks up the tough sod, but hardens the affection in his heart. He uproots briers and plants, but does not pluck out temptations to envy. Thus, in the harvest field of covetousness he gathers crops of jealousy and envy.

'And as he came and drew near the house, he heard the

8 *Historia*, the simple record of facts as opposed to the allegorical interpretation of Scripture. Cf. Introduction, pp. 19-23.
9 See Sermon 2 n. 7.
10 An allusion to the Eucharist.

music and dancing.' The music of devoted affection puts the envious brother in flight, the dance of affection keeps him outside. Natural affection prompts him to come to his brother and draw near to the house. But his jealousy does not let him arrive; his envy does not suffer him to enter.

Envy is an ancient evil, the first sin, an old venom, the poison of the ages, a cause of death. In the beginning, this vice expelled the Devil from heaven and cast him down. This vice shut the first parent of our race out of paradise. It kept this elder brother out of his father's house. It armed the children of Abraham, the holy people, to work the murder of their Creator, the death of their Saviour. Envy is an interior foe. It does not batter the walls of the flesh or break down the encompassing armor of the members, but it plies its blows against the very citadel of the heart. Before the organs are aware, like a pirate it captures the soul, the master of the body, and leads it off as a prisoner.

Therefore, if we wish to merit heavenly glory, or to possess the beatitude of paradise, if we wish to dwell in the house of our father and to escape the guilt of divine parricide, then let us by vigilant faith and the Spirit's light drive and keep away the foul tricks of envy. Let us suppress this envy with all the force of heavenly arms. For, just as charity unites us to God, so does envy cut us off from Him.

'His father, therefore, came out and began to entreat him.' The father's anxious heart is straitened by the diverse movements of his sons. In astonishment and love, he ponders their different fortunes, for he sees that one brother is soon driven away by the return of the other, and that through the safety of the one the other will perish. Because of the malice of envy, he perceives his long-felt grief, compensated by a short-lived joy, stirred up all over again.

O cancer of jealousy! A spacious house does not contain

two brothers! And what is strange about this, brethren? Envy has wrought this. Envy has made the whole breadth of the world too narrow for two brothers. For it goaded Cain to kill his younger brother.[1] Thus, the law of nature made Cain the first-born son, but envious jealousy made him an only son.

'But he answered and said to his father, Behold, these many years I have been serving you.' This is the view of one who dares to sit in judgment on the father's love. 'Behold, these many years I have been serving you.' See the service which this son pays back to the father in return for the gift of being born!

'I have never transgressed one of thy commands.' This is the result, not of your innocence, but of your father's forgiveness, because with deep love he preferred to cover up a son's transgressions rather than expose them.

'And yet thou hast never given me a kid that I might make merry with my friends.' An attitude of ill will to a brother cannot be pleasing to a father. And he who is oblivious of brotherly love cannot be mindful of a father's generosity. He says that no kid was given to him. Yet, at the time of the division, he received his complete portion of the property. For, at the time when the younger brother was asking that his share of the property be given him, the father soon divided the whole among the two brothers. The Evangelist's words are: 'He divided his means between them.'[2] But an envious man is always pretending something, always lying.

'And yet thou hast never given me a kid, that I might make merry with my friends.' He does not regard his father's friends as his own. He sees some men esteeming himself

1 Gen. 4.1-16.
2 Luke 15.12.

to please his father, and he regards these as strangers, not friends.

'But when this thy son comes, who has devoured his means with harlots, thou hast killed for him the fatted calf.' He is grieving because his brother has returned, not because the estate has perished. He is complaining,[3] not because of the loss, but because of his envy. He should have used his own means to improve his brother's appearance, and not have dishonored him thus because of what he lost. A father's whole estate is in his son. Hence, when the father recovered his son, he regarded nothing as lost. But the brother did believe it a loss when he saw his co-heir back home. When is an envious man anything but avaricious? He reckons whatever another possesses as his own loss.

'But he said to him, Son, thou art always with me, and all that is mine is thine; but we were bound to make merry and rejoice, for this thy brother was dead, and has come to life; he was lost, and is found.' O what the force of love accomplishes! To a son, however base, he knows not how to be, he cannot be, less than a father. He sees that the son has degenerated in spirit; that he possesses nothing of the father's devotion or character; yet he calls him son, he urges affection[4] upon him, he reawakens his attention to the kindness or the hope of his generosity, by saying: 'Son, thou art always with me, and all I have is thine. That is tantamount to saying: Bear with your brother's return to his father, bear with your father's welcome to his son. He did not seek anything else than his father. For he came with the request to be put in the place of a hired man, not of a son. 'Father, I have sinned against heaven and before thee.

3 *quaeritur*. The verb for 'complain' is often spelled thus in printed texts of S. Peter.

4 Reading *affectum*, not *effectum*, with Böhmer.

I am no longer worthy to be called thy son; make me as one of thy hired men.'[5]

Keep all your possessions; his father is enough for him. Moreover, to keep you from thinking that any of your present or former possessions has been diminished, I shall search for new ones for him in the future. Assuredly, if you observe your father's counsel and command, share your present goods with your brother, that the future possessions may belong to you as well as to him. So be glad and rejoice that he has been found, that he, too, may rejoice that you have not been lost.

But let us now conclude our narrative sermon, that afterwards, through the revelation of Christ, we may unfold the matters that are symbolic[6] and profound.

## SERMON 5

*The Two Sons as Types of the Gentiles and the Jews: The Allegorical Interpretation.*

Not to pay his obligations is often a trait of a clever and shameless debtor. By long and artful caviling he taxes his creditor's patience.

This is our fifth sermon on the departure and return of the Prodigal Son. In it we shall try, as we have promised,[1] to raise its historical sense[2] to a mystical[3] and extraordinary[4]

5 Luke 15.19.
6 The allegorical interpretation is given in Sermon 5.

1 At the beginning of Sermon 1 and the ends of Sermons 2, 3, and 4.
2 Cf. Introduction, pp. 20-21.
3 I.e., deep and symbolical, or allegorical, figurative. This sermon is an excellent example of the allegorical interpretation of Scripture. Cf. Introduction, pp. 20-21.

sense[5] which God gave[6] it.[7] In the case of so great a loan[8] entrusted to me, I am, through my own power, a rather unsuitable debtor. Therefore, pray that through God's power I may be found a payer acceptable to yourselves.

'A certain man had two sons,' the passage says. Since the time when Christ took upon Himself the burden of our flesh, and, being God, clothed Himself with human vesture,[9] God with truth calls Himself man. The Lord [i.e., God

---

4 I.e., Origen's 'spiritual sense' which he called by numerous synonyms: *anagagogé, allegoria, perinoia, pneumatiké ekdoché* in his Greek works, and *sensus mysticus, allegoricus, spiritualis intelligentia* in the works which have survived only in the fourth-century Latin translations of Rufinus and St. Jerome. See *Dictionnaire du Bible, s.v.* Origène, t. 4, col. 1876; *DTC* XI 2e, col. 1495.

5 From the time of St. Hilary (*c.* 315-376) on, *intelligentia* carried among its significations: sense, definition, meaning. See Souter, *Glossary, s.v.*, and also Sermon 36 (below, p. 78 n. 2) and Sermon 112 p. 180 n. 1).

6 Taking *deitatis* as a subjective genitive. Support for this interpretation lies in St. Peter's expressing similar thought in Sermon 96 below, p. 152): *Christ* veils His doctrine by parables and figures; and in Sermon 146 (below, p. 240), divine allegorical meanings. Cf., Sermon 36 (below, p. 78 n. 2).

An alternative rendering of these Latin words is: In it we shall try, as we have promised, to raise its historical meaning to a mystical [i.e., deep and symbolical] and extraordinary understanding of the Godhead. This rendering is possible as far as the Latin words go. but not so well supported by the similar passages of St. Peter.

7 It is interesting to compare an example of Origen's procedure in interpreting Scripture allegorically. In *Homilies on Genesis* he says (*PG* 12.260B): '"He washes his garment in wine, his robe in the blood of grapes" (Gen. 49.11). These statements, too, will be seen to signify by the historical explanation a field producing a grapevine, and by extended meaning an abundance of wine. But our allegorical (*mystica*) interpretation brings forth a nobler meaning. For the garment of Christ which is washed in wine is rightly understood to be His Church, having no spot or wrinkle, which He cleansed for Himself by His blood.'

8 His understanding of the mystical or symbolical meaning.

9 *Exuvias:* flesh, hide, form. An allusion in the language of rhetoric to Phil. 2.7.

the Father] truly calls Himself the father of two sons,[10] because the Deity mixed into the humanity, as also the human tenderness joined to the Deity, has mingled[11] man and God, and it united[12] the Lord to a Father.

Therefore, this man [in the parable], this father, had two sons. He had them through the bounty of the Creator, not because he was under any necessity to beget them, and he commanded their existence, rather than merited it. . . . For[13] Christ was a man before our eyes in such a way that He always remained God in the mystery of His Godhead.

'He had two sons,' namely, two peoples: the Jews and the Gentiles. Prudent knowledge of the Law made the Jewish people His elder son, and the folly of paganism made the Gentile world His younger son. For, just as truly as wisdom

10 The Jews and Gentiles, as the next paragraph shows. However, Böhmer in *BKV* 43, p. 218, takes the two sons to be Christ and the Jews. The first four paragraphs of this sermon form an example of the occasional obscurity of St. Peter, which is possibly due to imperfect texts.

11 *Humanitati permixta deitas,... miscuit hominem et Deum.* Here, either St. Peter is using *mixed* and *mingled* in a wide sense, or he is erring. He would scarcely have chosen these words, nor the similar *miscetur divinitas carni* in Sermon 156 (below, p. 267) had he spoken after the Council of Chalcedon (451), which defined: 'We teach that ... the one and the same Christ, the Son, the Lord, the only-begotten, is to be acknowledged as being in the two natures without mingling, change, division, or separation, with the difference of the two natures by no means destroyed because of the union, but rather with the characteristics of each nature being preserved and coming together unto one Person and Hypostasis.' (Denzinger, *Enchiridion Symbolorum,* 148). Christ said very simply (John 10.38): 'The Father is in me and I in the Father.' This and similar statements (e.g., John 1.14,18; 14.15) show that He is God's one and only natural Son, one Person distinct from the Father and possessing and acting by two united but unmixed natures. Standardized and philosophically accurate language to express all this was not yet common in St. Peter's time.

12 *Univit,* i.e., perhaps, made God the Father similar to a tender human father. Held in *BKV* 67, p. 52, translated 'turned God into a Father'; Böhmer in *BKV* 43, 'made God a Father.'

13 Logical connection of this statement with its context is not apparent. Quite likely, some statements have dropped out of the text.

brings venerable gray hairs,[14] so does folly take away the traits of an adult. So morals, not age, made the Gentiles the younger son; and not years, but understanding [of the Law], made the Jews the elder son.

'And the younger of them said to his father, Father, give me the share of the property which falls to me.' The younger son [representing the Gentile world] addressed this petition to the Knower of hearts by his desire rather than his voice. For, with us, it is our own will which gets us good things from God or bad. See the result. He who in company with his father possessed the whole property became through this use of his own will the possessor of only a fraction of it. That is what he got by his request: 'Give me the share of the property that falls to me.'

And what is that share? What? Conduct, speech, knowledge, reason, judgment—all those characteristics which in this earthly habitat belong to a man above other living beings; in other words, according to the Apostle, the law of nature.

But he carried out the division in this way. To the younger He gave those five gifts of nature which we have mentioned. For the elder He divinely wrote the five Books of the Law. Through these arrangements the divided property was to have unequal value, but a numerical parity. The one share of property was to hold together through human arrangement, the other was to stand firm by divine ordination. But each of these two laws was intended to lead the two sons to the knowledge of their Father. Each law was to bring reverence to its Author.

'And not many days later, the younger son gathered up all his wealth, and took his journey into a far country; and there he squandered his fortune in loose living.' We stated that not age, but morals, had made him the younger son.

14 Cf. Wisd. 4.8.

That is why the text said: 'Not many days later.' And rightly, because in the very beginning of the world the Gentile race hastened off to the Fatherland of idols. It sojourned into the foreign country of the Devil more in spirit than in place. Through its vain thoughts it roamed through all the elements,[15] and it was not by bodily motion that it was hurled from land after land. For, this younger son was in his Father's presence, yet he lacked this Father; although he was in his own house, he did not feel at home.[16]

Hence it is that these Gentile peoples—this loose-living son—through their desire of worldly eloquence, through the brothels of the schools,[17] through senseless disputation at the meeting places of the philosophical sects, dissipated the property of God the Father. By their conjectures they exhausted everything there was in the line of speech, knowledge, reason, and judgment. But, even after that, these poor wetches still suffered the greatest need and intensest hunger to know the truth. Philosophy enjoined the task of seeking God, but of that truth to be learned it gathered no fruit.

Consequently, these Gentile peoples kept on adhering to the chieftain[18] of that country. He kept on banishing them into that world of his; that is, into his one country house of multitudinous superstitions. He did this that they might feed swine, that is, the devils who say to the Lord: 'If thou cast us out, send us into the herd of swine.'[19] Yes, he sent them that they might feed the devils with incense, sacrificial victims, blood—and then get false replies from the oracles as

15 Cf. Wisd. 13.2.
16 *Cum in se esset, non erat secum.*
17 St. Jerome (*On Ezechiel* 16.31) also calls the schools brothels, because the philosopher 'through his immoderate appetite for philosophical knowledge, abuses the testimony of the Scriptures for the perversion of doctrine.' Cf. *PL* 52.198D.
18 The Devil.
19 Matt. 8.31.

the reward for all this labor. They killed many an animal in order to enable a creature which had no intelligence while alive to prophesy after being killed; to empower that which had never uttered speech with its mouth to speak with its entrails after death.

But in all this these Gentile peoples found nothing divine, nothing of salutary value. So they despaired of God, of His providence, of His judgment, and of all the future, and they betook themselves from the school down to the gluttony of the belly, eager to fill themselves with the pods which the swine were wont to eat.

The Epicureans knew this. When they were frequenting the Platonic and Aristotelian schools, and found there no elucidation of the divinity or of knowledge, they offered themselves to Epicurus, the most recent promoter of despair and pleasure. And they ate pods. In other words, they opened their mouths wide to the sinfully sweet pleasures of the body, and they themselves gave food to the devils who continually grow fat on the vices and filth of bodies. For, just as he who unites himself to God 'is one spirit with Him,'[20] so he who associates himself with the Devil becomes one devil with him.

Despite his desire, this younger son did not satisfy his belly with those pods. Why? Because no one was giving to him. Assuredly, the Devil was eager to use this hunger for knowledge and distress of pleasure, in order to make the Gentile son the more eager to get forbidden goods and to commit sins. But God, the Father, allowed the Gentile son to hunger for another reason: that the confutation of his error might become an occasion of salvation. He abandoned the Jewish son in just such a way as not to let him perish utterly, and He suffered the Gentile son to endure hunger that he might come back.

---

20 1 Cor. 6.17.

He does come back now to his Father and cries: 'Father, I have sinned against heaven and before thee.' Every day in her prayer the Church testifies that the younger son has returned to his Father's house, and is calling God his Father, for she prays: 'Our Father, who art in heaven,' 'I have sinned against heaven and before thee.'[21] He sinned against heaven when he said in blasphemy that the sun in the sky and the moon and the stars are gods, and when he profaned these same beings by adoring them.

'I am no longer worthy to be called thy son; make me as one of thy hired men.' This is to say: because I am no longer worthy of the glory of a son, or of pardon, I hope to earn the wages of a laborer's toil. May he who has lost the honor of being a son retain at least the sustenance of life in his daily bread.

But the father runs out, he runs out from afar. 'When as yet we were sinners, Christ died for us.'[22] The Father runs out, He runs out in His Son, when through Him He descends from heaven and comes down upon earth. 'With me,' the Son says, 'is he who sent me, the Father.'[23]

He 'fell upon his neck.' He fell, when through Christ the whole Divinity came down as ours and reposed in human nature. 'And he kissed him.' When? When 'mercy and truth have met each other: justice and peace have kissed.'[24] 'He gave the best robe,' that which Adam lost, the everlasting glory of immortality. 'He put a ring upon his finger.' The ring of honor, the title of liberty, the outstanding pledge of the spirit, the seal of the faith, the dowry of the heavenly marriage. Hear the Apostle: 'I betrothed you to one spouse, that I might present you a chaste virgin to Christ.'[25] 'And

21 Matt. 6.9.
22 Rom. 5.19.
23 John 8.16.
24 Ps. 84.11.
25 2 Cor. 11.2.

sandals upon his feet.' That his feet might be shod when he preached the Gospel, 'that the feet of those who preach the gospel of peace might be beautiful.'[26]

'And he killed for him the fattened calf.' About that David sang: 'And it shall please God better than a young calf, that bringeth forth horns and hoofs.'[27] The calf was slain at this command of the Father, because the Christ, God as the Son of God, could not be slain without the command of His Father. Listen to the Apostle: 'He who has not spared even His own son but has delivered Him for us all.'[28] He is the calf who is daily and continually immolated for our food.

But the elder brother—the elder son coming from the field, the people of the Law—'The harvest indeed is abundant, but the laborers are few'[29]—hears the music in the Father's house, and he hears the dancing, yet he does not wish to enter. Every day we gaze upon this same occurrence with our own eyes. For the Jewish people comes to the house of its Father, that is, to the Church. Because of its jealousy it stands outside. It hears the cithara of David resounding, and the music from the singing of the psalms, and the dancing carried on by so many assembled races. Yet it does not wish to enter. Through jealousy it remains without. In horror it judges its Gentile brother by its own ancient customs, and meanwhile it is depriving itself of its Father's goods, and excluding itself from His joys.

'Behold, these many years I have been serving thee, and have never transgressed one of thy commands; and yet thou hast never given me a kid.' As we already mentioned, this remark should be passed over rather than mentioned. For

26 Rom. 10.15
27 Ps. 68.32.
28 Rom. 8.31.
29 Luke 10.2.

the Jewish son is speaking, and the words are not those of a doer, but of a man venting his anger.

The Father steps outside and says to his son: 'Son, thou art always with me.' How? In the person of Abel, and of Henoch, of Sem, Noe, Abraham, Isaac, Jacob, Moses, and all the holy men from whom stems Christ's Jewish lineage read in the Gospel when it says: 'Abraham begot Isaac, Isaac begot Jacob,'[30] and the rest.

'And all that is mine is thine.' How? Because for you is the law, for you is prophecy, for you the temple, for you the priesthood, for you the sacrifices, for you the kingdom, for you the gifts, for you—and this is the greatest gift of all—Christ was born. But because you through your jealousy wish to destroy your Brother, you are no longer worthy to possess your Father's banquets and joys.

Within the narrow confines of this sermon we could not expound matters so extensive as fully as we desired. But the points which seem brief in our sermon form an ample field for you to exercise the power of perception which your own knowledge gives you. May this simple yet hidden comparison not be unpleasant. It has forced us to. unfold and explain these allegorical[31] and lofty matters, rather than to tell or declaim them.

30 Matt. 1.2.
31 *Mysticas*.

## SERMON 6

### *On Joy over the Call of the Gentiles to the Faith and to Grace*

(On Psalm 99.1-5)

At the return of the younger son, the whole household danced and sang heavenly music. Therefore it is fitting that today, at this great joy of God the Father, we, too, should take up the psalm, use the drum, set up the organ, play the zither; and make David's melody resound.

'Sing joyfully to God, all the earth.' What is it that an understanding of this great joy is likely to make clear? Why is it that, after God gave commandments so great, so terrifying, and so awesome, He now invites the earth to a shout of joy? 'Sing joyfully to God, all the earth,' the text reads.

What other reason is there than the following? The awesome God later on chose the role of a very gentle shepherd. He assumed this character in order to act as a merciful shepherd and gather together, like straggling sheep into one fold, those wandering peoples, those straying nations, those tribes scattered far and wide. Yes, more, He wanted to lead back to the use of milk and grass and restore those wild nations which were languishing after the prey of a carcass, the eating of flesh, the drinking of blood, and the fury of beasts. Briefly, He desired to make them once more sheep fully gentle.

'All the earth, sing joyfully to God,' He says, and by this command He imposes His shepherdly control on all the earth. The resounding trumpet draws the soldier forth to war. Just so does the sweetness of this jubilant call invite the sheep to pasture. How fitting it was to mitigate the din of fighting by shepherdly kindness, in order that grace so gentle might save the nations which their own natural wildness had long been destroying.

Furthermore, Christ Himself declared today[1] that the return of the shepherd was good when He came upon the earth: 'I am the good shepherd. The good shepherd lays down his life for his sheep.'[2] Therefore, the Master Himself is seeking helpers and companions to care for the whole world by His words: 'Sing joyfully, to God, all the earth.' Therefore, when He was on the point of returning to heaven, He gave Peter the trust of feeding His sheep in His place. 'Peter,' He says, 'dost thou love me? Feed my sheep.'[3] He does not want him, once appointed, to compel the tender firstlings of the flock by haughty power, but to encourage them by affection. So He repeats: 'Peter, dost thou love me? Feed my sheep.' He entrusts His sheep, He commends their younglings, because, like a far-seeing shepherd, He knows beforehand that the increase of his flock will be great. 'Peter, dost thou love me? Feed my sheep.'

As shepherd, Peter had Paul for his companion, and Paul, by his careful nourishing, was providing for the sheep from breasts full of milk. 'I fed you,' he says, 'with milk, not with solid food.'[4] The holy king sensed this. So he put himself in place of the bleating sheep, and exclaimed: 'The Lord ruleth me; and I shall want nothing. He hath set me in a green place. He hath brought me up on the water of refreshment.'[5]

So the next verse proffers joy to man. He is returning now, after life spent amid the constant groans and bloodshed of war, from his captivity to the pasture of Gospel peace. Man was the slave of sin, the captive of death, the possession of

1 The passage about the Good Shepherd (John 10.1-21) probably had been read in the liturgical service, as well as Ps. 99.1-5.

2 John 10.11.

3 John 21.16,17.

4 1 Cor. 3.2.

5 Ps. 22.1.2.

the devils. He was a servant of idols, a whipped scoundrel full of vices, a prisoner shackled for his crimes. This is how man was in evil and wretched slavery to such great and evil masters. When was he free from sadness while under the yoke of sin? When was he free from grief beneath the dominion of death? When not pale beneath the Devil's rule? When not trembling under the idols? When free from suspicion while encumbered by vices? When free from despair while charged with crime? That is why he uttered soul-piercing sighs while he so long endured such cruel tyrants! Rightly, therefore, does the Prophet express his joy when he sees us freed from such lords, and called back to the homage of our Creator, the favor of our Father, and the free service of the one good Lord. He exclaims: 'Serve ye the Lord with gladness. Come in before his presence with exceeding great joy.' Enter with your heart; there is not question of place here. 'Come in before his presence with exceeding great joy.' Because grace has led back and innocence has brought in those whom guilt had thrown out and conscience had driven away. 'Come in before his presence with exceeding great joy.' The man who enters God's presence with exceeding great joy is one who is free from guilt, and confident of his reward.

Yet, what is this which is urged? What is the Prophet striving to encourage here? 'Come in before his presence with exceeding great joy.' Who is free in the sight of God? Who acts falsely before His eyes? Who is joyful before God's awesome majesty? The archangels tremble, the angels fear, the powers are afraid, the elders of heaven prostrate themselves. The elements flee, the rocks break up, the mountains crumble, the earth quakes; and man of the earth, how will he enter without fear? Has he hitherto stood his ground in joy? Why does the Prophet dare to tell us to do all this? Why? Because of what follows in the text: 'Know ye that the

Lord he is God.' Because, indeed, the Lord is that God who was a tiny infant in our flesh. Hence, that Lord is God who, immense as He was, lay in our cradle, so sweet in His Mother's lap, so gentle in His conduct, so charming in His dwelling with us. Indeed, therefore, 'come in before his presence with exceeding joy.' For He has hid all the awesomeness of His divinity and His sternness as a judge, to appear like one of us and show His loving care. So we can enter His presence without fearing a judge's penalties; we may expect to get a father's embrace. How can a man fail to rejoice if he feared to encounter a scrutinizing judge, but finds him a father instead? 'Come in before his presence with exceeding great joy. Know ye that the Lord he is God: He made us, and not we ourselves.'

Futile is the act of the father and mother, unless the Creator's work and will also touch the offspring. 'Thy hands have made me and formed me.'[6] And elsewhere it is written: 'Thou has formed me, and hast laid thy hand upon me.'[7] Therefore, not to ourselves do we owe our birth and life, for we owe them wholly to our Creator.

'We are his people, and the sheep of his pasture.' It has been stated very often in Scripture that the Shepherd has come from heaven with His divine call, to summon back to life-giving pastures the sheep who were wandering and ill from poisonous grass.

'Go ye,' Scripture says, 'into his gates with praise.' This praise is the only acknowledgment which causes us to pass into the gate of faith. 'Go ye into his courts with hymns: and give glory to Him, praise ye His name.' As we mentioned before, surely we, who are already placed within the house of our Father—surely we should strike up the spiritual music of heavenly songs. Thus as we enter [the gate of the

6 Ps. 118.73.
7 Ps. 138.5.

Church] we can make an act of faith; we can sing hymns in its courts; and then we can utter full praises in its inner sanctuary, where the whole fullness of the Godhead dwells.

'Give glory to him, praise ye his name. Give glory to him, because he is God. Praise ye his name.' This is the Name through which we have been saved. This is the Name at which every creature in heaven, on earth and under the earth bends its knee, and loves the Lord God: 'for the Lord is sweet.'

Why? Because 'His mercy endureth forever.' He is indeed sweet through His mercy; through it alone He has deigned to blot out the dismal condemnation of all the world. Behold the Lamb of God; behold Him who takes away the sins of the world!

'And His truth endureth to generation and generation.' For God takes pity without harm to the truth. He forgives sins in such a way that in this merciful reckoning He saves full justice. Blessed is He forever and ever. Amen.

## SERMON 11

### *The Fast and Temptation of Christ*

(On Matt. 4.1-4)

God's Law[1] has made it easy for us both to know and not to know what neither human curiosity, nor the laborious study of the ancients, nor worldly wisdom in its long long seeking were able to discover. What is the origin of evil? Whence comes guilt? Whence the strength of vices, the whirling floods of crimes, the wars of bodies and the quarrels of minds, the great storm of life, and the shipwreck so cruel

1 The Law of Moses, Scripture in general. See Souter, *Glossary, s.v.*

that it kills? Man would not know all this unless God's revelation had exposed the Devil.[2]

The Devil is the origin of evil, the source of wickedness, the foe of the world, and ever the hater of successful man. He sets his snares, plans falls, digs ditches, arranges wrecks, stimulates bodies, pricks souls, suggests thoughts, stirs up enmities, makes virtues seem odious and vices attractive, sows errors, nourishes grudges, disturbs the peace, breaks up affection, tears unity apart, has a great relish of evil and none of good, profanes the things of God and disorders those of men.

Hence, as the narrative goes, the brash tempter made his way even to Christ: 'After fasting forty days and forty nights, he was hungry. And the tempter came and said to him, If thou art the son of God, command these stones become loaves of bread.'

Let not those who hear these words turn against God, nor blame nature.[3] They should not insult the Creator, nor accuse the flesh. They should not complain about their soul, nor attack the seasons, nor put the blame upon the stars. They should cease to debase the innocence of the creature. Let them perceive that evil is an accident, not something created; that God is the Creator of good, and the Devil the contriver of evil. Thus, they should ascribe evils to the Devil and good to God. They should avoid evil and do good. In this way they will have as their Helper in good deeds God, who gives the power to do what He commands, and does Himself what He commands. For just as the Devil urges men toward evil, so God leads them toward good.

Therefore, let no one acquiesce in the opinion that his vices have been co-created with himself. Let him not think that what pertains to sin should be ascribed to nature. Rather, let him

2 E.g., Rom. 7.7.

3 These two paragraphs are aimed at the Manichaeans.

take up with Christ the arms of fasting, let him drive off the attacks of sin, and raze the very camp of vices. With Christ fighting for him, let him gain a victory over the author of evil. Once the Devil has been overcome, the vices will have no power. Listen to the Apostle saying: 'Our wrestling is not against flesh and blood, but against the spiritual forces of wickedness on high.'[4]

'Then,' the text reads, 'Jesus was lead into the desert by the Spirit.' He was not led by the Devil, that this might be a divine course of action, not a human effort; a display of the Spirit's foreknowledge, not of human ignorance; of the power of God, not that of His enemy. The Devil ever disturbs the first beginnings of good, he tests the rudiments of virtues, he hastens to destroy holy deeds in their first origins, well aware that he cannot overturn them once they are well founded. Not unaware of this, Christ showed some patient compliance when the Devil tempted Him, that His foe might be held fast in his own trap, and might get caught himself by the very means by which he thought he might make a catch. Then, conquered thus by Christ, he was to yield to the Christians.

'After fasting forty days and forty nights, he was hungry.' You see, brethren, that our fasting in Lent is not a human invention; it arises from divine authority. It is mystic, not something arbitrarily set. It springs not from earthly usage, but the heavenly secrets. Lent, four decades, contains a squared[5] training in faith, because perfection is always something squared. Because we have not time now to unfold what mystical meanings[6] in heaven and on earth the number four and the number ten contain, let us explain the fast undertaken by the Lord.

---

4 Eph. 6.12.
5 I.e., 'perfected' according to Mita in *PL* 52.221C.
6 *sacramenta*. For this meaning, see Souter, *Glossary*, *s.v.*

'After fasting forty days and forty nights, he was hungry.' O man, God fasts in you,[7] He hungers in you. More, He fasts for your benefit, He hungers for your benefit. Just as He has no need to eat for His own benefit, so neither can He hunger. Therefore, when Christ fasts because of you, He is desiring you.

'After fasting forty days and forty nights, he was hungry.' This is not a sign of weakness, but a mark of strength. Because, when the text states: '*After* fasting, he was hungry,' it proves that *within* the forty days and forty nights He had no hunger whatever. To feel hunger and overcome it is a matter of human effort; to have no hunger at all is a mark of divine power. Therefore, Christ did not grow weary of His fast, nor hunger because of appetite. Rather, He experienced hunger to enable the Devil to find a matter for tempting Him. The Devil did not dare to approach Him while He was fasting, because he perceived the One thus fasting to be God, not man. Only then did he perceive Him as man, then did he believe Him mortal and think He could be tempted when he, clever spy, saw Him hunger.

'And the tempter came and said to him.' He came with the finesse of a tempter, not with the affection of a gracious servant. He approached with greater impudence than when he withdrew. But let us hear what he offered to the hungering Man. 'Command that these stones become loaves of bread.' Why, it is stones that he offers to the hungry man! That is always the nature of the enemy's kindness. That is how the author of death and the hater of life offers food.

'Command that these stones become loaves of bread!' O Devil, your cleverness undoes your plans. He who can change stones into bread can also change hunger into satiety. What need of your plan has He whose power is fully sufficient for

7 I.e., in a human nature like your own. The Son fasts by means of His human nature.

Him? 'Command that these stones become loaves of bread.' O Devil, you have both exposed yourself and failed to give food to your Lord.

'Command that these stones become loaves of bread.' You wretch! You wish to be evil, but cannot. You desire to tempt, and do not know how. You should have offered soft foods, not hard ones, to a famished man. You should have coaxed his appetite gently, with attractive viands, not rough ones. You should have driven his long long abstinence away by appetizing dishes, not disgusting ones. By these you could ensnare not even a son of a man, and much less the Son of God. O tempter, know that in the presence of Christ your wiles have been undone.

'Command that these stones become loaves of bread.' He who changes water into wine can also change stones into bread. But, miraculous signs should be given to foster faith, not wiles. They should be given to a believer, not to a tempter. And they should be worked for the salvation of the one who requests them, not for harm to him who performs them. O Devil, what good are miracles for you? Nothing helps toward salvation for you; everything remains for your punishment. Even miracles contribute to your downfall.

But receive your answer that you may know yourself and be subject to your Creator. 'Not by bread alone does man live, but by every word that comes forth from the mouth of God.' Here is your lesson: The Word of the Father hungers for the words of our salvation, not for bread. He acts that man may live always by the heavenly word, not always by earthly bread—indeed, that man may live for God in such a way as not to heed the toil. For that, indeed, is the true life. It knows not perspiration, has no pains, and has no end.

# SERMON 20

## *The Calming of the Storm at Sea*

## (On Matt. 8.23-27)[1]

By God's profound design, the passages read in the services of the Church are arranged in a wise order, that they may bring deeper penetration to the learned, and impart wholesome[2] grace of understanding to simple folk.

When Christ got into the boat, the text says, the weather made bold to stir up a great storm. 'He got into a boat, and his disciples followed Him. And behold, there arose a great storm on the sea, so that the boat was covered by the waves: but He was asleep.' The sea had offered its heaving back for Christ to walk upon it. Now it leveled its crests to a plain, checked its swelling,[3] and bound up its billows. It provided rocklike firmness, and He could walk[4] across a waterway.

Why did the sea heave so, and toss and pitch, even endangering[5] its Creator? Why did Christ Himself, who knows all the future, seem so unaware of the present that He gave no thought to the onrushing storm, the moment of its height, and the time of peril? But, while all the rest were awake, He alone was fast asleep—even then when utter doom threatened Himself and His dear ones. Why all this?

Brethren, it is not a calm sky but a storm which proves a pilot's skill. When the breeze is mild, the poorest sailor manages the ship, but in the cross winds of a tempest men

1 The speaker also draws details in this sermon from Matt. 14.24-33. Mark 6.45-52, and John 6.15-21.
2 Reading *salutarem intelligentiae gratiam,* with LaBigne.
3 Reading *motum,* with LaBigne.
4 Mark 6.48-52.
5 John 6.19.

want the best pilot with all his skill. The disciples' efforts as seamen, as they saw, had failed. The seas were trying to spend their fury against them, and the waves to swallow them. The twisting winds had conspired against them. So they ran in fear to the very Pilot of the world, the Ruler of the Universe, the Master of the elements. They begged him to check the billows, banish the danger, save them in their despair. At length, His mere command controlled the sea, struck back the winds, stopped the whirlwinds, brought back the calm. Then the men who were crossing the sea perceived, believed, and acknowledged that He is the very Creator of everything.

But, now, let us draw forth the inner meaning of all this. When Christ embarked, in the boat of His Church, to cross the sea of the world, the blasts of the Gentiles, the whirlwinds of the Jews, the tempests of persecutors, the storm clouds of the mob, and the foggy mists of the devils all descended in fury to make one storm over all the world. The waves of kings were foaming, the billows of the mighty seethed, the rage of subjects resounded, nations swirled like whirlpools, sharp rocks of infidelity came into view, groans resounded from Christian shores, the shipwrecks of the fallen-aways were drifting about, and there was one crisis, one shipwreck of all the world. 'So the disciples came to the Lord, and woke Him, saying, Lord, save us! We are perishing! But He said to them, Why are you fearful, O you of little faith?' Thus awakened by His disciples, Christ controls the sea, that is, the world; He pacifies the earth, softens the kings, placates the mighty, calms the waves, soothes the nations, and makes the Romans Christians. In their case, too, He brings the one-time persecutors of the Christian name to live out the word of the Christian faith. Christian princes preserve this tranquility, the Church holds it, Christianity possesses it, the Gentile world admires it.

'Then He arose,' the text goes on, 'and rebuked the wind and the sea, and there came a great calm.' 'And the men marvelled, saying, what manner of man is this, that even the wind and the sea obey Him?' The men who approach the Lord, and awake Him, and humbly beg Him to save them, are His disciples. But other[6] men are pointed out as those who marvel that the elements so obey Christ. They are indeed men, men of this world, who marvel that the world has thus been converted to obedience to Christ; who are astonished that their temple tops[7] have been cast down like the swells of the waves; who see that the froth of the idols and the whirlwinds of the devils have gone away. The deep and widespread peace of the Christian name[8] throughout the whole world makes these men utterly astonished. And truly, brethren, when Christ was in the sleep of His death, a great storm arose in the Church. But, when He arose from the dead, a great calm was given back to the Church, as has been written.

At present, Christ is asleep in us. Let us awaken Him, by a full groan from our hearts, by our voice of faith, by Christian tears, by deep-felt weeping, by apostolic shouts. Let us cry out: 'Lord, save us. We are perishing!' Furthermore, this passage applies very well to our own times. As it has been written: 'The north wind is a harsh wind,'[9] but by name it is called the 'wind at the right' which brings us such wild and bitter nations. So this harsh north wind from the right[10] hurls itself now to the southwest, now to the

6 Origen and some other Fathers thought that the men who expressed the marveling were not the disciples, but other men in the same or different ships. The speaker is following that opinion here.

7 Reading *vertices*.

8 I.e., Christianity.

9 Cf. Prov. 25.23: 'The north wind driveth away rain.' St. Peter is thinking of the north wind as a cold wind, and is manifestly alluding to the barbarian infiltrations from the north.

10 Possibly, St. Peter was facing west. Or perhaps he was stating that the north wind veers off toward the southwest.

south, now to the southeast. By its devastating cross winds it confounds the seas, blacks out the sky, wears down the mountains, swallows up cities, mingles provinces together, drives the whole world to one shipwreck. Consequently, the bark of Christ is now raised aloft toward the sky, now sinks into the troughs of fear. At one moment it is under the control of Christ's strength, at another it is tossed by terror. Now its decks are awash with billows of sufferings, now it makes its way by the oar strokes of divine praises. But let us cry out, dear brethren, again and again: 'Lord, save us! We are perishing!'

And, truly, brethren, if we were one, like one human body, if we believed our perishing fellow men to be parts of our very selves, then by afflicting ourselves with fasting, by the groans of our prayers, and by copious tears we would cry out unceasingly: 'Lord, save us! We are perishing!' Also, we would try to aid ourselves in the persons of our brethren. We would not be looking upon this sea of our blood amid this raging warfare. Neither would we be perceiving already such enormous shipwrecks of bodies and souls. But with humble voice we would be crying out: 'Lord, save us! We are perishing!'

However, no compassion, no piety, no fear, no shame whatever, or any remorse are stirring us up to sorrow. It is from God, it is from God that we are beset with evils, that we are always being lashed, that the nations wax strong, the hail falls, the mildew pays its visits, impiety flourishes, diseases stalk uncontrolled, death rages, the earth quakes. Yet, we neither tremble, nor fear, nor turn away from our sins, nor pursue the good. Avarice runs wild, ostentation goes on apace, sin brings pleasure, other men's goods seem attractive while our own go to ruin. The scourges of God come, but our faults provoke them.

If God is just, He is indeed also merciful toward us.

Brethren, let us return to the Lord, that God may return to us. Let us renounce evil, to get good in return. Let us serve the good God, that we may escape servitude to evil nations and wicked powers, through the help of our Lord and Pilot, Christ. His honor and majesty endure without end forever and ever. Amen.

## SERMON 22

### *Contempt of Earthly Goods. The Watchful Servants.*

(On Luke 12.32-38)

Prizes are always set up for those who are challenged to enter hard contests; the greater the contest, the bigger is the prize offered. That is why Christ makes it possible for His disciples to possess a kingdom. He desires to motivate them not to yield to danger or fear in the conflict. A man heading for a kingdom spurns danger. A man eager for victory knows no fear.

'Do not be afraid, little flock,' the text says, 'for it has pleased your father to give you a kingdom.' The flock is little in the eyes of the world, but great in the eyes of God; little, because He calls glorious those whom He has trained to the innocence of sheep and to Christian meekness. The flock is little, not as the remnant of a big one, but as one which has grown from small beginnings. This little flock denotes the infancy of His new-born Church, and immediately He promises that through the blessings of heaven this Church will soon have the dignity of His kingdom. 'Do not be afraid, little flock, for it has pleased your father to give you a kingdom.'

Then He added what the future rulers[1] should do: 'Sell what you have, and give alms. Make for yourselves purses that do not grow old, a treasure unfailing in heaven.' Sell what you have; no one can rule all men if he is hindered by his own possessions. The man becomes depressed in spirit who thinks of his private affairs when he is being called to a kingdom. The common, groveling soul values a little coin more than royal treasures. Poor judgment, brooding over trifles, loses great possessions. The man who sighs for the goods of earth loses concern for those of heaven.

'Sell what you have,' the text says, 'and give alms. Make for yourself purses that do not grow old, a treasure unfailing in heaven.' O man, Christ desired to enrich you by such advice, not to strip you. He wanted your goods to remain for you, not to perish. His order was that your purses should last forever, not get emptied out. He bade you to transfer them, not to lose them.

'A treasure unfailing in heaven, where neither thief draws near nor moth destroys.' He acts more like a fatherly counselor than like one enjoying the right to rule. He chides: Why do you store away your goods where thieves can plot and moths can nibble? You are advised not to bring yourself sleepless nights, anxious days, troubled times. The custodian of gold and guardian of silver has no security and knows not sleep. He who loses his security loses his sleep, too. He is rich with bother, not possessions.

'A treasure unfailing in heaven.' That is to say: Where I am, put it there. I save the things entrusted to me. O man, give to the Father, deposit with God. For, as a Father to an heir, and as God to man, He will not refuse to deliver the deposit. Surely, he cannot retain your possessions, since He gave you His own. Does He who bestows divine goods need human ones? He made us the heir of his riches; is He, then,

1 Reading *regnaturis,* with LaBigne.

covetous of ours? Is He likely to deny anything to those on whom He has conferred a kingdom?

O man, if you are going to remain here on earth, store up your treasures here. But, if you are going up to heaven, why do you leave them here below? The man caring for treasures destined to be left behind is caring for others' treasures, not his own. Living here below, where we are pilgrims, we find it rather hard to be poor, sad, and without honor, even for a while. Then, when we shall be among the eternal citizens of our everlasting country, what will it be like for us to endure pain because of our showing contempt, punishment because of ignobility, shame over our nakedness? What will it be like to be sentenced to torments when others are being promoted into possession of the kingdom? When the poor man is led to sit with God, and the rich man is dragged to the assembly of the damned? Oh, how lamentable will be the reversal of the situation when those whom men despaired of will acquire hope divine, and those who possessed human treasures will defraud themselves of the heavenly ones!

All this is what that treasure brings about. Either through alms-giving it raises the heart of a man into heaven, or through avarice it buries it in the earth. That is why He said: 'For where your treasure is, there your heart also will be.' O man, send your treasure on, send it ahead into heaven, lest you bury your God-given soul in the earth. Gold comes from the depth of the earth; the soul, from the highest heaven. Clearly, it is better to carry the gold to the abode of the soul than to bury the soul in the mine of the gold. That is why God orders those who will serve in His army here below to fight as men stripped of concern for riches and unemcumbered by anything. To these He has granted the privilege of reigning in heaven.

'Let your loins be girt about and your lamps burning, and

you yourselves like men waiting for their master's return from the wedding.' Let your loins be girt about: virtue should serve as a girdle in the place where passion should be checked. He who drops off the girdle of virtue cannot overcome the vices of the body. So girdled with the cincture of purity—it is the badge of membership in the Christian army—let us cut away the dissolute cowardice of the flesh. Alert while watching our king, let us have no part in the restless sleep of worldly minded men. For, 'They sleep not,' Scripture says, 'except they have done evil.'[2]

'And let your lamps be burning.' Blessed are they who hold in their hands the shining lamps of good works. For, thus does Scripture teach: 'Let your light shine before men in order that they may see your good works and give glory to your Father in heaven.'[3] Truly, a good work gleams before minds like a lamp before the eyes. A lamp furnishes light not alone to the bearer, but to many besides. Just so, a good work radiates from one deed and enlightens many men through example. A lamp repels the black darkness of night; a good work routs the darkness of evil. Let us by our good works light the lamp in our hands, if we wish ourselves to shine before God and men.

'And you yourselves be like men waiting for their master's return from the wedding.' Torches at weddings are always something pleasant and desired. That is why the purity of weddings is celebrated by a display of lights. Just as one who dares to do what is forbidden flees from the light, so is one who is seeking what is honorable happy to be bright in manifold light.

'And you yourselves be like men waiting their master's return from the wedding.' There are some men who await their master's arrival with unwearying watches, like those

2 Prov. 4.16.
3 Matt. 5.15.

who owe service. Now, those who are slaves to their bellies to such an extent that they no longer know the service of God, who are so devoted to the pleasures of the flesh that they have lost all concern about meeting God—these should be called not men, but beasts.

'And you yourselves be like men waiting for their master's return from the wedding.' Ever since Christ came to espouse His Church, the chamber of His bride has been a place of beauty. It is adorned with the gold of faith, the silver of wisdom, gems of virtues, curtains of holiness, roses of propriety, lilies of chastity, violets of modesty. This temple of purity, this pinnacle of virginity is raised to the heights of heaven. The harps of the Psalms are there, the organs of the Prophets, the voices of the Apostles, and all the music of the heavenly wedding feast. He whom such a loud shout does not arouse for the wedding of the heavenly King is indeed the slave of sleep.

'And you yourselves be like men waiting for their master's return from the wedding; so that when he comes and knocks they may straightway open to him.' He comes and knocks, the man of good conscience opens up his heart, the man of evil conscience closes his. The just soul opens up to receive the reward, but the unjust soul has stored up no merits and shuts itself tight. Therefore, let us be watchful, dearly beloved, that we may attain the blessedness which follows. 'Blessed are those servants whom the master on his return, shall find watching.' Let these promises of blessedness suffice. But, since Christ speaks about the high value of this very blessedness, let us put the matter off today. Thus we can hear at greater length what such a Father has promised to His children.

## SERMON 27

### *Scandal*

### (On Luke 17.1-2)

In a state of readiness for war, sentries are appointed in relays in such a way as to leave no chance for ambush or trickery. A foe who attacks in surprise is altogether too deadly. He either gains the advantage over his victims while they are still unaware, or catches them unprepared, or overwhelms them still asleep. That is why Christ, our King from eternity, has warned His soldiers to beware, by previously planned changes of watches practised throughout the night of life on earth, against the most clever deceit of the Devil, that is, the ancient foe; against the camouflaged onsets of vices, the deceptive attacks of crimes, the scandals which from various causes arise to endanger us, the temptations of the present life, the harassing pressure from the army of this world.

'Watch and pray,' His warning runs, 'that ye may not enter into temptation.'[1] To determine more in detail how we should watch, He added: 'And if he comes in the second watch, and if he comes in the third, and finds him so, blessed are those servants whom the master, on his return, shall find watching.'[2] Blessed indeed! For those who are alert and anticipate the deceitful tactics of the enemy will glory in the arrival of their Lord.

Today, however, the Lord has alerted our leaders as they keep guard, and armed them against scandals, by His words

1 Matt. 26.41.
2 Luke 12.38,37.

to His disciples: 'It is impossible that scandals should not come.'[3]

In other words: it is impossible that foes should not come. First of all, brethren, we should know what these scandals are. There are several kinds of these inducements to sin. The first kind consists of those which the craftiness of the Devil brings forth. The second is made up of those which human cleverness thinks up. The third is composed of those which our own suspicious and careless nature brings to birth from its own self.

From the Devil are those which have a deceptive appearance. They seem to proffer good, but really inflict evil. An example is the case of Adam.[4] While promising divine goods, the Devil snatched away our human ones. Another example occurred through Peter's exclamation: 'O Lord, this will never happen to thee.'[5] When he falsely represents himself to be aflame with intense love, Peter is tending to cast away the triumph of the Cross. For, while the Lord was speaking about the glory of His Passion, the Devil replied through Peter: 'Lord, this will never happen to thee.' How sweet is the poison of the serpent! He beguiles Peter, as a soldier, to deny his king's victory before he, as a servant, denies his Lord. Consequently, the Lord put the servant behind himself and sent the scandal back to its author. 'Get behind me,' He said to Peter; and to the Devil: 'Satan, thou art a scandal to me.'[6] And, truly Peter does go behind His Lord: to follow Him to heaven, he mounted the cross with his head turned downward.

Yet another scandal of this type is the one Satan con-

3 Luke 17.1.
4 Gen. 3.1-7.
5 Matt. 16.22.
6 Matt. 16.23

trived against the Jews. For he furrowed the wide rock on which to step, and roughened it till it was completely a hazard, and changed the rock of this whole footing into a stumbling-stone to make it a cause of ruin for unfortunate men. Scripture says: 'Behold I lay in Sion a stumbling-stone and a rock of scandal.'[7] Consequently, the Psalmist begs with anxious prayer: 'Keep me from the snare, which they laid for me, and from the stumbling blocks of them that work iniquity.'[8] Because he leaped across the hazard and overcame the stumbling block, he gloried thus: 'Thou hast exalted me on a rock, and Thou hast conducted me; for Thou hast been my hope.'[9]

We have treated the first kind of scandal. Now let us talk also about the second kind, which, we said, arises from human cleverness. The soothsayer Balaam[10] set up a scandal for the people of Israel when he went to meet their warriors, not with men in armor, but with women arrayed in all their finery. He hoped to make the men drop their arms for debauchery, change their triumph into disgrace, bring the avengers of guilt into guilt themselves, and—to put it briefiy—to profane all their holiness into depravity. As a result of it all, when Moses was meting out punishment, he sentenced Balaam thus: Kill Balaam the soothsayer, because he set up a stumbling-block before the children of Israel.[11]

Jeroboam raised up a scandal.[12] He set up as gods for the people golden calves—pitiful images—to keep them from seeking the living God, the true temple, God's law, the rightly appointed kings, and their ancestral rites. Consequently, the whole people thus delivered over to error became a source

7 Rom. 9.32; cf. Isa. 8.14.

8 Ps. 140.9.

9 Ps. 60.3,4.

10 Cf. Num. 31.8,15-17; Apoc. 2.14. St. Peter seems to regard Balaam not as a prophet but as a magician.

11 *Ibid.*

12 3 Kings 12.26-32.

of scandal like that given, according to the Apostle,[13] when a man eats, as harmlesss to his own conscience, the flesh of animals which were sacrificed to idols. He thinks that through such conduct he may well bring contempt upon the inanimate stones and wooden gods who can neither sanctify nor profane anything. But, what he thinks is an example of his faith becomes an occasion of error for uninstructed men, for its leads them not to contempt but to worship, and it causes the meal to appear to be a banquet of religious honor to those very inanimate gods whom he is intentionally diminishing by this ridicule. Consequently, the Apostle wisely concludes and explains: 'And through thy "knowledge" the weak one will perish, the brother for whom Christ died.'[14]

The third kind of scandal is that which our senses bring forth to us, when we are deceived by our eyes, beguiled by our hearing, taken in by an odor, corrupted through our taste. For example, Eve was harmed thus by the sight and taste of the forbidden, deadly food. 'Now the woman saw that the tree was good for food, pleasing to the eyes, and delightful to behold.'[15] Wisely, therefore, did the Lord add that our very senses give scandal, by saying: 'If thy eye is an occasion of sin to thee, or thy hand, cut it off, and cast it from thee; it is better for thee without an eye and a hand to enter into life than with thy whole body to go into hell.'[16] The Lord here commanded us to cut away our faults and vices, not our members. Nevertheless, if Eve, the mother of the human race, had done just what He ordered, she would have done better by coming to life without an eye and a hand, rather than have plunged her entire posterity into a pitiful death!

---

13 1 Cor. 8.7,8; cf. 1 Cor. 10.23-30.
14 1 Cor. 8.11.
15 Gen. 3.6.
16 Matt. 5.29,30; Mark 9.42,46.

Therefore, brethren, we should be careful neither to give scandal to others nor to take it ourselves when another gives it. It is scandal that troubles the senses, perturbs the mind, confuses our judgment otherwise sharp. It is a scandal that changed an angel into the Devil, an Apostle into a traitor; that brought sin into the world and allured man to death. Hear the Lord saying: 'Woe to the world because of scandals!'[17] Scandal tempts the saints, fatigues the cautious, throws down the incautious, disturbs all things, confuses all men. It is true that in this present passage the Lord is talking about the scandal of His Passion, and pointing out Judas through whose agency came the very scandal of scandals. Nevertheless, He uttered a warning to keep anyone else from coming to this, by saying: 'It is impossible that scandals should not come; but woe to him through whom they come! It were good for him if a millstone were hung about his neck and he were thrown into the sea, rather than that he should cause one of these little ones to sin.'[18]

Why not an ordinary stone, but a millstone? Because, while a millstone is grinding the grain, and pouring out the flour, and separating the bran from the meal, it is simultaneously furnishing bread to those who are dutifully toiling. Rightly, therefore, is a millstone tied to the neck of the man who chooses to be a minister of scandal rather than of peace, that the very same thing which should have drawn him to life may drag him down to death. For, he has changed those senses given to aid him toward life into a stumbling-block bringing death. Then they persuaded him to see something else, and hear, feel and relish something else than was in Christ and in His saving knowledge. In this way he has encompassed the cornerstone,[19] the stone symbolizing help,[20]

---

17 Matt. 18.7.
18 Luke 17.1
19 Isa. 28.16.
20 1 Kings 7.12.

the stone cut out without hands,[21] that is, Christ, and he has turned it into a stumbling-block for the weak. Consequently, he was preparing, not the bread of life, but that of tears and sorrow according to the testimony of the Prophet: 'You that eat the bread of sorrow.'[22] Therefore, it is well for him, as Scripture elsewhere says, 'To have a great millstone hung around his neck.'[23] Let him suffer for his punishment from that same place where he got his frame of mind. Let him be like the stupid beasts, since he did not care to be compared with men who relish heavenly things.

## SERMON 36

*The Daughter of Jairus and the Woman with the Hemorrhage as Types of the Synagogue and the Church*

(On Mark 5.22-34)

A gentlemanly borrower soon pays what he has promised. He does not tax his creditor's good will by frequently putting him off, or keep him in anxiety by long waiting. When the account of the ruler of the synagogue, or the related account which springs from it, that of the woman with the hemorrhage, was enticing us away from the customary brevity of our sermons, we preferred to cut our discourse[1] in half lest it seem to start anew to such an extent as to overburden your patience to listen.

21 Dan. 2.45.
22 Ps. 126.2.
23 Matt. 18.6.

1 Sermon 33 (*PL* 52.292-296). Sermon 36 is important because St. Peter here so clearly states his opinion on the allegorical interpretation of Scripture.

The ruler of the synagogue hastened to meet the Lord, and fell prostrate on the ground. He explained his case, manifested his grief, excited the compassion of his Benefactor, and begged Him to come with speed to effect a cure. In contrast, the Lord met the woman before He was entreated. While passing by, He gave her an occasion of recovering health; while silent Himself, He understood the case of the silent woman, and saw her wound even when she was hiding it. With her, it was in secret that the Lord carried on His important work of healing. And while He was making His way after being petitioned in public, her knowledge sprang from her faith, penetrated to His divinity, and discovered that great secret.

Oh, happy is that woman! In the midst of such a great multitude she was so much alone with Christ that only she was aware both of her restoration to health and His exalted power! Happy is she who found such access that no one could stop her. Happy she who by such a path struggled and crept up to her Creator, before she was upbraided by anyone because of her sore, and before she was free from its repugnance. She knew that with men and through their power the way to full health was closed to her. Men are more accustomed to shrink away from wounds than to cure them. God cleanses human wounds; He does not despise them. He does not shrink from human sores, but heals them. Nor does He detest the suppurations from the human body; rather, He cleanses them. God cannot, He cannot be soiled through contact with His creature.

But the Evangelist poses a problem when he states: 'And Jesus instantly perceiving in Himself that power had gone forth from Him, turned to the crowd and said, Who touched my cloak?' While He was asking as if professing ignorance, did He perceive that power had gone forth from Him, and fail to know to whom it had gone? Did He know that

He had let it go forth, without knowing to whom? Did He, who was certain that health had been conferred, doubt about the beneficiary?

No. The Lord asked here, not because of any error of one in ignorance, but with the majesty of Him who knows both the present and the future. He was not investigating something hidden to Him; rather, He manifested that it was well known to Him, in this way. He so asked His questions that He alone revealed the hidden matter to all those unaware of it. Not as an unknowing examiner, but as a questioner who knew everything beforehand, He drew His petitioner into the center of attention. She was silent, making suggestions only by her thoughts, in ready waiting behind His back for the measures by which He exercised His powers. He made her stand before all so that she who had gained health for herself might also bring faith for all; that she who had His power might acknowledge His majesty; that she who had made Him so fully known might not go away again unknown, herself, as she expected.

While she was blushing over her wound and with so much concern fearing Him as God, the woman found her faith getting darkened. Clouds of confusion obscured the light in her mind. Therefore, the voice of her questioning Lord, like a salutary wind, drove the clouds away, dispersed the mists, and enlightened her faith. It made her who had recently been in darkness of the night brighter than the very sun. For, she shines throughout the whole world, is resplendent in the whole of the Church, and is glorious among its members. Is she, then, less than a sun? If she had returned unseen—give me leave to say it—she would have escaped her Physician, not tested Him. She could have ascribed what she obtained to herself rather than to her Healer. She would have believed that she had drawn her cure from the hem of His garment, not from His penetrating understanding. For, what would she have believed to be truly His whose power she had experienced in her own case, but which in her wish she had deemed to be something outside Him?

Before her cure, perhaps it was because of her shame that she kept herself hid, and because of her humility that she thought herself unworthy. But after her cure, why did she not of her own accord run up to give Him thanks, and honor, and glory for such a great deed? After she saw that the Lord persisted in His questioning, that the disciples said that jostling from the crowd was the reason why He had been touched, and that she could not remain hidden, after fear and trembling in her own conscience began to trouble her, she came into the midst of them all. She wanted to profess public belief in Him whom she had privately recognized as her Physician, and to adore Him as God, and to become herself a remedy for sickness as great as hers, both to present and future men. As the Evangelist narrates: 'But the woman, fearing and trembling, knowing what had happened within her, came and fell down before Him, and told Him all the truth.'

However, the historical narrative should always be raised to a higher meaning,[2] and mysteries of the future should become known through figures of the present. Therefore, we should now unfold, by allegorical discourse, what symbolic teaching[3] is contained beneath the outward appearance of the ruler of the synagogue, or his daughter, or the woman afflicted with the hemorrhage.

In respect to His divinity, Christ cannot be moved from place to place; but walking by means of His human nature He comes, strides, and hastens to the daughter of the ruler of the synagogue. Without doubt, she is the Syangogue, for

---

2 *Intelligentiam*: meaning. See Souter, *s.v.*, and above, Sermon 5 n. 5.

3 *Quid sacramenti*: mystical meaning, or, the teaching which a symbolic type conveys. See Souter, *s.v. sacramenti*, and above, Sermon 2 n. 7.

Christ said: 'I was not sent except to the lost sheep of the house of Israel.'[4]

But, while Christ was hastening to her, His Church which was located out among all the nations was suffering a hemorrhage and losing the blood of the human race. The integrity of nature had been lost. While human skill kept trying to cure the weakness of the race, it increased it. For, the censure of human frailty, and the severity of the discipline of this world, did indeed continually shed the blood of nations. But it could not obliterate the enemy, nor check the wars of the citizens, nor blot out the insanity of crimes.

Therefore, as a result of such cares, this Church had a running wound. She saw that whatever substance she had possessed and still possessed was used up—that is, her soul, mind, power of discernment, ingenuity, toil, industry, and planning. (All these endowments can indeed be ascribed to her officials, the physicians trying to cure the sick.) When she perceived that Christ was present as He was passing by, she came up behind Him because, soiled with blood, she did not deserve to look upon His face.

She came up behind Him. That is, she follows the hearing of faith and getting very close she touches, so to speak, the very fringe of His garment. She does this while she is not honored among the fathers, is not sanctified by the Law, does not publicly bring herself forward among the Prophets, does not receive honor even from the very Body[5] of the Lord, while she is deemed a stranger even by the group of men reborn from Christ.

She follows Christ behind His back, that is, in this last age of time.[6] She is established as sacred by a hidden bond

4 Matt. 15.24.

5 Christ's mystical body, the Church. She does not get honor from all her own members.

6 The age or period from Christ to the end of the world. Cf. 1 John 2.18.

of faith, and she has truly touched his cloak (which she found in the Sepulchre) through this, that she has faith in these insignia of the risen Lord, and preaches them. But, while Christ is employing His powers in the case of his Church, He is not paying attention to the ruler's daughter. And the Synagogue dies—in order that she, too, who has died through the Law and perished through nature, may return to life through faith.

'While He was speaking, there came some from the house of the ruler of the synagogue, and they said, Do not trouble the Master, the girl is dead.' Today, also, the Jews do not want Christ to be troubled. They desire Him not to come. They have faithlessly destroyed their apprehension of His Ressurrection, and proclaim that He is dead.

But I see how that, too, is consistent with our assertion! For, as Scripture tells, the daughter of the ruler of the synagogue spent twelve years in life. So, too, it is recounted, did this woman endure her sore for twelve years, since the health of life both were to be restored at the latest and fulfilled time. That number twelve rounds off the time of human life. To make a year, the number twelve is divided and applied to the months. Consequently, the Prophet indicates[7] that Christ came in the acceptable year of the Lord. The Apostle, too, approves the teaching that Christ came in the fullness of time: 'When the fullness of the time came, God sent His Son.'

Pray, brethren, that just as the Synagogue has died to itself and the Law, in order to live to Christ, so we, too, may die in our sins in order to live in Christ.

---

7 Isa. 49.8; cf. 2 Cor. 6.2.

## SERMON 38

### *The Patient Endurance of Injuries*

### (On Matt. 5.38-41)

'If someone strike thee on the right cheek, turn to him the other also.' By these words the Lord has taught us today what greatness of soul is characteristic of a heavenly philosophy, and what strength belongs to those who fight the Christian warfare. Such conduct will seem hard to the man who does not know how great the rewards for patience are. If someone is unwilling to suffer a slap of the hand to get his crown, do you think he can endure the wounds necessary to gain the victory? Can he seek glory through death, if he deems an injury from man too high a price for the glory he will get from God? O man, when you were an infant, were you not taught your rudiments through means like those? Slaps are the beatings given to children, not to men. Hence it is that the infants of Christ are urged on by light commands, that when they are the men who live the Gospel out they may have the full strength to undertake its more serious precepts. They hope to obtain by these labors, pains, or even death what they could not get by little injuries throughout their infancy. To find proof that the commandments are not difficult, repeat the list of them.

'You have heard that it was said to the ancients, An eye for an eye, and, A tooth for a tooth. But I say to you not to resist the evildoer; on the contrary, if someone strike thee on the right cheek, turn to him the other also; and if anyone would go to law with thee and take thy tunic, let him take thy cloak as well; and whoever forces thee to go for one mile, go with him two.'

'You have heard that it was said to the ancients.' To what

ancients? Obviously, to the Jews. Malice rather than age made them ancient; their fury kept them so eager for vengeance that they demanded a head in return for an eye, and a life in payment for a tooth. Consequently, the Law was restraining their demand for vengeance. It aimed to bring those who were too weak to relish forgiving a fault, to relish, if you will, a portion of vengeance, that is, to demand vengeance only equal to the injury which the offender had inflicted in his anger.

This, however, was for the ancients. Let us hear what the divine Goodness enjoins upon us who have been renewed through grace. 'But I say to you.' To whom? Obviously, to the Christians. 'Not to resist the evil doer.' When He speaks thus, He wants us not to repay vices with vices, but to overcome them by virtues. He wants us to smother anger when it is still only a spark. If it grows to the full flame of its fury, it does not get checked without bloodshed. Mildness overcomes anger, meekness extinguishes fury, goodness coaxes malice away, affection lays cruelty[1] low, patience is the scourge of impatience, gentle words vanquish quarrelsomeness, and humility prostrates pride.

Therefore, brethren, he who wants to overcome vices should fight with the arms of love, not of rage. A wise man can readily see why endurance of injuries gives training toward a Christian way of living. Nevertheless, there are those who fail to understand that to do what follows is indeed a mark of strength, the summit of goodness, the pinnacle of piety, something characteristic of the divine outlook rather than the human: not to resist the evil-doer, but to overcome evil with good;[2] to bless the one who curses; to refrain from denying one who strikes you a chance to strike again; to give also your cloak to one who has taken your tunic, and

1 Reading *crudelitas,* with S. Pauli.
2 Cf. Rom. 12.21.

thereby to give a gift to the one who has snatched booty; to add compliance for two more miles to one who forces you to go a mile; to do all this that willingness may take precedence over force, and love may overcome impiety, and that the very thing which your adversary forces may become the virtue of the patient man. Those examples teach us how a soldier of Christ is trained by injuries to the strength to practice virtues. But, to make this still more evident, let us search more deeply why those practices have been enjoined upon us.

Brethren, when the disease of sin, the crime that springs from vices, and the madness of impiety permeated human minds and smothered whatever knowledge, perception, and reason were present, by its insane fury it brought the nations scattered over the earth to flee from God, follow devils, worship creatures, condemn their Creator, yearn for vices, shrink in horror from virtues, live under the pressure of the sword, and fall with wounds. It brought living men to perish in death.

The result was this. Men could not be healed save by arming themselves with all the long-suffering goodness of the heavenly Physician. Thus they could stand the injuries of those who suffered from madness, bear with curses, sustain blows, and be cut to pieces with wounds, until they could lead the evil-doers back to a sobriety of outlook, to sincerity of spirit, to sanity of mind. Through all this the evil-doers were to learn to seek God, flee the devils, grow aware of their apathy, relish health, cast off vices, acquire virtues, abstain from woundings, shrink away from blood, refuse to kill, and desire continuance in life.

If you want all this to become still clearer, let us use as examples the physicians who cure our bodies. Whenever the conflagration of cholera has set an unlucky man on fire, and made him delirious under the force of the fever, is not his intelligence disturbed and his mind undone? Does not rage approach and human conduct depart? To be brief, does not his madness live while the man is dying? Consequently, he gnashes his teeth, wounds his parents, scratches his relatives, inflicts cuts by his fist, carries on by biting, and injures his attendants.

Then the physician arms himself with his patience—to the praise of his virtue, the glory of his skill, and the increase of his reputation. He shows himself forbearing, makes no account of injuries, endures the bites, bears up under his efforts, and endures pains by no means light in order to free his patient from suffering. He uses applications of oil, plies his cures, dispenses medicine, sure that the sick man will pay him a reward of honor for his services, once he has recovered his health.

What greater madness is there, I ask, or what stronger force of rage than any of these: to slap a holy man on the cheek; to pummel the face of a meek brother; to spoil the charm or a placid countenance by making it a pitiful black and blue; to strip a man of the only garment covering him, and, to get some booty of little worth, to leave nothing to God, nothing to the man, nothing to nature, nothing to modesty; to exact service from a man already busy with his own pursuits; to regard another's pain as one's own solace?

Therefore, brethren, if we know that those who perpetrate such deeds are suffering serious madness, let us be obedient to Christ. Let us, through the virtue of piety in all its fullness, endure the bites, blows, and burdens of our frenzied brethren, in order to free them from their affliction, and to gain for ourselves the eternal reward which patience brings.

Neither should a servant disdain to receive from his fellow servants that which the Lord deigned to receive from servants for the sake of His servants. He did not refuse His face to their palms. When they took His tunic and cloak He delivered to them also His body. When some one forced Him to labor [up Calvary], He graciously and willingly followed even to death. Consequently, brethren, if the Lord deemed it worth while to suffer, how, how indeed, can it seem improper that His servant suffer? We are in error, brethren, we are in error. The man who does not do what the Lord commanded hopes without reason for what the Lord promised.

## SERMON 40

### *The Good Shepherd*

(On John 10.1-18)

Each year, when spring with its breezes begins to usher in the birth of so many sheep, and to deposit the numerous young of the fruitful flock about the fields, the meadows, and the paths, a good shepherd puts aside his songs.[1] He anxiously searches for the tender sheeplings, picks them up and gathers them together. Happy to carry them, he places them about his neck, on his shoulders, and in his arms. He wants them to be safe as he carries or leads them to the protecting sheepfolds.

That is the case with ourselves, too, brethren. When we see our ecclesiastical flock gaining rich increase under the favoring smile of the spring of Lent, we put aside the resonant tones of our treatise and the customary fare of our

1 Those by which he whiles away his leisure.

discourse.[2] Solicitous about our very heavy labor, we give all our concern[3] to gathering and carrying in the heavenly sprouts.

But, since we see that the lambs have been returned to the flock and that all are now within the enclosure of Christ, we are called back in joy to the divine declamations.[4] With full exaltation we set before you a life-giving abundance of the Lord's food, in order to have as sharers in our joy those whom we observed to be our companions in work.

Because this our preface has brought in mention of Him who alone is good, who alone is the Shepherd, and who alone is the Shepherd of shepherds, let the entire application of our discourse and treatise come to fulfillment and be deemed complete.

'The good shepherd,' the text reads, 'lays down his life for his sheep.' The force of love makes a man brave, because genuine love counts nothing as hard, or bitter, or serious, or deadly. What sword, what wounds, what penalty, what deaths can avail to overcome[5] perfect love? Love is an inpenetrable breastplate. It wards off missiles, sheds the blows of swords, taunts dangers, laughs at death. If love is present, it conquers everything.

But is that death of the shepherd advantageous to the sheep? Let us investigate. It leaves them abandoned, exposes them defenseless to the wolves, hands over the beloved flock to the gnawing jaws of beasts, gives them over to plunder

---

2 *Tractatus*: discussion, treatise, homily, sermon (see Harpers' *Latin Dictionary* and Souter, *s.v.*); and *sermo*: discourse, discussion, sermon. *Sermo* was used to render Origen's *lógos* (cf. *Catholic Encyclopedia* 7.448), which might have been rendered by *oratio*. Cf. Introduction, pp. 3, 4, 15; *PL* 52.312C n. i.

3 This is evidence that in Lent St. Peter, like other bishops of the time, omitted his customary preaching to devote his time to the instruction of the catechumens. Cf. *PL* 52.312D.

4 *cantus*.

5 Reading *superare*, with Held and Böhmer.

and exposes them to death. All this is proved by the death of the Shepherd, Christ. From the time when He laid down His life for His sheep, and permitted Himself to be slain through the fury of the Jews, His sheep have been suffering invasions from the piratical Gentiles. Like prisoners to be slain in jails, they are shut up in the caves of robbers. They are torn unceasingly by persecutors who are like raging wolves. They are snapped at by heretics who are like mad dogs with savage teeth.

The martyred choir of the Apostles proves this. The blood of the martyrs shed throughout the whole world proclaims it. The members of Christians thrown to the beasts, or consumed with fire, or sunk in the rivers clearly display it. And truly, just as the death of the Shepherd brought all this in, so could His life have prevented it.

In the light of all this, does the Shepherd prove His love for you by His death? Is He proving His love because, when He sees danger threatening His sheep, when He cannot defend his flock, He prefers to die before He sees any evil done to the sheep?[6]

But what are we to do, since the Life[7] Himself could not die unless He had decided to? Who could have taken life away from the Giver of life if He were unwilling? He Himself said: 'I have the power to lay down my life, and I have the power to take it up again. No one takes it from me.' Therefore, He willed to die—He who permitted Himself to be slain although He was unable to die. Hence, let us investigate the strength and the reason of this love, the cause of this death, and the utility of this passion.

Clearly, there is an established strength, a true reason, a

6 This sentence of the Latin is hard to understand in its context unless we make it a question. It is an example of the occasional obscurity in St. Peter.

7 Christ, who names Himself the Life in John 14.6.

lucid cause, a patent utility in all this blood. For, unique power sprang forth from the one death of the Shepherd. For the sake of His sheep the Shepherd met the death which was threatening them. He did this that, by a new arrangement, He might, although captured Himself, capture the Devil, the author of death; that, although conquered Himself, He might conquer; that, although slain Himself, He might punish; that, by dying for His sheep, He might open the way for them to conquer death.

The Devil, too, while he aimed at man, made an attempt on God. While he grows furious at the guilty one, he runs up against his Judge. While he inflicts pain, he incurs torture. While he is issuing a sentence, he receives one. And death, which lives by feeding upon mortals, dies while it is devouring the Life. Death, which swallows guilty men, gets swallowed while it is gulping down the Author of innocence. Death, accustomed to destroy all, perishes itself while it tries to destroy the salvation of all.

Therefore, by giving a pattern like this, the Shepherd went before His sheep; He did not run away from them. He did not surrender the sheep to the wolves, but He consigned the wolves to the sheep. For He enabled His sheep to pick out their robbers in such a way that the sheep, although slain, should live; although mangled, should rise again and, colored by their own blood, should gleam in royal purple, and shine with snow-white fleece.

In this way, when the good Shepherd laid down His life for His sheep, He did not lose it. In this way He held His sheep; He did not abandon them. Indeed, He did not forsake them, but invited them. He called and led them through fields full of death, and a road of death, to life-giving pastures.

But, someone will say: When will all this occur? Look, for the time being the sheep, that is, the Apostles, the prophets, the martyrs, and the confessors lie in their tombs. They have been plucked like flowers, and scattered all over the globe. Shrouded with their own blood, they lie shut up in darksome sepulchres.

And who doubts that these slain martyrs will arise, and live, and reign, since Christ Himself, though slain, has arisen, and lives, and reigns? Hear the voice of the Shepherd: 'My sheep hear my voice and follow me.' The sheep who have followed Him to death must also follow Him to life. They who have accompanied Him into the midst of insults must also accompany Him into honor. They who shared His passion must also share His glory.

'Where I am,' He says, 'there also shall my servant be.'[8] Where? Truly, above the skies where Christ is sitting at the Father's right hand. O man, let not living by faith disturb you, nor the long time you must hope fatigue you. Your destiny is a certain one, and is being kept for you with the very Author of all things! 'You have died,' Scripture says, 'and your life is hidden with Christ in God. When Christ, your life, shall appear, then you too will appear with Him in glory.'[9]

What the toiling sower does not see in his seed he will see in the harvest; and he who weeps while he sows[10] in the furrow will have great joy in the fruit.

---

8 John 12.26.
9 Col. 3.3,4.
10 Cf. Ps. 125.5-7.

## SERMON 43

### *Prayer, Fasting, and Almsgiving*[1]

We should speak to the populace in popular fashion. The parish ought to be addressed by ordinary speech. Matters necessary to all men should be spoken about as men in general speak. Natural language is dear to simple souls and sweet to the learned. A teacher should speak words which will profit all. Therefore, today let the learned grant pardon for commonplace language.

There are three things, brethren, three, through which faith stands firm, devotion abides, and virtue endures: prayer, fasting, and mercy. What prayer knocks for upon the door, fasting successfully begs and mercy receives. Prayer, fasting, and mercy: these three are a unit. They give life to one another. For, fasting is the soul of prayer; and mercy is the life of fasting.

Let no one cut these three apart; they are inseparable. If a man has only one of them, or if he does not have them all simultaneously, he has nothing. Therefore, he who prays should also fast; and he who fasts should also be merciful. He who wants to be heard when he petitions should hear another who petitions him. He who does not close his own ear to a suppliant opens God's ear to himself. The fasting man should realize what fasting is. If anyone wants God to perceive that he is hungry, he should himself take notice of a hungering man. If he hopes for mercy, he should show mercy himself. If he desires fatherly kindness, he should display it first. He who wishes someone to make an offering to him should make an offering himself. He is an unworthy petitioner who demands for himself what he refuses to another.

O man, have this as your norm of showing mercy. Do

---

1 This is a sermon rather than a homily. Cf. Introduction, pp. 3-4.

you yourself show mercy to others in the same manner, amount, and readiness with which you desire it to be shown to yourself.

Therefore, let prayer, mercy, and fasting be one petition for us before God. Let them be one legal aid in our behalf. Let them be a threefold prayer for us. These are the things, brethren, these are the things which hold fast the citadel of heaven, knock at the private chamber of God our Judge, follow up the cases of men before the tribunal of Christ, beg indulgence for the unjust, win pardon of the guilty. The man who does not have these as his aiding advocates in heaven does not have a secure position on earth. Since these have so high a post in heaven, they influence the generality of events on earth. They guide prosperity and ward off adversity. They extinguish vices and enkindle virtues. They render bodies chaste and hearts pure. They bring peace to the members of the body and ease to the mind. They make the senses a school for disciplinary control. They enable human hearts to become lofty temples of God. They make a man appear to be an angel, and even bring him honor from God.

Hence it is that through the influence of these three things Moses is made a god:[2] for the sake of his military triumphs he brings all the elements under his control. He bids[3] the sea to withdraw, its waves to solidify, its bottom to become dry, and the sky to drop its rain. He supplies food, compels the winds to scatter meats,[4] illumines the night with the splendor of the sun,[5] tempers the sun by the veil of the cloud. He strikes[6] the rock to make it yield from its fresh wound cool

2 Exod. 7.1. Magistrates had a share in God's powers, e.g., of judging. Therefore, in the Old Testament they were sometimes called 'gods', obviously in a wide sense. See also Exod. 22.8,9,28; Ps. 81.6; John 10.34.

3 Exod. 14.8-31.

4 Exod. 16.12-15; Num. 11.31.

5 Exod. 13.21,22.

6 Num. 20.2-13.

streams of water for those who thirst. He first gives[7] to the earth heaven's law, writes down the norms of living, sets the terms of disciplinary control.

Through these three—prayer, fasting, and mercy—Elias[8] does not know death. He leaves the earth, enters heaven, tarries among the angels, and lives with God. As a guest from earth he possesses the heavenly mansions.

Through these three John becomes an angel in the flesh, a citizen of heaven upon earth; by his hearing, his sight, and touch[9] he alone of men grasps, holds, and embraces the entire Trinity.

So we, too, brethren—if we wish to have a share in the glory of Moses, the life of Elias, the virtues of John, and the merits of all the saints, let us be fervent in prayer, let us have time for fasting, let us be attentive to mercy. The Christian armor-bearer and warrior of the Lord who has spent his life in these and has been fortified through them—he will not fear the javelins of sin, the weapons of the Devil, the strategems of the world, the wedge-like formations of vices, the evils of the flesh, and the snares of pleasures, or the arms of death.

But we who arise in the morning to meet we know not what, who pass the day in the midst of snares, who endure the vicissitudes of the hours, the changes brought by single minutes, the slips of words, and the dangers of deeds, why are we unwilling to enter the church in the morning? Why do we lack the will to beg protection for the whole day by our morning prayers? Why do we find pleasure in being with a man all day, but find none in presence with God for even a moment?

---

7 Exod. 20.1-17. Further details are given in Chapters 20-30.

8 4 Kings 2.11.

9 Mita (*PL* 52.332D) explains that John the Baptist *heard* the Father's voice coming from the cloud, *saw* the Holy Spirit descending as a dove, and *touched* the Son whom he was baptizing.

Not from ourselves, brethren, not from ourselves does that robbery spring. It takes its origin from the Devil. He is preparing to deceive those whom he does not suffer to be fortified by prayers. Why does the man who fails to pray for prosperity complain about adversity? Let us hear God's warning voice: 'Watch and pray, that you may not enter into temptation.'[10] He who does not go to prayer does go into temptation. Aware of this, the Prophet sang: 'Come let us adore and fall down before him; and weep before the Lord who made us.'[11] Do you think that he who disdains to utter words of prayer to the Lord will deign to weep before Him?

Let us come in the morning, let us pray, at least in human fear if not with divine love; at least compelled by evils if not enticed by benefits. Contempt for God brings evil times upon us; no mere passing of cycles fetches them. Therefore, let us seek by fasting what we have lost by our contempt. Let us immolate our souls by fasting, because we can offer nothing better to God. The Prophet proves this when he says: 'A sacrifice to God is an afflicted spirit: a contrite and humble heart God does not despise.'[12]

O man, offer your soul to God; offer the oblation of fasting. Do this to make your soul a pure victim, a holy sacrifice, a living victim, which remains yours while it is given to God. The man who fails to offer this gift to God will have no excuse, for he who will give himself is unable to suffer want.

But, to make those gifts acceptable, follow them up with mercy. Fasting does not germinate unless watered by mercy. When mercy dries up, fasting suffers drought, for mercy is to fasting what rain is to the earth. The man who is fast-

10 Matt. 26.41.
11 Ps. 94.6.
12 Ps. 50.19.

ing may prepare his heart, cleanse his flesh, pull out his vices, and sow virtues. Nevertheless, if he does not sprinkle his plants with streams of mercy, he does not gather his harvest. O faster, when your mercy fasts your field fasts, too. O faster, what you pour out in mercy comes back as storage in your barn.

Consequently, O man. lest you lose by saving, gather in by dispensing. O man, give to yourself by giving to the poor man. For you yourself will not possess what you leave to another.

## SERMON 44

### *The Counsel of the Ungodly, the Way of Sinners, and the Chair of Pestilence*

(On Psalm 1)

Whenever a skillful physician desires to administer adequate medicine to those sick with various ailments, he uncovers the inner causes of the diseases. He gives instructions about unsuspected attacks of a pestilence, and issues warnings about plague-ridden regions. He brings out as many kinds of remedies as possible, explains the powers of herbs, speaks about the qualities of the medicaments, and promises long-lasting health to those who obey him. In this way he persuades the sick, and leads them on to difficult, painful cures.

This is the reason why the holy Prophet, about to bring forth his heaven-sent medicine for body and soul, uncovers the deep recesses of impiety. He exposes the hidden diseases—sins. He lays iniquities bare, draws out in a marvelous way the hidden poisons, the very essences of the vices, the sources of the sins, and the roots of crimes. By such devoted manipulation and divine healing, he continually leads the sick souls of men to health, with a pious respect for their age, sex, circumstances, and ability.

The psalm which we sang today is the preface of the Psalms. Indeed, it is the Psalm of Psalms, the title of the titles. It is a theme suggesting other themes, and the basic subject matter of the hymns which follow. Once the key to a royal palace has opened the first door, it makes many interior living rooms accessible. Similarly, once that psalm has prepared an entrance for the understanding, it throws open the mystery of all the Psalms, and reveals their secret.

'Blessed is the man who hath not walked in the counsel of the ungodly, nor stood in the way of sinners, nor sat in the chair of pestilence.' 'Blessed is the man.' When a man is about to fight with the beasts and undergo the dangers of the most violent struggles, he is usually told beforehand about the prizes, rewards, and crowns. In similar fashion. the Prophet states a beatitude first, in order to stimulate man to overcome all the ferocity of the sins he will soon enumerate.

'Blessed is the man who hath not walked in the counsel of the ungodly, nor stood in the way of sinners.' Perhaps it seems absurd that he said, to *walk* in the counsel, and *stand* in the way. Men are more wont to *delay* about counsel, and to *walk* along a road. For perverse men, it is true, everything is perverted. Things which are not done in orderly manner cannot be kept in order. However, the Prophet is talking here about the movement not of the body but of the mind. He is working to prevent not slips of the foot but calamities of souls.

'Blessed is the man who hath not walked in the counsel of the ungodly.' The wicked man went away, away from himself when he receded from God; neither does he delay about counsel who lets his mind wander in evil thoughts.

At one moment he is raised up to the sky, at another he is cast back to earth. He is tossed about on the seas, lifted aloft on the billows, plunged into the troughs. And since his own thoughts stagger as if he were drunk, he takes account, not of himself, but of the sky. He who thinks that he knows everything does not know himself. For, if he knew himself, he would never adore the sky, the sun, the moon, bits of wood, or stones. All these have been given to him, subjected to his use. But he adores the stone and serves the wood, and he has disdained to serve the true and living God.

Review the deeds of wickedness from the beginning of creation. The counsel of the ungodly has dragged an angel from heaven to hell, and changed a messenger of divine revelation into a devil. It has expelled man from a regime of life to an exile on earth where he must die, and driven him from the delights of paradise to the troublesome labors of the world. It has brought woman from the glory of virginity to painful travail in the midst of groans. Therefore she has anguish before she rejoices, and pays the penalty of guilt before she exults over the birth of her child. As Scripture has it: 'I will make great your distress in child-bearing; in pain shall you bring forth children.'[1] When a beginning entails a penalty, of what sort is the termination? Whom will joy possess throughout the journey of life if he takes the beginning of his life from grief? The Prophet knew this when he said: 'I was conceived in iniquities, and in sins did my mother give me birth.'[2]

Brethren, if in this way we come forth from the womb to enter a way of sinners, if in every age of life we make a fast journey of sins, let us reflect on the vanities of infancy, the falls of youth, the disasters of manhood, and the infirmities of old age. Then we shall think we are traveling a way of

1 Gen. 3.16.
2 Ps. 50.7.

sinners rather than one of life. Christ has warned us about this road with His words: 'How wide and broad is the way that leads to destruction, and many there are who enter that way.'[3] It is wide for sins, spread out for turbulent traffic, broad for crimes. Truly, the present life is a way on which man comes and goes. 'One generation passeth away, and another generation cometh: but the earth standeth forever,'[4] Scripture tells us.

That is why it previously stated: 'Blessed is the man who has not walked in the counsel of the ungodly, nor stood in the way of sinners.'[5] It did not state 'has not come,' for there is no one who comes by another way than the way of sinners. The very law of nature and of death leads us along that way. What Scripture states is: Blessed is he who does not stand still on that way. He stands and loiters in that way who picks up burdens of sins, and arrives late like an overburdened traveler, and finds the heavenly mansion closed to him. The Prophet was encumbered by those loads when he exclaimed in tears: 'For my iniquities are gone over my head: and as a heavy burden have become heavy upon me.'[6] And because he was bearing these iniquities all the days of his life, he cried: 'I am miserable, and am bowed down even to the end.'[7]

The way of sinners is quickly traversed by the wayfarer who sees the evils of this life, but despises them. He perceives them, but treads them under foot. He endures them, but

3 Matt. 7.13.

4 Eccle. 1.4.

5 In the rest of this sermon, notice St. Peter's ingenious interpretation, arrived at by scrutinizing the three verbs of Ps. 1.1. We should not *sit* in a chair along the way of sinners which we all must travel, or *stand* on that way, or even *walk* along, but traverse it quickly toward heaven. No doubt, this ingenuity would be very pleasing to an audience of Roman rhetoricians.

6 Ps. 37.4.

7 Ps. 37.7.

conquers them. While he flees them he runs the more. Consequently, the keeper of the gates of heaven comes to meet him, and the heavenly mansion is not kept shut to him.

But, why did the sacred writer speak about the counsel of the ungodly before mentioning the way of sinners, in this order: 'Blessed is the man who has not walked in the counsel of the ungodly nor stood in the way of sinners'? Because, even if a man once born does enter into the way of sinners, he must beforehand lie supine as an infant. He does not run into that road of sin very soon. However, when he begins to taste the poisons of wickedness, then he relishes the fat of sins. The wicked man tends toward God, but he recoils from God when he sins. God despises sinners. He warned them beforehand that they should not sin. Darkness flees from the light, and when the light departs darkness returns. Just so, where God is there is no sin, and, where sin is, God is not. That you may know, O man, that before God's eyes man traverses a way of sins, listen to the Prophet: 'God is not before his eyes: his ways are filthy at all times.'[8] Therefore, man falls more seriously on this way of sins when he plunges down the steep slopes of godlessness.

'And he has not sat in the chair of pestilence.' He approves iniquity who does it and loves it. He who loves it cannot fail to teach it. Consequently, one who teaches iniquity is seated in the chair of pestilence, from which he dispenses, in honeyed language, the poison of doctrine fatal to his hearers.

By chair of pestilence the Psalmist meant philosophy, which has taught that there are many gods. It has held that He who is either does not exist or else cannot be discovered—even He who presented the gift of creation to nature, only to have nature deny its Creator.

The Pharisee[9] established a chair of pestilence, too. He

8 Ps. 9.26 (10.5 according to the Hebrews).
9 See Matt. 15.1-20.

made human traditions more important than God's laws, and dissipated the abundant light which the Jewish people had.

The heretic has taken his seat in the chair of pestilence. Under an apparent zeal for the faith, he tears, violates, and rends its unity asunder.

Therefore, 'Blessed is the man who hath not walked in the counsel of the ungodly, nor stood in the way of sinners, nor sat in the chair of pestilence.' Blessed, indeed, because by shunning those three errors he has merited to arrive at the beatitude of the Holy Trinity. Wherefore, let him meditate on the law of the Lord. Let him do this pondering day and night, that in the future he may deserve to see what follows, and at the proper time to hear something still more joyful.[10]

## SERMON 47

### *The Parables of the Pearl and the Net Cast into the Sea*

(On Matt. 13.45-50)

By the fact that Christ our Lord created the sky, earth, sea, and the great, many, and varied creatures in them, He gave wonderful evidence of His power. By the fact that He assumes human nature, acts the part of man, enters into the centuries, passes through the periods of life, teaches by word, works cures by His power, tells parables, gives examples, and manifests in Himself the burden of our emotions—by all this He reveals that he has an indescribable affection of human love.

For this reason, He makes heavenly goods appear attractive

10 Reading *laetius*.

through earthly examples. He uses beings of the present world to make us relish those of the future world. He represents invisible benefits by visible evidence. The parables which we hear from the Gospel today give forceful proof of all this.

'The kingdom of heaven is like a merchant in search of fine pearls. When he finds a single pearl of great price, he goes and sells all that he has and buys it.' Let no one who hears this take offense from the name merchant. Here Christ is speaking of a merchant who shows mercy, not of one who is always investing the profit from capital. He means one who provides the beauty of virtues, not the irritations of vices; one who brings forth seriousness of morals, not great weights of precious stones; one who has on a necklace of righteousness, not wantonness; one who wears the insignia of disciplinary control, not the trappings of pleasure.

Wherefore, that merchant displays these pearls of heart and body, not in human trading, but in heavenly commerce. He shows them, not to trade for a present advantage but for a future one—to trade in order to gain not earthly but heavenly glory; in order to be able to get the kingdom of heaven as the reward of his virtues, and to buy at the price of innumerable other goods, the one pearl of everlasting life.

The Lord added another parable in these words: 'Again, the kingdom of heaven is like a net cast into the sea and gathering in fish of every kind. When it was filled, they hauled it out and sitting down on the beach, they gathered the good fish into the vessels, but threw away the bad.' 'The kingdom of heaven is like a net cast into the sea.' This parable reveals why Christ chose fishermen to be His Apostles, and changed catchers of fish into fishers of men, that fishermen's practice might be recognized as a type of God's judgment.

The catch itself brings together fish of every sort, but the separation puts the chosen ones into vessels. Similarly, the vocation to the Christian faith brings together just and unjust, bad and good, but the divine election separates the good and the bad.

'The kingdom of heaven is like a net cast into the sea.' Christ sent His fishermen—Peter, Andrew, James, and John, all of them approved for their skill—to the sea of this world. It was a sea swelling with its vain display, proud of its confusion, stormy because of factions, fluctuating through uncertainty, noisy with grievances, roaring with anger, shipwrecked by sins, and sunk into impiety. 'Come, follow me,' He told them, 'and I will make you fishers of men.'[1]

Hence, He sent His fishers forth with nets woven of the precepts of the Law and of the Gospel, hemmed with counsels, expanded with gifts of virtues and with grace, fit to gather an unceasing catch into the shelter of the Gospel. Now, brethren, right now is the time of this catch. Christ's nets are being drawn through the tribes and nations now. Throughout the whole world they are bringing in teeming catches, without discrimination of persons.

However, because the end of the world is near, the nets are bringing to the beach the fish of our capture (that is, the men who wander about free and untrammeled while immersed in worldly concerns), they are disturbed by the dryness of the shore (that is, the nearness of the end), and they dash against one another because of the whole arrangement of things.[2] They see wicked nations wax prosperous through triumph after triumph, Christian peoples distressed in captivity all over the world. They see wicked men rejoice in success and prosperity, and pious men harassed unceasingly by one evil after another. They see masters reduced to slavery, slaves gaining the upper hand over their masters, sons rebellious against their parents, aged men held up in

1 Matt. 4.19.
2 I.e., they are scandalized at the order permitted by God.

contempt by youths. They see every condition of nature, every arrangement of order as something utterly perished.

However, although these facts are true, and perturb the weak [in faith], they do not unsettle the strong. They cannot perturb the strong because the strong increase their strength through parable, and build up their fortitude through aid from the figure.

The fish taken out of the deep toss about in their confusion for a little while on the shore, but the quick selection, while it discards the bad ones, separates the good. That brief confusion soon to pass makes them the good ones, rather than perturbs them. That heavenly selection consigns the evil to their penalties and quickly gathers the good to their honors. It leads the wicked below and places the faithful in the kingdom. It consoles[3] them all—fathers, the aged, the just, the elect—with everlasting glory in return for the short-lived insults they bore. The parable itself demonstrates this when it says: 'At the end of the world the angels of God will go out and separate the wicked from the just.'

'At the end of the world.' He who believes in the end of the world and discusses its deterioration, and has hope that the lasting possessions will be his later on—why does he seek to possess the perishable ones?

Brethren, the world takes a beginning from its very terminations. A creature is renewed by its end, not destroyed. It withdraws itself not from its Creator, but from sin. Not for the just, but for the sinners, do the elements come to an end [of their usefulness]. 'At the end of the world, the angels will go out to separate the just apart.' Let no one doubt that the angels will appear to the saints. Even Christ promises His service to the saints. His maxim is: 'I shall gird myself and minister to you.'[4]

3 Reading *consolatur,* with S. Pauli.
4 Cf. Luke 17.8.

'The angels of God will go out and separate the wicked from among the just.' Bear up, O just ones, endure for a while. Yea, more, even grant a truce to your opponents. This short-lived mingling with the unjust will be compensated by a long separation.

'They will separate the wicked from among the just and will cast them into the furnace of fire.' See what sort of abode those prepare for themselves who expel their neighbors and drive away their guests! See how great a fire those men kindle for themselves from their short-lived pleasure, who in this world prepare delights for themselves out of the hunger of the poor and the pain they inflict on others!

'There will be weeping and gnashing of teeth.' How woefully will that man gnash his teeth there who smiles in evil here! And he who has joy now from the misfortunes of the poor will then weep over their good fortune, because he had it within his power to rejoice with the poor, but would not. But you, my faithful ones, rejoice forever in the Lord.

## SERMON 57

### *On the Apostles' Creed: To the Catechumens*[1]

Blessed Isaias, an Evangelist no less than a Prophet, deplores his having unclean lips, and his dwelling in the midst of a people which has them too. 'Woe is me,' he says, 'because I am in remorse; because while I am a man, and have unclean lips, I dwell also in the middle of people that hath unclean lips. I have seen with my eyes the King, the Lord of hosts.'[2]

---

1 Sermons 56-72 form a series of instructions given to the catechumens in Lent.

2 Isa. 6.5.

Here he is struck with a sorrow more than human because he is unable to speak, proclaim, and avow all that he feels and sees about God. As much as the flesh is limited, just that much are the lips too narrow for their spirit, and the tongue too short to explain its mind. A roaring fire is shut up in the flesh. It fills the veins with steam, inflames the inmost members, and seethes in the marrow. It always enkindles a man's whole interior, because he finds himself unable to express adequately with his mouth what he contemplates in absorption of mind. He cannot pour it out of his lips, adorn it with his language, and put it like steam into his whole speech.

That is the reason why Isaias wept over his own and his people's unclean lips when he saw the King of heaven, that is, the Christ; also, when he saw with clear vision that He is the Lord of armies. For, just as confessing Christ's divinity enlightens hearts, washes mouths, and cleanses lips, so is denying His majesty a cause of pollution.

But let us hear what avail there was in that groan of the Prophet: 'And one of the Seraphims,' Scripture says, 'was sent to me, and in his hand he had a live coal which he had taken with tongs off the altar, and he touched my mouth, saying: Behold this hath touched thy lips, and hath taken away thy iniquities, and hath cleansed thy sins.'[3] This is not the time to tell why precisely one is sent, and who he is who is sent, and how great he is who thus fearlessly carries a live coal of heavenly fire in his hand; yes, more, who so tempers it by his touch that it purifies the lips of the Prophet and does not burn them. But let us at this time feel remorse with all the affection of our hearts. Let us admit that we are wretched in this misery of the flesh. Let us weep with holy groans because we, too, have unclean lips. Let us do all this to make that one of the Seraphims bring down

3 Isa. 6.6,7.

to us, by means of the tongs of the law of grace, a flaming sacrament of faith taken for us from the heavenly altar. Let us do this to make him touch the tip of our lips with such delicate touch as to take away our iniquities, purge away our sins, and so enkindle our mouths to the full flame of full praise that the burning will be one unto salvation, not pain. Let us beg, too, that the heat of that coal may penetrate all the way to our hearts. Thus we may draw not only relish for our lips from the great sweetness of this mystery, but also complete satisfaction for our senses and minds.

After the cleansing of his lips, Isaias told about that ineffable birth which the Virgin gave to her child: 'Behold, a virgin shall conceive in her womb and bear a son.'[4] In similar fashion let us tell about that mystery[5] of the Passion and the glory of the Resurrection.

'I believe in God, the Father Almighty.' That you have believed in God is something which you rightly confess today, when you rejoice over the fact that you have fled away from gods and goddesses of different sex, bewildering in their number, popular because moblike, base in their lineage, vile in their reputation, greatest in their wickedness, foremost in sin, and outstanding in evil-doing, convicted of all this even by their very countenance sculptured on the tombs[6] of their devotees. Your joy is proper, because to have such beings even as one's servants is wretched, painful, and unfortunate. Yet, up to the present, you endured them as your masters.

Rejoice that you have turned to the one, true, living, and only but not lonely God, by saying: 'I believe in God the Father.' The man who names Him Father should already acknowledge the Son. For He who has wished to be called

4 Isa. 7.14.
5 *sacramentum.*
6 The crimes of the gods were often portrayed by sculpture on tombs and sarcophagi.

a Father, to be denoted as a Father, is kindly making clear that He has a Son, whom he did not receive at any point of time, or beget in time, or have in His care merely for a time. Divinity does not take a beginning, or admit an end, or any succession; it is incapable of any waning. Not amid any pains does God bring forth His Son; He manifests that because of His powers the Son is existent. He does not make as something outside Himself that Being which is from Himself, but he generates that Being; while the Being is inside Himself, He discloses and reveals the fact. The Son has proceeded from the Father, but not withdrawn from Him. Neither has He come forth from the Father as one destined to succeed the Father, but as one who will remain always in the Father.

Hear John's words: 'He was in the beginning with God.'[7] And elsewhere John says: 'What was from the beginning.'[8] Assuredly, that which already was did not come by addition later on; clearly, that which was did not later take a beginning. 'I am the first, and I am the last,'[9] He says. He who is the first is not after someone else; He who is the last does not leave another behind Him. When He utters those words, He does not exclude the Father, but He concludes that all things are in both Himself and the Father.

Let us, however, take up the words that follow. 'And in Jesus Christ His only Son, our Lord.' Kings get new titles from their triumphs—multitudinous epithets derived from the names of the conquered nations. Similarly, Christ gets His names[10] from His titles to His distinctions. Because of the chrism of His anointing He was named Christ, who as the loving Physician poured the unguent of divinity into the

---

7 John 1.2.
8 1 John 1.1. 'He' and 'What' refer to the Word, the Son of God.
9 Isa. 44.6.
10 *A chrismate vocatus est Christus. Jesus vocatus est a salute.*

already withering members of mortal men. Just as He was called the Christ from the chrism, so from salvation was He called Jesus, [the Saviour], who moistened us with His divine unguent precisely to restore certain salvation to the sick and everlasting health to those in desperate need.

'And in Jesus Christ His only Son.' Yes, only Son, for, although there are many through grace, He is the one and only Son through His nature. 'Our Lord,' who seeks us out —once we have been freed from the control of such great, cruel, and base lords—not to place us in our original state, but to release us into everlasting freedom.

'Who was born from the Holy Spirit.' Precisely thus is Christ born for you, in such a way that He may change your own manner of birth as a man. Formerly, death awaited you as the setting sun of your life; He wants you to have a new birth of life.

'Who was born from the Holy Spirit of the Virgin Mary.' Where the Spirit is begetting, and a Virgin giving birth, everything carried on is divine; nothing of it is merely human. Neither is there any place for weakness where power is united to power. Adam was put into a deep sleep that a virgin might be taken from the virile half of the race;[11] now, the Virgin was amazed that mankind was to be renewed from a virgin. What will nature be able to claim as her own from such a great birth in which, while she sees her order being renewed and all her rights being changed, she perceives with wonder that her Creator has come into His own offspring? Let faithless men, if they will, think this something cheap. To believers it is a great mystery.[12]

'Who was crucified under Pontius Pilate and was buried.'

11 Gen. 2.21-23; Luke 1.29-38. St. Peter's Latin has an alliterative play on words: *ut de viro virgo sumeretur; . . . Virgo, ut vir reparetur ex Virgine.*

12 *sacramentum.*

You hear the name of the Judge that you may recognize the exact time of Christ's Passion. You hear that He was crucified, that you may acknowledge that the salvation once lost for us has been restored through exactly that,[13] through which it has been lost; also, that you may see the Life for believers hanging there where death had hung for faithless men. You perceive that He was buried, that His death may not be deemed something merely feigned. This is a sign of divine power: when death itself dies because of a death, when the author of death is maimed by his own sword point, and the pirate is captured by his own prey, hell is deprived of the life it has already swallowed.

'The third day He arose again from the dead.' Christ devoted the three days of His burial to the three abodes He was going to profit: the region beneath the earth, the earth, and heaven. He was going to restore the things in heaven, repair those on earth, and redeem those beneath the earth, in order that by this symbol of a three-day period He might open up the grace of the Trinity to men for their salvation.

'He ascended into heaven.' He ascended not to take Himself back into heaven—for He had always remained there—but rather to carry you there, whom He freed, bound as you were, and snatched away from hell. O man, understand whence and where God has raised you, in order to give a firm footing in heaven to you who on earth were on slippery footing and always liable to fall.

'He sits at the right hand of the Father.' The Father, however, has nothing at His left hand. Our profession of belief is

13 This passage is obscure. Its meaning seems to be: Salvation was lost through the wood of the tree from which Adam ate. On the wood of the cross hung Christ, who restored life for believers. Similar thought is found in stanzas 2 and 3 of the hymn *Pange lingua gloriosi* of Venantius Fortunatus (530-609), and in the Preface of the Cross in the Mass: 'O God, who placed the salvation of mankind in the wood of the Cross, that life might arise from where death came....'

giving, not the places where the divine Persons sit, but indications of their excellence. God cannot have places, and divinity admits nothing sinister.

'Whence He will come to judge the living and the dead.' Let it so be with regard to the living. But how will He be able to judge the dead? Why, those whom we regard as dead are living. Therefore, admit that those whom the pagan world thinks have perished will arise again to be judged; that those who have died and will be found to be living may give an account both of their deeds and their life.

'I believe in the Holy Spirit.' After you have acknowledged the mystery of the assuming of flesh, you should acknowledge the divinity of the Spirit, so that the unity and equality of the Trinity—of the Father, the Son, and the Holy Spirit—may through all things and in all things protect and hold firm the entire truth contained in our profession of faith.

'The holy Catholic Church'—yes, because neither are the members separated from the head, nor the spouse from her husband. But, by such a union, the Church becomes one spirit; she becomes all things, and God is in them all. Therefore, he believes in God who acknowledges the holy Church as something united to God.

'And the remission of sins.' He who is confident that his sins can be forgiven through Christ brings that forgiveness to himself.

'The resurrection of the body.' If you believe that through God's power you can arise from death, you believe well. For Him the elements always start anew; for example, season from season, day from night, seeds germinating from the spot where they were planted. Since these come back to life, surely you cannot perish utterly. Neither will it be difficult for God to do for you in your old age what you yourself do in the case of seed.

'Life everlasting.' This faith, this mystery, is not something to be consigned to note paper or written by letters,[14] because papers and letters remind us of objects to be cared for more than grace. But, where that divine gift, the grace of God, exists, faith suffices to serve as a contract, and the recesses of the heart are enough to contain the secret. Thus, the divine Witness can know [the terms in] this Creed of salvation, this contract of life, while the false witness remains ignorant of it. Sign yourselves. And may the Lord Himself, our God, guard your senses and your hearts. May He be present as your Supporter, to assist you in those matters which He has commanded.

## SERMON 61

### *On the Apostles' Creed: To the Catechumens*

I would scarcely believe it possible for you to be changed so easily from earthly lowliness to heavenly glory, if I did not find a consoling precedent in the sudden and unexpected conversion of blessed Paul.[1] For his quick profession of faith transformed him from a persecutor into an Apostle. It gave an outstanding teacher to the Church which had found him a furious destroyer of the Christian name. I am moved no less by the example of that eunuch whom faith snatched into grace before his chariot could take him back to his home in India.[2] There is, too, that remarkable instance of the thief,

14 St. Augustine also urged the catechumens not to write the Symbol or Creed, but to memorize it. Cf. *PL* 52.360D.

1 Acts 9.1-9.
2 Acts 8.26-40.

who stole Paradise at the very time when he was hung upon the cross to pay the penalty for his brigandage.[3]

The upshot of it all, my little children, is this. Since you have so arranged the time of your regeneration that neither we can say what is necessary nor you can hear what is proper, by way of adding more doctrine to that which you have,[4] we shall explain briefly what we cannot give at greater length. For, how can you, through our explanation, understand the mystery[5] of the Apostles' Creed, when you can hardly memorize its very formula? We give just this one admonition. Let no one put into writing what he is to put into his heart in order to believe it. For the Apostle has given this warning: 'With the heart a man believes unto justice, and with the mouth profession of faith is made unto salvation.'[6]

You are now about to hear the formula of the faith, the norm of believing, and the order of your profession. So make ready the hearing of both your body and your heart. As a spring gushes out of a small opening and broadens out with its copious flowing waters, just so does the doctrine in the compressed language of the Creed open up the widest paths of belief. And just as a root set deep into the earth sends its shoots far into the air, so does faith rooted deep in the heart spring up to the utmost height of belief. Therefore, purge the mud of unbelief out of your hearts, that the clear waters of faith may flow through you without hindrance. Cut the underbrush of unbelief in you at its very roots, that the

3 Luke 23.39-43.

4 *Fidem fidei committentes* seems to be a reference to the fuller explanation of the Christian mysteries given under the *disciplina arcani* after the catechumens were baptized. Possibly, however, it means: adding assurance to your belief.

5 *symboli sacramentum.*

6 Rom. 10.10.

stout young trees of your belief may grow to the heights. And, since the Apostle tells us that 'With the heart a man believes unto justice, but with the mouth profession of faith is made unto salvation,' pour now into the words of audible profession what you already believe in your heart.

'I believe in God, the Father Almighty.' He who believes in God should not rashly try to fathom Him. It is enough to know the fact that God is. He who inquires whence He is, how great He is, and what God is finds himself in ignorance. The sun blacks out an imprudent gazing, and his unpermitted approach to God becomes a blinded one. He who desires to see God should learn how to observe moderation in his gazing. If one wants to know his own God, let him not know the gods of pagans. He who calls them gods contradicts God. To serve the one God is liberty; but it is bondage to serve the many gods.

Believe Him to be a Father whom you have acknowledged as God, in order that, by believing Him to be a Father, you may learn that there is a Son. By calling Him a Son you recognize the fact that He has been begotten from the Father; recognizing the fact that He has been begotten, do not seek to know further how He was begotten, because you have said: 'I believe in God, the Father Almighty.'

The Almighty Being can do all things, and, if He can do all things, who will deny that He has a Son in Himself, from Himself, and always with Himself? God's generating has no beginning, is incapable of an end, and it admits no separating departure, since the One Begotten ever remains in the One Begetting, as the Lord Himself says: 'I am in the Father, and the Father is in me,'[7] and 'I and the Father are one.'[8] Now you have acknowledged the Father, and the

7 John 10.38.
8 John 10.30.

Son, and the secret doctrine of His divinity. Acknowledge, also, the mystery[9] of the Lord's Incarnation.

'And in Jesus Christ, His Son.' Christ is named from a heavenly anointing, for He is permeated with all the fullness of the divinity. The name Jesus is from salvation. At this name every being in heaven and under the earth trembles, bends the knee, and makes confession with bowed head.[10]

'And in Jesus Christ His only Son, our Lord.' Just as we acknowledge one divinity of the Father and Son, so let us confess their one domination over us.

'And in Jesus Christ His only Son, our Lord.' Just as we acknowledge one divinity of the Father and the Son, so let us confess their one domination over us.

'Who was born from the Holy Spirit of the Virgin Mary.' The Spirit and the Virgin—this is not an earthly union, but it is a heavenly mystery. This is a reason why that which is born is divine. Therefore, we must acknowledge the fact that He was born, but remain silent about how He was born. For, that which is secret cannot be known, that which is shut up admits of no opening, and what is unique cannot be represented by an example.

'Who was crucified under Pontius Pilate and was buried.' You hear the name of the judge, that you may not be ignorant of the date. You hear that He was crucified, that you may learn what kind of death He suffered, and what He paid for your sake. It was for you that He took upon Himself all the pain of such a death. You hear that He was buried, that you may know that His death was a true one, and not one unworthy to be taken seriously. To be reluctant to die is typical of human fear; to have arisen from death is a mark of divine power. So, do not be shocked at hearing

9 *sacramentum.*

10 Phil. 2.10.

of His death; in this case the glory of His resurrection blots out the harm done by death.

'On the third day He arose again,' because, just as the fact that He dies is a mark of His humanity, the fact that He arises is a testimony from the Trinity.

'He ascended into heaven'—carrying His human nature[11] there where it has always remained.

'He sits at the right hand of the Father.' He sits at the right hand, because Deity has nothing at the left.[12]

'Whence He will come to judge the living and the dead.' He will judge both the living and the dead. For those will arise for judgment who are thought to be non-existent after their death, and who in the opinion of the pagan world have perished utterly with their span of life.

'I believe in the Holy Spirit'—that you may believe and understand that there is one God in the Father and the Son and the Holy Spirit.

'I believe in the Holy Church'—that you may acknowledge that the Church, the Bride of Christ, will remain in everlasting union in Him.

'I believe in the remission of sins, the resurrection of the body.' He who does not believe in the remission of sins and the resurrection of the flesh takes away forgiveness from himself and robs himself of life.

Let your heart hold that which you have heard, and believed, and acknowledged. Let your memory retain it, but no paper know it. Do not let any secretary learn of it lest the sacred mystery of the faith be divulged in public, and the secret of the faith scattered to the infidel. May God Himself, who granted you both to hear and believe the mystery of the faith,[13] cause you to reach eternal salvation.

---

11 *hominem.*

12 *nil habet sinistrum*: i.e., has nothing bad.

13 Reading *fidei,* with S. Pauli.

# SERMON 67

## *The Lord's Prayer:*[1] *To the Catechumens*

### (On Matt. 6.9-13)

Dearly beloved, you have received the faith by hearing; now listen to the formula of the Lord's prayer. Christ taught us to pray briefly. He wishes us to put our petitions forward quickly. Why will He not give Himself to those who entreat Him, since He gave Himself to those who did not ask Him.[2] Or what delay in answering will He show who by formulating prayers has thus anticipated His suppliants' desires?

The angels stand in awe at what you are going to hear today. Heaven marvels, earth trembles, flesh does not bear it, hearing does not grasp it, the mind does not penetrate it, all creation cannot sustain it. I do not dare to utter it, yet I cannot remain silent. May God enable you to hear and me to speak.

What is more awesome: that God gives Himself to earth, or that He places you in Heaven? That He himself enters a union with flesh, or that He causes you to enter into a sharing of the Divinity? That He Himself accepts death, or that He recovers you from death? That He Himself is born into your state of slavery, or that He makes you to be free children of His own? That He takes your poverty upon Himself, or that He makes you His heirs, yes, co-heirs of His unique Self?

It is indeed more awesome that earth is transformed into a heaven, that man is changed by a deification,[3] and that

1 This sermon is a catechetical instruction to the catechumens. Cf. Introduction, p. 16 and *DTC* 12, 2e, col. 1920.

2 I.e., the Gentiles, as Mita remarks. The Jews often asked for the Messias in their prayers.

3 *deitate,* interpreted in the light of *consortium divinitatis* just above.

those whose lot is slavery get the rights of domination. All this is indeed something to fill us with fear. Nevertheless, the present situation has reference not to the one instructing but to the One who gives the command. Therefore, my little children, let us approach where charity summons, love draws, and affection invites us. May our hearts perceive God as our Father! Our voice should proclaim this, our tongue should utter it, our spirit should shout it aloud; and everything that is in us should be in tune with grace, not fear. For, He who has changed from a judge into a Father has wished to be loved, not feared.

'Our Father, who art in heaven.' When you say this, do not understand it to mean that He is not on earth, or that He who encompasses all beings is Himself contained in a place. But understand that you, whose Father is in heaven, have a lineage derived from heaven. So act, too, that you become your Father's image by your holy way of life. He who does not darken himself with human vices, but shines with virtues like God's, proves himself a son of God.

'Hallowed be Thy name.' We are called by the name of Him whose offspring we are. Therefore, let us beg that His Name, which is holy in itself and by its very nature, may be treated as holy by us. For, God's Name either gets honored because of our conduct, or blasphemed because of our misdeeds. Hear the Apostle's words: 'For the name of God is blasphemed through you among the Gentiles.'[4]

'Thy kingdom come.' Was there ever a time when God did not reign? Therefore we ask that He who always has reigned Himself may now reign in us, that we also may be able to reign in Him. The Devil has reigned, sin has reigned, death has reigned, and the human race has long been captive. Consequently, we ask that God may reign in His kingdom, the Devil may be subject, sin may fail, death

4 Rom. 2.24.

may die, and the captive human race may be captured in such a way that we may reign as free men unto everlasting life.

'Thy will be done on earth as it is in heaven.' This is the kingdom of God, when no other will than God's prevails, either in heaven or on earth; when in the case of all men, God is the directing mind, God is living, God is acting, God is reigning, God is everything, so that, according to that statement of the Apostle: 'God may be all in all of you.'[5]

'Give us this day our daily bread.' He who gave Himself to us as a Father, who adopted us as His sons, who made us the heirs of His goods, who raised us up in name and gave us His own honor and kingdom, He has directed that we should ask for our daily bread. In the kingdom of God, in the midst of His divine gifts, why does man in his poverty beg? Is it only when asked that a Father so good, so kindly, so generous gives bread to His children? And what are we to make of His statement: 'Do not be anxious about what you are to eat, or what you are to drink, or what you are to put on.'[6] Is he telling us to ask for that about which He forbids us to think? What do we hold?[7] The heavenly Father is encouraging us, as heavenly sons, to ask for heavenly bread. He said: 'I am the bread that has come down from heaven.'[8] He is the Bread sown in the Virgin, leavened in the flesh, molded in His passion, baked in the furnace of the sepulchre, placed in the churches, and set upon the altars, which daily supplies heavenly food to the faithful.

'And forgive us our trespasses, as we also forgive those who trespass against us.' O man, if you cannot be without

5 1 Cor. 15.28.
6 Matt. 6.31.
7 Reading, not *quatenus*, but *quid tenemus*, with Böhmer, *BKV* 43, p. 78.
8 John 6.41.

sin, and wish your whole debt to be forgiven you always, you yourself should forgive always. Forgive just as much as you want to be forgiven to yourself. Forgive as often as you want to be forgiven. Indeed, just because you want the whole debt to be forgiven to yourself, you yourself forgive the whole. O man, understand that by forgiving others you have given forgiveness to yourself.

'And lead us not into temptation,' because in the world life itself is a temptation. 'The life of man upon earth is a temptation,'[9] Job says. Therefore let us ask Him not to leave us to our own will, but to hedge us about in our own every act with His fatherly kindness, and by His guidance from heaven to keep us firm on the path of life.

'But deliver us from evil.' From which evil? Surely, from the Devil, from whom all evil comes. We ask that we be freed from evil, because he who has not been free from evil cannot enjoy the good.

If those [10] not yet born,[11] those still remaining in the womb, ask for bread and seek the kingdom, why is there complaint[12] because the Son of God always remained in the bosom of God the Father? If the Church begets[13]—that is not a doctrine based on reason, it is a heavenly mystery. The fact that the Son of God has been in God the Father—that cannot be explained by human reasoning. God must not be appraised in a human manner. You have heard the name, God; do not think of anything earthly or anything human. You have heard: Father of Christ; believe that He is this through His substance. You have heard that He is your Father; believe that He is this through His grace. He eternally

9 Cf. Job 7.1; the Vulgate has *militia,* not *tentatio.*

10 The catechumens.

11 By baptism.

12 Spelled *quoestio* in Migne; the normal spelling is *questio.* Cf. Sermon 4 n. 3.

13 I.e., begets spiritual children.

possessed the power that His Son should be existent; He recently allowed you to become His son. Therefore, so know that you are a son as not to become unaware of being a servant. So hear that you have been made into a likeness of Christ as to know yourself always as the servant of Christ.

## SERMON 70

### *The Lord's Prayer: To the Catechumens*

(On Matt. 6.9-13)

All the words and deeds which are reported as having God as their Author are intended to serve as a miracle, and stir up wonder. Mortals should be struck with fear at them, and the very dwellers of heaven should tremble. However, at nothing does heaven stand so much astonished, or earth tremble, or all creation fear exceedingly, as at that which you are going to hear from us today. The servant dares to call his Lord Father, the guilty man names his Judge his Parent, man in his earthly state brings himself by his own voice adoption as God's son. He who lost earthly goods deems himself the heir of Divinity.

But we do dare to speak thus, because the speaker is not rashly presuming in a case where one commanding him has authority. He who taught us to pray thus is the One who wished us to speak in this way today.

Yet, why is it strange if He has made men devoted sons of God, since He gave Himself and made Himself into the Son of Man? At that time He raised the nature of flesh into one divine, when He brought His divinity down to human nature. At that time He made man co-heir with Himself among the dwellers of heaven, when He made

Himself the sharer of the things of earth. He took upon Himself everything characteristic of man, even sin[1] and death; then what love, what gift, could He refuse man? Or can it be that He who made Himself the sharer of man's adversity will not let man be His companion in prosperity? O man, beloved thus by God, return to God. Give your whole self to glorifying Him who for your sake humiliated His whole Self to bearing all His suffering. Have confidence when you call Father Him whom you so lovingly accept, feel, and know as your Father.

'Our Father.' No one should be astonished that one not yet born[2] calls Him Father. With God, beings who will be born are already born; with God future beings have been made. 'The things that shall be,' Scripture says, 'have already been.'[3] Hence it is that while John was still in the womb[4] He perceived His creator; and he who was unaware of his own life served as a messenger to his mother. Hence, too, we read[5] that Jacob waged war before he was born, and triumphed before he lived. Hence, too, those who do not yet exist themselves are existent for God, that is, those who were chosen before the foundation of the world.

'Who art in heaven'—not that He is not on earth, but that you may know through this phrase that you are a scion of heaven. And if you acknowledge yourself to be a son of God, live like a son of God, that you can reflect so great a Father by your action, life, and virtues.

'Hallowed be Thy name.' Since you are named a Christian after Christ, you ask to have the privilege of having such

1 He took sins upon Himself not to retain them, but to delete them, as St. Peter states about John 1.29 in Sermon 45 (*PL* 52.327C).

2 A catechumen not yet reborn through baptism.

3 Eccle. 3.15.

4 Luke 1.44.

5 Gen. 25.21-24.

a name glorified in your own case. For God's Name, which is holy by its nature and in itself, is in our case either glorified by our conduct or blasphemed among the Gentiles through our misdeeds.

'Thy kingdom come.' He himself says: 'The kingdom of God is within you.'[6] If it is within us, why do we pray for it to come? It is present by faith, by hope, and by expectations, but we now pray that it may come in fact. Moreover, may it come to us, not to Him who is already and always reigning in company with His Father, reigning in His Father, but may it come for ourselves! 'Come, blessed of my father, take possession of the kingdom prepared for you from the foundation of the world.'[7] We say: 'Thy kingdom come,' that God may reign in us, and death and sin may cease to have dominion over us. 'Death reigned,' Scripture says, 'from Adam until Moses.'[8] And in another place, it says: 'Do not let sin reign in your mortal body.'[9]

'Thy will be done on earth as it is in heaven.' On earth, at present, many things take place in accordance with the will of the Devil, the wickedness of the world, and the desire of the flesh, but in heaven nothing is done except the will of God. So we beg that, once the Devil has been checked, the world renewed, our body changed, and the reign of sin destroyed—we beg that there may be in heaven and on earth, in God and men, only one and the same will of God.

'Give us this day our daily bread.' After asking for the heavenly kingdom, we are not[10] bid to ask for earthly bread, since He Himself forbids this when He says: 'Do not be

6 Luke 17.21.
7 Matt. 25.34.
8 Rom. 5.14.
9 Rom. 6.12.
10 Reading *non* with Migne, not *nos* with Böhmer *BKV* 43, p. 93. But, cf. Sermon 71 (*PL* 52.402C).

solicitous for your life, what you shall eat or what you shall drink.[11] But, because He is the Bread that has come down from heaven,[12] we beg and pray to take that same Bread on which we shall live daily—that is, eternally—in heaven. 'This day'—that is, we pray to take in the present life that Bread from the banquet of the holy altar, for the strength of our body and mind.

'And forgive us our debts as we also forgive our debtors.' By these words, O man, you have set the manner and measure of forgiveness to yourself. You ask the Lord to forgive you exactly as much as you forgive to your fellow servant. Therefore, forgive the whole offense to the one who wrongs you if you yourself wish to be liable to the Lord for nothing because of your own sins. For your own sake, be forgiving in the case of another man, if you wish to avoid the avenging sentence.

'And lead us not into temptation.' 'God tempts no one'[13] as Scripture says. But He is spoken of as tempting when He abandons those who stubbornly go into the snares of temptations. That is how Adam succumbed to the wiles of the tempter when he abandoned the commands of his Creator. However, Christ makes clear from what quarter and by whom man is tempted by the next words.

'But deliver us from evil,' that is, from the Devil, who is the author and source of all evil. The Devil was heavenly by nature. But now he is spiritual wickedness, older than the world, worn with his practice of harm, and highly skilled in the art of injuring. Consequently, he is called not precisely 'an evil one' but merely 'evil,' from which everything evil springs. Hence it is that a man tied with carnal bonds cannot be set free by his own strength. Therefore, we should

11 Matt. 6.25,31.
12 John 6.41.
13 James 1.13.

pray God to free us from the Devil, since God loaned Christ to the earth in order that He might conquer the Devil. Let man cry out, let him cry out to God, let him cry, 'Deliver us from evil,' that we may be freed from so great an evil and no one may conquer save Christ.

'Our Father who art in heaven.' In these few words He to whom you are to pray has Himself granted you the theme of praying, the subject matter to ask for, and the norm of making petition. He made this grant that from it you might get the feel of praying, obtain an understanding of how to request, gather a measure of your petitioning, and take most ample training from this brief instruction on prayer; also, because as a token of love the King Himself has performed the function of an advocate, in order to dictate the prayers which He intends to answer. Every hesitation in asking has been taken away; yes, more, full confidence of meriting an answer has been given, since He who is being asked finds His very self in the prayers. Fear has no place when a son desires to obtain holy gifts from his Father through the mediation of his own filial reverence.

## SERMON 74

### *Christ's Resurrection*

### (On Matt. 28.1-4)

Dearly beloved, the work connected with the vigils has prevented us from preaching for a while. Weakness from the fast contributed to this, too. Today[1] we shall give you a sermon on the Lord's resurrection. In relation to this, if Christ's birth from the Virgin is something divine, how much

1 This sermon was preached on Easter Sunday.

more so is His resurrection from the dead! Therefore, let not that which is divine be heard with merely human interpretation.

'Late in the night of the Sabbath,' Scripture says, 'as it began to dawn towards the first day of the week.' The evening of the Sabbath—the day of this world does not know this; the usage of the world does not contain it. The evening terminates the day, it does not begin it. The evening fades into darkness; it does not grow bright. It does not change into dawn, because it does not know the sunrise.

Evening, the mother of night, gives birth to daylight! It changes the customary order while it acknowledges its Creator. It displays a new symbolic mystery. It is eager to serve its Creator rather than the march of time.

'Late in the night of the Sabbath,' it says, 'as it began to dawn towards the first day of the week, Mary Magdalen and the other Mary came to see the sepulchre.' Earlier, a woman hastened to sin; now, later on, a woman hastens to repentance. In the morning a woman knew that she had corrupted Adam; in the evening a woman seeks Christ.

'Mary Magdalen and the other Mary came to see the sepulchre.' A woman had drawn a beginning of perfidy out of Paradise. Now, a woman hastens to draw faith from the sepulchre. She who had snatched death out of life now hurries to get life out of death.[2]

'Mary came.' This is the name of Christ's Mother. Therefore, the one who hastened was a mother in name. She came as a woman, that woman, who had become the mother of those who die, might become the mother of the living, and fulfillment might be had of the Scriptural statement [about her]: 'that is, the mother of all the living.'[3]

2 A woman took death from the tree of life; now, a woman takes life from the tomb, the abode of death.

3 Gen. 3.20.

'Mary came, and also the other Mary.' Scripture does not say *they* came, but *she* came. Two women of one name came through a symbolic mystery, not through chance. 'Mary came, and also the other Mary.' She came, but another, too. Another came, but the first, too, so that woman might be changed in life, but not in name; in virtue, but not in sex. A woman had been the intermediary of the fall and ruin, and a woman was to be the one to announce the Resurrection.

'Mary came to see the sepulchre.' The sight of the tree had deceived her; the sight of the sepulchre was to restore her. A guileful glance had laid her low; a saving glance was to raise her up again.

'And behold,' the Gospel continues, 'there was a great earthquake; for an angel of the Lord came down from heaven.' The earth trembled, not because an angel came down from heaven, but because its Ruler ascended from hell. 'And behold, there was a great earthquake.' The heart of the earth is stirred. The depths of the earth leap up. The earth trembles, the huge mountains quiver, the foundations of the earth are battered. Hell is caught, and set in its place. Death gets judged—death which, rushing against guilty men, runs into its Judge; death which after long domination over its slaves rose up against its Master; death which waxed fierce against men but encountered God.

Rightly, therefore, did the rule of hell perish, and its laws get blotted out. The power of death was taken away, and, in penalty for its rashness in attempting to harm its Judge, death brought the dead back to life. Thereupon bodies were yielded up. The man was put back together, and his life was restored, and now everything holds together through forgiveness, because the condemnation has passed over onto the Author of life.

'And behold there was a great earthquake.' Now there

was a great earthquake. Oh, if at that other time even some light whirlwind had blown down that death-bearing tree! Oh, if some smokelike cloud had darkened that woman's vision! Oh, if a dark cloud had enveloped the beauty of that deathly fruit! Oh, if the hand had trembled upon touching the forbidden fruit! Oh, if unholy night had darkened the day of sin, and taken away the sorrows of the world, the multiplying deaths, and the insult to the Creator! However, allurements always promote vices, and sweet things further sins, but austere and manly pursuits conduce to virtues.

'For an angel of the Lord came down from heaven.' Through the Resurrection of Christ and the defeat of death, men once more entered into relationship with heaven. Moreover, woman, who had entered into a deadly plan with the Devil, now enjoyed a life-giving conversation with the angel.

'For an angel of the Lord came down from heaven, and rolled back the stone.' Scripture did not say *rolled,* but *rolled back* the stone. When rolled forward it was a proof of His death. When rolled back, it was a proof of His Resurrection. Blessed is the stone which could both conceal Christ and reveal Him! Blessed the stone which opens hearts no less than the sepulchre! Blessed is the stone which produces faith in the Resurrection, and a resurrection of faith; which is a proof that God's body has arisen! Here, the order of things is changed. Here, the sepulchre swallows death, not a dead man. The abode of death becomes a life-giving dwelling. A new kind of womb conceives one who is dead and brings him forth alive!

'For an angel of the Lord came down from heaven and drawing near rolled back the stone, and sat upon it!" An angel does not weary. Then why did he sit? He was sitting as a doctor of faith and a teacher of the Resurrection. He was sitting upon a rock, that its very solidity might impart firmness to those who believe. The angel was placing the foundations of faith upon the rock, on which Christ was going to build His Church, as He said: 'Thou art Peter, and upon this rock I will build my Church.'[4]

'His countenance was like lightning,' the Gospel says, 'and his raiment like snow.' Is not brilliance of lightning enough for an angel? What did raiment add to the heavenly nature? But by such splendor he foreshadowed the beauty and pattern of our resurrection. For, those who arise through Christ are transformed with the glory of Christ.

'And for fear of him the guards were terrified, and became like dead men.' Wretched men! The fear of death struck them at the very time an assurance of life was being restored. But these ministers of cruelty, these executors of another's perfidy—how were they to gain belief about heavenly matters? They were guarding the sepulchre, setting obstacles to the Resurrection, and taking care to keep life from entering in any way, or death from perishing. The arrival of the angel rightly struck them prostrate. O wretched mortal men, always hostile to themselves! They grieve that they must die, yet they struggle to forestall a resurrection! It would have been far better to open up the sepulchre, and furnish anything possible to facilitate the Resurrection, that a miracle might shine forth from the fact, and hope might arise from this example, and full certitude about Him who returned, and belief in the future life. This is indeed colossal madness, that man should be unwilling to believe in that which he desires to come to him.

Let these remarks about these guards suffice for today. In order not to be tedious now, we shall later explain what our faith contains—through the help of our Lord Jesus Christ, who lives and reigns with God the Father forever, Amen.

---

4 Matt. 16.18.

## SERMON 80

### *Christ Appears to the Women Returning from the Tomb*

(On Matt. 28.5-20)

In the preceding sermon we restricted ourselves to the first part of the Gospel reading.[1] Today let us hear what is in the subsequent verses: 'But the angel spoke and said to the women, Do not be afraid; for I know that you seek Jesus, who was crucified. He is not here, for he is risen even as he said. Come, see the place where the Lord was laid.'

Do you think that Peter, John, and all the disciples are reproved for their absence and blamed for their cowardice through the fact that the alert women alone were the first who ran to meet the rising Christ? Was the male portion of the race thus branded with disgrace, that weak woman might be the first to arrive at the glory of the Resurrection?

Far from it, brethren! What happened is a cause, not a chance; a symbolic mystery, not an accident; planned arrangement, not a fault. For here, where man arises in the case of Christ, woman follows rather than precedes. Perceive, therefore, that Peter yielded place not to the women but to Christ; not to a handmaid but to the Lord; for the sake of a symbolic mystery,[2] not of sleep; of orderly arrangement, not of fear. To put it briefly, the male sex was already represented in Christ when the angel came to the women, in order that man might precede woman in honor as much as the Lord precedes the angel.

'Do not be afraid'—for love possesses the good, and dread harasses the evil. Fear terrifies the impious, and affection

1 I.e., Matt. 29.1-4. The statement applies to Sermon 74 better than to 79. No doubt, Matt. 28.1-20 formed the complete *lectio*.

2 *sacramento.*

warms the loyal. 'Do not be afraid.' This is tantamount to saying: Let the Jew fear who did the betraying, and Pilate who sentenced Christ, and the soldier who mocked Him, and the impious who crucified Him, and the cruel who gave Him cups of gall, and the heartless ones who guarded the sepulchre, and the scoundrels who paid for a fraud and tried to sell away a proof, who in their inhumanity grieved over the Lord's Resurrection, but not over having slain Him. You, in contrast, ought to rejoice, not fear, because He whom you sought as dead has arisen. He whom you mourned as one slain is alive.

'For I know that you seek Jesus, who was crucified.' That is, why do you seek the living One among the dead? Why do you seek life in the tomb? Rather, go to meet the Living One; do not assemble to do honor to the dead.

'I know that you seek Jesus, who was crucified. He is not here.' The angel spoke thus because he opened the sepulchre for a purpose: not to allow Christ who was already gone to go out, but rather to demonstrate that He was already absent.

'He is arisen even as he said.' Here we see a twofold power: to return from the dead, and to know the future in advance.

'Come, see the place where the Lord was laid.' Come, women, come. See where you laid Adam,[3] where you buried a human being; where by your design you thrust a man, inasmuch as you caused the Lord to lie there for the sake of His servants; and know that pardon exists in your favor, as great as was the insult given to the Lord.

'Come, see the place where the Lord was laid.' An angelic power announces that it is the Lord who was crucified. Then, does human weakness discuss whether it is the Lord who has arisen? Christ assumed human capabilities to suffer, but

3 I.e., the second Adam, Christ.

in such a way that He retained everything which pertained to His divinity.

'And go quickly and tell the disciples that he has arisen; and behold he goes before you into Galilee; there you shall see him.' Here, too, the Apostles are not made inferior to the women. Rather, woman is freed from guilt while she bears the news of life and of the Resurrection, just as she had borne the news of death and of ruin.

'And departing quickly,' the Gospel says, 'from the tomb in fear and great joy.' The women entered the sepulchre to become sharers of His burial and companions of His sufferings. They departed from the sepulchre that they might arise in their faith before they should arise again in their bodies. 'Departing in fear and great joy.' Where He is, do not be afraid. Fear was changed, not taken away. Fear arising from guilt departed, but the fear proper to servitude remained. Fear arising from guilt is evil; reverential fear is good. The women had lost the fear once given to Adam; now they were afraid of losing the fear restored to them.'[4]

'In fear and great joy.' It was written: 'Serve ye the Lord with fear: and rejoice unto him with trembling.'[5] 'In fear and great joy.' 'The fear of the Lord is holy, enduring for ever and ever.'[6] Wherefore, he who remains in the fear of God remains in holiness.

'They ran to tell his disciples. And behold, Jesus met them, saying, Hail.' Christ went to meet those who faithfully hastened, so that they might recognize by sight what they accepted through faith, and that He might strengthen by His presence the women who were still trembling from what they had heard.

'Jesus met them, saying, Hail.' He met them as the

4 Through the new Adam, Christ.
5 Ps. 2.11.
6 Ps. 18.10.

Lord, He greeted them as a Father. He enkindled their affection, and preserved them from fear. He greeted them, that they might serve Him through love, not flee through fear.

'And they came up and embraced his feet.' He who allowed Himself to be embraced wanted to be possessed. 'They came up and embraced his feet.' They were to know that man is in the head of Christ, women in His feet; also, that through Christ it was given to them as women to follow the man, not to take the lead.[7]

'Jesus said to them, Do not be afraid.' What the angel had said the Lord also said, to make still stronger those whom the angel had reassured.

'Go, take the word to my brethren that they set out for Galilee; there they shall see me.' When He arose from the dead, Christ reassumed the form of man, He did not relinquish it. Therefore, He gives the name of brethren to those whom He made to be brothers of His own self. He names those brethren whom He made adopted sons of His Father. He names those brethren whom He, the kind Heir, made His co-heirs.

But now hear how impiety also arises at the Resurrection of Christ. 'Behold, some of the guards came into the city and reported to the chief priest all that had happened. And when they had assembled with the elders, and had consulted together they gave much money to the soldiers, telling them, Say his disciples came by night and stole him while we were sleeping.' Those who disperse money seek goods to be saved, not lost. When Judas was selling, the Jews bought Christ in order to destroy Him; now they spend much money in order to lose themselves, their Law, Temple, and country. The bloody, deceitful men! They set a price for falsehood, draw up an agreement about perfidy. By wicked negotiations they buy a fraud against belief, and a robbery from

7 Cf. 1 Cor. 11.3.

truth. They bribe the soldiers to give the name of robbery to what was the mystery of the Resurrection.

'His disciples came by night and stole him.' Not content to have slain the Master, they plot how they can ruin the disciples. They pretend that the power of the Master is the crime of the disciples.

'His disciples came by night and stole him.' The soldiers clearly were the losers, and so were the Jews in their guile. But the disciples took their Master away not by theft but by faith; by virtue, not by fraud; by holiness, not by sin. They took Him away alive, not dead. That is why they are sent to Galilee—to be able to see Him, since God is not seen in a place of perfidy.

Now let us attend to His words: 'All power in Heaven and on earth has been given to me.' He declares that, in His case, He Himself had given it to Himself, as the Apostle testifies by stating: 'God was truly in Christ, reconciling the world to himself.'[8] The Son of God conferred on the Son of the Virgin, God conferred upon man, Divinity conferred on flesh that which He forever possesses along with the Father and Holy Spirit. Therefore He says: 'Go, baptize all nations, in the name of the Father, and of the Son, and of the Holy Spirit.' He wanted one and the same Power which had created all the nations unto life to create them again unto salvation.

'And behold,' He says, 'I am with you all days, even unto the consummation of the world.' He who is always with the Father is always with us; and He will come to us by means of that which He took from us.

Why should I say more, brethren? The fact that He was born, suffered, arose, and welcomed—all this does not spring from any need of His, but it pertains to our own salvation.

8 2 Cor. 5.19.

# SERMON 83

*Christ Appears to the Eleven Disciples at Table*

(On Mark 16.14-20)

Thus the holy Evangelist has told us today that within the very time of the Crucifixion the Apostles were concerned with the table; that they were gazing at foods, concerned about banquets, and forgetful of the Lord's Passion. He states: 'He appeared to the eleven as they were reclining at table.'

Reclining where? At the tomb of their Master, and then soon at table, these servants? Is this the loyalty of servants? Is this the charity of disciples? Is this the ardor of Peter? Is this the love of John who raised himself from Chirst's own bosom? Is this the affection they gained through so long a time, and through such great gifts and virtues? Right after His Passion, when His death still burns the mind and His burial still haunts the memory, when His enemies are rejoicing and all Judea scoffing—were the disciples then taking their meal with all the comforts of the banquet couches and all the pleasures of those who recline at table?

At the death of Moses the angels were present,[1] and God Himself took care of his burial. The Jews kept their camp in one place, halted their journey, endured a dreadful delay in the desert, enjoined thirty days of mourning and honored this body of a servant by these obsequies of thirty days.[2] Therefore, did not the true Christ, the one Lord, the Creator of the world, the Redeemer of all men—did not He deserve tears from His disciples three days after His tragic passion and death, the death of the Cross?

1 Jude 9.
2 Deut. 34.5-8.

The earth trembled, hell was disturbed, rocks were split, tombs were opened, the sun disappeared, the day was buried, everything became dark. And were the disciples alone feasting on delights, free from care, on high couches in one crowd, at perfect leisure? Is this, brethren, what the Master Himself found upon His return from below? 'Therefore he appeared to the Eleven as they were reclining at table; and he upbraided them for their lack of faith and hardness of heart, in that they had not believed those who had seen him after he had risen.'

O faithful Peter, Peter so devoted, what shall we say about these words? 'While they were reclining at table.' Were they also eating? Brethren, the whole case was not one of reclining at a feast, but of lying prostrate in grief. The Apostles were not a convivial crowd, but an assembly of mourners. The bread there was that of grief, not joy. The cups were filled with the bitterness of the Cross, not the sweetness of wine.

'The disciples,' says Scripture, 'were shut within for fear of the Jews.' If they were in fear and shut within, they surely were not feasting. And if they were not enjoying a meal, that was not a home but a jail. Theirs was not a banquet couch, but a tomb. At that time, all the distress of the Lord's passion had passed over to His disciples. The whole lance of sorrow was piercing not only their sides, but their very hearts. Their hands and feet were held fast by the nails of the clinging grief. The bitter spirit of the Jews was then giving them vinegar and gall to drink. For them the sun had set and the day had waned. At that time severe temptation of thought was dashing them against the crags of infidelity to shipwreck their faith. Despair, which is worse than all evils and is in adversity always the last one to arrive, was already laying them out in sombre tombs.

Consequently, as we mentioned, the Lord found the disciples not reclining to eat, not feasting, but lying in grief and buried. So He upbraided them for their lack of faith. They had given so much belief to their despair that they had none for the Resurrection foretold by the Lord, and none for His servants who announced its occurrence. Consequently, they retained nothing conducive to faith and salvation. Dead to the world, and buried as far as the world was concerned, they already believed that they all had but one abode, that is, one tomb.

Wherefore, when the Lord saw that they had withdrawn themselves from the world, He called them to the world. He sent them back into it by the words: 'Go into the whole world and preach the gospel to every creature.' Come into the world, that you who think you now lie prostrate in one abode may quickly see the whole world lying subject to you.

'Come into the whole world, preach the gospel to every creature.' This is to say: You be the hope of all, you who have been the cause of despair to your very selves. Test how great your unbelief has been. Test it then when you will see the world believing what you preach—you who could not believe your own sight. Know how great is your hardness of heart. Know it then when you will perceive the wildest nations throughout the world acknowledging Me although they have not seen Me—Me whom you denied when I was before your eyes. You will observe men scattered all over the earth—men secluded on islands, or dwelling on cliffs, or living in remote deserts; superficial magi of the East, quarrelsome Greeks, and skillful Romans—you will observe them seeking by faith alone the belief which you sought by inserting hand and finger into My open wounds. However, since I am sending you as witnesses of My Passion, Death, and Resurrection, I have allowed you to scrutinize those wounds more carefully—in the hope that your own hesitation will become a source of strength for those who will believe you.

'He who believes,' He continues, 'and is baptized will be

saved.' Brethren, faith is to baptism what the soul is to the body. Hence it is that he who is generated from the font lives by faith: 'He who is just lives by faith.'[3] Therefore, everyone who lacks faith dies.

'He who believes'—believes that the Trinity is one God; that in the Father and Son and the Holy Spirit there is one Majesty with full equality; that the Godhead is distinct in regard to the Trinity, not confused in the unity; rather, that it is clearly one with respect to the Godhead, and threefold with respect to the Persons; that God is the name of the Trinity; that the Father and the Son should not be thought such according to an order of dignity, but according to their relationship of love; that the Holy Spirit should not be regarded as a Being more or less inferior nor more or less exterior, since divinity cannot have exterior parts; that Christ became man in such a way that what is God remains, and He died in such a way that by His death He called the dead of the centuries back to life; that He arose not for His own sake, but for ours; that He raised us into heaven when He ascended there Himself; that He sits there to exercise the authority of judge, not as one weary and seeking rest; that He who, as far as movement goes, is already everywhere, will come, not in regard to place, nor will He who already possesses the whole world come to hold it fast, but He will come in order that the world may make itself more worthy to see its Creator.

Man should also believe in forgiveness of sins, because, although the heavenly region is very spacious, it does not admit the sinner. Neither should a man despair over the magnitude of his sins. For, if there is one sin which God cannot forgive, He is not omnipotent. Man should believe in the resurrection of the body, that is, that it is the man himself who arises. He who sins is to incur punishment and

3 Rom. 1.17.

he who labors is to get a reward. He should believe in everlasting life, to keep a second death from occurring.

In addition to this, the greatest indication of firm faith consists in the following signs. The devils, that is, the ancient foes, get exorcised from human bodies. One language intelligible in many others comes forth from one mouth. Serpents grasped in the name of Christ lose the power of their venom. Through Christ, cups of poison have no power to harm those who drink them. Bodily diseases are cured at the touch of one who preaches Christ. 'These signs,' He says, 'will attend those who believe: in my name they shall cast out devils; they shall speak in new tongues; they shall take up serpents; and if they drink any deadly thing, it shall not hurt them; they shall lay hands upon the sick and they shall get well.'

Therefore, O man, be a physician to yourself through your faith, to keep from being forced to employ other physicians at your expense and to buy at great prices what you already have free of charge. Pray, brethren, that in the present life we may always be aware of the medicine of faith. Pray that when we are awaiting Christ and He is on the point of coming, we may be free from anxiety and exult because of our good conscience.

## SERMON 88

### *The Angel Announces the Birth of John the Baptist*

(On Luke 1.5-17)

To be always in debt is disturbing, brethren. To be ever bound by the chains of paying interest is depressing. But it is my own promise which has often made me a debtor to you; and that promise gives me a certain amusement because of the nature and obligation of such a debt. For, he who promises gives; he does not receive. And he who owes through giving makes himself into a creditor who is obliged to pay to himself. Where the loaner is also the debtor, and the debtor is the one who has done the loaning, there the contract is evidently one springing from friendship, not necessity. Moreover, in such gaining of interest, the interest gets quickly paid as something not burdensome to the soul, but honorable and delightful.

After the Gospel described the appearance of the angel to the priest Zachary, it added: 'And Zachary, seeing him, was troubled, and fear fell upon him.' A man who always worries and trembles about the arrival of a public servant is fearful of the power of a judge. He estimates the merits of the command in accordance with the importance of the person who comes. Although his conscience is good he fears until he knows the reasons why the messenger came, and undrstands his quality. If all this is true, then what will the weak nature of man do, and with what trembling will it fear, when it perceives a heavenly power? When man gazes on an angel, and beholds a messenger from God's abode?

Flesh is never fully secure of its own conscience. This is proved by the case of Zachary of whom we now speak. He offended within the very time of propitiating. While he was believing he doubted, as the angel[1] made clear. 'Because thou has not believed my word.' While he was meriting an answer to his prayers, he committed a fault. He incurred blame while he was receiving the very gifts. While he was hearing a voice[2] he lost his own.

Consequently, before the angel disclosed his commission, or conferred the gifts, or gave the answers to the prayers,

1 Luke 1.20.

2 Or possibly: receiving 'the Voice,' namely, John the Baptist, the 'voice of one crying in the desert' (John 1.23).

he dispelled Zachary's fear, banished his awe, and comforted his spirit so disturbed by confusing thought. He wanted the mind which had fled from itself through excessive fear to return to itself and then to perceive and grasp such great bounty. 'Do not be afraid, Zachary,' he said, 'for thy petition has been heard, and thy wife Elizabeth shall bear thee a son, and thou shalt call his name John.'

Do you think that this distinguished priest forgot the people and the congregation to such an extent that he asked about his aged wife's conceiving, and about the childbirth of her who was barren beyond hope; that he, the advocate of all, prayed for himself alone; that he restricted this great function of his priesthood to his own domestic cares, shut it up within the narrow limits of his household and used it only there; that this veteran high priest applied the incense of the entire nation only to his personal desire to have a son; and that because of such a desire this old man, already looking back on his years, was enkindled to have a child long past the natural time?

Far from it, brethren, far from it! Let no faithful soul entertain such a suspicion about holy Zachary! Yet the angel does refer the effect of Zachary's entire prayer to this: 'Thy petition has been heard, and thy wife Elizabeth will bear thee a son.' If the angel is replying to a petition, the priest begged only for a son. If the priest made his supplication for all the people, why did the angel bring an answer only in regard to the son?

What do we hold? Why are we holding the minds of our hearers so long in suspense? How truly that venerable priest was present there, not for his own benefit alone, but for that of all! How truly the angel replied for all! In the case of that priest's son, how truly God looked far ahead! God had chosen that son for all parents and for all nature, unto this purpose: to give him to all men, to present him to the ages, and offer him to all nations; to be a son destined for sacred rites;[3] since his birth was announced amid the sacred precincts of the Temple and granted amid its sacred rites; to be a high priest sprung from a venerable high priest, an angel conceived into a holy womb at the voice of an angel; to be the voice of Christ: 'I am the voice of one crying in the desert';[4] to be the voice of Christ, preserved for Christ at His own hour; to be the herald who was to proclaim the presence of the Judge; to be one who would through penance summon the peoples of Christ to forgiveness.

Therefore, how truly did that priest Zachary act for all!—that priest already unaware of himself, already dead to himself, away from his wife, denied offspring. How truly did he get prayers answered for all! Let us learn this quickly from the angel's words: 'And many will rejoice at his birth.' He who was created for the joy of all was not born for one alone. 'For he shall be great before the Lord.' Who shall show how great among men is he who is great before the Lord?

'He shall drink no wine or strong drink.' He who was born from the holy body of a priest, and that in his old age when he was cleansed from all vices and free from the hot passions of youth—he knows not wine and keeps away from strong drink. They beget the excesses of drunkenness and vices; they dissipate all propriety of manners and beautiful virtues.

'He shall drink no wine or strong drink, and shall be filled with the Holy Spirit from his mother's womb.' How this conforms with the Apostle's admonition: 'Brethren, do not be drunk with wine, for in that is debauchery; but be filled with the Holy Spirit.'[5] 'And he shall be filled with the

3 Reading *sacramentis,* with S. Pauli.
4 John 1.23.
5 Eph. 5.18.

Holy Spirit from his mother's womb.' Fortunate is John, who through the spirit of God deserved to express his joy before he uttered any infant cries. Fortunate is he who deserved to possess divine benefits before he got human goods. Fortunate is he who deserved acquaintance with heaven sooner than with earth. Fortunate is he who deserved to announce future events before he saw any present ones. Fortunate is he who could receive God before he was received into his own body. Fortunate, yes outstandingly fortunate, is he who acquired merit before he knew how to seek it. Fortunate is he who did not come to grace through toil, but was ennobled by grace and then proceeded to his labors.

The text continues: 'And many of the children of Israel he shall bring back.' To whom? Let the angel tell, that the heretic[6] may be silenced in his blasphemies and denials. Let the angel tell, that the faithful soul may hear and rejoice. Let the heretic believe and return. 'He shall bring back.' To whom? 'To the Lord their God,' the text says.

Who is this God? He is the One of whom the Prophet states: 'This is our God, and there is no other apart from him. He found out all the way of knowledge and gave it to Jacob his servant, and to Israel his beloved.'[7] When did He give it? Then, indeed, when he wrote on the tablets of the Law a rule for the whole of life and a norm of disciplinary control. Be attentive, my hearer, that you may know who this our God is, apart from whom there is no other. Who is He? 'Afterwards He was seen upon earth and conversed with men.'[8]

Who else was seen upon earth save Christ, who conversed in our flesh? And who else conversed with men, save He who tarried with men in His human body? And if He is

6 He refers to the Arians. Cf. Introduction, pp. 10-11.
7 Bar. 3.36,37.
8 Bar. 3.38.

our God and there is no other apart from Him—O heretic, since you will not have Him, whom will you have? 'There is no other,' Scripture says, 'apart from Him.' And now do you not say: 'Where, therefore, is the Father?' The Prophet says: 'There is no other apart from Him.' And where is He [the Father]? Assuredly, in the Son, because the Father is not apart from the Son. 'I am in the Father,' He says, 'and the Father is in me.'[9] Wherefore, too, the Prophet did not say: 'There is no other'; what he said was: 'There is no other apart from Him.' This is to say: There is Another, but He is in Him.

But you object: 'And if He is in Him, how is He Another?' O heretic, He is Another in regard to His Person, in such a way that He Himself is the substance; and He Himself is the substance in such a way that the Trinity is not something put together. There is a unity of the Trinity in such a way that there is no separation in the Godhead. The Father is in Himself in such a way (and without Him the Trinity is not complete) that a distinct personality is in the Father and one in the Son and one in the Holy Spirit, but not a separate divinity.

'And he himself shall go before him.' Before whom? Before Christ, who is their God. Our God, the God of all, God apart from whom their is no other. 'In the power of Elias.' Let no one upon hearing this bring the transmigration of souls into his interpretation. Here the angel is speaking of that spirit which John gained through divine grace, not of that one which he acquired to vivify his body. Also, he is speaking of that power which he had from above, not that which he acquired for the sake of his bodily strength. Therefore, John comes in the spirit of Elias, and he walks in his power. To sum up, by his food, clothing, honor, chastity,

9 John 14.11.

abstinence, and all virtues, he represented both Elias and Christ.

'To prepare for the Lord a perfect people.' May our God and Lord deign to prepare this in your own case, too, unto the glory of His name.

## SERMON 93

### *The Conversion of Magdalen*

(On Luke 7.36-38)

Perhaps the hearer is surprised and troubled that Christ came to a dinner, and to the dinner of a Pharisee at that. However, He entered the Pharisee's house not to take the Jewish foods, but to dispense divine mercy. He reclined at table, not to partake of the cups made savory with honey and crowned with flowers, but to draw tears from other founts—the very eyes of a penitent. God's hunger is for the groans of delinquents, and His thirst is for the tears of sinners.

'Now one of the Pharisees,' the Gospel says, 'asked him to dine with him; so he went into the house of the Pharisee and reclined at table. And behold, a woman in the town who was a sinner, upon learning that he was at table in the Pharisee's house, brought an alabaster jar of ointment; and standing behind him at his feet, she began to bathe his feet with her tears, and wipe them with the hair of her head, and kissed his feet, and anointed them with ointment.'

You perceive that Christ came to the Pharisee's table not to be filled with food for the body, but to carry on the business of heaven while He was in the flesh. He came not to sample the viands placed before Him in the human fashion, but to give divine approval to the deeds done behind His back. For, we know that Christ always exercised divine virtues through human acts. All His deeds, even those which He performed in His body, were proved to be new and beyond the practices of men.

The Pharisee asked Christ to eat. What did the woman who was not asked seek there? A stranger does not burst into the interior of a house. An uninvited man does not dare to enter its private banquet room. A reckless spectator does not dare to disturb the foods made ready to relax spirits weary after labor. Why, then, does this woman, unknown—or rather of bad reputation—burdened with grief, weeping copiously, lamenting aloud, with the doorkeeper unaware, and everyone else, too, even the Shepherd Himself—why does she run through all the doors, pass through all the groups of servants, fly even to the private hall of the banquet, and turn the whole house of joy into one of lamentation and wailing?

Brethren, she did not come uninvited; she was under command. She entered not as one rashly daring, but as one ushered in. He who ordered her to be absolved by a heavenly judgment is the One who caused her to be brought to Himself. The well-dressed Pharisee was reclining at the first place on his banquet couch, swelling with pride before the very eyes of Christ. In order to please men, not God, he was gaily engrossed in his banquet. At that time the woman came. She came up from behind, because a guilty soul seeking pardon stands behind the pardoner's back. She knew that because of her guilt she had lost the confidence to stand before His face.

When she came, she came to make satisfaction to God, not to please men. She came to provide a banquet of devotion, not of pleasure. She set a table of repentance, served courses of compunction and the bread of sorrow. She mixed the drink with tears in proper measure, and to the full delight of God she struck music from her heart and body. She produced the organ tones of her lamentations, played upon the zither by her long and rhythmical sighs, and fitted her groans to the flute. While she kept striking her breast in reproach to her conscience she made the cymbals resound which would please God. While she set foods like these before God's sight, she received abundant mercy.

'Behold, a woman in the town who was a sinner.' The Evangelist enlarges her crime in order to magnify the forgiveness of her pardoner. 'A sinner in the town.' She had sinned in the town, because by her own reputation she had stained that of the whole town. Thus she was not only a sinner now, but she had become a source of sin[1] for the whole city. She knew that the sin of the town could not be taken away save by Him alone who alone had come to blot out sin.

'Upon learning that he was at table in the Pharisee's house' The sinner did not dare to approach when He was either standing or sitting. For, when God stands He is correcting, and when he sits He is acting as Judge. But when He reclines, He lies beside those who are prostrate in sorrow.

'Upon learning that he was at table in the Pharisee's house.' She learned that the heavenly majesty was prone to show mercy. Therefore, she believed He would be quick to show mercy to her—He who had been so quick to come to the Pharisee's table.

'She brought an alabaster jar of ointment.' She brought oil, because she sought from the heavenly physician medicine for a deadly wound.

'Standing behind him at his feet.' One who seeks pardon always hastens near to the feet. Well was she standing, for one who deserved to come to the feet of Christ could not

1 Either she brought that reputation upon the city; or her bad example unleashed sin, in the sense of concupiscence as in Rom. 6.6,12,14,17,20.

then fall down. 'Standing behind him at his feet'—that she who had traveled the way of death might follow the footsteps of Christ and travel the way of life.

'She began to bathe his feet with her tears.' See how the order of nature is changed. It is always the heavens which give rain to the earth. Yet, behold! now, the earth irrigates the heavens; even more, the rain of human tears has leaped above the heavens and all the way up to the Lord Himself. Consequently, the verse of the Psalmist may be sung also about the waters of tears: 'And let all the waters that are above the heavens praise the name of the Lord.'[2]

'She began to bathe his feet with her tears.' Oh, what power there is in the tears of sinners! They irrigate the heavens, wash the earth, extinguish hell fire, blot out the condemnation promulgated by God against every sin.

'She wiped them with the hair of her head.' She washed the Lord's feet with her tears, and wiped them with her hair. Poverty no longer suffices as an excuse; hard-heartedness will not be pardoned, for what we have from nature is altogether sufficient to do service to the Creator.

'She wiped them with the hairs of her head.' The water came back upon the head of the sinner to purge away her sins, in order that she might have a new baptism, and from her own fount wash away the silt of her sins.

'She wiped them with the hairs of her head'—that by this service—to use the Psalmist's terminology—she might turn into a means of satisfaction 'the hairy crown'[3] by which she had walked on in her sins.

'And she kissed his feet.' Her interceding tears had gone beforehand, that the kisses of her devotion might follow. For tears are an evidence of satisfaction, and kisses are a proof of reconciliation.

---

2 Ps. 148.4,5.
3 Ps. 67.22.

'And she anointed them with ointment.' We know from another Evangelist[4] that a woman poured the oil on the Lord's head. Consequently, what this woman did was not a matter of soft pampering of the flesh, but a sacred function of whole-souled human kindness. For, God is in the head of Christ, and in the feet of those who preach the gospel of peace.[5]

Pray, brethren, that we, too, may deserve somehow to be reckoned as part of the unguent of Christ, and be anointed with the ointment which flows from the feet of the Saviour. For, just as there is an oblation when an ointment is offered, so is a chrism perfect when it flows back from the feet of the Lord.

With God's help we shall explain what it is of which that woman is a type,[6] or how great a mystery she prefigures, when we set forth the matters in the following sermons.

## SERMON 95

### *The Conversion of Magdalen Allegorically Interpreted*

(On Luke 7.36-50)

All the deeds which Christ is reported to have performed while He was in His body on earth are based on historical truth in such a way that they are always found to be replete with heavenly symbols. In our two preceding sermons we have already treated what was on the surface of the Gospel text. Therefore, pray that through the light of the Holy Spirit we may, as we promised, lay open its deeper meanings.

4 Matt. 26.7.
5 Rom. 10.15.
6 She is a type of the Church, as Sermon 95 makes clear.

A sermon is unworthy if it uses nothing more than human exposition to penetrate what God has done.

The text says: 'Now one of the Pharisees asked him to dine with him.' Brethren, the Pharisee is called the Catholic of the Jews, for he believes in the resurrection, and disagrees with the Sadducee who denies it. That is why this Pharisee invited Christ, that is, the Author of the resurrection, to dine with him. For, he who dines with Christ cannot die. Indeed, he lives forever.

'He asked the Lord to dine with him.' You ask, O Pharisee, to dine with Him. Believe, be a Christian, that you may feed upon Him. 'I am the bread,' He says, 'that has come down from heaven.'[1] God always gives greater gifts than He is asked for. He was being asked to give the hope of eating with Him, and He gave Himself as food to be eaten. Moreover, He granted all this in such a way that He did not refuse that which He was asked for. Does He not promise[2] this of His own accord to His disciples? 'You who have continued with me will eat and drink at my table in my kingdom.' O Christian, what that is His can He, who here gave Himself to you to be eaten, refuse to you in the future? He who prepared such great provisions to sustain you on your journey, what has He not prepared for you in that everlasting abode? 'You will eat at my table in my kingdom.' You have heard about the banquet of God; do not be anxious about the quality of this banquet. He who deserves to be present at a king's table will eat whatever the king possesses through his power and control of his kingdom. Similarly, he who comes to the banquet of the Creator will have among his enjoyments whatever is contained in creation. But, let us return to what we intended to say.

'So he went into the house of the Pharisee.' Into what

1 John 6.51.
2 Cf. Luke 22.28,30.

house? Assuredly, it was into the Synagogue that He went and reclined at table. Brethren, Christ reclined at table in the Synagogue during the time when He reposed in the grave, but He transmitted His body to the table of the Church, that this flesh from heaven might be a help to salvation for the nations who would eat it. 'Unless you eat the flesh of the Son of Man, and drink of his blood, you shall not have life in you.'[3] Those who have been instructed in the heavenly mysteries[4] know how the flesh of Christ is eaten, and how His blood is drunk.

'And behold,' it says, 'a woman in the town who was a sinner.' Who is this woman? Beyond any doubt, she is the Church. 'A sinner in the city.' In what city? In that one of which the Prophet had said: 'How is the faithful city, Sion, become a harlot?'[5] And elsewhere he said: 'I have seen iniquity and contradiction in the city, and in the midst thereof are iniquity, labor and injustice. And usury and deceit have not departed from its streets.'[6] Therefore, the Gospel text refers to a city full of perfidy; a city surrounded by walls, fortified by towers of pride, criss-crossed by streets of iniquities, locked up by gates of quarrels, blackened by the smoke of deceit, hardened by flintstones of usury, aggravated by vexations of business, and disgraced by houses of ill repute, that is, by temples of the idols. It was in this city that this woman, that is, the Church, was bearing up under the depressing guilt which sprang from the heavy silt of so many past sins.

But then she heard that Christ had come to the house of the Pharisee—that is, to the Synagogue. She heard that

---

3 John 6.54.

4 *sacramenta,* referring to the *disciplina arcani.* In many cases the catchumens were not told about the Eucharist.

5 Isa. 1.21.

6 Ps. 54.10,12.

there—that is, at the Jewish Pasch—He had instituted the mysteries of His Passion, disclosed the Sacrament of His Body and Blood, and revealed the secret of our Redemption. She ignored the Scribes like contemptible doorkeepers. 'Woe to you lawyers! you who have taken away the key of knowledge.'[7] She broke open the doors of quarrels, and despised the very superiority of the Pharisaical group. Ardent, panting, perspiring, she made her way to the large inner chamber of the banquet of the Law. There she learned that Christ, betrayed amid sweet cups and a banquet of love, had died through the fraud of the Jews, according to the Prophet's statement: 'For if my enemy had reviled me, I would verily have borne with it. And if he that hated me had spoken evil things against me, I would perhaps have hidden myself from him. But thou, a man of one mind, my guide, and familiar, who didst take sweetmeats together with me: in the house of God we walked with consent.'[8]

'Upon learning that he was at table in the Pharisee's house' —that is, that in the Synagogue He had been sentenced altogether unjustly through every conceivable pretext, had suffered, been crucified, and buried. Nevertheless, the Church does not let that great injury inflicted on Him deter her from fervor of faith. Instead, she carries her ointment, she bears the oil of Christian chrism. She has not deserved to see the bodily face of Christ. Therefore, she stands behind Him, not in place but in time. She clings to His footsteps that she may follow Him. And soon she pours out tears of desire more than of regret, that she may deserve to see Him when He returns, whom she did not deserve to see when He was going away. Therefore, with welling love she sheds her tears upon the feet of the Lord. With her hands of good works she holds the feet of those who preach His kingdom. She washes them with tears of charity, kisses them with prais-

---

7 Luke 11.52.
8 Ps. 54.13-15.

ing lips, and pours out the whole ointment of mercy, until He will turn her—(what means this word, turn? It means, come back)—until He will come back to her and say to Simon, say to the Pharisees, say to those who deny, say to the nation of the Jews: 'I came into thy house; thou gavest me no water for my feet.'

And when will He speak these words? When He will come in the majesty of His Father, and separate the just from the unjust, like a shepherd who separates the sheep from the goats, and will say: 'I was hungry and you did not give me to eat; I was thirsty and you gave me no drink; I was a stranger and you did not take me in.'[9] This is tantamount to saying: But this woman while she was bathing my feet, anointing them, and kissing them, she did to the servants[10] what you did not do for the Master, she did for the feet what you refused to the Head, she expended upon the lowliest members what you refused to your Creator. Then He will say to the Church: Your sins, many as they are, are forgiven you because you have loved much. For the remission of sins will take place then when all occasion of sin will be taken away, when all the matters conducive to sin will be gone, when corruptibility will put on incorruptibility, when mortality will take a place behind immortality, the flesh of sin will become flesh altogether holy, earthly slavery will be exchanged for heavenly domination, and the human army will be raised aloft into the divine kingdom.

Pray, brethren, that we, too, placed in a section of the Church, may merit to arrive at the benefits we have enumerated, through the gift of Christ Himself. To Him, along with the Holy Spirit, is there honor and glory forever. Amen.

9 Matt. 25.42.
10 The 'least of the servants' referred to in Matt. 25.42.

## SERMON 96

### *The Parable of the Cockle*

(On Matt. 13.24-30)

If the words or deeds of Christ would always be completely grasped by our bodily powers of perception, my mind would grow weary, my ingenuity would be unchallenged and dormant, my heart would pine away, and whatever human vigor or energy I have would be extinguished.

The Gospel text states: 'He set a parable before them.' A potential spark is cold in the flint, and lies hidden in the steel, but it is brought into flame when the steel and flint are struck together. In similar manner, when an obscure word is brought together with its meaning, it begins to glow. Surely, if there were not mystical meanings,[1] no distinction would remain between the infidel[2] and the faithful, between the wicked man and the devout one. The devout man would be like a proud one, the lazy man like a toiler, the watchful man like a sleeper. But, as things are, when the soul asks, the mind knocks, the power of perception seeks, piety hopes, faith demands, and studious attention deserves it, the one who labors in perspiration does see fruit appear. The lazy man, by contrast, is seen to suffer a penalty. The uprightness of a giver appears, too, because things received as gifts give more pleasure than those already possessed, and those newly discovered delight us more than those we have long understood. This is why Christ veils His doctrine by parables, covers it with figures, hides it under symbols,[3] make it obscure by mysteries.

---

1 *Mystica,* meaning symbolical, typical. Cf. Sermon 2 nn. 7,9.
2 Reading *infidelem fidelemque,* with S. Pauli.
3 *sacramentis.* On this meaning, cf. DeGhellinck, *Pour l'histoire du mot sacramentum* 54, and Souter, *Glossary.*

'He set a parable before them.' Before them, that is, not before His own, but before strangers who are His enemies, not His friends; before those gazing intently to find a cause of calumny, not before those listening to gain salvation. 'This is why I speak to them in parables,' the Gospel relates, 'because seeing they do not see, and hearing they do not hear, neither do they understand.'[4] Why? Because he who misrepresents past benefits does not deserve to see present ones, and one who hid the Law to keep it from becoming known is not worthy to recognize Grace. 'Woe to you lawyers!' another Gospel warns. 'Because you have taken away the key of knowledge; you have not entered yourselves, and those who were entering you have hindered.'[5]

'He set before them a parable, saying, The kingdom is like to a man.' In what respect did Christ give offense when He was made like unto man,[6] in order to help the perishing human race? Does the Lord give scandal if, to free His slaves, He appears in the form of their slavery? Then look! Does He give scandal when He compares His future majesty, His second coming, and His kingdom to a man?

'The kingdom,' it says, 'is like a man who sowed good seed in his field; but while men were asleep his enemy came and sowed weeds among the wheat, and went away.' You have heard how the Sower of the world sowed the good principles of things and how no evil proceeded from the Author of the original sowing. The evil is an addition sowed by an Enemy. The evil was not brought forth by the parent of things. 'God saw that all he had made was very good,'[7] Scripture relates. Good, and very good. For, when God

---

4 Matt. 13.13.
5 Luke 11.52.
6 Phil. 2.7.
7 Gen. 1.31.

made the universe He called it clean; and when the Enemy was striving to undo it, he made it unclean. God placed man in Paradise that he might have a life of delights. But that foe dragged man down into this life of toil, and brought him to death. God implanted affection as something natural in human flesh. But that foe through his envy changed that affection into parricide. Cain[8] proves this, for he was the first to stain the earth with a brother's blood. He was the genuine originator of murder to get rid of a brother. That is how death which springs from strife always splits human love and keeps it asunder.

To take up all the cases would be tedious. Hence, we feel compelled to show at least by a few examples how the enemy has always sowed evil plants among the good, vices among virtues, deathly things among the life giving, in order to achieve our destruction.

Did not God people the whole earth from one man? Did not this loving Sower start the human race from one seed and multiply it until it became an extensive and promising harvest? But soon the enemy reduced all the men to one again. By sowing evil on top of what had been well sown, he got that promising harvest blotted out by the Deluge, rather than merely watered. In similar manner, the Law was sown of divine and true precepts. But he got it obscured by human and deceitful machinations. Consequently, the priest became a persecutor, the teacher became a corrupter, and the defender of the Law became an enemy.

Creatures were made in order to bring about recognition of their Creator. But, to make God go unknown, the Devil told the lie that these creatures were gods. In this way he turned the wise men of this world into fools. He taught the contemplators of this world to see nothing. He caused the professors of wisdom to have no knowledge. He sent the

8 Gen. 4.8.

investigators of all things away ignorant. On top of the growing crop of the Gospel, sown with the seed from heaven, he sowed heretical cockle. Thus the Enemy caused a puzzling mixture, that he might make the sheaves of faith bundles for hell, that no wheat might get stored in the barns of heaven. Why should I say more? After he himself was changed from an angel into a devil, he hastened to use ingenuity, tricks, devices, and deceit to keep any creature[9] from remaining secure in its own state.

But now let us open up the words of the present parable 'The kingdom of heaven is like to a man.' To what man? Assuredly, to Christ. 'Who sowed good seed'—because the nature of the Creator can put no evil in the very seed of things. 'In his field'—that is, in the world, as the Lord Himself says: 'The field is the world.[10]

'But while men were asleep'—that is, the holy fathers, patriarchs, prophets, apostles, martyrs, who were resting for a time in the deep sleep of death. For, the death of the saints is a sleep, but that of the sinners is truly a death, in so far as in hell they live only for punishment. As far as life is concerned, the sinners perish.

'His enemy came,' that is, the Devil. 'And sowed weeds.' He sowed the weeds on top of the good seed; he did not sow them above themselves. The good things of the Creator precede, the evil things of the Devil follow afterwards, so that the evil which is from the Devil may be an accident, not a nature.

'He sowed weeds among the wheat'—because the Devil has become accustomed to sow of his own accord heresies among the faithful, sin among the saints, quarrels among the peaceful, deceptions among the simple, and wickedness among the innocent. He does this not to acquire the weeds

9 Reading *creatura,* with S. Pauli.
10 Matt. 13.38.

of cockle, but to destroy the wheat; not to capture the guilty ones, but to steal away the innocent. An enemy seeks the leader rather than a soldier. He does not besiege the dead but attacks the living. Thus, the Devil is not seeking to capture sinners whom he already has under his dominion, but is laboring thus to ensnare the just.

'He sowed weeds among the wheat, and went away'—because with great might the Devil drives men towards destruction. But, after he has prostrated someone, he abandons him. The Devil seeks not the man, but his destruction. Brethren, he rejoices over our evils, he swells with pride over our ruin, he grows strong from our wounds, he thirsts after our blood, he is sated from our flesh, he lives by our death. The Devil does not wish to possess a man, but to destroy him. Why? Because he does not wish, he does not dare, he does not allow the man to arrive at the heaven from which the Devil fell.

Our sermon is detaining us rather long today. Therefore let us postpone what remains, in order that this work, our common task, may be lighter for us all, and also that we may give fuller consideration to the matters yet to be said. May our God deign to give me the grace of speaking and you the desire of hearing.

## SERMON 98

### *The Parable of the Grain of Mustard Seed*

(On Luke 13.18,19)

Today, brethren, you have heard how all the greatness of the kingdom of heaven has been compared to a grain of mustard seed. This analogue is something so small, so tiny;

indeed, it is the tiniest of tiny things. How can it contain such great power? The Lord says that it does: 'What is the kingdom of God like, and to what shall I liken it?'

When He says: 'What is it like?' He shows and works up the attitude of one who is searching. He alone is the Word, the Fountain of knowledge, the River of copious speech; He waters the hearts of all, opens their powers of perception, augments their talent. Is He now having difficulty in finding a comparison?

But let us hear what He did find. 'The kingdom of heaven,' the text says, 'is like a grain of mustard seed.' Searching in heaven and on earth, does He find nothing except the grain of mustard seed by which to indicate the full power of the heavenly kingdom? That kingdom is uniquely mighty, blessed with everlasting duration, resplendent in its divinity, spread throughout heaven, and expanded over all the earth. Does He force and insert it within the narrow limits of a grain of mustard seed?

'The kingdom is like a grain of mustard seed.' Is that the complete hope of those who believe? Is that the highest expectation of the faithful? Is that the happiness which the virgins gain by their long struggles for continence? Is that the glory acquired by the shedding of all the blood of the martyrs? Is that what 'eye has not seen nor ear heard, nor has it entered into the heart of man?'[1] Is that what the Apostle promises has been prepared, through an indescribable mystery, for those who love God?

Brethren, let us not be easily troubled over the Lord's words. For if 'the foolishness of God is wiser than men, and the weakness of God is stronger than men,'[2] this tiniest creature of God is found to be something more magnificent than all the greatness of the world. Oh, if we would only

---

1 1 Cor. 2.9.
2 1 Cor. 1.25.

sow this grain of mustard seed in our minds in such a way that it will grow into a great tree of knowledge, and through the full height of understanding be raised toward the sky; that it will spread out into all the branches of the sciences; that it will burn our tingling mouths with the pungent taste of its seed! Thus it will burn for us with all the fire of its seed, and break into flame in our heart, and through the pleasure of taste it gives us take away all the insipidity of our ignorance.

'The kingdom of heaven is like a grain of mustard seed, which a man took and cast into his own garden; and it grew and became a large tree, and the birds of the air dwelt in its branches.' As the text says, the kingdom of God is like a grain of mustard seed, because the kingdom is brought by a word from heaven, is received through hearing, is sown by faith, takes root through belief, grows by hope, is diffused by profession, expands through virtue, and is spread out into branches. To these branches it invites the birds of heaven, that is, the powers of spiritual insight. In those branches it receives them in a peaceful abode.

Let the heretic come, let him come, for entrance into the Church is always open to those who return. Let him come, let him hear, and let him now cease to bark against the Lord's love. If all the majesty of the heavenly kingdom is like a grain of mustard seed, why does the heretic complain[3] that God came down into human nature, that the Lord descended into the form of a slave? For, He came in such a way, O heretic, that the whole matter should grow in importance to you through your faith, just as it waned when you relied on nature.

'The kingdom of heaven is like a grain of mustard seed.' Let us revert to the grain of mustard seed. The full perfec-

---

3 *quaeritur,* in place of the more usual spelling *queritur.*

tion of a kingdom remains and consists in the kingdom of heaven. Christ is the kingdom of heaven. He was planted, like a grain of mustard seed, in the Virgin's body. He grew into the tree of the cross spread throughout the world. He emitted the pungency of its seed when He was abraded by His Passion. Consequently, by a mere touch He gave savor and seasoning to anything which sustains life. When a grain of mustard seed is still whole, its power lies hidden inside it; if the grain is abraded, its power becomes forcefully evident. Similarly, Christ wanted His Body to be abraded, because He did not want His power to lie hidden inside it.

Brethren, let us abrade that grain of mustard seed, that we may discover its force in this parable. Christ is a king, because He is the full Source of authority. Christ is the kingdom, because the full majesty of His kingdom is in Him. Christ is the man, because every man[4] is renewed in Christ. Christ is the mustard seed, because in His case, the full greatness of God appears in miniature inside the tininess of man.

Why should I say more? He became all things in order to restore all men through Himself. Christ as man received the grain of mustard seed, that is, Christ as man received that kingdom of God which He as God had always possessed. He cast the seed into His garden, that is, into his spouse, the Church. He is often mindful of this garden in the Canticle of Canticles, when He speaks of 'a garden enclosed.'[5] The Church is the garden, spread through her worship[6] over all the world by the plow of the Gospel. She is a garden enclosed by the goads of her discipline, and cleared of all rank weeds by the labor of the Apostles. She is a garden beautiful to see because of the young trees of the faithful, the lilies of the

4 That is, all mankind. For *every* as the meaning of *totus,* cf. Souter, *s.v.*
5 Cant. 4.12.
6 *cultura*; cf. Souter.

virgins, the roses of the martyrs, the verdure of the confessors. She is fragrant with unfailing flowers.

Accordingly, Christ cast this grain of mustard seed into His garden, that is, because of the promise of His kingdom. The seed had its roots in the Patriarchs, was born in the Prophets, and grew in the Apostles. In the Church it became a great tree, and through the gifts it produced numerous branches which the Apostle enumerates when he says: 'To one is given the utterance of wisdom; to another the utterance of knowledge; to another the gift of healing; to another the working of miracles; to another prophecies; to another the distinguishing of spirits; to another various forms of tongues.'[7]

Brethren, you have heard how that grain of mustard seed expanded into a tree. You have heard what roots it sent down, and into what kind of great seed-bearing branches it soon spread itself. In those branches the birds of heaven, not those of air, rest in the security of faith after their flight upon the wings of wisdom and prudence.

You, too, be attentive, if you wish to be free from fear of earthly beasts, if you wish to avoid the rapacious birds and voracious vultures; that is, the birds of the air. All these are spiritual vices. Raise yourself up above the earth, and abandon earthly goods. Take to yourself the silver-colored wings of the Prophet's dove,[8] take the wings shining with the brilliance of the divine Son. In this way, fly away as a gold-colored dove, to rest in such great branches, to be there as a dove which can no longer be allured into any traps, strong because of your flight, and free from care because of such an abode.

In the following sermon, through the instruction of the Lord, we shall explain the following parable.[9]

7 1 Cor. 12.8-10.

8 Ps. 67.14.

9 That of the leaven. Cf. Sermon 99 (*PL* 52.477-479).

## SERMON 101

### *Christian Fearlessness of Death*

### (On Luke 12.4-6)

Brethren, you have heard how Christ, in an address worthy of a king, urges His soldiers to despise death and to have no fear of those who kill the body. Thereupon He bestows the rights of friends on those who, through their pursuit of this triumph and their love of liberty, have shed their blood with joy and intrepidity. His words are: 'But I say to you, my friends, Do not be afraid of those who kill the body, and after that have nothing more that they can do. But I will show you whom you shall be afraid of; be afraid of him who, after he has killed, has power to cast into hell.'

'But I say to you, my friends: Do not be afraid'—because virtue proves liberty, and fear reveals slavery. A free man was born for glory, but the slave for fear. Therefore, the man who for God's sake intrepidly spurns death and knows no fear is rightly raised to a friendship with God. If imitation of habits makes men friends, and similarity of habits keeps them together, rightly, then, does Christ call those His friends upon whom He gazes and foresees that in imitation of Himself they will tread under foot the javelins of the world and the very fear of death.

'But I say to you'—that is, not all men, but to my friends. 'But I say unto you'—those whom that death does not exterminate, but sets free. 'I say to you'—those whom the death of the body does not lead to torments, but promotes to something better. 'I say to you'—for whom life is not ended by death, but begun. 'I say to you'—whose death becomes precious not because of its nature, but for this reason: it is finding additional benefits of life, rather than losing its enjoyment.

But let us hear what it is that He says to His friends.

'Do not be afraid of those who kill the body.' Let those readers hear this who have conned the old tomes which the ancients wrote about the benefit of death, but could not take any courage from them, or find consolation. There was a reason for this. With all the powers of eloquence those ancients roused souls to the endurance of death; they dried up tears, stopped sighs, put an end to groans, and hemmed in sorrows. But, for their readers they found nothing about well-founded hope, or everlasting life, or true salvation.

Who would say this to a man, especially to a man of sense? To die is a matter of nature; it is necessary to perish. Our ancestors lived for us; we live for future men; no one lives for himself. It is the part of virtue to will what cannot be avoided. Willingly accept that to which you are being pressed with reluctance. Before death arrives it does not exist, but, when it has come, one no longer knows that it has arrived. Therefore, do not grieve about the loss of something about which, once you have lost it, you will have no more grief.

But, when they utter statements like these, all they say is about the philosophical maxims; they do not talk about life. They do not know from what quarter death has come, or when, or how in your own case, or through whom. For us, however, the Author of life has exposed the author of death. For, God made life, but the Devil schemed against it, as the divine revelation makes clear. 'For God made not death.'[1] 'But by the envy of the devil, death came into the world.'[2]

But you object: 'Why did God allow His own work to perish through the activity of the Devil?' O man, if you truly wanted the answers to your questions, you would set

1 Wis. 1.13.
2 Wis. 2.24.

yourself at leisure for a while, give them your attention, and open your ears. You yourself, so full of curiosity, would want to act as the judge scrutinizing this matter of chief importance. But you are always busy about other men, and never about yourself. As one idle and sluggish, always busy about others and never about yourself, why do you blame the blind causes of things, all the difficulties of the centuries, the depth of judgments, and some inscrutable mystery?

In order to know the forms of the letters and the rudiments of education, were you not assigned to a master and enrolled in a school? Then, completely ready to endure toil or pain, did you not forego visits to your home or your parents? How profitable for you is that for which a teacher is assigned to you, and a school is put at your service. By his work and the punishments he inflicts on you, the teacher begs you to conceive a desire to know those rudiments and to deign to listen to such important matters. The Apostles express their approval of this procedure—especially Paul. He taught by getting whipped, not by whipping, in order to be an outstanding teacher and to receive and bear sufferings as numerous as the customs of men. Then, should we, in a mere moment of time, learn the beginnings of things, and the causes of the world, just because we are ordered to do so? And how are we ordered? Moreover, you do not listen as you ought; that bondage—such a necessity—excuses us. Such complete liberty, such a resolution, accuses you without any doubt. What we say is the part of our duty. That we say but little arises from your being bored.

Do you ask, O man, why God did not soon destroy death along with its author? Why did He not in His providence then carefully prevent that fatal poison from working the ruin of the whole world, especially of His image?

The sky which you behold, O man, made completely of air, carries many waters and is not itself supported by anything else, since a mere command hung it up, and the sole force of a precept supports it. The divine revelation states: 'Who stretchest out the heaven like a pavillion: who coverest the higher rooms thereof with water.'[3] The great weight and burden of the mountains rests upon the earth which is made solid by its own mass; and that earth floats upon a foundation of liquid, as the Prophet testifies: 'Who established the earth above the waters.'[4] Consequently, the fact that it stands arises from a commandment, not from nature. 'He spoke, and they were made: he commanded, and they were created.'[5] Therefore, the fact that the world holds together is a matter of divine operation, not of human understanding. The sea rolls along with the high crest of its own waves, and is raised aloft toward the clouds. Yet, light sands hem it in. Hence we see that its great might yields not to the sand, but to a precept. All the beings in the sky and earth and sea move and live after they have been made by one sole command. The Prophet affirms that they will be dissolved again by a mere command, when he says: 'In the beginning, O Lord, thou foundest the earth: and the heavens are the works of thy hands. They shall perish but thou remainest: and all of them shall all grow old like a garment: And as a vesture shalt thou change them, and they shall be changed.'[6] How? In such a way that their great age may fail through time, but not that creation will perish before the eyes of its Creator.

But, already you say—whoever you are who does this asking—that we have strayed from our subject. For, you asked why God allowed death to remain and destroy His creature, and we have described at great length how the sky and earth and sea were made from nothing and will

3 Ps. 103.2,3.
4 Ps. 135.6.
5 Ps. 148.5.
6 Ps. 101.26-28.

again be dissolved—because of nothing.[7] We have only given you more and more matter to ask about.

So you urge: 'I asked why man perishes, and you have pressed the declaration that the very elements will perish also. You wanted to give to the wearied minds of mortals not repose of mind through reasoning, but merely some solace through the thought that everything perishes—just as if there were not a cause of sorrow in the fact that the sky perishes, and the earth gets dissolved, and the whole appearance of things is being blotted out because of the law of mortality. I ask (you urge), what is prettier than the sky? What more splendid than the sun? What more pleasing than the moon? What more ornamental than the stars? What more healthful than the earth. What more useful than the sea? Or what failure through age is there in all these? They remain just what they were produced or made. Certainly, their enduring would be something more pleasing than their perishing.'

O man, perhaps it would be more pleasing, but not more useful. For, while they have been enduring, you have let your attention falter. While they gleamed, you were blinded so as not to see. The brilliance of the sky has dulled your senses, and the brightness of the sun has blinded your eyes. Deceived by the beauty of these things, you have denied their Maker. You have acknowledged them as rulers of the world. You have called gods those beings which the true God has made subject to you. That is why they must all be dissolved and renewed, so that at least then you will believe they have been made, when you see that they have been repaired. So, do not think that we strayed from our subject. You see that we ran through all creation in order to bring conviction to your understanding.

O man, you did not see it when your Creator made you from dust. For, if you had seen yourself made, you would

7 Not any creature will destroy them, but age and God's mere command.

never have bewailed thus the fact that you were going to die. You saw yourself as one fully made; you saw yourself living; you saw yourself beautiful; you saw yourself like to your Creator. Since you saw yourself neither being born nor dying, were you unaware of whence you came, and what manner of man you were? That is why you attributed your whole self to nature or to yourself, and nothing to God. Wherefore, by means of nature God reduced you to your pristine state. From nothing[8] He has permitted you to be recalled again to dust. Thus He wants you to see what you once were, and to give thanks because you will rise again—you who once lived in such ingratitude despite the fact that you had been produced and made.

Therefore, brethren, as the Lord said, let us not fear those who kill the body. For, they do not annihilate that life, but merely pull it down while they are changing it from temporary life into something everlasting. Brethren, why should I say more? God, who has power to raise the dead, is the One who then permitted us to die. He who can restore life is the One who permitted men to be killed. To Him is honor and glory for ever and ever. Amen.

## SERMON 108

### *Man as Both a Priest and a Sacrifice to God*

(On Rom. 12.1)

This is an unusual kind of piety, which requests both that it may pray and give a present. For, today, the blessed Apostle is not asking for human gifts, but conferring divine ones, when he prays: 'I exhort you, by the mercy of God.' When a physician persuades the sick to take some bitter

8 I.e., nothing save age and God's command. Cf. n. 7, above.

remedies, he does so by coaxing requests. He does not use a compelling command. He knows that weakness, not choice, is the reason why the sick man spits out the heathful medicines, whenever he rejects those which will aid him. Also, a father induces his son to live according to the severity of disciplinary control not by force, but by love. He knows how harsh discipline is to a youthful disposition.

If one sick in body is thus enticed by requests toward getting cured, and if a boyish disposition is with difficulty thus coaxed to prudence, is it strange that the Apostle, always a physician and a father, prays with these words, in order to entice human souls which bodily diseases have wounded to accept divine remedies? 'I exhort you by the mercy of God.'

He is introducing a new kind of adjuration. Why does he not exhort through God's might, or majesty, or glory, rather than by His mercy? Because it was through that mercy alone that Paul escaped from the criminal state of a persecutor, and obtained the dignity of his great apostolate. He himself tells us this: 'For I formerly was a blasphemer, a persecutor and a bitter adversary; but I obtained the mercy of God.'[1] A little further on he continues: 'This saying is true and worthy of entire acceptance, that Jesus Christ came into the world to save sinners, of whom I am the chief. But I obtained mercy to be an example to those who shall believe in him for the attainment of life everlasting.'

'I exhort you, by the mercy of God.' Paul asks—rather, God Himself is asking through Paul, because God has greater desire to be loved than feared. God is asking because He wants to be not so much a Lord as a Father. God is asking through His mercy, that He may not punish in His severity. Hear God asking: 'I have spread forth my hands

1 1 Tim. 1.13-16.

all the day.'[2] Is not He who spreads forth His hands asking by His very demeanor? 'I have spread forth my hands.' To whom? To a people. And to what people? 'To an unbelieving people,' yes, more, to a contradicting one. 'I have spread forth my hands.' He opens His arms, He enlarges His heart, He proffers His breast, He invites us to His bosom, He lays open His lap, that He may show Himself a Father by all this affectionate entreaty.

Also hear God asking in another way: 'O my people, what have I done to thee, or in what have I molested thee?'[3] Does He not say the following? 'If My divinity is something unknown, at least let Me be known in the flesh. Look! You see in Me your own body, your members, your heart, your bones, your blood. If you fear what is divine, why do you not love what is characteristically human? If you flee from Me as the Lord, why do you not run to Me as your Father? But perhaps the greatness of My Passion, which you brought on, confounds you. Do not be afraid. This cross is not Mine, but it is the sting of death. These nails do not inflict pain upon Me, but they deepen your love of Me. These wounds do not draw forth My groans; rather, they draw you into my Heart. The extending of My body entices[4] you into My bosom; it does not increase My pain. As far as I am concerned, My blood does not perish, but it is something paid down in advance as a ransom price for you. Therefore, come, return and at least thus have experience of Me as a Father whom you see returning good things for evils, love for injuries, such great charities for such great wounds.'

Let us now hear the contents of the Apostle's exhortation.

---

2 Isa. 65.2.
3 Mich. 6.3.
4 *dilatat*, influences. Cf. Souter, *s.v.*

'I exhort you to present your bodies.' By requesting this, the Apostle has raised all men to a priestly rank. 'To present your bodies as a living sacrifice.' O unheard of function of the Christian priesthood, inasmuch as man is both the victim and the priest for himself! Because man need not go beyond himself in seeking what he is to immolate to God! Because man, ready to offer sacrifice to God, brings with himself, and in himself, what is for himself! Because the same being who remains as the victim, remains also as a priest! Because the victim is immolated and still lives! Because the priest who will make atonement is unable to kill! Wonderful indeed is this sacrifice where the body is offered without [the slaying of] a body, and the blood without bloodshed.

'I exhort you,' says the Apostle, 'by the mercy of God, to present your bodies as a living sacrifice.' Brethren, Christ's sacrifice is the pattern from which this one comes to us. While remaining alive, He immolated His body for the life of the world. And He truly made his body a living sacrifice, since He still lives although He was slain. In the case of such a victim, death suffers defeat. The victim remains, the victim lives on, death gets the punishment. Consequently, the martyrs get a birth at the time of their death. They get a new beginning through their end, and a new life through their execution. They who were thought to be extinguished on earth shine brilliantly in heaven.

'I exhort you, brethren,' he says, 'by the mercy of God, to present your bodies as a sacrifice, living, holy.' That is what the Prophet sang: 'Sacrifice and oblation thou wouldst not, but a body thou hast perfected for me.'[5] Be, O man, be both a sacrifice to God and a priest. Do not lose what the divine authority gave and conceded to you. Put on the robe of sanctity, gird yourself with the belt of chastity.

5 Ps. 39.7, as quoted in Heb. 10.5.

Let Christ be the covering of your head. Let the cross remain as the helmet on your forehead. Cover your breast with the mystery of heavenly knowledge. Keep the incense of prayer ever burning as your perfume. Take up the sword of the spirit. Set up your heart as an altar. Free from anxiety, move your body forward in this way to make it a victim for God.

God seeks belief from you, not death. He thirsts for self-dedication, not blood. He is placated by good will, not by slaughter. God gave proof of this when He asked holy Abraham for his son as a victim.[6] For, what else than his own body was Abraham immolating in his son? What else than faith was God requiring in the father, since He ordered the son to be offered, but did not allow him to be killed?

Therefore, O man, strengthened by such an example, offer your body. Do not merely slay it, but also cut it up into numerous members, that is, the virtues. For, your skills at practicing die as often as you offer these members, the virtues, to God. Offer up faith, that faithlessness may suffer punishment. Offer a fast, that gluttony may cease. Offer up chastity, that lust may die. Put on piety, that impiety may be put off. Invite mercy, that avarice may be blotted out. That folly may be brought to naught, it is always fitting to offer up holiness as a sacrificial gift. Thus your body will become a victim, if it has been wounded by no javelin of sin. Your body lives, O man, it lives as often as you have offered to God a life of virtues through the death of your vices. The man who deserves to be slain by a life-giving sword[7] cannot die. May our God Himself, who is the Way, the Truth, and the Life, deliver us from death and lead us to life.

---

6 Gen. 22.1-18.

7 Reading *gladio*.

# SERMON 109

## *The Whole Man, Body and Soul, as a Reasonable Sacrifice to God*

(On Rom. 12.1)

Our preceding sermon touched merely the opening words of the Apostle's passage. Today let us hear what the Lord inspires us to say about the words which follow. He began thus: 'I beseech you,' the text says, 'by the mercy of God to present your bodies as a living sacrifice.' By these words has the Apostle said with approval that bodies alone are worthy to be victims offered to God? And does he either fail to mention, or pass over, or abandon souls as something disapproved for this purpose? Is not the soul from heaven and the body from earth? Is not the body ruled, while the soul rules? Does not the soul reign, and the body serve? Does not the body live, and the soul vivify? Does not the soul remain, and the body decay? Does not the body suffer age, while the soul cannot? Finally, is not death itself, which has power over the body alone, unable to occur while the soul is present? Then what is the reason why the soul gets no mention, and only the body is thus summoned to be a victim of God?

Brethren, in this passage the Apostle honors the body without diminishing the importance of the soul. Sins master the body, crimes bind it fast, and transgressions depress it. Vices corrupt it, and passions weigh it down. Therefore, the Apostle desires to release the body. He is eager to set it free, he is striving to elevate it, and he is hastening to purify it by expiation. He wants the body to rise up to where the soul took its origin, rather than to have the soul descend to the nature of the body. He desires the body to accompany the soul to heaven, rather than to have the soul follow the body to the earth. Hear Scripture describe the type and magnitude of the vexations which burden the soul: 'For the corruptible body is a load upon the soul, the earthly habitation presseth down the mind that museth upon many things.'[1] Clearly, therefore, the Apostle desires not a degradation of the soul but an elevation of the body. He wishes both the body and the soul, that is, the whole man, to become a holy victim, a sacrifice pleasing to God. The Psalmist declares that the soul, too, is a sacrificial offering to God when he says: 'A sacrifice to God is an afflicted spirit.'[2]

'To present your bodies as a sacrifice, living, holy, pleasing to God.' Because man pleases by the fact, not that he lives, but that he lives well. He becomes a sacrificial victim not merely by offering himself to God, but by offering himself to God in a holy manner. A spotted victim makes God angry just as much as an unblemished victim placates Him. Hear God saying: 'Do not offer to me anything lame, or half-blind, or polluted because it is intended for death, but something mature without blemish.'[3] Hence it is that the Apostle seeks a living sacrifice for God. Therefore, brethren, if we as the incense of that propitiation . . .[4]

Cain is proof of this. As an ungrateful priest, he so shared his few possessions with God, from whom he had received everything, that he offered the worst of them upon the altar. He kept back for Himself what was best, and thereby gave offense. The upshot was that when he evilly arranged this

---

1 Wisd. 9.15.

2 Ps. 50.19.

3 Cf. Lev. 22.18.

4 There is a gap in the text here. Held (*BKV* 67 130) conjectures that the passage meant this: 'If we bring ourselves as incense to propitiate God, let us bring with our gift not merely our lower part, the body, but also the nobler part, the soul, in order to offer them both to God.'

division with his Maker, he separated himself and his descendants both from life and from the human race.[5]

Therefore, let us follow Abel to his reward, and let us not accompany Cain to his punishment. Abel, bringing a lamb to be sacrificed to God, was accepted as a lamb. Cain, bringing his stubble, found it to be tinder for himself, fuel through which he himself was to be set afire.

'To present your bodies as a sacrifice, living, holy, pleasing to God, your reasonable service.' A service which is not reasonable makes God angry to the same extent as one which is based on reason appeases Him. A service is reasonable when it is not disturbed by presumption, or disordered by rashness, or profaned by transgressions, or colored by pretense. To show service to a king, all the soldiers in a military outpost stand in fear. Human power demands a punctilious service. The obeying servant watches in fear to discover the whim of his master who commands. For, alert devotion brings a reward of just remuneration, while presumptious service does not escape the penalty of its rashness. Who rashly undertakes to serve in a king's palace if he is not invited? Who without a title has dared to profess himself a soldier? Who without the fillets indicating a dignity rashly assumes title to it? If these are matters of anxiety and caution among men, if they stand because of reason,[6] if they prosper through orderly arrangements and if they are preserved because of reverence, then how much more in our relations with God is devotion something to be cautious about! How much more should we be reverent in our service, and solicitous in our worship, that we may offer a reasonable service to God?

'Your reasonable service,' the Apostle says. A service which is warm because it is reasonable is true fervor, but one

---

5 Gen. 4.1-17.

6 Reading *ratione*.

which is not restrained by reason is fanaticism. Consequently, the Jewish nation, when it sought a god for itself in an unreasonable way,[7] lost God to whom it had been giving a reasonable service. The sons of Aaron,[8] unmindful of making their service reasonable, and presuming to add earthly fire to that ordained by God, changed the flame used on the sanctifying sacrifices into a flame of vengeance against themselves. When Saul,[9] swollen with pride at the height of his kingly authority, thought that what was permitted to the priesthood was permitted also to himself, he became a rash violator of the altar, and lost the kingly authority he had received. The Jew, while he cultivated the Law without the reasonableness of the Law, put the Author of the Law to death. The Gentile, unmindful of reasonableness while serving monstrous gods and whole clans of gods, did not deserve to come to the service of God who is one and true. Arius thinks that he does a service to the Father by blaspheming the Son. And while he is attributing a beginning to the Son, the pitiful man is putting a limit upon the Father. Photinus, while denying that the Son is co-eternal with the Father, is elaborately explaining how the Father was not always existent precisely as Father. So it is with all the heresies. While they are spread to the insult of God, and lie about the Trinity through their terms, they further blasphemies.

In contrast, brethren, let us make our bodies fit to be a living sacrifice to God. Let us take care that our service be reasonable, that our faith be true, our conscience pure, our minds well balanced, our hope firm, our heart pure, our flesh chaste, our senses holy, our spirit pious, our reason prudent, our charity undiluted, our mercy generous, our

7 I.e., by adoring the golden calf. Cf. Exod. 32.1-35.
8 Nadab and Abiu. Cf. Lev. 10.1-7.
9 1 Kings 15. 1-35, especially v. 23.

life holy, our appearance modest. To the perfect service of Christ, let humility always accompany our steps.

## SERMON 111

### *Original Sin*

### (On Rom. 5.12-14)

'Therefore as through one man sin entered into the world and through sin death, and thus death has passed into all men because all have sinned—for until the Law sin was in the world, but sin is not imputed when there is no law; yet death reigned from Adam until Moses even over those who did not sin after the likeness of Adam, who is a figure of him who was to come.'

Brethren, the selection[1] from the Apostle for today tells us that through one man the whole world received its sentence. This passage impels us not to preach a sermon, but rather to weep with a renewed and heartfelt sorrow. Renowned prophets have bewailed at length the plight of the Chosen People, and of one city, and sometimes of a single man. If this is the case, then what mind would not be suffering from a total darkening, or what senses would not be getting confused from a complete dulling, or what eyes would not be converted into flowing springs of tears at this fact: The downfall of all men has issued from the fall of one, and the fault of one man has flowed out to become a punishment of all, and the vice of the parent has brought a sad catastrophe upon the whole race? That is what the Apostle states: 'Therefore as through one man sin entered into the world and through sin death.' Oh, what grief I feel! The very man

1 The *lectio;* cf. Introduction, p. 17.

who was a source of all our goods has become the entrance letting in all our evils!

'Sin entered into the world.' Into this world. Are you in wonderment that he who by his sin brought condemnation on the world proved harmful to his descendants? But, you ask: 'How did sin enter? Through whom did it get in?' How? By means of a fault. Through whom? Through a man. And what is sin, a nature or a substance? It is neither a nature nor a substance, but an accident. It is an unfavorable power which is observed in its operation and felt in the punishment it brings on. It attacks the soul, wounds the mind, violates and disorders the nature itself.

And why should I say more, brethren? Sin is to nature what smoke is to the eyes, what fever is to the body, what a bitter salting is to the sweetest springs. The eye indeed is faultless and lucid through nature, but becomes confused and disordered through the injury brought on by smoke. The body, too, thrives by means of its parts, members, and senses, because it was formed into a unit by God. But, once the stormy force of fever has begun its control, that whole units becomes weak. Then there is bitterness in the man's mouth and confusion before his eyes. The path of his steps is uncertain. Then, too, a gentle breeze causes pain, and his dear ones are burdensome, and even helpful attentions bothersome. Too, springs are very pleasant through their natural sweetness, but they become just as unpleasant when they receive foreign matter from outside to spoil them.

But, let us get back to the theme we began. 'Therefore as through one man sin entered into the world and through sin death.'

There is the entrance, brethren! Through a man sin came, and clearly through this sin we are seen to have come under the control of death. O sin, you cruel beast—and a beast not content to vent your fury against the human race from merely one head. We have seen this beast, brethren, devouring with a triple mouth all the highly precious sprouts of the human family. Yes, brethren, with a mouth that is triple: as sin this beast captures, as death it devours, as hell it swallows down.

And as we stated, what copious tears we should surely shed over such a parent! How great are the miseries he left us for our inheritance! Not only did he lose the goods conferred on himself, but he left all his descendants at the mercy of such fierce creditors. O bitter and cruel inheritance! Oh, how unfortunate we were! We found no pleasure in getting that inheritance, but could not disclaim ourselves as the heirs!

Hear what follows. 'And thus death has passed into all men.' However, do not by any chance think it something unjust when through one man death has passed into all men, because all men have their existence through that one. You are deploring your condemnation through him through whom you glory for having received your birth to the light of day.

But, you object: If I owe to my ancestry the fact that I was born, do I also owe to its transgression this, that nature should make me guilty, before any fault of my own? The very next words of the Apostle give a reply to this question of yours. 'Because[2] all have sinned.' If because of him [Adam] all men have become sinners, then rightly through him have all men received the penalty.

'As through one man sin entered into the world and through sin death, and thus death passed unto all men, because all have sinned.' Whether it be in the case of the man, or in the case of his sin, through him and because of him all have become sinners. Therefore, sin has not been

2 *In quo omnes peccaverunt*. The older Douai version translates: in whom all have sinned.'

changed into a nature. But while sin brings on death, it requires that the penalty due to itself be paid through a nature. God had made man's nature such that He was creating man for life. However, when this nature reluctantly generates [offspring] destined to death, it acknowledges that it is subject to sin, and serves as the minister in this life of the penalty due to sin. For, brethren, who would hold opinions like these—that nature would desire its infants to perish, and those young so dear to itself to be killed? Rather, while she groans in her grief, she sighs and longs to see her lost liberty again.

But it is John who first clearly shows through whom nature received this liberty. When he sees Christ he proclaims with loud shouts: 'Behold the Lamb of God, who takes away the sin of the world.'[3] The sin of the world—namely, brethren, that sin which the Apostle testifies to have entered through one man. Therefore, brethren, rejoice! Because the sin which by its heavy mass was depressing toward hell has by Christ been taken away and already sunk into hell. And the grace of this second and divine Parent has restored us from this punishment back to life—us whom the fault of our first parent had sentenced to death. Therefore, man could not be saved without Christ, because before His coming the sin of the whole world had an enduring position.

You, however, admit that you are justified through Christ. Then do you object to your having received sentence through Adam? And do you complain that the penalty due to another man has also hurt you—you who see that the injustice of another man has helped you? Is not the whole tree contained in the seed? Therefore, a defect of the seed is a defect of the whole tree. If the nature itself had been able to help itself through its own power, the Creator Himself would never

3 John 1.29.

have assumed this nature to work its repairing. Do you believe that it has been created for life, if you still doubt that it has been repaired by its Creator?

'For until the Law,' the text states, 'sin was in the world.' When you hear the words 'until the Law,' understand them to mean all the way until the end of the Law, that is, up until the coming of our Lord Jesus Christ. 'Because sin is not imputed,' it says, 'when there is no law.' And when was the law, which began with man himself, non-existent? If there had been no Law, Adam indeed would not have been a transgressor, as the same Apostle makes clear: 'Yet death reigned from Adam until Moses.' Both of them had received a law. But Adam transgressed soon after receiving it, and Moses, once he had received the Law, promulgated it to transgressors. As the Apostle says: 'The Law was enacted on account of transgressions.'[4] Therefore, death reigned through the Law, because in its fierceness death devoured the transgressors more eagerly than the mere sinners. It devoured those men now fallen through their own sin, not only through that of their parent.

'But death reigned,' it says, 'from Adam until Moses, even over those who did not sin after the likeness of the transgression of Adam'—because it kept on devouring not only the adults, but also the children. It kept on striking down not only the guilty, but also the innocent—I mean those free from their own personal guilt, not from their parent's. Consequently, their state was all the more pitiful, since the infant was paying the penalty of that father whose life he had scarcely begun to enjoy. And he who did not yet understand the world was expiating its sin.

Therefore, brethren, let us acquiesce in the fact that death has reigned through one man and because of one man's sin, if all of us wish to be set free through One Man, and to

4 Gal. 3.19.

have our very being through Christ. For, he who lives owes it to Christ, not to himself; and he owes to Adam the fact that he must die.

## SERMON 112

### *Death through Adam; Life and Grace through Christ*

(On Rom. 5.15-21)

If someone gives a cup of cold water to a thirsting traveler, he indeed refreshes the spirit of the heated voyages somewhat, and he clearly does a favor to a fellow man, but he does not quench his thirst completely and forever. Similarly, our sermon, adapted to the present occasion and the need of haste, is insufficient for those who wish to fathom the depths of theological knowledge. If the whole life of man is short for learning human science, what time do we believe enough to understand the divine meaning?[1] So, forgive me, brethren, if within a short period of time, and that scarcely one hour,[2] I cannot in every way elucidate what is obscure, open up what is locked, firmly establish everything doubted, treat the profound subjects, and explain that indescribable mystery[3] of so many centuries. Forgive me, too, if I cannot speak cautiously to our adversaries, off-handedly to our children, confidently to believers, and firmly to unbelievers. To-day, however, the whole passage of the Apostle pours itself

1 *divinam intelligentiam.* Cf. Sermons 5 n. 5; 36 n. 2.

2 In Patristic times a period of one hour was often allotted to the sermon. Cf. *PL* 52.508, note d, and 533, note c. St. Peter, however, usually preached a quarter of an hour. Possibly, he preached one quarter hour homily on the Epistle of the Mass, and another on the Gospel. Cf. the end of Sermon 120 n. 11, and the beginning of Sermon 115 (below p. 189).

3 *sacramentum.*

with clear light into the minds of the hearers. It leaves nothing ambiguous to Catholic minds, when it says: 'For if by reason of the one man's offense death reigned through the one man,' Therefore, let us set aside the pursuit of declamation, and strive to devote our attention with all simplicity to the statements themselves which the Apostle made, that our sermon may beget no obscurity for those who want to know the truth.

'If,' as the text states, 'by reason of the one man's offense death reigned through one man,' why does the authoritative Scriptural writer strive to insist and prove that from this one and first man death has come upon his descendants? Although this statement is clear enough, 'God did not make death,'[4] some men insist, beyond my understanding, that it was God who established death as something so harsh, so cruel, so merciless. No one thinks, without sin, that God, so pious and good, could have created death. Its author is accused and detested by the whole world with unceasing sorrow, groans, and tears. If even among men death is the penalty for crimes, with what daring is death believed to have been created by the guiltless God simultaneously with man, and set up for his punishment earlier than life?

But let us hear the Apostle: 'If by reason of one man's offense death reigned through the one man, much more will they who receive the abundance of the grace and of the gift of justice reign in life, through the one Jesus Christ, our Lord.' Behold, the one man and the other, Adam and Christ. Through the former sin has reigned to promote death; through the latter grace has reigned to serve life. Next, these two sources of life and of death, of liberation and of punishment, of longed-for freedom and final damnation, receive clarification and confirmation from the following statement of the Apostle. 'Therefore as from the offense of one man

4 Wis. 1.13.

the result was unto condemnation to all men, so from the justice of one the result is unto justification of life to all men.'

Through the one man and the other either death reigns or life is granted. What can an interpreter's words add here? If you merely keep silent here, every attack of the adversaries fails.

'From the offense of the one man the result was unto condemnation to all men, so from the justice of the one the result is unto justification of life to all men.' Like a river in relation to its source, or the fruit in relation to its seed, so does the posterity depend on its ancestor for its condemnation or liberation. These words which the Apostle added prove this more fully: 'For just as by the disobedience of the one man the many were constituted sinners, so also by the obedience of the one the many will be constituted just.' Let man be the sinner, that God may be just, because the guilt reflects upon the judge if he forces a guiltless man into a penalty. That is why the Apostle said: 'For just as by the disobedience of the one man the many were constituted sinners'—that men might know that they were participants in the fault of him whose punishment they see themselves sharing.

But, now, let the lovers of the Law hear what the Law availed according to the Apostle: 'Now the Law intervened,' he says, 'that the offense might abound.' See, as the Apostle tells us, the Law did not bring on a lessening[5] of crimes, but an abundance of them. The Law did this, brethren, not because of its own character, but because of him who was too weak to endure the Law. The brilliance of light is not what dulls eyes; light was created by God only for eyes. But it is the weakness of eyes which cannot sustain the whole of light, and bear its splendor. So it is with the Law, brethren. In itself it was just and holy enough. But, while it demanded

5 Reading *imminutio.*

rigid self-control from fragile man, it more and more burdened him and revealed his delinquency.

And why this, brethren? That through the grace and forgiveness of his Creator he might return to life—he who through his swelling pride and ignorance was being led into the debt and penalty of his ancestor, even when he was wickedly boasting about his innocence. So, an undetected disease was hiding within him. Through it the inmost parts of his bones and the blood coursing through his veins were tending to destroy his vital organs. He was generating a contagious infection in his interior members. The Law came to reveal the sore and tell that a heavenly Physician was coming for his long-standing disease. The Law came to bring up to the skin, by means of the poultices of the commandments, that sore that was developing so fatally inside. The Law came to open up that long-standing ulcer by the knife of the commandments, and to effect a healthy draining of the long-gathered pus.

However, brethren, the Law could not by its own power either close up the wound or give perfect health to the patient. When the poor patient saw this and at length recognized his unfortunate state, he began to hasten to the Physician. He hoped that this great Physician's skill and grace would cure that sore which the Law had revealed and long aggravated. We say that the wound was aggravated because, after the lancing, brethren, foulness, stench, noisomeness, and distress are produced in the wound itself as a result of the incision. Through this care his pitiful appearance of weakness grows worse than it was when he was unaware of the danger. So the Physician came, and by the mere assurance of His voice He aided the man who was tired of cures and wearied of their vexations. The centurion acknowledges this when he says: 'Say the word, and my servant will be healed.'[6]

6 Matt. 8.8.

Consequently the prophetical statement was fulfilled: 'He sent his word, and healed them.'[7] That is why this follows: 'Where the offense has abounded, grace has abounded yet more'—as if it were saying: 'Where the wound was opened wide, health has been poured in.'

Let no one, therefore, be ungrateful to the Law, because it lifted up and nursed man whom it found prostrate and sick. Hoping to restore him to health, it led him with healthful joy all the way to the Physician. So that, as the Apostle said: 'As sin has reigned unto death, so also grace may reign by justice to life everlasting through Jesus Christ our Lord.' Grace reigns unto life, sin unto death. Correct faith attributes to God, man's Creator, not death or destruction, but salvation. Let death be from man, let it be from sin, in order that life may be believed to have been created and restored only through Christ!

## SERMON 114

### *Slaves to the Law and to Grace*

(On Rom. 6.15-21)

A traveler always finds it sweet and pleasant to return to his own home. The courtyards of his ancestral house are attractive to him after an absence. Similarly, after these intervals, I find it sweeter to return to my series of passages[1] from the Apostle. Some necessity of religion often compels us to depart from the order of discourses which we had intended, and from the straight path which our discourse

---

7 Ps. 106.20.

---

1 *The lectiones.*

was to follow. For, we must so control the sequence of our instruction that one matter does not hinder another.

Wherefore, let us hear what the holy Apostle has told us today. What does he say? 'Have we sinned because we are not under the Law but under grace? By no means.' Brethren, this question reveals the inexperience of those who, captivated by their custom of living according to the Law, cannot perceive the powers we get from the gift of grace. They were an unyielding people, as we learn from the long series of the precepts of the Law, and the benefits they gained from their sacrificial gifts and the splendor of their festivals made and kept them obstinate in vain observances. When the passage of time will bring the Law to its end, what will one do who has cultivated the Law and been wrenched away from it?

O Hebrew, what is there that you have not lost? And if you have lost it, why do you glory as if you had not lost it? Where is your temple? your priest? your sacrifice? your incense? your purifications? the devout celebration of your festivals, which you thought should never be omitted?

Rightly are you circumcized that you may be a Jew, because you have been cut away from all those goods mentioned above. For it is written: 'Cursed be he that abideth not in all the precepts which have been written in the books of the Law.'[2] If the man who offends against one precept is cursed, how often will he be cursed who will stand convicted of having observed none of them?

'Have we sinned,' he says, 'because we are not under the Law but under grace?' As if he were asking, brethren: 'Have we sinned because, already cured, we have not kept ourselves under the treatment? Have we sinned because, already healed, we have abandoned cauterization, the iron, and the medicants?' The sick man is indeed unfortunate who after

2 Cf. Deut. 27.26.

a cure is unwilling to trouble himself about the painful instruments.[3]

Why should I say more, brethren? He who seeks and awaits a sick man's desires never effects a cure. A cold humor always produces a veritable fire in the body. Excessive firmness irritates and strikes the members, makes and begets a sharper burning sensation. Consequently, when the sick man impatiently requests that cold water be given him, the effect is an increase of the fire which is ever seething and panting in his veins. He is unaware that at such a time fever-heat is extinguished by heat; and that the fire is nourished by what is cold.

Therefore, when the Law anticipates and restrains man's inclination, and when man, impeded by his load of sin, is not strong enough to obey the precepts of the Law, the Law does not free its devotee from the bond of sin. Rather, it binds him the more by bringing a charge of transgression upon him. That is why the Apostle added: 'Do you not know that to whom you offer yourselves as slaves for obedience, to him whom you obey you are the slaves, whether to sin unto death or to obedience unto justice?'

How is it, brethren, that the very fact of our speaking about the Law has revealed that man was the slave of sin? 'Whether to sin unto death,' the text says, 'or unto justice?' A little earlier[4] the Apostle had said that sin was not to have dominion over you, since you are not under the Law but under grace. Clearly, therefore, those who are under the Law of sin are weighed down and bent by its domination; wretched men that they are, they cannot be liberated from this base slavery to sin unless grace sets them free.

The Apostle continues: 'But thanks be to God that you were the slaves of sin.' Is he giving thanks as one who rejoices

3 I.e., to put them away.
4 Rom. 6.14.

because man was the slave of sin? Far from it. He is giving thanks not because we were previously slaves of such a cruel master, but because we are slaves no longer. He expressly makes that point clear by his next words: 'but you have now obeyed from the heart that form of doctrine into which you have been delivered, and having been set free from sin, you have become the slaves of justice.' We have become obedient, brethren, through the gift of Him who calls us, not through our own will, for we were being held as captives by it.

'You have now obeyed from the heart that form of doctrine.' What form? Beyond question, that of the Gospel, where the slavery has not been abolished by a new kind of freedom, but changed, because a devoted service is better than a capricious and headstrong freedom.

'You have become the slaves of justice.' Brethren, this slavery does not restrain, it liberates. It does not burden, it honors. It does not brand a man with the stain of slavery, but removes it. Here, where one form of slavery expels the other form, where one state drives out another state, where death dies because of a death, where loss is healed by a loss, and—to say it properly and briefly—where all adversity is laid low by a sword of adversity, what is there here, I ask, that is not divine? The Apostle expresses this: 'I speak in a human way because of the weakness of your flesh; for as you yielded your members as slaves of uncleanness and iniquity unto iniquity, so now yield your members as slaves of justice unto sanctification.'

He shows the greatness of his love when he reduces the doctrine of the Gospel to such humble and almost shameful examples, so that he recommends that you now devote yourselves as much to holiness as you once did to uncleanness, as much to justice as formerly to iniquity. Consequently, he gains control over slavery.

Brethren, that comparison seems absurd and unbecoming. It would have man subject only as much to glory as to depravity. And would that he were subject only as much, and no more! Yet, when does human frailty give as much service to God as to the world? as much to heaven as to the earth? as much to virtue as to vices? Wretched man is so entirely given over to the flesh, so occupied with present affairs, that he relinquishes nothing in him which might be of service to his future life, to supernatural well-being.

In one phrase the Apostle fittingly described the force of temporal allurement upon the human conscience. He properly stated that the human members should yield themselves as eagerly to justice, purity and cleanness as they had once yielded themselves over with vehemence and madness to depravity and vices. The man who wishes to withdraw from his property after losing his right of ownership demands little or perhaps nothing. Likewise, he takes away your excuse who enjoins upon you only insignificant and ordinary payments[5] which you ought to pay back in return for great benefits.

Therefore, O man, give to God as much as you once gave to your flesh and vices. Why do you keep yourself bound to vices rather than to God, since it is only because of His love for you that God asks so much of you?

The text continues: 'For when you were the slaves of sin, you were free as regards justice. . . . But now set free from sin,[6] you have become the slaves of justice.' Previously you were slaves of sin, now you are slaves of justice. Behold, according to the Apostle one kind of slavery follows upon another. O obstinate man, now show the time of your liberty! Sin previously told the lie that you, the unhappy man whom it was holding captive, were free. Now, grace calls you its slave; and that it might make you truly free it has made

5 *repensor* is here being used as a deponent verb.
6 Apparently quoting from memory, he reverts from Rom. 6.22 to 6.18.

you the adopted son of God Himself. Therefore, Christ's statement has been fulfilled: 'Whoever wishes to become the master, let him be the servant.'[7] Blessed is this slavery! It begets an everlasting reign. For, that former liberty brought upon us a penalty as its fruit, and unbearable confusion, as the Apostle says: 'For what fruit had you then from these things of which you are now ashamed? For the end of these things is death.'

Behold how the Devil does his liberating! See the reward with which he honors that slavery! He wants death simultaneously to end your life and begin your punishment.

But those who serve Christ, brethren, contemn death and its wages; and they are transferred into an everlasting life of holiness. For death in Christ does not admit a termination, because it does not kill a man, but brings him to his perfection.

## SERMON 115

### *The Abrogation of the Law in Favor of the New Covenant of Grace*

(On Rom. 7.1-6)

After we have soothed your minds and hearts by playing upon the Davidical harp with a plectrum of spiritual understanding and an accompaniment of rhythmical chant, and after we have expounded awesome principles of the resounding Gospel to quicken your powers of perception,[1] we have thought that we should soon come back to the teaching of

7 Cf. Matt. 20.23.

1 A reference to previous homilies which explained Psalms and passages from the Gospel.

the Apostle. Thus, each section of our threefold division of the preaching of the Christian doctrine can retain and impart its salutary instruction. For the chant relaxes your minds from constant effort, and the authority of the Gospel refreshes them again and stirs them up to labor, and the Apostle's vigor does not permit your minds to be drawn off the direct road and to wander.

Today, we find that we are to follow this passage of the Apostle with continuous running comment: 'Do you know, brethren,' he says, '(for I speak to those who know law) that the Law has dominion over a man as long as he lives?' Then he enters upon a comparison: 'For the married woman is bound by the Law while her husband is alive; but if her husband die, she is set free from the law of the husband. Therefore while her husband is alive, she will be called an adulteress if she be with another man; but if her husband dies, she is set free from the law of the husband.'

Brethren, you perceive this great pronouncement of the Apostle's heavenly instruction. He expounds how the time of the Law, by the Law's own testimony, has passed away; he has voided the Law's place of privilege, through his striking example of marriage.

And rightly does he compare the Law to a marriage in the flesh, because the Law did not possess a spiritual union with the Synagogue. For, when the Law had accepted her as its bride for the promotion of discipline, the abundance of holy offspring, the increase of modesty, the protection of chastity, the sacred and revered inner sanctuary of the heavenly chamber, and the mystical unity of the heavenly couch—then it found in her the defilement of complete infidelity. For, she came to meet such a great man, that is, the Law, and she was not elegant in her manners, nor arrayed with the jewels of virtues, nor stately in her pace, nor covered with that truly brilliant veil of virginal modesty. Rather, she was wanton in her eyes, loose in her steps, forward with her seductiveness, completely illusive with guile and pretense.

When such a great man saw her, he justly looked down on her with indignation. He kept her far from any association with himself, and execrated her with all the full weight of his condemnation. However, she neither blushed when despised, nor corrected herself when contemned, nor came to herself in repentance. But, when she was repulsed, she flew altogether headlong to the brothels of the idols. She preferred to undergo the infamy of fornication and incur the crime of adultery than to cease to be horrible because of the baseness of her habit which so evilly pleased her.

Consequently, the Prophet rightly deplores her: 'How is the faithful city become a harlot?'[2] Holy Ezechiel, too, describes her adulteries in almost his whole volume. Hence it is, brethren, that in the Gospel when she was being accused[3] before the Lord as an adulteress by the scribes and doctors of the Law, the Lord turned away His face, and stooped down to the earth, in order not to behold a crime which He was to punish. And He preferred, brethren, to write forgiveness in the sand rather than to utter a condemnation about the flesh.

The Apostle is striving to recall this adulteress to union with Christ. He does not allow her to be retarded by fear over her former fall. While her husband was alive she was rightly called an adulteress because she was with another man. But now she is not deserting the Law when she is taking recourse to the Author of the Law. Rather, although she is under the condemnations of the Law, she is dying to the Law, in order that she may live unto grace and in order that she who through the Law was intemperate and made to die may arise again through forgiveness.

2 Isa. 1.21.
3 John 8.1-11.

Finally when the Apostle asserts that she is set free from the law of her deceased husband, he testifies by his following words that she, rather than her husband, has died. For, the Law does not die to a man, but a man dies to the Law. The precept does not pass away, but he who slips away from the precept breaks loose from its control. Listen to what follows: 'Therefore, my brethren, you also have been made to die to the Law.'

Did he say: 'The Law has died to you'? His words are: 'You also have been made to die to the Law.' And well did he add, 'Through the body of Christ,' because the Law binds only a guilty man, restrains only a harmful man, punishes and executes only a criminal. Therefore, he who has been freed from every crime through the body of Christ is fortunately dying to the Law, in order to live unto innocence and grace. 'So as to belong to another who has risen from the dead,' the Apostle continues. 'To another.' He [Christ] became that 'other' when He changed our corruptibility into incorruptibility, and raised our mortality into the glory of immortality.

'In order that we may bring forth fruit unto God,' he continues. He asserts that those who have become, through Christ, partakers of a heavenly nature should bring forth fruit not unto the earth, but unto God; not unto death, but unto life; and not unto the flesh, but unto God. 'For when we were in the flesh,' the Apostle continues, 'sinful passions, which were aroused by the Law, were at work in our members so that they brought forth fruit unto death.' When he says 'when we were,' he indicates a time during which, placed in the flesh alone, or rather, more exposed to it, we were being compelled to relish, do, and will only those things which pertain to the flesh, according to the Apostle's statement: 'They who are carnal cannot please God.'[4]

4 Rom. 8.8.

'For when we were in the flesh, the sinful passions which were aroused by the Law.' I shall say what was said by the Lord: 'If the light that is in thee is darkness, how great is the darkness itself?'[5] If sinful passions which were aroused by the Law dominate the human members, what will those passions do through their own power? They unfortunately and painfully attach themselves to a man soon after his birth. When anxieties depress one born like that—and one is born like that—and when dangers beset him, and pains exert their influence on him, the passions, brethren, are the cause. Through them infancy is spent in weakness, boyhood is dragged along, youth acts in folly, young manhood and old age are burdened with many sorrows. It is the passions which, abetted by the Enemy's disturbing turmoil, beset the whole life of man even until his death. While the Law was prohibiting them, it incited them to action; while it was investigating them, it enlarged them; while it was accusing them, it made them more beloved; and through the knowledge which the Law gave it made those which were lying hidden through ignorance better known.

And just as thorns grow the more when they are cut by the sickle, so the passions put forth more sprouts when they are trimmed through the Law, since they are internally strengthened because they are implanted, as it were, in a root of flesh. The Law has within it a sufficiently proper cultivation of faith, but it does not make efficacious progress; consequently, by its prodding, it brings the human flesh, like soil, to produce fruit of death. The text reads: 'Sinful passions, which were aroused by the Law, were at work in our members so that they brought forth fruit unto death.' The passions in us vindicate for themselves unto the fruit of death that which was an instrument of life. Therefore, wounded thus, we are set free by the grace of Christ

5 Matt. 6.23.

from the Law of death, and we receive within ourselves the Holy Spirit as warrior and victor over vices; that the passions, shut outside, may rap and try to provoke, but be defeated before the glory of our triumph. For us, for us does He desire to conquer, who, when He was ruling us, condescended to fight for us, as He stated.[6]

Therefore, already free from the slavery of the flesh, let us 'serve in newness of spirit,' because to serve in God-given sanctity is true domination. For the 'old man'[7] and the old letter[8] corrupted and destroyed all discipline.

## SERMON 116

### *The Law as an Occasion of Sin*

(On Rom. 7.7-12)

Whenever the mystical chant[1] resounds—different in its kind but always harmonious—it fills and delights the ears with its soothing sweetness. Similarly, when the divine and heavenly doctrine—different in its manner of expression, but one in its spirit and meaning—it brought up for consideration, it opens up and unfolds the mystery of the knowledge in the Gospel more pleasantly and with the greatest sweetness. Consequently, after the prophetical song and the astonishing miracles worked by Christ's powers, let us return to the series of readings from the Apostle.

---

6 A quotation from Scripture has apparently been lost from the manuscripts.

7 Adam.

8 The letter of the Jewish Law, which St. Paul contrasted in 2 Cor. 3.6 with 'the new covenant, not of the letter but of the spirit; for the letter kills, but the spirit gives life.'

---

1 No doubt, that of the Psalms, as can be inferred from the beginning of Sermon 115.

Today, the continuation of the reading is this: 'What shall we say then? Is the Law sin? By no means! Yet I did not know sin save through the Law. For I had not known lust unless the Law had said, Thou shalt not lust. But sin, having thus found an occasion, worked in me by means of the commandment all manner of lust.'

Brethren, you have heard in what a state of sickness the human race lay without Christ. How much a captive human frailty was without grace! It was not being restrained from crime by the Law and Commandments, but rather armed to commit them. It kept itself attentive and learning, not in order to overcome sins, but to commit them. 'I did not know sin save through the Law.' Not to have known vices is happiness. To be acquainted with them is dangerous. To have overcome them is virtue. A noble, strong king goes to meet his foes afar off. Thus he anticipates the ruses of his assailants. Consequently, the confidence of his soldiers cannot be diminished, or the constancy of his subjects disturbed. In similar manner, through the grace of Christ a noble soul breaks through the unfortunately narrow limitations of the body. Thus, with all its power, it anticipates sins. It treads vices under foot, and by ruthless slaughter lays crimes low with all its might, in order that the vices may not be able to fool the understanding[2] by deceitful measures, or to corrupt anyone's character by wiles, or to dissolve wretched, weak hearts by interior storms, or through the heat of passion and bloodshed to fan the occasions of sin, still smoking like embers, into full flame, or by different kinds of passions to harass the members naturally weak. Vices are to the human body what fire is to a dried-up grain field. They are overcome rather securely only by being kept at a distance; they are killed by being ignored; and if they are ignored, they happily vanish. If these vices penetrate the mind and the senses; if

2 Reading *sensus*.

they make their way into souls, and once enter the members of the body, an unextinguishable fire is conceived and fanned. Then, unless heavenly water will flood the hearts, pour itself into the minds, and drench the members, everything which goes to make up a man's strength is overcome and reduced to ashes.

'Is the Law sin? By no means. Yet I did not know sin save through the law.' This is as if he were saying: 'Gold is not avarice, yet I did not know avarice save through gold. Wine is not drunkenness, yet I did not know drunkenness save through wine. Bodily beauty is not concupiscence, but beauty of shape snatched me into the power of concupiscence and brought me to fall.'

Thus, it is clear that those things—which God created for their usefulness, for salvation, and for grace—are not evil by their nature. Yet, an occasion of sinning is furnished through them. The upshot is that the miser blames the gold, and the drunken man the wine. The licentious man or the fop wants to attribute to beauteous form that which brought on his downfall. Thus, too, the Law which had been given by God for salvation, which was by its own nature heavenly and holy, was made through man an instrument of wretched man's downfall. The Apostle proves this by the following words: 'So that the Law indeed is holy and the commandment holy and just and good.'

Clearly, that which was good did not bring in death. Rather, it was sin which chiefly brought in death—sin which had made human nature fragile and weak and prone to falls and vices. Sin was lurking in the human body and waxing strong. The Law reprehended it and exposed it while it instructed man about innocence, holiness, justice, virtue, and faith, and while it censured him about vices, offenses, and crimes. However, man began to hear about the virtues, and he began to will them, but he did not attain them. He began to detest the vices, but to follow them; to hate the offenses, but to commit them; to stand aghast at the crimes, but to carry them out. Consequently, he slowly perceived that he was a captive slave, condemned to the evil of madness, and he began to cry out: 'Unhappy man that I am! Who will deliver me from the body of this death?'[3] He received the reply: 'The grace of God through our Lord Jesus Christ.'

After hearing that, he began to seek freedom through his Creator, salvation through forgiveness, and to hope for life through grace alone. For long he had failed to know where difficult innocence comes from, and arduous justice, and toilsome sanctity, and laborious virtue, and faith completely full of dangers. He had not known whence the offences get such great force, whence vices grow strong even while they are being pruned, why virtues fail even while they are being cultivated. The Law opened this up, and taught it, and showed with full light that in human hearts and human minds crimes rule through sin and virtues through God. It made evident that offences cannot be overcome until their source has been extinguished, that is, sin which Christ took away, as John testifies: 'Behold the lamb of God, who takes away the sin of the world.'[4]

'For without the Law sin was dead,' the Apostle continues. 'Once upon a time I was living without law, but when the commandment came sin revived, and I died, and the commandment that was unto life was discovered in my case to be unto death. For sin, having taken occasion from the commandment, deceived me, and through it killed me.' Sin was dead, not in that it was non-existent, but in that it was unknown. Rightly was it said: 'Sin revived.' For it lay buried under human ignorance. It was not the commandment which

3 Rom. 7.24,25.
4 John 1.29.

revived through sin; rather, sin revived through the commandment, in so far as the commandment made him who had previously been a sinner [unknowingly] a [knowing] transgressor [of the Law]; in so far as it made the guilty man obstinate, too, and excited him to be a rebellious apostate. Consequently, when man recognized from what source, and why, and through what he was dying, he rightly exclaimed that he was then already dead. We now see, brethren, how cruel a tyrant sin is.

'Sin, having taken occasion from the commandment, deceived me, and through it killed me'—because it stretched the instrument of salvation into a snare, made the means of cure a means of sickness, changed the means of health into a deadly wound, converted life itself into a death-dealing sword.

'Sin, having taken occasion from the commandment, deceived me, and through it killed me.' But, since man had been killed, how could he, as one already slain, now provide for himself? For, who was able to help a slain man save Christ, who by His death restored life? It was He who through His death inflicted a dead man's retaliation in kind. He destroyed death. He betrayed it as being a haughty creature which, although ordered to exact penalties only from guilty men, dared to attack the Judge Himself. It presumed to assault the Author of innocence Himself. Consequently, death rightly died, and not I myself live, but Christ lives, acts, reigns, and commands in me.

# SERMON 117

## *The First Adam, and the Last Adam, Born of a Virgin*

(On 1 Cor. 15.45-50)

The holy Apostle today recounts that two men gave an origin to the human race, namely, Adam and Christ. They are two men alike in body, but different in worth; truly similar in the structure of their members, but truly dissimilar in their own beginnings. 'The first man, Adam,' the text says, 'became a living soul; the last Adam became a lifegiving spirit.' That first one was made by this last One, from whom he got his soul to be alive. This last One was fashioned by His very Self, that He alone might not await life from another, but give it to all men. The first one was moulded from the cheapest earth; the last One came forth from the Virgin's precious womb. In the case of the former, earth is changed into flesh; in that of the latter, flesh itself is raised up to God.

Why should I say more? This last is the Adam who placed His own image in the first one when He made him. That is why He both plays the same role as the former and receives his name, in order not to let perish, as far as He was concerned, that which He had made to His own image. The first Adam, and the last Adam. That first one has a beginning; this last One has no limit. For, in truth, this last One is Himself first, as He says: 'I am the first, and I am the last.'[1] 'I am the first,' that is, without a beginning; 'I am the last,' assuredly without an end.

'But it is not the spiritual that comes first,' the text says, 'but the physical and then the spiritual.' Surely the earth exists before the fruit, but it is not as precious as the fruit.

1 Isa. 48.12.

The earth exacts groans and toil, but the fruit gives substance and life. The Prophet rightly glories over such fruit: 'Our earth has yielded her fruit.'[2] What fruit? Clearly, that of which he says elsewhere: 'Of the fruit of thy womb I will set upon thy throne.'[3]

'The first man,' the text continues, 'was of the earth, earthy; the second man is from heaven, heavenly.' Where are they[4] who think that the Virgin's conception and giving birth to her child are to be likened to those of other women? For, this latter case is one of the earth, and the Virgin's is one from heaven. The one is a case of divine power; the other of human weakness. The one case occurs in a body subject to passion; the other in the tranquility of the divine Spirit and the peace of the human body. The blood was still, and the flesh astonished; her members were put at rest, and her entire womb was quiescent during the visit of the Heavenly One, until the Author of flesh could take on His garment of flesh, and until He, who was not merely to restore the earth to man but also to give him heaven, could become a heavenly Man. The Virgin conceives, the Virgin brings forth her child, and she remains a virgin. Consequently, her body is conscious of strength, not pain. By her child-bearing she receives an increase of her integrity, and suffers no harm to her modesty. She is, rather, the witness of her motherhood who suffered none of its customary pains. The new mother marvels at her having a part in heavenly mysteries. Well does she understand that the birth[5] of her Son has nothing which ordinarily occurs among men. If the Magus through His gift acknowledges that God is thus being born, and makes

2 Ps. 84.18.
3 Ps.131.11.
4 Cerinthus, Ebion, and the Carpocratians.
5 Reading *originem*. If *ordinem* is correct, 'birth' should be changed to 'dignity.'

his acknowledgment while he is adoring, think what a Christian ought to feel and believe!

But, let us hear what follows: 'As was the earthy man, such are the earthy; and as is the heavenly man, such also are the heavenly.' How will it be possible for those who were not born thus as heavenly men to be found heavenly men? Not through their remaining what they were born, but by continuing to be what they were when reborn. Brethren, that is why the heavenly Spirit by a mysterious injection of His light fecundates the womb of the virginal Mother. He desired to bring forth as heavenly beings those whom an origin from an ancestral stock of earth had brought forth as earthy men, in a wretched state. He wanted to bring them to the likeness of their Creator. So, let us who have already been reborn, and reformed to the image of our Creator, fulfill what the Apostle commands.

'Therefore, even as we have borne the likeness of the earthy, let us bear also the likeness of the heavenly.' Let it be granted that all this was a necessity: that we, formed from earth, could not produce heavenly fruits; that, born from concupiscence, we could not avoid concupiscence; that we, born from the powerful attractions of the flesh, had to carry the base load of its attractions; that we, accepted into this world for our home, were captives to its evils. Yes, let us who have been reborn to the likeness of our Lord (as we mentioned), whom a Virgin[6] conceived, and the Spirit enlivened, and modesty carried, and integrity brought to birth, and innocence nourished, and sanctity taught, and virtue trained, and God adopted as His sons—let us bear the image of our Creator in a perfect reproduction. Let it be a reproduction not of that majesty in which He is unique, but of that innocence, simplicity, meekness, patience, humility, mercy, and

6 Inasmuch as we are part of Christ's Mystical Body; or, perhaps, as Böhmer says in *BKV* 43.285, the Virgin is the Church.

peacefulness by which He deigned to become and to be one with us. May the bothersome itch of vices cease, and the fatal allurements of sins be overcome, and damnable rage, the source of crimes, be checked. May all the fog of wordly display be dispelled from our senses. May all the illusion of worldly desire be cast out of our minds. May we desire Christ's poverty which stores its everlasting riches in heaven. May we preserve complete holiness of soul and body, that we may bear and enhance our Creator's image in ourselves, in regard not to its size, but to our way of acting.

The Apostle confirms what we have said by his words: 'Now this I say, brethren, that flesh and blood can obtain no part in the kingdom of God.' See how he preaches the resurrection of the body. There, the spirit will possess the flesh, not the flesh the spirit, as the next words make clear: 'Neither shall corruption have any part in incorruption.' You see that not the flesh perishes, but the principle of corruption; not the man, but his fault; not the person, but his sin; in order that the man living in God and before Him alone may rejoice over arriving at the end of his sins.

We should devote a complete sermon to the resurrection, brethren. It is not right for us to speak only in passing, and that at the end of our sermon, about that which sends us into the endless ages and everlasting life.

# SERMON 120

## *Two Patterns: Wordly Life and Christ's Life*

(On Rom. 2.2-21[1])

Today, Christ made it clear that His Apostles are salt, by His words: 'You are the salt of the earth.'[2] Let no one be impatient with us if we abraze the words of the holy Apostle like grains of divine salt, in order that, seasoned[3] more deeply ourselves, we may improve our understanding of his meaning. For, unabrazed grains of salt produce their seasoning effect through getting broken up and descending more deeply into the substance being seasoned. Similarly, the Apostle's passage, if read in an ordinary manner, yields its surface meaning. But it gives up its profound meaning if it is reread with careful attention to the matters we previously observed.

Today, the holy Apostle tells us: 'Be not conformed to this world.' Do you think that by this statement the blessed Apostle Paul is exhorting us not to make ourselves like the shapes of the elements? or not to be like Persian kings? Sometimes they put a globe beneath their feet in order to be deemed controllers of the world and to simulate the functions of God. Again, they sit with a shape and appearance like the sun, with rods protruding like rays from their heads, that they may not seem to be men. Sometimes, as if to express grief that they are men, they wear horns, and make themselves women with the appearance of the moon.[4] At times, they put on various appearance of stars, in order to lose

1 This sermon continues the homily begun in Sermon 109.
2 Matt. 5.13.
3 Reading *saporati*. If *soporati* is right, the phrase is: in order to improve, by this seasoning, the penetration possessed by our now slumbering mind.
4 The Persians sometimes worshiped the moon as a woman; cf. *PL* 52.527, note c.

the shape of men—yet they acquire nothing of heavenly brightness. But all those practices spring from the vanity of the world. Wise men ought to have nothing to do with them and to laugh at them.

However, when the Apostle says: 'Be not conformed to this world,' he is correcting the manner of the life of the world, disapproving its practices, passing judgment on its mode of life, denouncing its inclinations, and condemning its luxury. He is warding off all the pomp of wordly vanities, putting them to flight, striving to keep them out of Christian minds. Yet, in this way he is forcibly reminding us, in an abridged manner, of what he stated more at length at the beginning of this Epistle, where he gives this picture of the figure of the world in its vices: 'Being filled with all iniquity, malice, immorality, avarice, wickedness; being full of envy, murder, contention, deceit, malignity; being whisperers, detractors, hateful to God, irreverent, proud, haughty, plotters of evil; disobedient to parents, foolish, dissolute, without affection, without mercy. Although they have known the ordinance of God, they have not understood that those who practise such things are deserving of death. And not only do they do these things, but they applaud others doing them.'[5]

Brethren, you have heard what the form of the world is, you have learned its appearance, and seen its figure—if we should call that a form and not a shapeless monster, where through the disorder of crimes the whole appearance of things has been made hideous; where through a sinful marriage the whole figure of the world has become loose-jointed; where the very image of the Creator has been ruined by the diseases of sins; where man is buried under vices; where crimes of a corrupted body abound; where a man is the sepulchre of his true self; where in man is discerned not

5 Rom. 1.29-32.

a true man but a corpse. This, therefore, is the form or pattern of the world to which the Apostle forbids us to be conformed. He prohibits us to become like this figure. He does not permit us to be images of this model. Rather, he transforms us to the form of God. He calls us back to likeness to Christ. He allures us towards the whole pattern of our Creator, with the words: 'But be transformed in the newness of your minds.'

That is, cast away the pattern of this world, and be renewed in your minds through Christ. Discard the unshapeliness of the antiquated form, and make your nature[6] one modeled upon that of your Saviour, that the newness of your minds may shine forth in your deeds, and the man of heaven may walk the earth with a heavenly deportment.

Let it now become clear how the Apostle draws up the pattern of the new man: 'For just as in one body we have many members, yet all the members have not the same function, so we, the many, are one body in Christ, but severally members one of another. But we have gifts differing according to the grace that has been given us.'[7] He is struggling and taking care that the body, to which he assigns a heavenly function, may through the harmony and co-operation of the members hold fast its life which is characteristic of heaven and its practices of holiness. He wants neither the foot to interfere through perverse conceit in the functions of the eye, nor the eye in those of the foot. Rather, he desires the holy members to be content with the gifts conferred by the Giver. He wishes all the members to regard what any one member has done as their own. For, no member which has the honor of being part of the whole body can be of less importance. Hence, the Apostle portrays the functions

6 For this translation of *formam,* cf. Phil. 2.5,7.
7 Rom 12.4-6.

by means of the members, and the members by means of the functions:

'Or he who teaches, in teaching; he who exhorts, in exhorting; he who gives, in simplicity; he who presides, with carefulness; he who shows mercy, with cheerfulness. Let love be without pretense. Hate what is evil, hold to what is good, anticipating one another with honor, being kind to one another. Be not slothful in zeal; be fervent in spirit, serving the Lord, rejoicing in hope. Be patient in tribulation, persevering in prayer. Share the remembrances of the saints, practising hospitality. Bless, and do not curse. Rejoice with those who rejoice; weep with those who weep. Provide good things not only in the sight of God, but also in the sight of men. Be not wise in your own conceits. To no man render evil for evil. If it be possible, as far as in you lies, be at peace with all men. Do not avenge yourselves, but give place to the wrath. "If thy enemy is hungry, give him food; if he is thirsty, give him drink." Be not overcome by evil, but overcome evil with good.'[8]

Brethren, the Apostle revealed above the vice-laden members. Now, he has shown us the virtuous members. He wants the body meant for heaven to be strong with such great virtues, and robust with such sinews, that it can easily prostrate the wars of the world and overcome the Devil's assaults.

If a man lives according to the Apostle's teaching, does he not lay the world low? Does he not subdue his flesh? Does he not conquer the Devil? Does he not become like the angels? Is he not greater than the sky? Clearly he is, because the sky does not move itself by its own power. It does not act by free will. It does nothing through judgment, but functions always through necessity, because its function was appointed to it once for all. Not by its own strength or

8 Cf. Rom. 12.7-21.

effort does it keep itslf undefiled. Consequently, it is not subject to punishment, but neither can it expect a reward. But, when man, a creature put together from earthly stuff, overcomes his earthly stigma, vanquishes the urges of his blood and overwhelms the passions of his flesh, he mounts above the sky and flies to the very abode of God. Thus he becomes greater than the heavens. He excels the angels, not by his nature, but by his merits.

The example of Paul the Apostle is proof of this. While he was winning quite a victory over the world, he penetrated the sky, and passed through the second heaven, and deserved to get all the way to the third one. All this was right. For, surely, he who by his word and example had so well taught others how to enter the heavens should himself be the first to rise into them. He who will live according to Paul's teaching, he, too, will surely be greater than the sky. He who thus shines throughout the world by the rays of his virtues so that he does not let himself be darkened by any night of vices, he will be brighter than the sun. He who mitigates this darkness not by any dimmed light, but banishes all the night by the strong brilliance of his merits, he will surely be more luminous than the moon. He will not, like the moon, experience daily diminutions of his light, but by the steadily glowing lantern of his deeds he will remain in the illumination of a heavenly light. Neither is he, like the moon, changed by a monthly waning. Rather, he will bask forever in the uninterrupted love of God. If the moon is great because it moderates the night, how much greater is this man whose life admits no darkness of night into itself! I say nothing about the stars, because the saints shine with as many virtues as the sky is spangled with stars. 'You are the light of the world,' said the Lord; 'shine like lamps in the world.'[9] At the end of the world, as God has told us, the sky, the

9 Matt. 5.14,16.

sun, the moon, and the stars will pass away, but the just man will remain in the bright light of God.'[10]

Brethren, I should like to make single comments on the Apostle's every word. But repeated reading begets weariness of hearing, and we cannot longer remain silent about the virtues recounted in the Gospels.[11] Therefore, may you in your charity find it satisfactory that we have terminated our comments on the present reading by this abridged sermon. May our God Himself deign to imbed in your holy minds both the matters we have said and those we have left unmentioned.

## SERMON 122

### *The Rich Man and Lazarus*

### (On Luke 16.23-24)

Today, brethren, our sermon ought to treat adequately the virtues of St. Andrew.[1] However, we promised to go back

10 Matt. 24.29-35.

11 The sermon of the bishop sometimes preceded the reading of a passage of the Gospel, as *PL* 52.529, note a, points out. However, St. Peter's statement here may be evidence that he gave one homily of fifteen minutes on the Epistle, and another a little later during the same Mass on the Gospel, and perhaps even one on the chanted verses of the Psalms. Cf. the beginning of Sermon 112 (and note 2) and of Sermon 115; also, Introduction, p. 17.

1 St. Peter treats the entire parable of Luke 16.19-31 in Sermons 121-124. Sermon 122 was selected because it is a good homily, and also because its introduction throws much light on the Fathers' manner of preaching. They spoke not only on Sundays but on other feasts, too, especially those of the martyrs. Cf. *PL* 52.533, note d. St. Peter was unwilling either to depart from his custom of preaching only for fifteen minutes or to interrupt his series here to preach about St. Andrew, about whom he did speak on another occasion. (Sermon 133).

and treat the remainder of the subject of the rich man and Lazarus, the poor man of the Gospel. Furthermore, the prerogative of St. Andrew's apostolate and martyrdom suffice—yes, more than suffice—for his glory. Therefore, if it is agreeable to you, we shall, with the aid of the Lord, give you what we promised and owe.

Aware that weariness begets aversion in both the hearers and the speaker, in our previous treatise we postponed [treatment of] the greatest part of the passage which is set forth. This was to enable us to refresh the strength of our mental faculties and then, with full vigor and proper attention, grasp the remainder of the salutary word.

After the words we spoke come these: 'And lifting up his eyes, being in torments, the rich man saw Abraham afar off, and Lazarus in his bosom.' 'And lifting up his eyes.' Late does the rich man lift up his eyes toward heaven; he has always kept them intent upon the earth. O rich man, those very eyes you lift up are your accusers. Those eyes you lift up do not placate your Judge, but enkindle Him to anger. They gain you, not forgiveness, but a feeling of guilt. They call for the full measure of penalties, not solace. Whither do you raise your eyes? Why do you still cry out, O rich man? Whither do you cast your glance again and again, O rich man? There is Lazarus, there is the betrayer of your impiety, the witness of your crimes, the herald of your cruelty.

'And he cried out,' the text says, 'Father Abraham, have pity on me.' Now you recognize him as a father. But in the person of Lazarus you spurned Abraham as a father, and you cannot now know him as a father toward you. Now you see him as a just man who then, to be kindly to you, long allowed Lazarus to be tormented. Unhappy is he whom his own ancestor thus accuses, whom the one responsible for his seeing the light of day thus condemns. Unhappy is he whose crimes were so great that in the judgment his ancestor could not show mercy to him, or his father forgive him, or his father's affection help him.

Why do you still cry out, O rich man? You are still rich, but in crime, not in wealth; not in possessions, but in guilt. Why do you cry out? What do you ask for? Here we see no more petitioning, but a controversy in which the one who suffered is one of the opponents. The participants are in separated places. The one speaks from nearby; the other, from afar. The ones carries on from a bosom; the other, from hell. The one pleads from a place of repose; the other complains from amid his torments.

What does the rich man say? 'Father Abraham, have pity on me.' Well would you be speaking, O rich man, if Lazarus, reposing in Abraham's bosom, were not holding the very heart of the judge. Well would you be speaking if Lazarus did not possess all the secrets of this perfectly just reviewer. He whom an innocent Confessor thus accuses petitions the judge to no purpose. He believes in vain that the judge can help him when the very man who endured so much is talking through the judge's mouth.

'Have pity on me, and send Lazarus.' Are you still so cruel to Lazarus? 'Send Lazarus.' Whither? From Abraham's bosom to hell, from his lofty throne to the deepest abyss, from the holy repose and deep silence of the blessed to the din of the tortures? 'And send Lazarus.' As I see the matter the rich man's actions spring not from new pain, but from ancient envy. This is enkindled not so much by hell as by Lazarus' possession of heaven. Men find it a grave evil and an unbearable fire to see in happiness those whom they once held in contempt. The rich man's malice does not leave him, even though he already endures its punishment. He does not ask to be led to Lazarus, but wants Lazarus to be led to him. O rich man, the loving Abraham cannot send to the bed of your tortures Lazarus whom you did not condescend to admit to your table. Your respective fortunes have now been reversed. You look upon the glory of him whose misery you once spurned. He gazes upon your tortures who then wondered at you in your glory.

Let us see, brethren, why he thus begs in tears to have Lazarus sent to him. 'Send Lazarus to dip the tip of his finger in water and cool my tongue.' You are in error, O rich man. This fire is not so much in your tongue as in your mind; not so much of the tongue as of the heart. That heat is still one of the conscience, not that extreme flame which waits in readiness for you. For, if the full fire of the Last Judgment were already surrounding you, if the sentence of that hopeless condemnation already held you, you would never be lifting your eyes. You would never be presuming to speak with your father, or to ask for yourself, or to intercede for your brothers. Surely, if all the fire of hell already holds you, and the flame of Gehenna enwraps you, why do you want help only for the burning in your tongue?—unless it is because, when your breast is heaving with the flame of your crime and guilt, your tongue which insulted the poor man and refused mercy to him is burnt the more, and catches fire, and violently burns. The tongue precedes to the Judgment. It first tastes and suffers tortures. It is the first member of all the body to sense heat. For, when it was the first member to taste here on earth various delicious foods and to sample the perfumed cups, it refused to order generosity. It did not command mercy to be shown, but, when others were showing it, the tongue complained.

This is he who used to clothe himself in purple and fine linen. What is the matter, rich man? Does the fine linen fail to protect you from the heat? Does the purple fail to resist hell? Those goods remained behind. They deserted you, and yourself, who once mocked at the heat while clothed with garments ingeniously light, you are now naked and sweat and burn.

'And send Lazarus to dip the tip of his finger in water and cool my tongue.' Why this, rich man? Where are the torrents from your wine presses? Where are your barns, expanded not less by your greediness than by your supplies, as far as the poor man's hunger is concerned? As far as his need is concerned, where are those wines preserved so long because of their age and oblivion of their dates? Where are all the prodigalities, bustlings, and pourings of your servants? All this exists no more for you; it is no more an occasion of sin. Now you have thirst for the drop on a finger tip. If you had given only this to the poor man, you would not have this thirst. A drop made you unmerciful, and a crumb made you inhuman. Drops and crumbs make up the whole sustenance and life of a poor man.

I should like to know, O rich man, if you in your suffering excuse even your own self. You would not have come to these evils if on earth you had given a crumb from your huge barns and a drop from your great wine presses. What the flesh needs, and nature demands, and suffices for life, is little. Avarice is the reason why a man stores up many great possessions, not for himself but for others, and that clearly to his present or future suffering.

But, you object, O rich man: 'Even if I did refuse to give wine, what I ask for is water, which the Creator Himself of all beings and nature gave as something common to all human beings.' I think, O rich man, that you refused even water to the poor man. You exposed him to as many dogs as you could to keep him from entering your door and coming to your well.

'Send Lazarus to dip the tip of his finger in water.' What is the meaning of this which you say if he is not to bring the water? Evidently, that water is nearby, to you. And if it is near, why do you not take it from nearby? Why? Because your hands are rightly bound, O rich man. Because you spurned to give help to Lazarus' hands when they had lost their strength through weakness. Man should certainly share his members with the weak. When Job was not so much giving them as giving them back, he spoke as follows: 'I was an eye of the blind, and a foot of the lame. I was the father of the weak.'[2] O man, if you do not have a coin, give a poor man your hand, because he shows greater mercy who by his own hand, leads a poor man who is weak to his table. He gives his very self to the poor man who devotes himself to his service, makes himself the poor man's servant.

Again, brethren, let us postpone the completion of the present discourse, in order to expound in a third sermon what sentence the rich man endured from holy Abraham.

## SERMON 129

### *Saint Cyprian, Martyr*

Today, we have assembled in the sight of God on the birthday of St. Cyprian the Martyr. On this date he triumphed over the Devil in an admirable struggle. Moreover, he has left us a glorious example of his virtues. For these reasons it is proper for us to exult and rejoice. Dearly beloved, when you hear about the birthday of the saints, do not think that mention is being made of their birth from flesh into life on earth. There is a question of their birth from earth into heaven; from toil to repose; from temptations to rest; from tortures to delights which are not fleeting, but strong, firm, and everlasting; from worldly hilarity to a crown of glory.

2 Job 29.15,16.

Such birthdays of the martyrs are celebrated in a fitting way. Therefore, when a festival of this kind is being kept, do not think, dearly beloved, that birthdays of the martyrs should be celebrated only by meals and more elegant banquets. Rather, what you celebrate in memory of a martyr is something proposed for your imitation. Consequently, dearly beloved, observe the ardor of the congregation which is present. At one time on this date a mob of evil men stood by, when, through the tyrant's orders, St. Cyprian was being maltreated. There were crowds of evil-doers and bands of onlookers. Now, a devout multitude of the faithful has assembled to rejoice. Then, there was a crowd of furious agitators; now, one of those who rejoice—then, a band of men without hope; now, one of the men who are full of it.

It is for a purpose that the birthdays of the martyrs are celebrated every year with joy: that that which happened in the past should remain in the memory of devout men of every century. The festival is carried out, dearly beloved, that you may not say you do not know about it. The festivities are celebrated annually to keep you from saying: I forgot. Therefore, animate yourselves to imitate these deeds, dearly beloved. Desire this grace of magnanimity. Ask that what he merited to obtain may be given you. For all those who desire heavenly goods cannot let themselves be enmeshed by the snares of earthly goods. They have determined that their citizenship is in heaven, after the teaching of the holy Apostle: 'But our citizenship is in heaven.'[1] Therefore, let our hearts direct their desires to the heavenly abode, where your heart will be after you have distributed your treasures to the poor. Christ is the treasure of all good men. May He, with the Father and the Son and the Holy Spirit, deign to heap heavenly gifts upon you and fill you with them, both now and forever.

---

1 Phil. 3.20.

## SERMON 132

*The Unity of the Faithful in Prayer*

(On Matt. 18.19,20)

If nature begot and brought forth all things as fully developed, hardy, and in want of nothing, all love would perish. Natural inclinations would fail, and skill would pass away.

Gold would remain in the earth, unpolished; the sparkle of the gem would be left hidden in the uncut stone. However, the craftsman finds them both through his skill. He cleanses, enhances, and polishes them. He artfully works on them to evoke all the beauty and charm of a perfect necklace. Similarly, what the earth sprouts forth from nature's bounteous supply either gets bruised by brambles or grows like a wild grapevine with the luxuriance of virgin country, unless the farmer by skillful work brings it under the control of his cultivation. That I may not wander longer, let us bring out our labored point by one household example. When a newborn infant lies in the cradle, a man is in that human nature, but he is not yet fully apparent. There is a body, yet there is not. The members are seen, yet they are practically nonexistent. They are alive, yet not alive with sensation. Then, love turns itself upon the infant. It applies its industry to the point of perspiration, and exercises its skill. To speak more fully, as many arts of instruction are put to work to make him a developed man as he has members. And why should I say more? Love nourishes, industry develops, and ingenuity embellishes everything which nature generates or produces.

Then why should we be astonished, brethren, if God, who willed to suffer for man's sake, willed that man's nature, too, should be weak in regard to what we are considering today? He wanted to bring honor to human industry.

Hence, too, arises the fact that the meaning lies hid in the letter; that a divine mystery is concealed in human speech. The future things which are already clear to believers are to be made obscure to heretics and unbelievers—just as if the penal blindness of the unbelievers redounded to glory of the faithful. For, it is quite trying not to comprehend the things seen, not to understand those heard, to reject as harmful those which are salutary, to shun virtues as if they were vices. Christ Himself has said: I speak in parables, 'That seeing they may not perceive, and hearing they may not understand.'[1] To the faithful He said: 'To you it is given to know the mystery of God.'

Wherefore, brethren, let no one in his simplicity deem the Gospel text common or cheap, especially in that verse where the resounding trumpet of its reading predicts that nothing[2] is to be refused to those who ask well and desire piously. The verse states 'that if two of you shall agree on earth about anything at all for which they ask, it shall be done for them by my Father in heaven.'[3] You have heard what power and efficacy arises from group agreement in a holy petition. Christ did not mention one thing or another, but He promised to give everything—whatever the united request desires. His words are: 'about anything at all for which they ask, it shall be done for them.' Of course, that reverent caution should not be disregarded: that we should ask of God things worthy of God. He who asks evil things of God judges and supposes that God is the author of evil. And he who asks for cheap and unworthy things is an ignoble petitioner and ignores the power and might of the

1 Mark 4.2,12,11; cf. Luke 8.10; Matt. 13.11.
2 Supplying *nihil*; cf. *PL* 52.461, note c.
3 Matt. 18.19.

Giver. Consequently, we should always ask from such a Giver not unholy gifts, but holy ones; not earthly, but heavenly ones; gifts compatible with virtues, not dangerous attractions; not things likely to stir up hatreds, but those consonant with virtue.

Christ promises that He will be in the midst of two or three who are gathered, and that He will give everything they request of Him.[4] If this is so, where are those who presume that the congregation of the Church can be disregarded, and assert that private prayers should be preferred to those of an honorable assembly? If He denies nothing to so small a group, will He refuse anything to those who ask for it in the assemblies and congregation of the Church? This is what the Prophet believed, and what he exults over having obtained when he states: 'I will praise thee, O Lord, with my whole heart, in the council of the just, and in the congregation.'[5] The man who hears that everything he will ask for in the council of the saints will be granted praises with his whole heart.

Some, however, endeavor to excuse under an appearance of faith the idleness which prompts their contempt [for assemblies]. They omit participation in the fervor of the assembled congregation, and pretend that they have devoted to prayer the time they have expended upon their household cares. While they give themselves up to their own desires, they contemn and despise divine arrangements. These are men of the sort who tear apart the [Mystical] Body of Christ and scatter its members. They do not suffer the form of its Christlike appearance to develop to its full beauty—that form which the Prophet saw and then sang about: 'Thou are beautiful in form above the sons of men.'[6]

4 Matt. 18.20,19.
5 Ps. 110.1.
6 Ps. 44.3.

It is true that the individual members have, each one, their own function to perform. But they will fulfill these respective functions best if they are joined together and compacted and attain to the full beauty of the fully developed Body. This, therefore, is the difference between the glorious richness of a congregation and the presumptious vanity of separation which springs either from ignorance or negligence: that from the health and praiseworthiness of the entire body a beautiful unity arises, while from the separation of its members there springs base, deadly, and hideous ruin.

O man, consider either the separation of the joints in your own body or the joining together of the separate members. Has it taught you anything else than this, that you should live both as one man compounded of many parts and as one man in many members? The eye is precious for the healthy functioning of the members—but only if it remains in the body. Otherwise, when it fails the body it also fails itself. All the other members are indebted to the eye for the service of light which it furnishes. But the eye itself perceives, too, that it owes to the body the fact that it is a light. When united with the members it provides a service for them; plucked out of the body, it itself does not see.

Whoever he is who thinks that he is something, let him be instructed by such an example and remain in the Church, that he may be something. Otherwise, when he fails the Church, he soon terminates his own importance. If anyone desires a more extensive understanding of this, let him read the Apostle's treatise in which he speaks about the [Mystical] Body of Christ.[7] The desirable brevity of our sermon does not permit us to run through it. The Law was given not for one, but for all. So, too, Christ came not for one or to

7 1 Cor. 12.4-31; cf. Rom. 12.4-13,21.

one, but to all and for all. He desired to bring all things together into a unity which alone is good and pleasant. The Prophet, aware of the future, assures us: 'Behold how good and pleasant it is for brethren to dwell together in unity.'[8] For, not singularity, but unity, is acceptable to God. The Holy Spirit descended upon the Apostles with all His welling fountain when they were assembled together.[9] This occurred after the Apostles had been instructed by the Lord's own commandment to wait in a group for the Spirit's coming.

Brethren, suppose that a man is evil to himself, and because of his shortcomings foolishly self-sufficient. Suppose that thus he seeks life outside the Church. He loses divine gifts, he spoils the outpouring of grace, he cheats himself of the benefits of charity. The blessing of that unity will not await him. The Prophet testifies that that life is only in the Church: 'Behold how good and pleasant it is for brethren to dwell together in unity. . . For there the Lord hath commanded blessing, and life forevermore.'[10]

## SERMON 133

### *St. Andrew the Apostle*

Today is rightly considered St. Andrew's birthday. He did not come to birth from his mother's womb today, but we recognize that through the conception of faith and the childbirth of martyrdom he was brought forth into heavenly glory. His mother's cradle did not receive him today as a softly crying infant, but the heavenly abodes welcomed him in triumph. He did not draw the soft mild nourishment of milk

8 Ps. 132.1.
9 Acts 2.1-4.
10 Ps. 132.1,3.

from his mother's breast, but as a devoted soldier he valiantly shed his blood for his King.

He lives, because, as a warrior in the heavenly army, he slew death. Sweating and sighing after his expiring Lord, he follows along and strives to walk with the full vigorous stride of his virtue. Nature had made him similar to his brother,[1] his vocation had made him a companion, and grace had made him an equal. He did not want this journey to make him dissimilar.

At one word of the Lord, Andrew had, like him, left his father, his country, and his possessions. Through Christ's own gift, he offered himself without wearying as the companion of his brother in labors, reproaches, journeys, insults, and vigils. The only blemish is that he fled at the time of the Lord's Passion. However, his fleeing does not give him an inferior rank. If to deny one's Lord is deemed a fault of some importance, surely it is not more serious to flee than to deny.

We should pass over the other matters in silence, brethren. The forgiveness put on a level those whom their fault had separated. And the fervor with which they afterwards suffered martyrdom proved the devotion of those men who had previously incurred dishonor through their fear. Later on, they eagerly embraced with all their hearts that cross from which they had shrunk, so as to ascend to heaven and gain their reward and crown from the same cross from which they had once derived guilt.

Peter mounted a cross, and Andrew a tree. In this way they who longed to suffer with Christ showed forth in themselves the kind and manner of His suffering; redeemed upon a cross, they were made perfect for their palms. Thus, even if Andrew is second in dignity, he is not inferior in regard to the reward or the suffering.

---

1 Simon Peter.

# SERMON 134

## *St. Felicitas, Martyr*

Time does not allow us to enumerate the diverse and manifold victories of the martyrs which the cruelty of persecutors, so often foiled, has multiplied. Therefore, we bestow all the eloquence of our sermon on her who deserved to have as many sons as the world had days.[1]

She is indeed a mother of lights and a source of days who shines throughout the whole world through the flashing brilliance of her seven sons. Blessed is she[2] who not only suffered for the Law, but as a holy mother has merited to produce a lampstand of seven candles—yes, brethren, a seven-branched candlestick meant to illumine with its holy light not the sanctuary of one temporary tabernacle,[3] but, rather, the everlasting Church. Blessed is she who deserved to bear as many virtuous children as the ark carried sacred volumes of precepts. She was to teach by her example just as they were by word.

She bore them as martyrs even then, brethren, when she dedicated those childbirths by a sevenfold and mystical number. Hither, let St. Paul come hither, he who is still in labor until Christ be formed in man.[4] Look, a mother again and again gives birth to a child, until her weakness is changed into strength, flesh passes over into spirit, earth is transferred into heaven. She was eager, she sighed in longing to give them a birth as holy martyrs on one day, whom it took her a course of years to bring forth as infants. See this woman!

---

1 I.e., seven days of creation. St. Felicitas had seven sons who underwent martyrdom with her.

2 An allusion to the mother and her seven sons martyred under King Antiochus; cf. 2 Mac. 7.1-42.

3 Exod. 25, especially vv. 8, 31-40.

4 Gal. 4.20.

Look at this mother whom the life of her sons made anxious, and their deaths made secure.

Blessed is she! As many candlesticks stand ready for her in her future glory as she had sons! Blessed is she who sent so many sons ahead of herself into the Kingdom. More blessed still is she who here below did not lose[5] anything that was hers! She moved with greater joy among the transpierced bodies of her sons than she had done amid their cherished cradles. With her interior eyes she saw as many prizes as there were wounds; as many rewards as there were torments; as many crowns as there were victims. Why should I say more, brethren? She who does not know how to love her sons like this is not indeed a true mother.

## SERMON 135

### *St. Lawrence*

This day is renowned because of the martyr Lawrence's crown of baptism.[1] No part of the Roman world is ignorant of the merits of this outstanding martyr. He suffered in the very capital of the nations, that is, in the city of Rome itself. For he ministered there as a deacon, and there in the flower of his youth he purpled his youthful beauty with his blood. His suffering is extraordinary and much to be admired. With the Lord's help, I shall briefly narrate it.

He was an archdeacon when Blessed Sixtus was bishop, whose triumphal martyrdom occurred three days earlier. When the holy Lawrence was following his bishop, Sixtus, on his way to martyrdom, he was sustained by his faith

5 She did not lose her sons, but sent them ahead as deposits into heaven.

1 The Fathers often called martyrdom a baptism; cf. *PL* 52.565, note d.

and sad at heart—not because Sixtus was about to suffer, but because he himself was being left behind by the bishop. Sixtus, the venerable old man, looked back at the youth and said: 'Do not be sad, my son. You will follow me three days from now.' After Lawrence heard this prophecy, he was soon fully prepared in his heart and intoxicated with spiritual joy. He had hope that what he who knew had predicted would certainly come to pass.

After a while, he was seized and led away. Since he was an archdeacon, he was believed to have the resources of the Church in his possession. The persecutor desired to get these, motivated more by anger than by avarice. He hated the man he was putting to death, but in him he admired his attitude of contempt. However, the holy Lawrence was poor in goods, but rich in virtues. He did not deny that he had the riches of the Church, but requested a delay of three days in order to display them. Thereupon he ordered groups of the poor to be assembled. When he was summoned to his trial on the very day he won his crown, as if he were about to display what his judge wanted, he showed what he had. The persecutor asked: 'Where are the riches of the Church.' But Lawrence extended his hand toward the poor and said: 'These are the riches of the Church.'

He spoke what was true, but bitter. Is it strange if this truth increased the hatred? Angry over being ridiculed, the cruel tyrant and avaricious enemy, who perhaps would have thought up a penalty less severe, ordered his men to kill the admirable young man by the sword and to prepare flames. He was afire himself rather than setting fire to another. He was applying fire to another's flesh, but blazing in his own heart. And his torture was as much more serious as it was interior.

Next, some one brought out the well-known gridiron for martyring Lawrence by parching him—or, to speak more truly, by roasting him. He was bound fast by iron, but he regarded that gridiron of torture as a bed of rest. I used the word torture. It was torture according to the mind of the torturer, but not according to the outlook of the victim. There is no torture of a condemned man where there is not a penalty for sin. Consequently, the most blessed martyr, showing how quietly he was resting on that red-hot iron, told the bystanders: 'Turn me over now. If one side is cooked, begin to eat.'

We admire his patience. Let us admire this as a gift of God. In this case his faith was not burning painfully in him; it was even consoling the man who was being roasted. Why was faith consoling him? Because it was keeping faithful the One making promises. God was bestowing on Lawrence all these as His gifts: that his faith might not fail, that his hope might not be quenched, that his charity might be enkindled the more amid his bodily punishments of fire.

My brethren, let no one arrogate to his own ability that which no one save God gives. When the Apostle was addressing the martyrs, rightly did he say what you heard when his Epistle was read today: 'You have been given the favor on Christ's behalf—not only to believe in him but also to suffer for him.'[2] Therefore let us honor and esteem the merits of the martyrs as being the gifts of God. Let us beg for them, and add the inclination of our own will. For, our will follows; it does not take the lead.[3] Nevertheless, charity is not lacking if our will is not lacking, for the eager will itself is called charity. Who is there who willingly fears? Who is there who unwillingly loves? May prayer be fervent, and let the feast of this martyr be celebrated. But let everyone who celebrates also imitate him, that the celebrating may not be idle.

2 Phil. 1.29.
3 This is the opposite of Pelagianism; cf. Introduction, pp. 13, 14.

# SERMON 138

## *Peace*[1]

Dearly beloved brethren, it would have been better if our common father and chief[2] had allowed our lack of ability to lie hidden. It would have been better if he had not made public our mediocrity, which we have so far kept concealed beneath the veil of our modesty. It would be better if he who has such an abundant supply of the spiritual riches of doctrine did not request the contribution of a weak discourse from the little ship of a poor man. For, what can a needy man confer on the rich, or a pilgrim on the citizens, or an uninstructed rustic on scholars?

Nevertheless, since we feel obliged to obey his orders, the same course of humility which seems to excuse us compels us to speak and obey. What is there, therefore, O devout people of the Lord, which we can fittingly offer you, even though we are poor and very unlearned? Beyond any doubt, peace, that peace which our Lord Jesus Christ bids us to offer every house we enter.[3] Hence, at the very beginning of our greeting we, too, prayed for peace to you from the Lord. It should be possessed always, and prayed for continually. We are not speaking about that faithless, unstable peace of this world, which is either sought for its advantages or preserved through fear. Rather, there is question of the peace of Christ which according to the statement of the Apostle Paul surpasses all understanding,[4] and preserves the hearts of the faithful.

This peace is nourished from the rich fruitfulness of charity.

---

1 St. Peter probably preached this sermon as a visiting bishop outside his own diocese of Ravenna; cf. *PL* 52.572, note e.

2 Probably the presiding bishop.

3 Luke 10.5.

4 Phil. 4.7.

It is the nursling daughter of faith, the supporting column of justice. Peace is a suitable pledge of future hope. Peace, which unites those present, invites the absent. This peace reconciles earthly things with the heavenly and human matters with those divine. For, that is what the Apostle states: 'that our Lord Jesus Christ established in peace through His blood all things whether on the earth or in the heavens.'[5]

These, therefore, are the viands which a traveling pilgrim has set before you, in proportion to his strength as a poor man on a journey. He was hoping rather to dine with you at the heavily laden table of a powerful master. May the God of peace, who joined earthly things to the heavenly, grant us to relish the same things one with another, and to rejoice in our complete concord, through Jesus Christ our Lord, through whom glory is given to God, the Father Almighty, forever and ever. Amen.

## SERMON 140

### *The Annunciation to the Blessed Virgin Mary*

(On Luke 1.26-29)

Dearly beloved, our present desire should be to have eyes sufficiently strong, unimpaired, and penetrating to look upon the brilliance of a divine origin. Even when our bodily eyes are fully sound and well preserved, they can scarcely endure the radiance of the rising sun. What firm strength, then, must we prepare for our interior vision, to enable it to gaze upon the splendor of its rising and brilliant Creator?

'Now in the sixth month,' we read, 'the angel Gabriel was sent to a town of Galilee called Nazareth, to a virgin

5 Cf. Col. 1.20.

betrothed to a man named Joseph.' The holy Evangelist points out the place, the time, and the person, that the truths of his account may receive confirmation from the clear evidence furnished by the very details he sets down.

'The angel was sent to a betrothed virgin.' To this virgin God sends a winged messenger. He who bears this gift of grace is giving her a pledge, and he is carrying back a dowry from her. He receives her promise, and hands over to her the gifts of God's overshadowing power—he who sets free the promise of the virgin's consent. The swift mediator flies in haste to the maiden, to keep away the completion of her human engagement from the spouse of God, and to hold it in suspension. He does this, not to take the virgin away from Joseph, but to restore her to Christ, to whom she was pledged when she was beginning to exist in the womb.[1] Christ, then, receives His own spouse; He does not take away the spouse of another. Neither does He cause the breaking of an engagement with someone else when He unites her, His creature, exclusively to Himself in one body.

But let us hear what the angel did. 'When the angel had come to her, he said: Hail, full of grace, the Lord is with thee.' This salutation contains a giving, a giving of a present, and not merely an expression of greeting. 'Hail.' This means: receive grace. Do not be alarmed or worried about your nature.[2] 'O maiden full of grace.' Grace exists even in other men. Then, surely, the whole fullness of grace will come upon you.

'The Lord is with thee.' Why is the Lord with you? Because He is coming to you not merely to pay a visit, but He is coming down into you in a new mystery, that of

1 I.e., in the womb of her mother. Mita took this sentence as evidence for the doctrine of the Immaculate Conception; cf. *PL* 52.676, note f. However, the Latin can also mean: 'to whom she was pledged when He was beginning to exist in her womb.'

2 I.e., that your nature is merely human.

being born. Fittingly did the angel add: 'Blessed art thou among women.' Through the curse she incurred Eve brought pains upon the wombs of women in childbirth. Now, in this very matter of motherhood, Mary, through the blessing she received, rejoices, is honored, is exalted. Now, too, womankind has become truly the mother of those who live through grace, just as previously she was the mother of those who by nature are subject to death.

'When she had seen him she was troubled at his word.' Why is it that she gazes upon her angelic visitor, but it is only at his word that she is troubled? Because the angel had come as one of pleasing appearance, strong in war, meek in his bearing, terrible in his speech, uttering human words, but promising things divine. Hence, the angel by being seen disturbed the virgin only a little, but the sound of his words troubled her deeply. The presence of the one sent had moved her but slightly, but the authority of the Sender struck her with full force. Why should I say more?

She soon realized that she was receiving within herself the heavenly Judge, there in that same place where with lingering gaze she had just seen the harbinger from heaven. It was by a soothing motion and holy affection that God transformed the virgin into a mother for Himself, and made His handmaid into a parent. Nevertheless, her bosom was disturbed, her mind recoiled, and her whole state became one of trembling when God, whom the whole of creation does not contain, placed His whole Self inside her bosom and made Himself a man.

'And she kept pondering,' the Scripture continues, 'what manner of greeting this might be.' Notice in your charity that, as we said, the virgin gave her consent not to a greeting of mere words, but to the realities of which they told her. Notice, too, that the salutation was not one of ordinary courtesy; rather, it contained the full might of heavenly power. So she gives the matter careful thought. For, to make hasty replies is characteristic of human levity, to think deeply is the mark of the greatest constancy and of judgment fully mature. The man who sees no reason to be astonished at her attitude or to marvel at her spirit does not truly know how great God is. Before Him the vault of heaven shakes and the angels tremble. No creature bears Him up, nor can all nature bound Him. Yet this one young maiden takes Him into an inner chamber of repose, her bosom. She receives Him, and delights Him with her hospitality. Thus she gives Him a dwelling that she may request in payment, and get as the price for use of her very womb peace for the earth, glory for heaven, salvation for the lost, life for the dead, for those on earth relationship with the saints—even union of God Himself with man. She does all this, too, to fulfill the Prophet's statement: 'Behold, the inheritance of the Lord are children: the reward, the fruit of the womb.'[3]

But let us close this sermon for the present. Thus, through God's grace, we may have sufficient time to tell with greater satisfaction of the birth of a child from the virgin.

## SERMON 141

### *The Incarnation of Christ*

How secret are the sleeping quarters of a king! The place where the nation's head, who is powerful, takes his rest is wont to be viewed only in a spirit of reverence and awe. No alien, no sullied man, no unloyal subject, gains access and entrance to it. How clean, how chaste, how faithful are the services expected there! The resplendent trappings of a royal court make all this clear to us. And what com-

3 Ps. 126.3.

mon or unworthy person dares to approch the gates of the king's palace?

Surely, no one is admitted to the inner chamber of a bridegroom except a relative or an intimate friend. He must be a man of good conscience, praiseworthy reputation, and upright life. Thus, too, it happens that God takes into His inner chamber only this one virgin; she alone, with her virginity unimpaired, is received there.

These examples, O man, are for your instruction. Realize from them just who you are, how great you are, and of what character you are. Then ponder this in your heart: Can you fathom the mystery of the Lord's birth? Do you deserve to enter into the resting place of that bosom, where the heavenly King, with all the full majesty of His divinity, finds His repose? Ought you, as a rash witness with human eyes and bodily senses, to gaze on the virgin's conceiving? Can you, as a bystander, contemplate with daring reverence the very hands of God fashioning for himself the holy temple of a body within the womb of the mother? Can you by your gaze lay bare that mystery hidden through the ages, and unveil for yourself that sacrament invisible to the angels themselves? Can you act as an overseer in the workshop of the heavenly Artisan, so that you may clearly observe how God has entered the shrine of her unbroken flesh? Can you observe how without this virgin's awareness He has produced the outlines of His sacred body in her venerable womb; how, without any sensations on the part of her who was conceiving, He made firm those bones which will last forever, how, beyond any arrangement of man, He produced a genuine human form; how, without any fleshly desire, He assumed the whole nature of man; how, apart from the way human flesh operates, He has taken on its every quality?

Even if you did not enjoy free access to knowledge of all

these marvels, would you think that God was unable at that time to assume from flesh what in the beginning he took from mud? Indeed, since everything is possible to God, and it is impossible for you fully to understand even the least of His works, do not pry too much into this virgin's conceiving, but believe it. Be reverently aware of the fact that God wishes to be born, because you offer an insult if you examine it too much. Grasp by faith that great mystery of the Lord's birth, because without faith you cannot comprehend even the least of God's works. 'All his works' says Scripture, 'are [understood] by faith.'[1] But, here is a matter which depends completely upon faith, and you want it to stand by reason. It is not, indeed, without reason that this matter holds true; it holds true by the reasoning of God, O man, not yours. What is so much according to reason as the fact that God can do whatever He has willed? He who cannot do what he wills is not God.

So, what God commands an angel relates. His spirit fulfills it and His power brings it to perfection. The virgin believes it, and nature takes it up. The tale is told from the sky, and then proclaimed from all the heavens. The stars show it forth, and the Magi tell it about. The shepherds adore, and the beasts are aware. As the Prophet testified: 'The ox knoweth his owner, and the ass his master's crib.'[2] You, O man, if you did not recognize Him soon along with the angels, do acknowledge Him now, even though very late, in company with the beasts. Otherwise, while you loiter, you may be deemed less than those very animals with whom you were previously compared. Look, they give homage with their tails, they manifest their pleasure with their ears, they lick with their tongues, and with whatever sign they can they acknowledge that their Creator, in spite of His nature,

---

1 Cf. Ps. 32.4. The Hebrew meant: All God's work is trustworthy.
2 Isa. 1.3.

has come into yours. Yet, you argue and quibble along with the Jews who turned away from their inns their Master whom the beasts welcomed in their cribs. If, therefore, you will at length give reverent ear at least to the angels, at least properly, if not joyfully, receive from us the message which the angel will speak.

You need a sermon about this, holy brethren, but today we find it necessary to postpone this matter and treat it in our next discourse.

## SERMON 145

### *The Birth of Christ, and Joseph's Desire to Put Mary Away*

(On Matt. 1.18-23)

Brethren, today you will hear the blessed Evangelist's account of the mystery of the Lord's birth.[1] The text reads: 'Now the origin of Christ was in this wise. When Mary his mother had been betrothed to Joseph, she was found, before they came together, to be with child by the Holy Spirit. But Joseph her husband, being a just man, and not wishing to expose her to reproach, was minded to put her away privately.'

How is he a just man who deemed it wise not to investigate the motherhood of his spouse? How is he just who does not seek the reason of her self-consciousness which he has suspected, or does not vindicate the reputation of his marriage, but lets the matter drop?

'He was minded to put her away privately.' This seems to be characteristic of a man in love rather than of a just man—but according to human judgment, not divine. Before

1 On *generatio* meaning birth, cf. Souter, *s.v.*

God, piety does not exist without justice, nor justice without piety. According to the heavenly meaning of the terms, justice does not exist without goodness, nor goodness without justice. If these virtues are separated they vanish. Equity without goodness is savagery; justice without love is cruelty.

Rightly, therefore, was Joseph just, because he was loving; he was loving because just. While he nourished his love, he was free from cruelty. While he kept his emotions under control, he preserved his judgment. While he postponed vengeance, he escaped crime. While he refrained from being an accuser he escaped condemnation.

His holy mind, shocked at the novel situation, was in turmoil. His spouse stood, pregnant yet a virgin. She stood large with the child she carried, yet not free from the cause for blame. She stood in concern about her pregnancy, but free from fear about her integrity. She stood dressed as a mother, yet not excluded from the honor of virginity. What was the husband to do in such a case? Was he to accuse her of sin? But he himself was witness of her innocence. Should he publish her fault? But he himself was the guardian of her purity. Was he to press a charge of adultery? But he was the herald of her virginity. What was he to do in such circumstances? He thought of putting her away, since he could neither reveal outside what had happened, nor keep it inside. He thought of putting her away, and he told it all to God, because he had nothing to tell to men.

We, too, brethren, whenever something troubles us, or some appearance deceives us, or the outward color of a transaction makes us unable to know its substance, let us restrain our judgment. Let us withhold punishment, refrain from condemnation, and tell the whole matter to God. Otherwise, while we perhaps easily impel an innocent man toward a penalty, we shall pronounce a sentence of condemnation upon ourselves. The Lord says: 'With what judgment you judge, you shall be judged.'[2] But, if we keep silent, the Lord will surely speak aloud. The angel will reply who by these words prevented Joseph from deserting the innocent maiden: 'Do not be afraid, Joseph, son of David, to take to thee Mary thy wife, for that which is begotten in her is of the Holy Spirit. And she shall bring forth a son, and thou shalt call his name Jesus; for he shall save his people from their sins.'[3]

'Joseph, son of David.' You observe, brethren, that the race is named in the person. The whole stock is indicated in one man. The whole series of the Davidical ancestry is cited in the person of Joseph.

'Joseph, son of David.' Born in the twenty-eighth generation after him,[4] how is he called the son of David, unless the secret of the race is being opened up, the object of the promise is being fulfilled, and the God-given conception of the heavenly birth in the virgin's body is already being signified?

'Joseph, son of David.' With this statement the promise of God the Father had been given to David: 'The Lord hath sworn truth to David, and he will not make it void: of the fruit of thy womb I will set upon thy throne.'[5] In this canticle he glories that it has been fulfilled: 'The Lord said to my Lord: Sit thou at my right hand.'[6] 'Of the fruit of thy womb.' Truthfully of the fruit of thy flesh, truthfully of the womb, because the heavenly guest, the inhabitant of heaven, so descended into the hospice of the womb that He did not harm the enclosure of the body. He so departed from the abode of the womb that the virginal door did not open, and what is sung in the Canticle of Canticles was ful-

2 Matt. 7.2.
3 Matt. 1.20.
4 Cf. Matt. 1.6.
5 Ps. 131.11
6 Ps. 109.1.

filled: 'My sister, my spouse, is a garden enclosed, a garden enclosed, a fountain sealed up.'[7]

'Joseph, son of David, do not be afraid.' The bridegroom is admonished not to fear the condition of his spouse. A soul which truly loves has greater fear when it suffers along with someone else.

'Joseph, son of David, do not be afraid.' Otherwise, while troubled in mind, you may fail to understand this mystery.

'Joseph, son of David, do not be afraid.' What you see in her is virtue, not sin. This is not a human fall, but a divine descent. Here is a reward, not guilt. This is an enlargement from heaven, not a detriment to the body. This is not the betrayal of a person, it is the secret of the Judge. Here is the victory of Him who knows the case, not the penalty of torture. Here is not some man's stealthy deed, but the treasure of God. Here there is a cause not of death, but of life. Therefore, do not be afraid, for she who is bringing forth life does not deserve to be slain.

'Joseph, son of David, do not be afraid to take to thee Mary thy wife.' This is a part of the divine Law,[8] that an engaged girl be named a wife. Therefore, just as she is a mother while her virginity remains, so is she called a wife while her modesty remains.

'Joseph, son of David, do not be afraid to take to thee Mary thy wife, for that which is begotten in her is of the Holy Spirit.' Let those come and hear who ask who He is whom Mary brought forth. 'That which is begotten in her is of the Holy Spirit.' Let those come and hear who have striven to becloud the clarity of the Latin tongue by a whirlwind of Greek,[9] and have blasphemously called her

7 Cant. 4.12.

8 Cf. Gen. 29.21.

9 St. Peter is berating the followers of Theodore of Mopsuestia and the Nestorians.

***anthropotókon*** [mother of the human nature] and ***Xristotókon*** [mother of Christ] in order to rob her of the title ***Theotókon*** [mother of God].

'That which is begotten in her is of the Holy Spirit.' What is born of the Holy Spirit is spirit,[10] because God is a spirit. Therefore, why do you ask who it is who is born of the Holy Spirit, since God Himself replies to you that He is God, since John reprimands you with his words: 'In the beginning was the Word, and the Word was with God; and the Word was God.... And the Word was made flesh, and dwelt among us. And we saw his glory'?[11] John saw His glory, and also the insult He receives from the unbeliever. 'That which is begotten in her is of the Holy Spirit.' 'And we saw his glory.' To whom does that 'his' refer? To Him who was born of the Holy Spirit, to Him who as the 'Word was made flesh, and dwelt among us.' 'That which is begotten in her is of the Holy Spirit.' She conceived as a virgin, but from a Spirit. As a virgin she brought forth her child,—but that child of whom Isaias had predicted: 'Behold a virgin shall conceive in her womb, and bear a son, and they shall call his name Emmanuel, which is interpreted, God with us.'[12] He is God with us, but He is man with them [the heretics]. And Scripture says: 'Cursed be the man that trusteth in man.'[13] Let those hear this who ask who He is who was born from Mary.

'Thou shalt bring forth a son,' the angel continued, 'and thou shalt call his name Jesus.'[14] Why Jesus? The Apostle says: 'That at the name of Jesus every knee should bend of those in heaven, on earth and under the earth.'[15] And

10 John 3.6.
11 John 1.1,14.
12 Isa. 7.14; Matt. 1.24.
13 Jer. 17.5.
14 Cf. Luke 1.31.
15 Phil. 2.10.

you, O guileful judge, do you now ask who Jesus is? Every tongue now confesses 'That the Lord Jesus Christ is in the glory of God the Father.'[16] And do you still ask who Jesus is?

'Thou shalt bring forth a son, and thou shalt call his name Jesus; for He shall save his people.' Not someone else's people will He save. From what will He save them? 'From their sins.' O most faithless man, if you do not believe the Christians when they say that He who forgives sins is God, believe at least the Jews when they say: 'Because thou, being a man, makest thyself God,'[17] and 'Who can forgive sins, but God only?'[18] They who did not believe that He was forgiving sins were denying that He is God. Do you believe that He forgives sins, yet hesitate to admit that He is God?

The Word was made flesh, that man's flesh might be raised to the glory of God, not that God might be drawn into the humiliation of the flesh. As the Apostle says: 'He who cleaves to the Lord is one spirit with Him.'[19] And how shall not God be one [with him] when God unites Himself with man? Human laws invalidate all contested questions within thirty years;[20] is Christ made an occasion of debate some five hundred years after His birth? Does He endure controversies about His origin, and bear with investigations about His state? O heretic, cease to judge your Judge, and adore Him as God in heaven whom the Magus adored on earth.[21]

16 Phil. 2.11.
17 John 10.33.
18 Mark 2.7.
19 1 Cor. 6.17.
20 St. Peter restated most of the matter of this last paragraph in his Letter to Eutyches; cf. below, pp. 285, 286.
21 Matt. 2.11.

## SERMON 146

### *The Birth of Christ, Joseph the Affianced Husband, and Mary the Betrothed Mother*

(On Matt. 1.18)

Every time a year reaches the finishing point of its course and Christmas Day arrives; every time the splendor of the Virgin Birth is spread like flashing lightning throughout the world, we are silent—through our own desire, not through fear. What mind dares to intrude at the very birth of the divine King? Human vision is dulled when the rays of the sun stream down. Then, how can the vision of souls escape all injury when God radiates His light? When we gazed on Christ's birth in the flesh, our senses received a shock from all the new light. But they have recovered now. Therefore, the time has come for us to contemplate even the secrets of His divinity.

'The origin of Christ was in this wise,' the Evangelist tells us. Brethren, if we desire to understand what is said, let us not use merely human procedure to ponder the divine words. Human comprehension must be set aside when all that is said is divine. Thus, the fact that Christ is born is not an ordinary occurrence, but a sign. It is not something natural, but extraordinary power; not the regular succession of events, but something mighty. It is a miracle of heaven, not an ordinary human event. What will worldly understanding gather here? Or what will the sagacity of the flesh seek here?

'The origin of Christ was in this wise,' the Evangelist says. He did not say: 'was made in this wise,' but: 'was in this wise,' because, at the time when Christ was being produced from His human mother, His generation was already existent in His Father. What He was, He was eternally. What He was made, that was given to Him. He was God; there was given to Him a human nature.[1] From the womb He received the nature of us[2] whom He had made from clay.

'When Mary his mother had been betrothed.' It would have been sufficed to say: 'When Mary had been betrothed.' What is the significance of 'a betrothed mother'? If she is a mother, she is not an engaged maiden; if she is engaged, she is not yet a mother. 'When Mary his mother had been betrothed.' She was a fiancee because of her virginity, and a mother because of her fruitfulness. She was a mother who had not known man, but neverthless was conscious of motherhood. After the birth of her Son she was a virgin mother; how, then, was she not a mother before she conceived? Or when was she not a mother, she who gave a human birth to the Creator of the world, and gave to things their King?[3] Just as virgin nature is always a mother, so is she, when corrupted, a stepmother. Therefore, it is a part of a virgin's performance that with God's help she should give a second birth to that to which a virgin [i.e., nature] with His help gave its first birth.

There is a heavenly union between God and integrity; virginity joined to Christ is the pperfect union of virtue. The fact that a virgin conceives is the honor of the Spirit, not a burden of the flesh. The fact that she gives birth as a virgin is a mystery of God, not an activity of marriage. The fact that Christ is born is a matter of divine majesty, not of human weakness. The full glory of the Deity is present where there is no lesion of the flesh.

---

1 Literally, a man.

2 Literally, he received us.

3 Reading *principem*, with Böhmer, *BKV* 43.18, not *principium*. If *principium*, the reading of S. Pauli, is right, the meaning is: 'Or when did the mother, who gave a human birth to the Creator of the world, not give to things their beginning?'

'When Mary his mother had been betrothed to Joseph, she was found, before they came together, to be with child by the Holy Spirit.' How is it that the secret of heavenly innocence is destined for an engaged maiden and not to a girl still free? How is it that thus through the anxiety of the fiance a danger is created for the fiancee? How is it that such great virtue is deemed a sin, and such certain health is thought a danger? How is it that among the innocent modesty is thus distressed, shame wastes away, chastity grows weary, fidelity is wounded, an accusation stands ready, the case becomes pressing, and plausibility is taken away from every excuse? Who excuses a fiancee whom her own child-bearing accuses? Or what will an outside defender accomplish when an accuser from within the house stands by as a witness of the deed?

What do we hold, brethren? Neither the tips of the letters, not the letters themselves, nor the syllables, nor any word, nor the names, nor the persons in the Gospel are free from divine allegorical meanings.[4]

An engaged maiden was chosen, that even then the Church might be signified as the Spouse of Christ, according to the statement of Osee the Prophet: 'I will espouse thee to me in justice, and judgment, and in mercy, and in commiserations. And I will espouse thee to me in faith.'[5] Hence John says: 'He who has the bride is the bridegroom.'[6] And holy Paul: 'I betrothed you to one spouse, that I might present you a chaste virgin to Christ.'[7] Truly she[8] is a spouse who by a virgin birth[9] gives life to the new infancy of Christ.

4 For this meaning of figura, cf. Souter, *s.v.* For a discussion of this statement, cf. Introduction, pp. 19, 20.
5 Osee 2.19,20.
6 John 3.29.
7 2 Cor. 11.2.
8 The Church.
9 I.e., through baptism.

Joseph, the bridegroom, was chosen as her guardian that he might fulfill the type of Christ's Passion foreshadowed in that former Joseph. Joseph incurred anger through his prophetical dreams. Christ, too, sustained hatred because of His prophetic visions. Joseph was cast into a pit of death,[10] but came out of it alive. Joseph was sold; Christ was appraised at a sum. Joseph was led into Egypt; Christ fled there, too. Joseph abundantly supplied the hungry peoples with bread; Christ satisfies with the Bread from heaven the nations dwelling throughout all the world. Thus it is clear how that former Joseph furnished a type of the bridegroom from heaven, how he bore His image, walked as a symbol.

Mary was the name of His mother. And when were the seas[11] not a mother? 'The gathering together of the waters, he called seas,'[12] says Scripture. Did not this water of the sea conceive in its one womb the people fleeing from Egypt, that it might merge as a heavenly offspring reborn into being a new creature? As the Apostle said: 'Our fathers were all under the cloud, and all passed through the sea, and all were baptized in Moses, in the cloud and in the sea.'[13] Moreover, in order that Mary might ever be the pathfinder of human salvation, in the Canticle she rightly preceded the people whom the water like a mother brought into the light of day. As Scripture says: 'Mary, the sister of Aaron, took a timbrel in her hand, and said: Let us sing to the Lord, for he is gloriously magnified.'[14]

This name is related to prophecy and salutary to those reborn. It is the badge of virginity, the glory of purity, the indication of chastity, the sacrificial gift of God, the height

10 Gen. 37.24.

11 St. Peter uses a play on the words *Maria* meaning Mary and *maria* meaning seas.

12 Gen. 1.10.

13 1 Cor. 10.1.

14 Exod. 15.20,21. This text also says that she was a prophetess.

of hospitality, the sum total of sanctity. Righty, therefore, is this motherly name that of the mother of Christ.

We have explained why a betrothed maiden was the mother, why Joseph was the bridegroom, why the mother's name was Mary, in order to show that everything connected with the birth of Christ was symbolic.[15] Now let us bring out, for other reasons, why a betrothed maiden was chosen to give birth to Christ.

Isaias had foretold that a virgin would bring forth the God of heaven,[16] the King of the earth, the Lord of all regions, the renewer of the world, the slayer of death, the restorer of life, the Author of perpetuity. The very occurrence of the Lord's nativity proved how sad this was for worldly men, how frightening to kings, and how terrifying to the Jews. For, when Judea heard and Herod learned from the words of the Magi that Christ was born, the Jews and Herod quickly devised means to destroy and kill Him. While they feared a successor, they tried to slay the Saviour of all men. At length, since they could not find Him, they devastated His country, mixed mothers' milk with blood, and beat to death the infants of His own years. They dismembered the companions of His innoocence, because they could not find for punishment sharers in any guilt of His. If they did all this after Christ was already born, what would they in their wild fury have done to Him when He was conceived?

That is why a bridegroom was provided, and an appearance of marriage. It was all done to conceal[17] the miracle, cover up the sign, veil the virgin's parturition, give no place for accusation, and in this way to elude the madman's wiles. If Christ, although destined to die, had been slain in

15 Or: allegorical, figurative. The whole sermon brings out that this is the meaning of *mysticus* in this context.

16 Isa. 7.14.

17 Reading *celet,* with S. Pauli.

the womb, death would have taken away before the appointed time Him who had come for our salvation.

That passage can, if read, benefit us so much, brethren. Therefore, let it suffice for us today to have taken merely a foretaste of this mystery[18] of the Lord.

## SERMON 147

### *The Mystery of the Incarnation*

Some time ago we heard, brethren, what caused the Lord Christ to enter into a union with an earthly body, to submit to the narrow limitations of human flesh, and to dwell in the mansion of the Virgin's womb. Let us hear about this more fully today. You are my life, my saving encouragement, and my glory. Therefore, I cannot suffer you to remain ignorant of what God gave me to know.

The Evangelist knew God when he said: 'No one has at any time seen God.'[1] Therefore, the creature acknowledged and perceived [the activities of] God whom he knew. But, because he could not see Him, he was carried along in a hard slavery. He gave a service sadly unworthy of God's invisible majesty. Fear had permeated all things, dread had disrupted the universe, terror had battered everything. In heaven God's splendor had prostrated the angels, and on earth thunder and lightning were shaking the hearts of men.

But, as the matter stood, fear did not fully shut out the Ruler's love.

Fear chased the angels down to earth, drew men to idols,

18 *sacramentum*.

1 John 1.18.

filled the world with empty errors, brought everyone to flee the Creator and worship creatures. He who has enough fear cannot love. That is why the world preferred to perish rather than to fear; death itself is lighter than dread.

When Cain[2] began to be harassed with terror of his paricide, he sought death, thinking that he would find rest in it. And why mention Cain? When Elias[3] perceived himself overwhelmed with complete fear, he again wanted the death he had escaped, deeming it better to give in to death than to fear. Peter, too, besought Christ to depart from him when he was awestruck at the Lord's power: 'Depart from me, for I am a sinful man, O Lord.'[4] He uttered this because the dead weight of fear had extinguished whatever love and faith he had. In this way fear, if not tempered with love, turns servitude, however devout, into insolence.

Therefore, God, seeing the world falling into ruin because of fear, continuously acts to recall it with love, invite it back by grace, hold it tight in charity, and embrace it with affection. Therefore, He washes the earth, steeped in evils, with His avenging flood. He calls Noe the father of a new world, addresses him with pleasing language, gives him kindly confidence and fatherly instruction about the present, consoles him with good hope for the future. And now, not so much by commands as by a sharing of work, He shuts into one ark the seedling creatures of the whole new world, that the love of fellowship may banish the fear characteristic of bondage, and a common love preserve what a common toil had saved.[5]

This is the reason, too, why He summons Abraham from the heathen nations, lengthens his name, makes him the father of believers, accompanies him in his travels, preserves him

---

2 Gen. 4.13-15.
3 3 Kings 19.1-15.
4 Luke 5.8.
5 Gen. 7.1-24.

amid foreigners, enriches him with possessions, honors him with triumphs, places Himself under promises, snatches him from injuries, hospitably entertains him, astonishes him with offspring no longer hoped for. God wanted Abraham, favored with so many benefits, and drawn by the striking sweetness of God's charity, to learn to love God rather than to fear Him, and to do his worshiping by loving rather than by trembling.[6]

This is the reason why He consoles the fleeing Jacob in his sleep, prepares him for a conflict on his return, and encircles him with a contestant's embrace, to make him love, not fear, the father of the conflict.[7]

This is why He summons Moses by His fatherly voice, addresses him with paternal love, and invites him to be the liberator of his people.[8] Why should I say more? He makes him a god;[9] He sets him up as a god before Pharao. He makes him a god, fortifies him with signs, arms him with virtues, wins wars through mere commands, grants to him as a soldier victory gained by a mere word. By His orders He concedes him a triumph and leads him through all the crowns of virtues to His own friendship, gives him an opportunity to share in His heavenly kingdom, and allows him to be a legislator. However, Moses received all this that he might love—that at length he might be so inflamed with the love of God that he would burn with it himself and encourage others to have it, too. 'Thou shalt love the Lord thy God with thy whole heart, and with thy whole soul, and with thy whole strength.'[10] He wanted the love of God to possess whatever heart and soul and strength there are, to

6 Gen. 12.1-20.
7 Gen. 28.10-22; 32.24-32.
8 Exod. 3,4.
9 The magistrates who administered the Law were called 'gods' in the terminology of the Old Testament. Cf. Ps. 81.6 and John 10.34.
10 Deut. 6.5.

such an extent that love of worldly things would have no chance to displace this love for God.

Yet, in all these wonders which we mentioned, when the flame of divine love enkindles human hearts, and the intoxication of the love of God overflows into men's senses, they begin, with impaired mind, to want to see God with their bodily eyes. How could the restricted human sight take in God whom the world does not contain? The faculties of love give no second thought to what will be, what ought to be, or what can be. Love has not judgment, heeds not reason, knows not measure. Love accepts no solace because the object it desires is impossible, nor cure because the object is difficult.

Unless love gains its desires it kills the lover. That is why it goes where it is led, not where it ought. Love brings forth desire, it swells with ardor; and ardor extends itself to illicit objects. Why should I say more? Love cannot stand not to see what it loves. That is why all the saints deemed everything they merited of little worth if they should not see the Lord. And truly, brethren, how will one render homage in return for benefits received if one does not see the giver of the benefits? Or how will one believe that he is loved by God if he does not merit the vision of Him?

This is why love which longs to see God, even if it lacks judgment, does have the spirit of devotion. This is why Moses dares to say: 'If I have found favor in thy sight, show me thy face.'[11] This is why another man says: 'Show us thy face.'[12] Finally, this is why the very Gentiles fashioned idols. In their errors they wanted to see with their eyes what they were worshiping.

Therefore, God, aware that men were suffering torture and weariness from their longing to see Him, chose as a

---

11 Exod. 33.10.
12 Ps. 79.4.

means to make Himself visible something which was to be great to the dwellers of earth and by no means small to the dwellers in heaven. For, could something which God made like Himself on earth fail to be deemed honorable in heaven? 'Let us make mankind in our image and likeness,'[13] Scripture says. What perfect devotion owes to a king it owes also to his picture. If God had assumed an angelic nature[14] from heaven, He still would be invisible. If from the earth He had assumed something less than human nature,[15] He would have suffered an insult to His divinity, and He would have depressed, not elevated, man.

Therefore, most dearly beloved, let no one deem it an insult to God if God came to men through a man,[16] and assumed something from ourselves, in order to be seen by us—He who lives and reigns as God now, and through all the ages of ages. Amen.

## SERMON 148

*The Mystery of the Incarnation*

Today, brethren, we should take up again the same subject as yesterday. Today we should repeat our joy over the Lord's birth. When a virgin conceives, a virgin brings forth her child, and she remains a virgin, this is not an ordinary occurrence, but a sign;[1] not something easily understood,

13 Gen. 1.26.
14 Literally, an angel.
15 Literally, a man.
16 I.e., by means of a human nature.

1 I.e., a miracle, proof, as in the Gospels; e.g., in John 4.48.

but a power;[2] the Creator, not nature. It is something unique, not common; divine, not human.

Wherefore, let philosophy cease from her fruitless toil. Christ's birth was not a necessity, but a sign of might. It was an honor, not an injury. It was a mystery of love, not a lessening of His Deity. It was the restoration of man's salvation, not any diminution of the divine substance.

He who made man from undefiled earth, without any process of birth, He Himself by being born fashioned His human nature from an undefiled body. The hand which with dignity raised earth to our image also with dignity assumed flesh for our restoration. Therefore, the fact that the Creator is found in His creature, and God in flesh—this is an honor to the creature, not an insult to the Creator.

The one who deems this an insult is he who values earth as something more precious than flesh. Is he perhaps pained about the insult to the earth when it was raised to the honor of flesh and the glory of a man? O man, who are so precious to God, why do you seem so cheap to yourself? Honored thus by God, why do you do yourself such dishonor? Why do you ask from what you have been made, and not seek to learn for what you have been made? That whole house of the world you see—has it not been made for you? For you the streams of light dispel the encircling gloom. For you the night has been softened. For you the day has been measured off. For you the sky has been made to drop down the varied brilliance of the sun, the moon, and the stars. For you the earth has been bautified like a picture, with flowers, groves, and fruits. For you has been created that marvelous multitude of living creatures, containing so many beautiful

---

2 *Virtus* here means the power of working miracles, as in Mark 5.30. The Fathers aften used *virtus* to signify the divinity; cf. *PL* 52.595, note b, and Souter, *s.v.*

beings in air, fields, and water, to keep sad solitude from spoiling the joy of the new world.

This is why God fashioned you from earth: to make you the Lord of earthly creatures, like to them in the sharing of a common substance. However, earthly though you are, He did not level you with the earthly creatures in such a way as to fail to make you also equal to the heavenly creatures, through your soul granted from heaven. That you might possess reason in common with God, and a body in common with the beasts, He gave you your soul from heaven, and your body taken from earth, that in your case a harmony between heaven and earth might be established and preserved.

However, your Creator is yet thinking up what to add to your honor. He puts His own image in you,[3] that a visible likeness may make the invisible Creator present on earth. Also, in these earthly creatures He gave you His representations, so that this extensive possession of the world might not be lessened for the vicegerent of the Lord.

If that is the case with all those beings, why is it thought an insult when God kindly took to Himself what He made through His power in you and willed Himself to be truly seen in human nature,[4] in which He previously willed Himself to be visible as in an image? When He granted that that human nature which formerly received the privilege of being God's image might now become His very possession?

A virgin conceived, and a virgin brought forth her child. Do not be disturbed at this conception, or confused when you hear of this birth. If there is any human shame, her virginity excuses it. Or what injury is there to modesty when the Deity enters into union with that virginity always dear to Himself? Where an angel is the mediator, faith the

3 Gen. 1.26.
4 Literally, in man.

bridesmaid, chastity the betrothal, virtue the dowry, conscience the judge, God the cause, integrity the conception, virginity the birth, a virgin the Mother?

Therefore, let no one judge in a human way what is done in a divine mystery. Let no one try to penetrate this heavenly mystery by earthly reasoning. Let no one treat this novel secret from his knowledge of everyday occurrences. Let no one employ an example to evaluate what is unique. Let no one manipulate the work of love into an insult, or run the risk of losing salvation.

But, let him who wants a deeper knowledge betake himself to the Law. Let him seek from the Law his understanding of the Law. Let him understand the Author's work from His authority. The Law recounts[5] that God made man to live his own life; that He bade the earth to bring forth produce in willing service to man; that He ordered the beasts and herds and flocks to be subject to man's control, not to his artful devices, that man might know no toil, be free from all pain, and possess his delights in joy.

But, that angel who once was among God's best envied man his possession of all these goods. To avoid seeing man so full of glory he preferred to be changed into a devil. Afire with this envy, he approaches the woman with his guile. He entices the virgin to taste the forbidden fruit. Once beguiled herself, she entices the virgin young man who was soon to be her husband. While she proffered the food of death, the fodder of sin, she debased the state of his life. She who had been made to be man's singular comfort became the occasion of his complete ruin!

The upshot of it all was the first sin, and the beginning of death, and toil, and suffering, and groans. From here has been passed on all the bitter state of our servitude. Man, formerly the lord of all creatures, was cast down into slavery

5 Gen. 2.8-25.

by them all, and he who was feared by all now fears them all himself. He who was ruling by his authority can now scarcely exercise control by his artful devices.

This is the reason, brethren, this is the reason why the succession of events is what it is in the birth of Christ. The Devil had come to a virgin, an angel came to Mary, that what the bad angel had cast down the good angel might raise up. The first one urged infidelity, the latter fidelity. The first woman believed the Tempter, the latter one her Maker. Christ is born, to renew our corrupted nature through His birth. He accepted infancy, allowed Himself to be fed; He went through the ages of life to restore the one, perfect, abiding age which he had made. He supports man, that he may be unable to fall now. He made into a heavenly being him whom He had made an earthly one. He vivifies with a divine life man once animated with human life. Thus He raises the whole man toward God, to leave in him nothing of sin, or of death, or of labor, or of suffering, or of earth. All this is offered by our Lord Jesus Christ, who lives with the Father, and reigns in unity with the Holy Spirit, as God now, and forever, indeed, through all the undying ages of ages. Amen.

## SERMON 149

### *The Birth of Christ and the Peace of Christians*

(On Luke 2.8-14)

When our Lord and Saviour came to earth and made Himself bodily present, the angels appeared in chorus and gave the good news to the shepherds: 'I bring you good news of great joy which shall be to all the people.' We, too, borrow this hymn from these holy angels and announce great joy to you.

For, today, the Church is in peace, and the heretics in anger. Today, the ship of the Church is in port, and the fury of the heretics is tossed about on the waves. Today, brethren, the pastors of the Church are in security, and the heretics in consternation. Today, the sheep of the Lord are in a safe place, and the wolves rave in anger. Today, the vineyard of the Lord has abundance, and the workers of iniquity are indigent. Today, very dearly beloved, the people of Christ has been exalted, and the enemies of truth have been humbled. Today, dearly beloved, Christ is in joy, and the Devil in grief. Today, the angels are in exultation, and the demons in confusion.

Why should I say more? Today, Christ, who is the King of peace, has come forth with His peace and routed all discord, banished dissensions, and dissipated conflicts. As the brilliance of the sun lights up the sky, so He illumines the Church with the splendor of peace. 'For,' the text says, 'there has been born to you today a Savior of the world.' O how desirable is the very name of peace! How firm a foundation peace is for the Christian religion, and what a heavenly ornament for the altar of the Lord!

What can we utter worthy of peace? Peace is a name of Christ Himself, as even the Apostle says: 'For Christ is our peace, He it is who has made both one.'[1] The two were at variance, not over conflicting opinions or faith, but because of the Devil's envy. But, just as the streets are cleansed when the king comes forth, and the whole city decked with myriad flowers and banners to keep out of sight anything less worthy of the king's countenance, so also now, when Christ the King of peace comes forth, let

1 Eph. 2.14.

everything depressing be removed from our midst. While truth is shining, let falsehood be banished, and discord flee, and concord be resplendent. We often see that when the pictures of kings or of brothers are painted, the skillful painter, to produce symbols of unity between them, portrays Concord attired in feminine dress behind the back of the two. Embracing them both with her arms, she is meant to indicate that these who seem separated in body are in agreement of opinion and will. Just so, at present, the Peace of the Lord standing in our midst, and with palpitating bosom joining both of us together, teaches separated persons to come to agreement in spirit by linking elbows. In all this is fulfilled, no doubt, the prophetical statement which says: 'And the counsel of peace shall be between them both.'[2]

Yesterday, indeed, our common father[3] uttered a preliminary prayer in the Gospel language of peace. Today, to be sure, we make our declarations by means of a message of peace. With upturned hands he received us yesterday. So, with expanded heart and outstretched arms we today hasten to him bearing gifts of peace. Wars have now been destroyed. The beauty of peace holds everything. The Devil is in mourning, and all his cohort of demons in lamentation. But the heavenly beings now have joy, and the angels who hold peace especially dear are in exultation. An unfailing spring of peace is found among the heavenly powers, and they admire peace. And the dwellers of earth are refreshed by at least some drops falling from this spring. For this reason, even if peace is praised by the saints on earth, the splendor of that praise has an effect of overflow into heaven. The angels of heaven praise

2 Zach. 6.13.
3 Perhaps some bishop. Cf. Sermon 138 n. 2.

that peace and say: 'Glory to God in the highest, and peace on earth among men of good will.'[4]

You see, brethren, how the dwellers of heaven and of earth mutually send gifts of peace. The angels of heaven announce peace to the earth. The saints on earth praise Christ our peace, again restored among the dwellers of heaven, and in mystical choirs they exclaim: 'Glory in the highest.'[5] So let us also say with the angels: 'Glory in the highest to God,' who humbled the Devil and exalted His Christ. 'Glory in the highest to God,' who has banished discord and established peace. You perceive, brethren, that the angelic hymn is sonorously vibrant. 'Glory to God in the highest, and peace on earth.'

To be sure, I mention the Devil's cunning. You are not unaware how clever he is. Satan observed the solidity and stability of the faith. He saw it hedged about with God's kind gift of doctrine, and abounding in fruits of good works. Therefore, in the sight of all he fell into madness, and burned in a rage of fury, in order to shatter concord, uproot charity, and tear peace asunder. But may peace be always with us.

## SERMON 152

### *The Slaughter of the Holy Innocents*

(On Matt. 2.16-18)

Today, Herod's inhuman cruelty has exposed how far jealousy tends to go, and spite leaps, and envy makes its way. While this cruelty was jealously seeking the narrow

4 Luke 2.14.

5 Luke 19.38. Knox translates: 'Glory in heaven above.'

limits of temporal reign, it strove to block the rise of the eternal King. The Evangelist has told us the account: 'Then Herod, seeing that he had been tricked by the Magi, was exceedingly angry; and he sent and slew all the boys in Bethlehem and all its neighborhood.'

'Seeing that he had been tricked by the Magi.' Impiety grieves that it has been tricked. Cruelty is in a rage because it has been warded off. Deceitfulness roars because it has been deceived. Trickery has turned against itself and been dashed to naught. Herod hisses in rage while falling himself into the net he has spread. Consequently, he unsheathes the iniquity he has hidden. His trust in perfidy is the arsenal from which he takes his arms. In his earthly fury he hunts Him whom he does not believe to be born from heaven. He moves the soldier's camp to the bosoms of mothers, and attacks the citadel of love among their breasts. He tests his steel in those tender breasts, sheds milk before blood, causes the infants to undergo death before experiencing life, brings darkness on those just entering into the light of day.

That is how he deports[1] himself—that master of evil, minister of deceit, craftman of anger, deviser of crime, author of impiety, pirate of love, enemy of innocence, foe of nature who is evil to all men, worse to his own relatives, worst to himself. Christ fled from him not to get away from him but to escape seeing him. Making his way up high, he falls from aloft. Knocking at heaven, he enters hell. He who rushes against God attacks himself. He tries to kill life and kills himself, because salvation cannot be gained by murder, or life by killing, or eternity by termination. O ambition, how blind you always are! O presumption, how dastardly you always are! Oh, how he who

1 Reading *agit,* with Held (*BKV* 713).

grasps what is not granted loses what is! Herod, possessing an earthly kingdom, attacks the heavenly one. Gazing intently on his earthly goods, he rushes for those divine, and with all his impiety he pursues Piety Himself.

He had heard that the King was born. He had asked where, when, from whom, and for what purpose. But he did not seek as he should have, because he had a love of sinning, and his love of innocence had gone. Impelled to crime, prone to sins which cry for expiation, ready for atrocity, he disregarded the proofs of innocence, abrogated right, confused the lawful with the abominable. Wickedness was his companion, and he hated equity. Iniquity was always dear to him who lived through murders, strengthened his own position through bloodshed, and practiced cruelty. Everything he possessed stood through fear, nothing through love.

Thereupon, Herod blindly sought to kill Christ by his swords. He hunted for Him by means of blood, and thoroughly searched by means of cruelty. In fear of a successor, he moved against his Creator. He slew the innocent babies, with intent to kill Innocence Himself. He was ruler of the people, guardian of morals, censor in charge of discipline, investigator of justice, defender of equity, preserver of innocence, developer of the people. Yet, he made the case of the Innocent One into a crime of the innocent babies. He changed the service of the prophetical wise men[2] into an occasion of punishment, commanded the birth of the Creator to become the death of the new-born babies, and the work of the Saviour to become the hazard of those who were to be saved.

A judge summons hearers, questions speakers, cross-questions those who deny, presses plaintiffs, dismays the guilty, reproaches accomplices, sentences confederates, de-

2 The Magi are probably meant.

livers those convicted to their sentence. But, what has he to do with infants? Their tongue has been silent, their eyes have seen nothing, their hands have done nothing. No act has proceeded from them; then, whence do they have any guilt? They who did not yet know how to live got death. The period of their life did not protect them, nor did their age excuse them, nor their silence defend them. With Herod, the mere fact that they were born was their crime. And in truth, why were they not to return the loan [of life] which nature gave them? It was the welfare of the Saviour which was being asked from them. The unhappy man! All his preparations turned out to be charges against himself. He left not even a while for excuse, but prepared everything for pain! Who will excuse him whom innocence blames, infants attack, milk accuses as if it were blood? All this is against Herod.

But Christ foreknew the future and all secrets. He was the Judge of thoughts and the examiner of minds. Why did He desert those whom He knew were being searched for because of Himself, and whom He knew would be killed for His sake? Born as a King, yes, as the King of heaven, why did He neglect those little soldiers of His innocence? Why did He contemn that army of infants of His own age? Why did He abandon these guards deputed to keep watch at their cradles, in such a way that the foe who was to seek only the King advanced against His every soldier?

Brethren, Christ did not contemn His soldiers; He promoted them. He enabled them to triumph before living. He caused them to gain a victory before fighting. He gave them their crowns before their members.[3] He willed that they should overcome vices by their virtues, possess heaven sooner than earth, and not become enmeshed in human

3 I.e., before their members had grown strong.

affairs before possessing the divine benefits. Therefore, Christ sent His little soldiers ahead; He did not lose them. He did not abandon his front line troops, but took them to Himself.

Blessed are they! They were born for martyrdom, not for the world, as we have seen. Fortunate are they! They have changed their labors into rest, their sufferings into refreshment, their sorrows into joy. They live, they are alive. They are the ones who truly live, they who merit to be slain for Christ. Blessed are the wombs which bore such babes, blessed are the breasts which nourished them, blessed are the tears which were shed for them, and conferred on the weeping ones the grace of baptism. For, by one gift, but in different ways, the mothers were baptized in their tears and the infants in their blood. The mothers suffered in the martyrdom of their children. The sword which transpierced the members of children penetrated to the hearts of the mothers. Moreover, those who were companions of the suffering must be sharers of the reward.

The infant smiled at his slayer. The child made fun of the sword. The babe in arms saw, in place of his nurse, the frightfulness of the man ready to strike. The tender-aged boy so soon to die, and scarcely aware of the light, rejoiced. An infant son looks on every man, not as a foe, but, as a parent.

The mothers bore whatever anguish and sorrow that came to them. Therefore, they who shed the tears of martyrdom will not lack its joy.

At this point, let the hearer consider and notice carefully, that he may know that martyrdom cannot be bought by merit, but comes through grace. In the case of the infants, where nature itself was still held captive, what will power was present, or what act of decision? Therefore, in the case of martyrdom, we owe it all to God, and nothing to ourselves. To conquer the Devil, give up one's body, hold its members unimportant; to ponder the thought of the rack, tire out the torturer, take glory from insults and life from death—all that is not a matter of human ability, but a gift of God. He who runs to martyrdom by his own power does not arrive at the crown through Christ.

But may He lead us to heavenly nourishment who condescended to repose in a stable of ours, Jesus Christ of Nazareth, our Lord, who lives and reigns for ever and ever. Amen.

## SERMON 154

### *St. Stephen, the First Martyr*

The titles set upon boundary marks announce the owner of the farm lands. In similar fashion, the very names of saints often indicate their merits and reveal their outstanding deeds.

This was the case with Abraham. When his name was changed by divine intervention from Abram to Abraham, he showed by an addition to his name that he believed by faith. This was done that he who was to be multiplied in his offspring might have his name enlarged first. The Lord said: 'You shall no longer be called Abram, but your name shall be Abraham; for I will make you the father of a multitude of nations.'[1]

Thus, too, when his holy wife was changed from barrenness to fruitfulness she had her name changed from Sarai

1 Gen. 17.5.

to Sarah,[2] that she, too, might grow in name[3] before she grew large with child. Through the Lord's permission, laughter was provoked by the very thought that so aged a woman, already furrowed with wrinkles, should conceive a child; that she whose fruitfulness was long past hope should give birth to an infant; that she whose barrenness was deemed certain because of her extreme age should become pregnant. Therefore, she named the child she soon brought forth Laughter. By this name she indicated her disposition[4] when she laughed: 'And he called him Isaac'[5] which means laughter.

This was the case with Jacob, too. While still in his mother's womb, he began to struggle sooner than to see; and to conquer by his mental abilities sooner than by his members. Not yet separated from his mother's body, he was named The Supplanter.[6] For, before he was born, he was known to have overthrown his divinely disapproved brother.

To go into all such examples would take too long. Peter got his name from a rock because by the firmness of his faith he was the first to deserve to be a foundation of the Church. Similarly, Stephen got his name from a crown because he was the first to deserve to undergo the conflict for the name of Christ, the first to merit to inaugurate martyrdom by that bloodshed so characteristic of the soldiers of Christ. Let Peter retain his long-standing headship of

---

2 Gen. 17.15-19. According to Mariana (cited in *PL* 52.607, notes d and e), Abram means Exalted Father (*pater excelsus*), and Abraham, Father of a Throng (*pater turbae*); Sarai means *my* lady or mistress, and Sarah, lady or mistress in general, with a connotation of her numerous descendants.

3 In Hebrew spelling her name grew by one consonant, from SaRai to SaRaH.

4 Cf. Gen. 18.10-15.

5 Gen. 21.3; cf. Gen. 21.1-8.

6 Or, The Tripper. Gen. 25.25.

the Apostolic[7] College. Let him unlock the kingdom of heaven for those who enter it, bind the guilty by his power, and mercifully absolve the repentant. But Stephen is the first of the martyrs. Let him be the leader of that purpled army, for he was an eager warrior who shed his blood for the still warm blood of his Lord.

He procured for himself a purple robe, dyed with his own blood. Therefore, later on, he rightly received a crown from his King. And this was he who at his birth got his name from a crown. Clearly, God foreknew and predestined him; now He called him as the first one to come to the glory of martyrdom.

## SERMON 155

### *The Desecration of New Year's Day by Pagan Practices*

When Christ was lovingly born for our salvation, the Devil also soon brought forth many pernicious wonders in the sight of the divine goodness. He wanted to fabricate something ridiculous out of religious observance, to turn holiness into sacrilige, to prepare an injury to God from the very attempt to honor Him. This, brethren, this is why the pagans today[1] bring out their gods. With planned defile-

7 Reading *apostolici,* with S. Pauli.

1 This is manifestly a sermon for New Year's Day. The Roman festival of the Saturnalia, celebrated through many days in late December, was a season of extravagant merriment and even of license. Similar orgy marked the celebration of New Year's Day, and its excesses often drew the reprimands of the Fathers of the Church, as the Feast of the Fools in the Middle Ages drew the condemnation of one provincial council after another. St. Augustine preached two sermons (197, 198, *PL* 38.1021-1026) *De Kalendis Januariis contra Paganos.* A decree of Bishop Atto of Vercelli against celebrating January 1 *ritu paganorum* is in *PL* 134.43.

ments and premeditated disgrace they pull them hither and thither as beings appearing baser than baseness itself, and drag them about. They make them unworthy to look upon.

What vanity! What silliness! What blindness! To recognize them as gods, and dishonor them with all this derision! Those who mock the gods they venerate are scoffers, not adorers. Those who thus deform the gods by whom they think that they themselves were made do not honor them, but load them with insults. Those who fashion their gods after their own disorder do not glorify them, but shame them.

Truly, indeed, as the Apostle says, 'As they have resolved against possessing the knowledge of God, God has given them up to a reprobate sense, so that they do what is not fitting.'[2] When they attribute divine prerogatives to those beings whom they deprive of the qualities of men, when they deem them worthy of heaven and make them unworthy of earth itself, they have indeed been given up to a reprobate sense. And this is not a matter of human judgment, but one of the wisdom of God, in order that those who are recognized as the authors of this discredit may be themselves the avengers of the insults offered to God. What [other] anger, what avengement, would follow upon an offense from the idols against God in just this manner, so as to bring the following result? Antiquity, through its altars, incense, victims, gems, and gold, lyingly asserted that those beings are gods; posterity, through its debasing cult, judged them to be disgraceful men, and signified its opinion of their life, morals, and deeds by their very countenances. Posterity has taught that such beings should be fled rather than worshiped.

Brethren, let us weep over those who follow such practices, and let us rejoice that with heavenly aid we have

---

2 Rom. 1.27.

escaped them! The pagans represent the adulteries of these beings in their images; they perpetuate their fornications in their likenesses, make their incests the titles of their paintings, display their cruelties as patterns in books, make their parricides a matter of tradition, act out their base deeds in their tragedies, and mimic their obscenities. With what insanity would they believe these beings to be gods, were it not for the following fact! They are themselves possessed by a desire of crimes and a love of enormities, and wish to have gods who are criminals, too. He who wants to sin worships and venerates the authors of sins. That is why the adulterer attaches himself to Venus, and the cruel man becomes devout to Mars.

We have mentioned these matters, brethren, to reveal why the pagans today make their gods commit such deeds as we endure; why they make their gods such as to inspire horror and shame in those who see them; why they bring it to pass that sometimes even those who fashion these gods abandon them in horror, and Christians glory in their liberation from such beings through Christ.

If only these Christians would not be defiled by these pagan spectacles, or stained by contact[3] with them! If only they would flee the danger of showing approval of such practices, since approval is always equal to the deeds themselves, as the Apostle says with approval: 'and not only they that do them but they also that consent to them that do them.'[4]

Now, if such terrible condemnation arises from approving them, who can sufficiently bewail those who play the role of idols?[5] Have they not lost the image of God, and

3 Reading, with Böhmer, *inquinentur attactu*, not *inquinent thura tactu*.
4 Rom. 1.32 (Douay-Rheims version). The statement preceding the words cited by St. Peter are: 'They who do such things are worthy of death.'
5 Some Christians still participated in these pagan practices. St. Peter here reprimands them. Cf. Introduction, pp. 7-9.

destroyed His likeness? Have not those who dressed themselves as the sacrilegious characters of idols put off the garment of Christ?

But, someone will object: 'All this is not practice of the sacrilegious rites, but only a desire to take part in the sport. It is joy over the new era, not the folly of the old. It is the beginning of the year, not the insult of paganism.'

O man, you are in error. These actions are not sport, they are sins. Who sports over impiety? Who jokes about what is sacrilegious? Who calls an act requiring expiation a laughing matter? He who maintains that objection deceives himself quite completely. He who puts on the tyrant's robes is a tyrant himself. He who makes himself a god stands as one contradicting the true God. He who has been willing to masquerade as an idol has refused to bear the image of God. He who has been willing to joke with the Devil will not be able to rejoice with Christ. No one plays with a serpent without danger, and no one jokes with the Devil with impunity.

Therefore, if we have any love in our hearts, any regard for our fellow men, any zeal for our brethren's salvation, let us restrain those who are thus running to perdition, being snatched away to their death, dragged toward Tartarus, and hastening to Gehenna. Let the father restrain his son, the master his servant, the parent any other parent, the citizen his fellow citizen, the man any other man. Let the Christian restrain those who have made themselves equal to beasts, put themselves on a level with asses, made themselves up as cattle, masqueraded as demons. The man who thus acts as a liberator merits a reward, and he who is negligent commits an offense. Blessed is he who is the the guardian of his own life, and a caretaker of his brethren's salvation, too.

# SERMON 156

## *Epiphany and the Magi*

## (On Matt. 2.1-12)

When cautious physicians skillfully prepare a remedy of salutary juices against deadly diseases, and if the patient rashly takes it differently from the directions, or in amount not conducive to healing, or with improper timing, that which was planned to bring health becomes a cause of danger. So, too, if the hearer rashly tries to understand the word of God without the teaching authority, and learning, and the doctrine of the faith, that which is the nutrition of life becomes an occasion of perdition. We must strive, brethren, that what has been divinely written for our progress may not turn out, through our lack of skill in hearing, to be something detrimental to our souls.

Do you think that the Evangelist taught that the Chaldaean watchers of the stars, the Magi journeying with the aid of the stars, studying the affairs of the heavens in the darkness of the nights, attributing the causes of birth and death to the movements of the stars, asserting that good or evil comes to men through the decision of these luminous bodies—do you think that the Evangelist taught that it was by the mere natural guidance of a star that they today discovered the birth of the Christ hidden from the ages?

Let no one have such a thought! That is what the world thinks, what the pagans understand, what the reading yields at first blush. But the Gospel text speaks matters not human, but divine; matters not ordinary, but new; matters not deceptive through cleverness, but based upon truth; matters not illusory to the eyes, but rooted in hearts; matters not fluid through conjectures, but firmly established by authority;

matters coming from God, not fate; matters not gathered by reckonings, but acquired by the practice of virtues.

'When Jesus was born in Bethlehem of Judaea,' the text says, 'in the days of king Herod, behold, there came a Magi from the east to Jerusalem, saying, Where is the newly born king of the Jews? We have seen his star in the east, and have come to worship him.' When Jesus was born, the Source of things arose, the Maker of the race was begotten, the Creator of nature was born, in order to repair nature, restore the race, re-establish the original state. The first man, Adam, the father of the race, the origin of all posterity, lost by his sin the good of nature, the freedom of his race, and the life of his offspring. Consequently, his unfortunate posterity endured the evil of nature, the slavery of the race, the death of their offspring. Hence it came about that Christ by His birth restored nature, took away death by dying, summoned life back by His resurrection. He who had given man his soul from heaven now enabled him to stand firm in the flesh, lest some earthly stain might again overwhelm his spiritual insight and bring him to a fall of the body. As the Apostle said: 'The first man was of the earth, earthy; the second man is from heaven, heavenly. As was the earthy man, such also are the earthy; and as is the heavenly man, such also are the heavenly.'[1] John the Evangelist also stated: 'No one who is born of God commits sin; but the Begotten of God preserves him.'[2] Thus it is that Christ was born to elevate those prostrate in an earthy seed up to a heavenly nature.

'When Jesus was born in Bethlehem of Judaea.' Bethlehem, brethren, is called in Hebrew the house of bread. These words indicate the house of Juda; they name the race, that the pledge of the promise may be fulfilled, and also

1 1 Cor. 15.47,48.
2 1 John 5.18.

the truth of that prophecy which Jacob spoke: 'Juda, your brothers shall praise you; your hand shall be on the neck of your enemies; the sons of your father shall bow down to you.'[3] Later, the text continues: 'The sceptre shall not be taken away from Juda, nor a ruler from his thigh, till he come for whom the things have been stored up, and he shall be the expectation of nations.' Wherefore David also said: 'Juda is my king.'[4]

'When Jesus was born in Bethlehem of Judaea in the days of King Herod.' What means this, that it was in the time of a very wicked king that God descended to earth, divinity entered into[5] flesh, a heavenly union occurred with an earthly body? What does this mean? When does one not truly a king come to drive out a tyrant, avenge his country, renew the face of the earth, and restore freedom? Herod, an apostate,[6] invaded the kingdom of the Jewish race, took away the Jews' liberty, profaned their holy places, disrupted the established order, abolished whatever there was of discipline and religious worship. Rightly, therefore, did divine aid succor that holy race which had no human help. Rightly did God support the race which had no man to be its helper.

In just this way will Christ come again, to undo the Antichrist, free the world, restore the fatherland of Paradise, perpetuate the liberty of the world, take away all the slavery of this world.

'Behold, there came Magi from the East.' The Magi came from the East to the Orient,[7] that He who had bade them come might receive them on their arrival. For, when

3 Gen. 49.8,10.
4 Ps. 59.9.
5 *miscetur divinitas carni.* Cf. Sermon 5 n. 11, on *humanitati permixta deitas.*
6 *refuga;* cf. Souter, *s.v.*
7 Cf. Luke 1.78: 'the Orient from on high has visited us.'

would a Magus have sought God save by God's command? When would a star-gazer have found the King of heaven, save by God's revelation? When would a Chaldaean, who served as many gods as there were stars in the sky, have adored the one God without God's aid? The Magi themselves are more of a heavenly sign than the star, for a Magus recognized the King of Judaea and the Author of the Law, while the Judean does not; Chaldaea pays deference while Judaea does not; Jerusalem turns away and plays apostate, Syria follows and adores.

'Behold there came Magi from the East to Jerusalem, saying, Where is the newly born king of the Jews. We have seen his star.' And what is that which is seen? Truly, what the Apostle said: 'Being rich, he became poor.'[8] When He was rich in his divinity, He became a poor man in our flesh; He who made, owns, and sustains all creation began to have one star.

'We have seen his star.' At length the Magus sees Him who owns the star, and is not possessed by it. He is not moved by the course of the star, but He Himself moves the star, and He so directs its course through the sky, and controls its pace, and choses its path, that it serves and is sent for the Magi's advance. For, when the Magus moves on, the star does, too. When he sits, the star stands still. When he sleeps, the star keeps watch. Thus, the Magus perceives that those who journey under a common condition are under a common necessity of rendering service. Now, he does not believe the star to be a god, but he believes it to be his fellow servant, bound, as he sees, to giving service to himself.

'Where is the newly born king of the Jews? For we have seen his star in the east, and have come to worship him.' By saying: 'Where is He who was born king of the Jews,'

8 2 Cor. 8.9.

they do not ask a question, but taunt. When those who know question those who do not know, they themselves do not lack knowledge. Rather, they are reproving the negligent, challenging the lazy, betraying the evil, and chastizing the haughty. They are lodging the charge that the servants have not met their Lord in welcome. Why should those address questions to men who already knew from God what they were asking about? What good would human information do them, who for their purpose were receiving service from the stars of heaven? What good was the light of the Temple for them who had marvelous light from a star of heaven?

'Where is the newly born king of the Jews?' This is tantamount to saying: Why does the king of the Jews lie in a manger, and not repose in the Temple? Why is He not resplendent in purple, rather than poorly clad in rags? Why does He lie hidden in a cave, and not on display in the Sanctuary? The beasts have received in a manger Him whom you have disdained to receive in His house. As it has been written: 'The ox knoweth his owner, and the ass his master's crib.'[9] But you, O Israel, have not sought out your Master.

'We have seen his star.' The star appeared not of itself, but by command; not because of the gravitation of heaven, but by an impulse of God; not because of the law of the stars, but of the novelty of signs; not because of any clear climate in the sky, but because of the power of Him being born; not from art, but from God; not because of an astrologer's knowledge, but the Creator's foreknowledge; not by an arithmetical reckoning, but by a divine decree; through heavenly care, not Chaldaean curiosity; not through art of magic, but because of Jewish prophecy.

Thus, when the Magus saw that human cares had come

9 Isa. 1.3.

to naught, that his own arts had failed, that the labors of worldly wisdom had been exhausted, that the perspiration of all the sects had congealed and the treasures of all philosophy had been emptied out, that the night of paganism had fled and the clouds of opinions dissolved, that the very shadows of the devils had skulked into hiding, that the star was not, like a comet with its surrounding tail, hiding what it was announcing, covering up what was shining—when the Magus saw all this, he spoke: 'It is a divine decree that I see you in Judaea, resplendent with a new ray, a significant light, and a steady splendor, and there—above the law of the universe, above the arrangement of flesh, above the nature of men—there pointing out the King now born.'

With his error thus dispelled, he follows, he runs, he arrives, he finds, he rejoices, he falls prostrate, he adores. For, not through the star, not through his skill, but through the help of God has he found, in astonishment, God in human flesh. Therefore, brethren, the passage read today does not establish the error of magic, it dissolves it. Let these remarks suffice for today, that with God's help the matters which follow may become clear.

## SERMON 165

### *On the Consecration of Projectus, Bishop of Forum Cornelium*[1]

I acknowledge that I indeed owe veneration to all the churches, and a very faithful service, too. But I am com-

1 Forum Cornelium is the modern Imola, near Ravenna.

pelled to show special devotion to the Cornelian church because of my love of its very name. For, Cornelius was renowned for his life of blessed memory, illustrious everywhere through all his titles to virtues, known to all men because of his great achievements; and he was a father to me.[2] He begot me through the Gospel. Devout himself, he devoutly nourished me; holy himself, he trained me in the holy service. As a bishop, he brought me to the sacred altar and consecrated me. Consequently, the name of Cornelius is to me something distinguished, venerable, wonderful.

Therefore, my love of the name urges me eagerly to comply with the desires of the Cornelian church, and with deeper affection consecrate the venerable Projectus as its bishop. I have used the word Projectus, not Abjectus, in accordance with the Scriptural phrase: 'I was cast upon thee from the womb. From my mother's womb thou art my God.'[3] Truly, this man, projected from the womb of his human mother, has remained without interruption in the womb of the divine mother;[4] not frequenting his own house, he has perseveringly dwelt in the house of God. It would be tedious for me to tell you, brethren, how from the very cradle he has risen up through the ranks and offices of the Church's army. Therefore, as the Lord says: 'He is of age, let him speak for himself,'[5] through our Lord Jesus Christ who lives and reigns with the Holy Spirit forever. Amen.

---

2 Perhaps through baptizing him; certainly, through educating and conferring some Orders.

3 Ps. 21.11: *In te projectus sum ex utero. Projectus* means: the one advanced, made prominent; *abjectus*: the one rejected.

4 The Church.

5 John 9.21.

## SERMON 166

### *The Lenten Fast*

Simplicity has indeed the charm of its own innocence and the fruit of its own faith, but it cannot possess the reward which learning gets, or the palm which virtues gain. It is one thing to live for leisure and one's own security; another, to endure watches and labors for all men. Simplicity makes a good citizen, it does not make a brave soldier. Hence it is that the citizen pays what he is assessed, the soldier receives wages and honors. The citizen either retreats or falls before adversity; the soldier endures it and drives it away. The former has not learned how to fight; the latter has learned not to fear. The former is always on his guard; the latter wins the battle.

We have mentioned these matters in order to point out the distance between the man who with simplicity accepts and follows the sacred mystery of the Christian faith and him who is zealous to grasp the mystery of that faith intelligently and understand it profoundly.

Consider the fast of Lent, which the whole Church takes up tomorrow with solemn devotion. Many think that it has been handed down to us, or that the Lord observed it, solely for the practice of abstinence; that it does not contain a symbolic mystery[1] for a deeper understanding, but has been given us merely for the chastisement of our bodies, the uprooting of vices, and the restraining of our hearts. Now, that number forty is something so sacred from antiquity, and it is found to be so mystical,[2] that by some unbreakable law it is written as a number which is always used to accomplish divine projects and to explain impor-

1 *mysterium.*
2 Or: symbolical.

tant affairs of God. That this fact may shine to the clear sky, let us illustrate it with many examples.

In the unfortunate infancy of the human race, when the world was growing foul with an undescribable squalor of vices, and stank in its entirety with horrible crimes, and was tending almost to cloud up the great brightness of the sky with the smoke of its wickedness, for forty days and nights rain was poured out to purify the earth.[3] This happened that the world (which should have been already on the point of perishing, since it was but a creature) might rejoice over this second birth by such a baptism; that it might know that it owes the fact of its existence not to nature, but to the gift of its Creator; that the earth, the source of our body, might have a foretaste of the very form of our baptism; and, finally, that the earth, which previously was producing men born for death, might produce them now as men reborn unto life.

Notice, brethren, how important that number forty is. Then, it opened up the heavens for the cleansing of the earth; now, through the font of baptism,[4] it opens the world for the renewal of the nations. Rightly we do run through the fast of forty days to arrive at the font of baptism and salvation.

The rain of manna fed the Jewish people for forty years[5] in the desert. It did not by its customary service cause an increase of sprouts from the earth, but streamed on the earth like harvested grains. It took away all the toil of human labor, and by its pleasant dew[6] offered and spread out heavenly produce for the hungry.

For forty days an exploring party, sent out by God's

3 Gen. 7.1-24.
4 Baptism was solemnly administered on Holy Saturday at the close of the Lenten fast.
5 Exod. 16.1-36.
6 The manna appeared as dew; cf. Exod. 16.13.

command, traversed the Promised Land.[7] Thus, this sacred number was to summon the Israelites to the Promised Land, just as it now by its forty periods of fasting summons us, and leads us to heaven. Now, an investigation from heaven explores and traverses the land of our body for forty days, to attack and expel the tribes of vices and enable a legion of virtues to possess the region of our heart.

We should omit nothing. Moses himself was so purified and freed from his body by a fast of forty days[8] that his whole self took on a glorious appearance of divinity. Still in the darkness of our body, he gleamed with the full radiance of divinity. The eyes of mortals could not gaze upon him who, long nourished by the substance of God, had forgotten all about the aids provided by mortals' food. From this he learned that the sustenance of life does not fail those who live in God's sight and with Him. Truly, brethren, he who has God for his bread and life runs no risk of growing weak or dying. Rightly did Moses, being one like this, deserve to promulgate the Law, since he had lost whatever the Law could force in the case of man. Perhaps his protracted fast brought all this to Moses. But it would not have made him such as he was if this sacred number of forty had been lacking.

A fast raised Elias to heaven,[9] and brought to his body so purified the services of the fiery chariot, to show how much the hell fire which burns the guilty does service to the innocent. To become fit for all this Elias first runs the course of the mystical way of the number forty.[10]

By lying on his one side for forty days (I am speaking to those who know the Law), Ezechiel, who is eminent among the Prophets, prefigured the future captivity and

7 Num. 13.26.
8 Exod. 24.18.
9 4 Kings 2.11.
10 3 Kings 19.7,8.

fixed its term.[11] That sacred number takes on the iniquities to blot them out, enters the days of captivity to terminate them, accepts bonds to break them.

Therefore, all this is the reason why the Lord, Author from eternity of the symbolic mystery[12] hidden in this number, [kept His own fast] within that number of forty days of fast,[13] that Truth itself might bring to fulfillment these deeds and beginnings which He had already outlined in the case of these servants; that He might strengthen what was tender, complete what was begun, and strengthen by His example what He had set us by commands. For, it would not have been enough to command by words this great symbolic mystery of this important number, had He not also recommended it by His deeds.

However, brethren, we have tried to expound the mystery of this sacred sign from the time of the deluge on, without daring to touch on previous events, or to pry into the more ancient ones, or to speak the unmentioned, or to utter matters certainly hidden away for so long. We have done this especially because I see that to explore such important beginnings would be rash for me and unnecessary for you. It is the part of true devotion and loyal service to ask what the Master wants done, not why He wants it to be done.

Therefore, if a simple, unadulterated, unvarying fast of forty days is taught us by such great evidence, as something handed down by the Lord under the number of so important a symbol, whence arises that variety and novelty? Whence come those weeks: now relaxed, now rigid; now too indulgent and now too severe? Whence that use of immoderate fasting, which either afflicts a person without his obtaining forgiveness, or drives him back to excessive indul-

11 Ezech. 4.6.
12 *sacramentum.* See De Ghellinck, *Pour l'histoire du mot Sacramentum* 149. A verb is missing from the text printed in Migne.
13 Matt. 4.2.

gence? This is a case of applying exclusively to their single uses hot measures and cold ones, remedies of salt and of food, while completely neglecting the Maker of Life.[14] Surely, those who season the foods of our body should learn how to compound the food of the soul wisely and properly, lest something too salty or completely unsalted beget a fatal distaste of all nourishing food.

Let the fast be one properly measured. And, as we received from tradition, let it be observed for the discipline of both the body and the soul. Surely, let not the one who is unable to fast start some innovation. Rather, let him acknowledge that it is through his personal weakness that he mitigates his fast, and let him redeem by almsgiving what he cannot fulfill by fasting. For the Lord does not require groans from him who has thus acquired the cries of the poor as pleadings for himself.

## SERMON 170

### *Christ, Our Example in Manifold Ways; The Vocation of the Apostles; The Counsel of Poverty*

(On Mark 6.7-13)

When blessed Mark told us today that the Lord went about in the villages of Galilee, he revealed His unspeakable love toward us. The text states: 'And Jesus made a circuit of the villages, teaching.'

You have heard how He traveled; how for your sake He sought you everywhere with His indefatigable love. He who upholds all things and is Himself upheld by no crea-

14 Or possibly: 'while neglecting Him who gives balanced seasoning to our life.'

ture, He enters your body. He constrains Himself in it, compresses Himself in this abode of yours. The voice of the faithful daily acclaims His majesty with the shout: 'Heaven and earth are full of Your glory';[1] and He for your sake makes a circuit of your localities. He appears in them, is seen in them, is pressed to remain in them.

To where does His immovable fullness move itself? All beings are full of Him. Then, where does He approach, or from what does He withdraw? He does go and return, descend and ascend. He, O man, being God, endures your whole nature[2]—and that for your sake—because He loves you intensely, and has so much benevolence for you. He has assumed various appearances, varied His forms and changed His favors.

At one time He appears all aglow in a bush.[3] For, you are cold with the perfidy of infidelity, and He wants to enkindle you with the heat of faith. At another time He glows like fire in a pillar[4] extending toward heaven, that the darkness of your ignorance may be removed, and that you can follow the way of saving knowledge through the wilderness of this world. At yet another time He is changed for you into a pillar of cloud, in order to restrain the burning ebullitions of your passions. Again, like an eagle, He covers you with the wings of His wisdom, to stimulate you to fly toward heaven. In the words of Moses: 'As the eagle guards its nest and is undaunted above its young; extending its wings it takes them up and puts them on its back. The Lord alone illuminated them, and there was no strange god with them.'[5]

1 Preface of the Mass.
2 Literally, endures you.
3 Exod. 3.2.
4 Exod. 13.21,22.
5 Cf. Deut. 32.11.

Now, like a hen,[6] He leads you forth and round about. He calls you, receives, protects, fondles, carries, encircles, and embraces you. As a hen forgets for a time her own flight and freedom and rolls about in the dust, so does He live in your sanctuary—that he may nourish you, rear you, and instruct you with native, familiar, homemade foods.

Now, as a good shepherd,[7] He alone seeks you as you stray in the mountain heights. He alone finds you, puts you on His shoulders. To keep you from being seized[8] in earthly pastures by the teeth of the wolves, He carries and leads you to the sheepfolds of heaven. In these ways, as we said, He has assumed various appearances, varied His forms of activity. To change you for the better He so frequently changes and replaces His roles. The Enemy had long gone about to catch and devour you. Therefore, Christ necessarily goes about to vindicate and rescue you. As Scripture states: 'Your adversary, as a roaring lion, goes about seeking some-one to devour.'[9]

'And he summoned the twelve,'[10] the text says. After the long centuries of dreadful night, the eternal day, our Christ, shone forth. The world had long awaited the splendor of His dawning. In the case of His twelve Apostles He desired to signify the twelve hours of this day.[11] The blessed Psalmist saw this day in spirit when he sang: 'This is the day which the Lord hath made: let us be glad and rejoice therein.'[12] Consequently, the Apostle, too, calls the believers children

6 Matt. 23.37.
7 John 10.1-18.
8 For *pervadaris* meaning seize, cf. Souter, *s.v.*
9 1 Pet. 5.8.
10 Mark 6.7.
11 The Romans divided the day into twelve equal parts or 'hours' between sunrise and sunset. The length of an hour naturally varied with the seasons.
12 Ps. 117.24.

of light and of faith: 'You are children of the light and children of the day.'[13]

'And he summoned the twelve.' That number twelve, through division into groups of four, shows to us and forms three teams, each with four horses. By these teams the whole Trinity is carried throughout the world through the Apostles' journeys. The meek Warrior is to subdue the Devil, the gentle Victor is to reduce the pride of the world, the peaceful Fighter is to blot out the discords of nations, in order to destroy hell, that is, the grave of sin, to set captivity free from its long imprisonment, and to lead the souls of the human race to the glory of His triumph. In his prophetical spirit the Psalmist saw this chariot of the Holy Trinity when he said: 'Thou hast ascended on high, thou hast led captivity captive; thou hast received gifts in men.'[14] The Lord was preparing this chariot for Himself, His Father, and Holy Spirit when He said: 'Take my yoke upon you, because my yoke is easy and my burden light.'[15] He who bears mercy and carries love does not know how to grow weary.

The twelve patriarchs destined to become twelve tribes[16] were arranged to be a type[17] and pattern of the number of the Apostles. So were the twelve fountains[18] in the desert, and twelve stones[19] taken from the bed of the Jordan. We leave it to the student of the Law to find deeper proof of all this. For, the progression of our intended reading brings us now to the effort to explain why the Lord sent His disciples to preach two by two.

---

13 1 Thess. 5.5.
14 Ps. 67.19.
15 Matt. 11.29,30.
16 Gen. 49.1-32.
17 For *figura* meaning type, allegory, cf. Souter *s.v.*
18 Exod. 15.27.
19 Jos. 4.3.

'And he began to send them forth two by two.' He sent them two by two that no one of them, being abandoned and alone, might fall into a denial, like Peter, or flee, like John.[20] Human frailty quickly falls if it proudly relies on itself, despises companions, and is unwilling to have a colleague. As Scripture says: 'Woe to him that is alone, for when he falleth, he hath none to lift him up.'[21] The same Scripture testifies how much one is strengthened by another's aid, when it states: 'A brother that is helped by his brother is like a strong city.'[22]

'And he began to send them forth two by two.' It is not strange, brethren, if the Trinity which employed the three teams, of four horses each, which resulted from dividing the number twelve, now mounts also a chariot drawn by two horses. This was done that the vocation of the two peoples might be clearly shown by two messengers, as the Apostle states: 'Is God the God of the Jews only, and not of the Gentiles also? Indeed of the Gentiles also.'[23] It was done, too, to fulfill the prophesy of Isaias, who testified that he had seen a rider of a two-horse chariot, when he heard it said to him: 'What dost thou see? And he replied: I see a rider of a two-horse chariot.'[24] Because of this he cried out right away that Babylon had fallen, and all its graven gods.

Who doubts, brethren, that by this two-horse chariot Christ was riding upon His saving journeys, since he sees that through the Apostles' preaching temples have fallen, idols have perished, the bleatings of herds have ceased, and the victims, along with even the very altars with their per-

20 Mark 14.66-72; 50-52.
21 Eccle. 4.10.
22 Prov. 18.19.
23 Rom. 3.29.
24 Cf. Isa. 21.7,9.

fume of incense, have already disappeared through all the centuries. Habacuc had seen these chariots when he exclaimed: 'Who will ride upon thy horse: and thy chariots are salvation.'[25]

'And he gave them power over the unclean spirits,' the text says. This is a badge of divine power. This is the trophy of an outstanding triumph. The pirate himself is now handed over to his prey, the captive himself to his own captives, and the Devil, bound himself, is surrendered to those he once held bound, in order that he should be subjected to the sway of those over whom he once acted as slave master and tyrant. Rightly does he grieve, rightly does he groan, rightly does he howl. He who had long been persuading men by lies that he was a god now perceives himself struck down by the sentence of men and the power of men.

'And he instructed them to take nothing for their journey, but a staff only—no wallet, no bread, no money in their girdles.' When a man invites laborers to work, he supplies not merely the necessities of food, but even banquets with extensive preparations. He desires the banquet provided by the human kindliness he lavishes to win a victory over the burden and toil of the work. If God invites a man to work, and the man comes burdened and anxious with a wallet, bread, and wages, how inhuman he believes God to be! That man approaches the work either as a tired or sluggish worker, or perhaps he cannot even approach! God promises abundant rewards, by His numerous signed bonds and His witnesses. He promises a generous reward. Do you think that, in a niggardly spirit, He will supply neither bread nor clothing? He granted you existence when you were not. Whatever you have, O man, He gave to you. When you were living for yourself and your own

25 Hab. 3.8.

pleasures, He did not refuse the necessities of food. Do you think that He will not give bread or clothing to one applying himself to His virtues and tasks? Who gave you the very contents of your wallet and girdle? Why do you hasten to insult Him over His own gifts? He knows that you are rich.

O man, give up your resources! Divine poverty is enough for you. Put off the packs of your riches; a burdened man cannot make his way along the narrow road all the way to the work of the Lord's harvest. Come unencumbered, come free to the tasks, before you get stripped and robbed, and arrested for punishment as a worker unfaithful to all. For, as it is written: 'Riches do not go along with a dying man.'[26]

Let your conscience be your wallet, let your life be your bread, in order that the true bread in your life can be Christ, who said: 'I am the bread.'[27] Regard your heavenly reward as your salary. For, if in order to follow Christ a man has dispossessed himself of everything and faithfully scorned and despised what he had, he can ask a reward from Christ without any anxiety.

---

26 Cf. Ps. 48.7.
27 John 6.35.

## APPENDIX

### *The Letter of Saint Peter Chrysologus to Eutyches*[1]

### *Introduction*

Eutyches, an ardent opponent of Nestorianism but a rather unskillful theologian, fell into an opposite error. Aged seventy, and ill, he was summoned before Bishop Flavian and his standing council of bishops at Constantinople. He professed before the council that in Christ, after the union of the divine and human natures, there is but one nature. The council excommunicated him. His chief fault at that time seems to have been ignorance and stubbornness rather than malice, and the treatment of the council seems rather severe and untactful.[2] Eutyches wrote letters of complaint to St. Peter Chrysologus and Pope St. Leo the Great. His letter[3] to the Pope, written shortly after November 22, 448, restates his doctrine. However, Pope Leo found the letter too obscure[4] to understand the case, until he had further information from Flavian. Eutyches' letter to St. Peter Chrysologus is not extant. Probably enough, its contents were similar to what he wrote to the Pope.

Pope Leo received Eutyches' letter in February, 449. It was probably then or shortly later that St. Peter Chrysologus

---

1 The Latin text with an ancient Greek translation is printed in two chapters in *PL* 54.739-744 as Letter 25 among the Letters of Pope St. Leo the Great. Probably, Chapter 1 is St. Peter's original Latin and Chapter 2 is a retranslation into Latin from the Greek version; cf. *PL* 54.737-740. The Latin is also in *PL* 52.24-25.

2 Cf. Cayré, *Manual of Patrology* II 53.

3 Printed as Letter 21 in *PL* 54.713-720.

4 Cf. Letter 34, *PL* 54.801.

received Eutyches' letter and wrote his own Letter to Eutyches in reply.[5] He takes a very kindly attitude toward Eutyches, and declines to express a decisive opinion because he does not fully know the case. The letter shows his esteem of the authority of the Bishop of Rome as the successor of St. Peter the Apostle. When St. Peter Chrysologus wrote his letter, he manifestly had no knowledge of Pope Leo's long and justly famous dogmatic letter to Flavian,[6] which was written in June, 449, and condemned the doctrine of Eutyches as heretical.

5 Cf. *PL* 54.739-740.
6 Letter 28, *PL* 54.755-782.

*Peter, Bishop of Ravenna, to the Dearly Beloved son and Rightly Honorable Priest, Eutyches*

## *Chapter 1*

I have read your sad letter with deep grief, and run through the details you have written with a sympathetic regret corresponding to their sorrowful nature. For, just as peace among the churches, mutual harmony among priests, and the tranquility of the people cause us to rejoice with heavenly joy, so fraternal dissension afflicts and depresses us, especially when it arises from causes such as these.

Human laws cancel human questions unsolved within thirty years,[1] yet, after so many centuries, Christ's origin,[2] which the divine Law calls indescribable, is still bandied about in rash disputation! In your prudence, do not fail to notice what Origen, the Investigator of Principles,[3] incurred, nor how Nestorius slipped into error while disputing about the natures.

By their symbolic[4] gifts the Magi acknowledged Jesus in the cradle as God,[5] yet priests by their lamentable debating dispute about who He is who was conceived from the Holy Spirit and born by a virgin birth! When Jesus uttered His infant cries in the cradle, the heavenly host sang: 'Glory to God in the highest';[6] and is the subject of His origin

1 St. Peter repeated this and other matters from his Sermon 145 (cf. above, p. 237) against the Nestorians; he probably suspected because of the incomplete details in Eutyches' letter that Eutyches was falling into Nestorianism.
2 *generatio.* Cf. Isa. 53.8.
3 An allusion to Origen's work *On Principles.*
4 *mysticis.* Cf. Sermon 2 nn. 7, 9.
5 Matt. 2.1-12.
6 Luke 2.14.

stirred up now, when 'at the name of Jesus every knee is bent of those in heaven, on earth and under the earth'?[7] Dear brother, we affirm with the Apostle: 'Even though we have known Christ according to the flesh, yet now we know Him so no longer.'[8] Neither can we turn this matter over and over again in our minds in detrimental fashion. We are ordered to honor Him, and fear Him, and await Him, not to debate about Him whom we acknowledge as our Judge.

## *Chapter 2*

I have made these brief replies to your letter, dear brother. I would have written more if our brother and fellow bishop Flavian had sent written details about this case. For, if, as you write, you are displeased that a hearing had not been given you,[9] how shall we be able to pass judgment about these men?[10] Because of their absence, we do not see them; because of their silence we do not know what their view of the case was. He is not a just mediator who listens to one party in such a way that he leaves no case for the other party. However, we give you this exhortation in regard to everything, honorable brother: obediently heed these matters which the most blessed Pope of the City of Rome has written, because blessed Peter who lives and presides in his own see proffers the truth of faith to those who seek it.

7 Phil. 2.10.
8 2 Cor. 5.16.
9 Reading *ut scribis, tibimet ipsi sublatam audientiam,* with *PL* 54.742, note j. The other reading, *electum judicium* (*PL* 54.741), would mean: 'If the council which was chosen displeases you.' This does not square well with Eutyches' Letter to Pope St. Leo (*PL* 54.714-720).
10 Flavian and the members of his council.
11 *audire* has the force of *dijudicare,* as is clear from the Greek in *PL* 54.744A.

For, in accordance with our pursuit of peace and of faith, we cannot decide upon cases of faith without the harmonious agreement of the Bishop of Rome.

May the Lord long deign to preserve your love unharmed, very dear and honorable son.

# SAINT VALERIAN

## HOMILIES
## AND
## LETTER TO THE MONKS

## INTRODUCTION

ABOUT 455, DURING THE PONTIFICATE of Pope St. Leo the Great, St. Valerian was the Bishop of Cimelium, the present day Cimiez. During the period of the Roman Empire, Cimelium was long the capital of the Province of the Maritime Alps. Today, Cimiez is a hill within the city of Nice; then it was the important city and Nice was but a port town a little over a mile away. Cimiez had a Roman amphitheatre for about 6,500 spectators. Its remains can still be seen. The city was made illustrious by the death about 258 of the martyr Pontius in the persecution of the Emperor Valerian. Nice was a bishopric in 314; we do not know when Cimiez became an episcopal see. Pope Leo united the two sees, perhaps in 451. St. Hilary (Pope, 461-468) separated them, and shortly later again united them.[1]

Very little of the life of St. Valerian is known with certainty. No clue to the date of his birth exists. It is quite probable that in his youth he was a monk of the monastery of Lerins[2] which supplied so many bishops to the Church of southeast Gaul. His *Letter to the Monks*[3] shows a cordial and sympathetic understanding of the monastic life which would be natural in one who had lived it.

The name of Valerian appears[4] among the bishops of southeast Gaul who assembled at the Councils of Riez in

1 *DACL* 12 1er, cols. 1170-1172, *s.v.* Nice-Cimiez; *Catholic Encyclopedia* 11 48, *s.v.* Nice.
2 Cf. *PL* 52.762.
3 Below, pp. 437-440.
4 *PL* 54.884 (*Ep.* 66), 966, 969 (*Ep.* 99), 985 (*Ep.* 102).

439, of Vaison in 442 under St. Hilary, Bishop of Arles, and at Arles under St. Hilary's successor Ravennius in about 455.[5]

Hence, it is clear that the milieu of those councils formed that of Valerian's life. In the first half of the fifth century, largely as a result of the struggles with the Arians and the migrations of nations, the Church in Gaul was in great disorganization, and a strengthening of the ties between its bishops and Rome was an obvious necessity. Arles was an extensive papal vicariate claiming rights over numerous other dioceses of southeast Gaul. A council of bishops assembled at Riez in Provence in 439 to deal with disciplinary matters, and prescribed that semi-annual synods be held in the metropolitan district, that of Arles.[6] In 442, another such council, presided over by St. Hilary, then Bishop of Arles, was held at Vaison, and dealt with doctrinal and disciplinary matters.[7]

Shortly after Pope Leo began his pontificate in 440, he determined to make use of the papal vicariate of Arles in an effort to set up a center for the Gallican episcopate in immediate union with Rome.[8] At first, he fell into temporary conflict with St. Hilary. Hilary had been making excessive use of his authority over the neighboring ecclesiastical provinces, and of metropolitan rights over the Province of Vienne. In 444, he deposed a certain Bishop Cheldonius, who hastened to Rome, successfully pleaded his case, and was reinstated by Pope Leo. The Pope saw fit to restrict the rights of St. Hilary, and deprived him of authority over the Province of Vienne.[9] After the death of St. Hilary, Valerian was among

5 G. Bardy, *DTC*, fasc. 144-145, col. 2521, *s.v.* Valérien; *PL* 52.760; *Dictionary of Christian Biography, Literature, Sects and Doctrines during the First Eight Centuries* (London 1887) 4 1102.

6 *Catholic Encyclopedia* 11 266d.

7 *Ibid.* 16 78b, *s.v.* Vaison.

8 *Ibid.* 9 155d, *s.v.* Leo the Great, Pope.

9 *Ep.* 10 (*PL* 54.634); *Catholic Encyclopedia* 7 349.

the Gallic bishops who approved the choice of Ravennius as his successor and who signed a petition to Pope Leo to restore all the former privileges of the See of Arles.[10] The Pope praised their zeal, but did not see fit to grant their request.[11] On this occasion, he also sent to these bishops a copy of his celebrated dogmatic letter on the Incarnation against Eutyches,[12] written in 449 to Flavian of Constantinople, in order to disseminate its contents among the bishops of Gaul.[13] In 451, the bishops replied that they received the Pope's letter as a symbol of the faith.[14] Bishop Valerian was one of the forty-three signers of this reply, and thus we learn of his loyal devotion to the Pope in matters of doctrine and discipline.

Duchesne thinks that the reception of this letter in 451 was the occasion when Pope Leo issued a rescript joining the two sees of Cimiez and Nice, which had hitherto been separate despite their proximity.[15]

Valerian is one of the bishops whom Pope Leo congratulated in 452 for their orthodoxy.[16] A little later, probably about 455, St. Valerian was one of the signers of the acts of a council held at Arles[17] to deal with a dispute about jurisdiction which arose between the monks of Lerins under Abbot Faustus and the neighboring bishops.

After this council we hear no more about him. Hence, his death is conjectured to have occurred about 460. An entry in a monastic martyrology for the ninth day before the Kalends of August reads: 'At Nice in Provence, the burial of Saint Valerian, Bishop and Confessor, who as a

10 *Ep.* 65 (*PL* 54.879-883).
11 *Ep.* 66 (*PL* 54.884-885).
12 Cf. above, pp. 283, 284.
13 *Ep.* 67 (*PL* 54.886-887).
14 *Ep.* 99 (*PL* 54.966-970).
15 Bardy, *loc. cit.*
16 *Ep.* 102 (*PL* 54.983-988).
17 Bardy, *loc. cit.*

monk of Lerins was elevated to the episcopacy, zealously strove to fulfill the office of a good pastor, was brought into the joy of the Lord, and deserved to hear the words: Well done, thou good and faithful servant.'[18] The cult of St. Valerian is an approved one, and his feast is still celebrated on July 23.[19]

The homilies of St. Valerian of Cimiez, like those of St. Peter Chrysologus, were delivered after the reading of a passage (*lectio*) from Scripture in a liturgical service, probably the Mass.[20] Although we can only guess the beginning and end of each of these passages, even this conjecture greatly helps us to understand the discourse. But, while St. Peter usually gave a running commentary on the entire passage or a goodly portion of it, St. Valerian generally selected one or two verses, and made them the point of departure for a sermon on the subject they suggested, as, for example, in Homily 6. Hence, if the distinction between sermons and homilies be strictly observed,[21] St. Valerian's discourses could be named sermons. Some of his discourses, such as Homilies 15, 16, and 17, seem to be not homilies upon a liturgical *lectio,* but sermons on some subject which the occasion demanded, such as 'The Excellence of Martyrdom.'

Homily 1 was long published among the works attributed with doubt to St. Augustine.[22] The true author was learned when Melchior Goldastus of Haiminsfeld found this discourse on an old manuscript of the Monastery of St. Gall, with the title *Liber S. Valeriani Cemeliensis,*

18 Quoted in *PL* 52.762.

19 *The Book of the Saints,* comp. Benedictine Monks of Ramsgate (London 1947) 589.

20 Cf. opening sentences of Homilies 2.1 and 6.3, below.

21 Cf. above, pp. 3, 4.

22 So printed in *PL* 40.1219-1222.

and published it with notes in Germany in 1601.[23] In 1612, James Sirmond, S.J., found nineteen other homilies and a *Letter to the Monks* in a codex of Corby. These works had a fluent style, a diction, and a content all so strikingly similar to Valerian's Homily 1 that he attributed them to Valerian also, even though the manuscript did not bear his name.[24] No one has yet found serious fault with this attribution. Sirmond first published the entire set of homilies and the *Letter* in Paris in 1612.

The homilies give explicit treatment chiefly and almost exclusively to matters of morals and asceticism. But matters of doctrine, like the necessity of good works as well as faith (2) and of help or grace from God for the performance of every good work (7,11), receive treatment in passing. St. Valerian forcefully condemns drunkenness, the source of unchastity, and avarice, the source of pride (6). Homily 6 is an interesting early treatise on the capital sins. He gives special praise to generosity toward the poor (7-9), to traveling along the straight and narrow path (1,2), and to martyrdom (15-18). His sermons reveal quite a little wild, coarse living in the private and public life of his contemporaries.

Some readers will perhaps find some of his homilies heavy, but others are light and beautiful, such as those on martyrdom. Still others, such as those on parasites (10) or on the termination of Lent (19), are interesting and even entertaining to a modern reader. One must be dull at heart if he listens to St. Valerian berating his contemporaries' follies and does not reflect that human nature is ever the same. He is always a sincere and forceful speaker, and he employs imagery and example well. If his voice

23 Cf. *PL* 52.682C, 686-688.
24 *PL* 52.688,699.

and delivery were at all good, he no doubt effectively held the interest of his audience.

His style is correct, sometimes elegant, and in general carefully worked out, as is shown by the fact that it can so easily be arranged in sense lines. Thus it reveals that he pursued the studies of the rhetoricians in his youth. The continual recurrence of chiasma, and of balanced sentences, arises from rhetorical training, not chance.

Shortly after Sirmond published his edition in 1612, someone delated them as teaching that we can of ourselves begin good actions, although we need God's grace to bring them to fulfillment. Sirmond successfully defended St. Valerian against this charge of Semi-Pelagianism before the members of the Holy Office in Rome, which permitted continuance of their publication. However, someone apparently renewed the charge, for in 1633 T. Raynaud, S.J., published a lengthy refutation against a certain Nicholas Chicon.[25] The charge was based on isolated statements, especially in Homily 11, which apart from their context can be understood in a Semi-Pelagic sense. Even if St. Valerian's doctrine were proved to contain Semi-Pelagianism, he would be materially rather than formally heretical, since the condemnation of Semi-Pelagianism did not occur until the Council of Orange in 529, about seventy years after St. Valerian's death. But such proof is wanting. In fact, his homilies are an arsenal of ammunition against both Pelagianism and Semi-Pelagianism. Homilies 7 and 11, in particular, are abundantly full of the doctrine that all our good works must be ascribed to God.

The charge has been renewed in modern times. In 1947, De Labriolle stated, without footnote or discussion, that St.

25 *PL* 52.681-684, 686, 758-836.

Valerian's homilies are 'strongly tainted with Semi-Pelagianism.'[26] Far nearer the truth, it seems to us, is the opinion of G. Bardy that, in view of St. Valerian's frequent recognition of our need of God's help for the performance of good deeds, it is an excess to make too much of the isolated statements which can be given a heretical meaning out of their context.[27]

It is a misfortune that no translation of St. Valerian's works has hitherto been published. Sincere and elevating, they deserve to be better known. At present, there is no critical text. The best printings seem to be those of Margarino de La Bigne in the *Maxima Bibliotheca Patrum* (Lyons 1677) and of James Sirmond, as reprinted at Augsburg in 1758 The present translation is based chiefly on the Sirmond text. The handiest text is that in Migne, *PL* 52.691-758.

---

26 P. de Labriolle, *Histoire de la litterature latine chrétienne,* ed. 3e, rev. G. Bardy (Paris 1947) 2 654.

27 *DTC,* fasc. 144-145, col. 2522. For further discussion, cf. Homily 11 and notes.

## HOMILY 1

### *Discipline*

(On Prov. 3.11,12)

(1) Many persons opposed to sound doctrine find fault with justice. They regard disciplinary control as haughtiness, and attribute a just punishment to an overbearing nature. However, there is no haughtiness unless something unjust is ordered; and there is no overbearance except in the one who spurns discipline. Discipline, therefore,[1] is a teacher of religion and of true piety; she does not threaten in order to inflict pain, or chastize in order to work injury.

In fact, when discipline is angered she corrects the habits of men, and when she is aroused she keeps them under control, as Solomon tells us: 'My son, do not remove yourself from the correction[2] of the Lord, and do not faint when thou art chastised by Him. For whom the Lord loveth, He chastiseth; and He scourges every son whom He receives.'[3] Indeed, there is nothing which correction fails to remedy or save. If anyone is wise enough to accept the correction, he neither loses the pleasantness of friendship [with his corrector], nor runs the risk of condemnation.

---

1 Reading *igitur*, with Sirmond, not *initur*.

2 The Latin word is *disciplina*, which St. Valerian took from various passages of Scripture. In his homilies, as in the Scriptures, the word has various shades of meaning according to context, such as: discipline, control, correction, training with moulds, orderly conduct, loyalty or obedience to the law of God, conduct according to that law. Cf. Souter, *s.v.*

3 Cf. Prov. 3.11,12, which probably was part of the *lectio* which preceded the homily.

No one ought to deem disciplinary control unreasonable. It is under control, as he clearly sees, that all the elements in Almighty God's great plan hold together, once He has arranged them in heaven and on earth by His creative word. In the very beginning of His creative activity God established nothing sooner than control. When by His wisdom He raised up the sky, and prepared the earth, and hemmed in the seas, and set both the circling sun and the disc-like moon in their own places and times, He set everything under this control. If all the elements did not lie beneath established laws, would they not all be darksome, disarranged, and erratic? Does the sun run its course free from control? Without wearying, it completes its appointed journey every day, yet every morning it comes back ready for duty again, and daily presents itself in the eastern heavens in its readiness to illumine all the corners of the earth.

So vast is the system of control that even the constellations run their courses, with all those recurring changes of their unwearying journey, inside the confines of periods set by law. Consequently, the moon does not escape the losses caused by her waning, nor does the sun's daily flame die down. Or is it without control that the waves of the great ocean are shut in by the low-lying beaches? Or that the water, though frequently stirred by the winds till it overtops the shore, is yet contained in its own basin? Clearly, nature, having no intelligence of her own, would be throwing everything into the greatest confusion, were not the system of control governing the world.

(2) We have mentioned these matters for a definite purpose: that you may learn to keep the Gospel precepts and obey the divine commandments. When a man sees that even the elements observe the sacred laws of their discipline established by God's holy will, it is quite easy for him to understand what is befitting a rational nature, made according

to God's image. Listen to the Prophet who tells us: 'Serve ye the Lord with fear: and rejoice unto Him with trembling. Embrace discipline, lest at any time the Lord be angry, and you perish from the just way.'[4] In all lawsuits fear rightly submits to disciplinary law. The man who in view of this very fact knows how to guard against the threatening misfortunes of dangers, or the wrath of judges, has acquired the power of maintaining his safety.

If disciplinary law did not keep the explosive rage of men in check through their fear of punishment, what would be chaste before an adulterer? What would be safe before a thief? What inaccessible to a robber? Who would not be deeply afraid at the caves at the seaside, or the recesses of the forest? What is there which men would not appropriate in their rash presumption?

Clearly, unless some orderly way of living had been established, our nature would never put a limit upon sinning. There is nothing which gluttony would fail to urge, if control should give way to it. There is nothing which lust would fail to destroy, if through your love of vice your self-restraint should leave you. There is nothing which your heart, naturally covetous to get and to keep, would leave unappropriated if discipline should cease to condemn the vice of avarice.

All vices lie prostrate beneath the fear of discipline. Why, there is not a man on earth whose faith would have to blush over his deeds, if he would only look to God's coming judgment, and think of the account he must render there. Nor is there any one against whom the avenging fires will flare if, through regard for discipline, you will now meditate virtuous deeds, and cast out of your heart those that are shameful. In a case[5] where for the sake of discipline a thief receives punishment to make up for the commission of the crime with

4 Ps. 2.11,12.
5 Reading *Multi ibi nomen crudelitatis ..., ubi ...,* from *PL* 40.1220A.

which he is charged, many men hurl the charge of cruelty, even though the sentence of the judge is in accordance with just laws, and extends help to men not only of the present but also of the future.

(3) Who, therefore, would not with reason think that he may as well sin freely, if no judge were prescribing disciplinary measures for shameless, wicked deeds? Let us recall what the law states: 'Thou shalt not kill. Thou shalt not commit adultery. Thou shalt not steal. Thou shalt not bear false witness.'[6] These commandments are the disciplinary controls which the Law exercises; even the severity[7] of a condemnation in the courts of the world conforms itself to these when it attacks base deeds and retrenches crimes. For, Scripture adds: 'A judge is appointed as the avenger not of the good work, but of the evil.'[8] Consequently, the Law even demands a punishment like in kind when it states: 'Eye for eye, tooth for tooth.'[9] But we can easily avoid that severity inflicted under the Old Law, if we only think of the flames of the judgment which is to come.

The Apostle Paul teaches that the punishments of the civil court can be completely avoided. He states: 'If you wish, then, not to fear the authority, do what is good.'[10] These words should not be taken lightly. While the Apostle's teaching is treating explicitly of these earthly powers, it is insinuating to our understanding the function of a heavenly court. Surely, when he teaches that we must observe civil laws, he is necessarily warning us to have a care for the future. 'If you wish,' he says, 'not to fear the authority, do what is good.' This is tantamount to saying: 'You desire to have no fear of a future condemnation?' Then, 'Decline from evil

6 Exod. 20.13-16.
7 Reading *districtio,* with Sirmond and LaBigne.
8 Rom. 13.3.
9 Lev. 24.20.
10 Rom. 13.3.

and do good.'[11] Here his command is expressed in a formula which is not dealing with the laws of the world. Therefore, we ought to take heed of the first sentence of his admonition, and to win our victory in such a manner that we also ward off a condemnation to death in the future life. For, there are some men whom the temporary punishment of this world does fail to overtake, but the insatiable pain of everlasting torment pursues them forever.

So, let no one think that a man has really escaped the charge of murder if he has gained his acquittal from some civil court which was corrupted. Neither should anyone think that his offence of adultery has been fully overlooked if he got arrested, indeed, but then went free again through some easy-going custom of pardoning. Let no one judge that the penalties due by law to a culprit have been omitted merely because he sees his right hand still healthy after perjury. Dead men have their sins still clinging to them, unless before their demise they purged them away through the intercession of their tears before God. Hell, armed with due punishments, awaits its prisoner.

The authority of a civil sentence pertains more to the disorder of the present life, but not to the cleansing of the sin. Therefore, we ought above all to ponder chiefly those punishments in which the man lives with uninterrupted pain, where torments never fail to afflict his body and the arms of the torturer never weary. We can easily avoid all these afflictions if we hold fast to the reins of discipline, as the Apostle reminds us: 'Dost thou wish not to fear the authority? Do what is good, and thou wilt have praise from it.'[12]

(4) What man, if he is wise, will not joyfully turn his attention to these benefits of discipline? Through them he can not only escape the punishment of his sins, but also gain the

11 Ps. 36.27.
12 Rom. 13.3.

reward of being praised. Listen to the words of the Prophet: 'Embrace discipline, lest at any time the Lord be angry, and you perish from the just way.'[13] In this passage, I think, the sense pertains to those whom discipline has not yet reached. They are still tarrying in the byways, held fast by the old error of paganism. The very fact that they are warned to embrace discipline shows that they have never lived under the Law.

Then the psalm goes on to say: 'lest at any time the Lord be angry, and you perish from the just way.' Now, if the Prophet deems those men guilty whom discipline has never reached, what should we think of those whom she has abandoned? Discerning between the acts of these two classes of men, the Prophet authoritatively regards the fault of never having come to discipline as one less serious than that of having rejected her law. Notice his words: 'He that rejecteth instruction, despiseth his own soul.'[14] The case truly is just what he says. For, the man who has spurned the warnings of discipline in order to occupy himself with the Devil's business is indeed the foe of his own soul.

(5) Some complain that discipline is composed of laws that are quite hard. Let some men—those poor wretches whom the Devil, the author of death, is enticing to every crime—speak thus if they want to. They are those who have an insatiable gluttony possessing their souls; they lie under the sway of drunkeness; they have base lust holding them as its captives, and an unbearable pride which never leaves them.

But, there are other men who are striving to keep faithful to honorable continence, and to practice humility and piety. They find the burden of discipline sweet, and the yoke of the Lord light. It is not heavy for anyone except those who have been or will be lost.

---

13 Ps. 2.12.
14 Prov. 15.32.

I blush to explain why—to the shame of human negligence—discipline counts so little among some men, although we see that its governing control does prevail among the mute animals. Why, horses with their docile spirit should teach us how to observe the orderly arrangements of discipline. Led in a circle, they adapt their limbs to their winding steps; controlled by only one rein, they consent to be allowed to run free in precisely such a way that it is under a certain control of law that they run for a time and halt for a time. This is how nature takes creatures diverse in number and unites them through their obedience to discipline.

Observe, too, how the strong-bodied oxen are hitched to a wagon. They prepare their spirits for control to such an extent that, though naturally wild, they submit their necks to a light yoke. This is the way in which even the beasts, born wild as they are, submit to the controls of discipline.

Consequently, I am often astonished at the conduct of man. He is endowed with wisdom and prudence, yet at whim he lightly rejects the precepts of discipline. How different is the conduct which we see in the beasts! They avoid vices, carry out commands, submit to control, and mould their spirits to perfect obedience. As a result, when need arises, they run against armed legions, and charge head downward against the javelins of the foe.

In this matter, too, listen to the Prophet: 'The ox knoweth his owner, and the ass his master's crib, but Israel hath not known me.'[15] I fear to speak further, lest that passage may be upbraiding our own negligence. For, truly, the man who is not aware of the obligation flowing from his condition of creaturehood simply does not know God.

(6) I shall explain how the Lord can be found and known, if only a man desires to see. If you desire to see God, seek out the beggar, receive the pilgrim, visit the sick, hasten

15 Isa. 1.3.

to the prison. If you desire to see God, break the bonds of captivity, cut the knots of iniquity. Listen to Christ Himself speaking on this subject: 'I was hungry and you gave me to eat; I was thirsty and you gave me to drink; I was a stranger and you took me in; naked and you covered me; sick and you visited me; I was in prison and you came to me.'[16] So I, too, advise you: Do not despise the naked, or withdraw the helping hand from the blind, or scorn the man clothed in rags. In precisely such clothing was the Lord found when the Magi first sought Him.

Since we have mentioned the discipline under which the Christian faith flourishes, we must remind you of all the trappings of life. This will help each one to realize that he will gain little from the mere reputation of having been converted to a good life if he does not, in spite of the world, have a true love of discipline.

Therefore, if a man desires to follow Christ, let him first of all receive the clothing of his heart no less than of his body. Every life by which one lives out the religion he professes ought to be adorned with a reputation for complete blamelessness, in order that the crown of virtue may not smite with a damaging embarrassment him for whom it is in waiting.

May health of the body give him strength in his life, and may an unblemished faith lend protection to this health. In this way may this faith, through lasting benefits of body and soul, bring this unsullied man to reign with Christ.

(7) But the proof of our conversion lies in this one fact, that we are good men. Therefore, everyone who is striving to pursue goodness ought also to endeavor above all to have men regard him as good. Even if a man keeps his body pure and unspotted, but his deeds bring a blush to his face, he carries a tattered life to God. I grant, of course, that conscience alone can suffice to make our acts good. But, is it

16 Matt. 25.35,36.

not something better still for you also to have a good reputation with the man who often sulks about your door with groundless suspicions?

Men in general are naturally prone to judge ill of good persons. But you, who cherish good report among men, strive hard to gain the benefit of a reputation for complete moral righteousness.

Let our lives be exemplary enough to be known to all men. Let our complete righteousness of life do a service to religion, and our modesty to humility. If a man is eager to preserve his integrity, above all let him also ward off even the report of insinuated sin. Never to have admitted evil acts into one's life is indeed something great, something glorious, something for all men to shout up to the very sky. But, never even to have been subject to false suspicions is something greater still.

For, how much will sobriety profit you, if you practice the vices characteristic of a drunken man? Who will not think that you yourself are drunk, if in the midst of flowing wine cups you imitate the weavings of the dancers? Who will think that you are chaste, if he observes you taking part in a play about harlots, and uttering foul language or sounding off smutty words in the language of actors? Indeed, I do praise the fact that your conscience approves your chastity, but I detest your conversation characteristic of a harlot.

(8) At this point, someone may object: 'A clear conscience is enough for me.' True, it is enough for you as an individual, with respect to your own personal innocence. But you ought to take care lest someone else sin as a result of your easy-going ways, in such a manner that his sin falls back upon yourself. Scripture warns you about this: 'Woe to the man through whom scandal comes.'[17] You may clothe your body in precious silk, and cover your limbs with white fleece; even

17 Matt. 18.7.

so, you will not pass the day unsullied if you handle the doors of a blazing furnace.

Wherefore, may discipline be the companion of your life in your every deed. If you are eager to please Christ, strive that your trustworthiness may make your profession more acceptable, and that your reputation may recommend it. Also, may patience, the companion of humility, precede you, and may modesty, the teacher of complete uprightness, assist you. May greediness flee from you, and drunkenness blush at your approach. May lust grieve over its own acts, and pride depart in confusion. Whoever, therefore, is eager to know God will be able to find our Christ through this orderly conduct which springs from discipline.

Dearly beloved, many matters still remain which this theme of discipline has been prompting me to explain. But, as I proceeded, I decided to postpone them, lest my sermon grow too long and tedious. Yet, I do not want to appear to have withdrawn anything of moment from my homily. So, on a later occasion I shall strive to discourse on the characteristics which religious deeds ought to have.

## HOMILY 2

### *The Narrow Way*

(On Matt. 7.13,14)

(1) Dearly Beloved: As you have just heard the Evangelist[1] state, our Saviour has set up our Christian way of

1 Probably, in the *lectio* or passage read in the Mass before the homily or sermon. This homily seems to have been preached about Matt. 7.13,14, or even about a longer passage from which these two verses were selected for explanation.

life by establishing many, even innumerable, disciplinary precepts. In different ways has He pointed out the road of salvation to His people who are being regenerated. He desired nothing to remain hidden which might have a bearing on a soul's salvation or its damnation. He did not want a soul, bought for so great a price, to be deceived through the vice of ignorance and to be subject to diabolical superstitions.

But, here is something that is worse. Medicine brings little benefit to those who will soon die. Similarly, the salutary way of salvation seems hard because the way leading to death is easier to travel. As Scripture tells us: 'How wide and broad is the way that leads to death, and many there are who enter that way. How narrow and close the way that leads to life, and few there are who find it.'[2] Perhaps some wonder why the Evangelist calls the way of death wide and easy to travel, since the journey through life is hard at every step. But, who ever found the descent to a lower level hard? A man, overcome by the load of his own baggage, finds himself pulled down that slope by his own weight. Many obstacles obstruct the way to salvation, desirable as it is.

On the way death tries to work its harm especially against those whose lives are dominated by vanity and cruelty. Other factors, too, work together to prevent a man from coming to eternal life: dissensions, rivalries, fights, quarrels, sacrileges, sins of adultery, murders, fraternal hatred, parricidal counsels, and perjury armed with lies. These vices not merely retard a man's ascent; they also cast him into the depths of hell. When, then, can any man easily reach heaven, if such vices retard him?

'Narrow and close is the way that leads to life.' This is

2 Matt. 7.13,14.

that road, dearly beloved, along which the just travel, and the holy and unstained souls progress. Along it lies the journey of those who possess humility, complete righteousness of life, and holiness, and then follow our Christ without giving in to fatigue.

(2) So we ought to select this approach as our road, and improve it. For it is passable, even though difficult. It even becomes easy to travel for those who resolve firmly, if only they do not let vanity or a deceitful attraction of this world hold them back.

The man who undertakes a journey up a steep mountain ought to be free, and unencumbered by any baggage. As we often see, a man who carries too big a pack staggers with uncertain steps. Just so, a soul preoccupied with sinful pursuits is sure to experience many a fall. Consequently, one trying to climb the steep heights ought to lighten his person[3] burdened with worldly desires; otherwise, the danger of death will paralyze his effort, or despair over his labor will grow too intense.

What man of sense will drive his pack animal bearing a huge load along a narrow path, where the poor beast has a towering mountain pressing it on one side and a sheer cliff threatening it on the other? But, if his rashness has brought him to such a place, he must either turn back or go on. Similar is the case of the man who has entered the way of religious living. He who desires his soul to arrive at heavenly glory must continually prune away whatever seems base or foul. With good reason does Christ say: 'Abandon your possessions and follow me.'[4] Dearly beloved, those possessions, increased through our worldly deeds, are our

---

3 *corpus;* St. Valerian often uses this word where he means person, man. In dialects and colloquialism, the English word body is also used to denote person, man. Also, cf. Souter, *s.v. corpus.*

4 Cf. Matt. 19.21.

misfortunes. While devoting too much attention to them, many men have lost the goods of heaven.

(3) If, then, you wish the gate of heaven to open for you, you must give up all your goods. If you have employed any of them negligently or improperly to the detriment of your spiritual life, you must devote them to penance. Only with great difficulty will you arrive at those blessings which the Lord has prepared for those who believe in Him, unless you lighten your heart of its burdening vices, and bring all your faults of injustice within the control of religious discipline.

Fruitlessly do you fancy yourself to be keeping to the paths of the hard journey along the rough road, if you are impeding your soul through error. Imagine, if you will, two men who are striving for the heights. One of them is making his way while laden with a heavy burden; the other proceeds with only a light staff on which he leans. You will soon see who will reach the top with greater ease.

Look first at him who is heavily laden. You will observe that where he is climbing his steps often slip suddenly backwards, and that his knees are so bent that you might think he is returning. At one moment he seems to be coming down; at another, to be falling. Minute by minute he is so swayed by the whole weight of his body from side to side on his winding path that the very need of his keeping himself in motion seems to arise more from despair than from desire to climb.

Now look at him who carries no load on his back. You observe how freely he proceeds, how easy it is for him to maneuver even those rocky heights where plants cannot grow, and to cling upon cliffs where the footing is insecure. At one moment by his easy mounting he is on top of a ridge;

at another he moves with eager spirit through the ravines.[5] Consequently, he shows that even rugged spots are not blocked for unencumbered men,[6] and that journeys, even though very steep, are not too difficult for anybody, if only he will unburden his mind of excessive loads.

The case is similar, dearly beloved, with those whom sinful habits burden, and those who have shaken off their old faults and have their tears of repentance to commend them. The man who desires to reach the judgment free from anxiety must cast off everything burdensome. He who wants to possess heaven must despise the goods of the earth.

(4) Truly, dearly beloved, in order more easily to surmount the difficulties of that steep road, we must display the zeal which springs from sincerity of purpose. If an unfortunate conversation has served to stir up quarrels, or a tongue full of poison for the injury of another has brought reproach on one's household, these vices should be repressed. It is impossible to estimate how much the vices which spring from uncontrolled language check one's progress on the road to life. While such language wags its tongue with too much talking, it excites against itself all the enmity which springs from idle gossip. Our Lord mentions that an account will have to be given for idle conversations.[7] If one cannot carry even light faults to the judgment without danger to his soul, consider what will happen to him who has cause for serious blame standing against him.

'Narrow and close is the way that leads to life.' Therefore, if anyone is wise, let him rid himself right away of the encumbrances of this world, and let him make his journey easier by leading a disciplined life. Let him remove by repentance whatever blemishes he has incurred through negli-

---

5 Reading *demersa,* not *diversa.*
6 *corporibus.*
7 Matt. 12.36.

gence. If worldly glory has put any burdens on his back, let him not think them worth carrying with him. For, such burdens are by nature heavy, and they grow heavier still through the difficulty of the journey.

Perhaps in this world the exigencies of this narrow and hard way beget despair in some rather delicate souls. Reason holds this, and truly, too: an inexperienced soul feels intense fear before dire hardships. But what are we to do, since no gate to virtue opens up before delicate soldiers? What fruit would your effort be producing if you were but running over a level course? Or, when would you have satisfaction over your arrival at an appointed place, if you were reaching it without any hurt to your body? What lover of ease ever set up a trophy of victory? Or, who ever gained a victory by sleeping while the enemy's legions were surrounding him on every side?

A crown for virtues which has not been gained through effort merits little praise. The man who gets a crown like this does indeed get his palm, but he does not have glory. When did an ease-loving farmer fill his barns? Who ever gathered in his harvest in the proper season if he did not first prepare the hard earth by many a furrow? The account taken of great virtues[8] is this: the more a man works, the greater reward does he get.

(5) Now let us turn our attention to the nature of that way of death which the Evangelist calls wide and broad and full of traffic. Innumerable deaths occur on it, yet new lawbreakers are ever turning into it. It is just the kind of road which soon attracts men likely to die. It seems to be so easy to travel to those who have cast off all regard for disciplinary law. But, if we compare this route to that humble and narrow one, we see that nothing brings more danger

8 Reading *magnarum,* with Sirmond.

to a traveler than these wide roads, because, where horses are given free rein, they run without control. Thus it comes about that the gate of death receives many men, for a man arrives more easily when he travels without any check.

Hear the Lord's words: 'Take up your cross and follow me.'[9] Clearly, a man does not fear the easy approach to that hard road. Why should the difficulty disturb him when another is extending him a helping hand? Anyone who is guided through difficulties at the side of another praises the necessity which made him undertake the trip because that companion shares its labors. That is why anyone who hastens to the heights in company with the Lord can without any doubt arrive at the promised rewards of his kingdom.

But first, as we mentioned before, dearly beloved, we must cast off whatever burden the unfortunate error of worldiness has placed on our human bodies. Otherwise, this error, by casting a burden of sins in our way, will not let us arrive at those days of remuneration. Or, if we do arrive, it will not let us enter the heavenly gates.

(6) But, you object: 'We simply cannot arrive. This is urged by certain tests. For we see that often many men—as any door could witness—depart without having greeted the master of the house.' They have been rendered odious by their wickedness, or malice, or faithlessness, or lust, or pride. Let everyone of you contemplate that sin of diabolical presumption. Then you will understand how much pride burdens a man who wishes to scale the heights, or in what condition that man finds himself who lets a spirit of pride

9 Matt. 16.24.

rule his life. Pay heed to the Lord's words: 'God gives grace to the humble, but resists the proud.'[10]

The vice of avarice is hardly less a hindrance to those who must undertake this climb. While it allures the rich man to take too much pleasure in his excessive store of money, it excludes him from the kingdom of heaven. As the Lord says: 'Amen I say to you that it is with difficulty that a rich man will enter into the kingdom of heaven.'[11] Drunkenness, too, accessory to so many sins of lust, imposes a heavy burden on human bodies. While it makes acts of impurity easy, it excludes the unhappy man from his share in the heavenly kingdom.

Another vice which blocks the sequestered regions of the narrow way is cruelty accompanied by impiety. While it has remained faithful to the bloody laws of Mars,[12] it has closed the way to heavenly glory. The Apostle has stated: 'Neither thieves, nor the covetous, nor drunkards, nor the evil tongued, nor the greedy will possess the kingdom of God.'[13]

Therefore, we must struggle against these vices we have mentioned in order to arrive at the abode of life. On our journey we must especially practice piety, mercy, humility, complete righteousness of life, purity, sobriety, peace, faith, and charity. You will not arrive at the place of the promised inheritance, unless in your pursuit of life you first strip your body of the vices which burden it.

---

10 Cf. James 4.6.
11 Matt. 19.23.
12 Following the reading *Martis institit.*
13 1 Cor. 6.10.

## HOMILY 3

### *The Narrow Way*[1]

### (On Matt. 7.13,14)

(1) Every man who is concerned to see God and attain to the heavenly kingdom can easily understand two facts: the requirements of the hard and narrow way have a bearing on the sum total of our life; and the hope of our getting the glory of heaven lies in our effort. There is nothing which effort does not overcome, if only we do not let our courage decay to its opposite, as it all too easily does. It is abundantly clear that innumerable difficulties occur to the man who finds his delight in the errors of that broad way. Listen to the Evangelist's words: 'How wide and broad is the way that leads to destruction, and many there are who enter that way. How narrow and close is the way that leads to life, and few there are who find it.'

I have no doubt that some who are taking part in the warfare which wins heaven experience a feeling of despair. It arises from this, that the very entrance to the laborious journey of the celestial warfare is distressingly narrow. True, indeed, dearly beloved, for those who tend toward the heights, that journey is not merely laborious, but also difficult and more toilsome. On the other hand, those who are unwilling and lazy, and those who are busy but negligent[2] —they also certainly find that their need of effort grows greater even when they travel through level regions. Lofty destinations are indeed vexatiously hard to attain, but, with-

1 The true subject is: The Contrast between Willing and Reluctant Service to God.

2 I.e., negligent of what is truly worth while.

out doubt, travelers who refuse to despair do at length reach an open field.

Therefore, dearly beloved, willing service is necessary for every task in which human activity must be vigorously employed. If a man's inclinations deceive him in matters of the greatest necessity, there is no way to estimate how great their difficulty grows. If despair gains sway over him, he will never make even a good beginning of his journey up the difficult mountain. When can a man's body grow accustomed to toil unless his willingness goes along with the toiler? Look about you and see how quickly the man who mounts a horse in fear jumps off again to the ground, or what anguish that man suffers who is reluctantly putting out to sea in order to cross it.

(2) The religion named Christian, to which we have been called, has undertaken service which springs from a free will. If anyone takes up this pattern of life unwillingly, he adds a burden upon a burden, and upon his body just stripped of an ancient law he places the load of a life which brings despair. That is why the gate of death receives many men, for the difficulty of living always looms big to those soon to die. Consequently, if a man is coming to the way of freedom, he must prune away any remnant of infidelity that may be in him and store up heavenly merit by giving a willing service to God. Otherwise, the man who is obligated to God for such great benefits may find himself ungrateful even in regard to small duties. The negligent and inexperienced will perhaps judge the service due to God burdensome because there can never be a period of vacation from this service. God has not merely called every man to freedom; He has also given him the highest dignity of His creatures. But the man who gives a reluctant service brings a state of slavery upon himself. For, if you should make

your service a willing one, you would find yourself to be not God's servant, but His son. That is what the Prophet tells us by the Lord's own words: 'I will be a Father to you, and you shall be my sons and daughters, says the Lord Almighty.'[3]

(3) Dearly beloved, the service which men in our condition ought to give is such as this. We should always praise God our Lord in His works, and with unfailing voice exalt Him in the splendor of his majesty. What else than this does He, in the power of His invisible, incomprehensible, and inconceivable glory, want from men? Or, in what is bodily service needful to Him who receives homage from the choir of the angels?

That, indeed, is an intolerable slavery which is inflicted on us by the haughty domination of the tyrant, that is, the Devil; it is an injury of captivity unjustly inflicted. But, to offer willing service to a superior person is not slavery; it is deferential respect.

Listen to the Prophet's voice: 'I will freely sacrifice thee, O Lord.'[4] Learn how different an inflicted servitude is from a voluntary one. A man who finds his own negligence accusing himself of suffering self-inflicted servitude can never pass a day without regret. A man who obeys his Lord because of some solemn promise and thus reluctantly gains grace—he has stored up an injury for himself, since the Prophet says: 'Cursed be he that doth the works of the Lord negligently.'[5] If each of you reflects upon the wonderful gift of the acquired liberty which our Christ has granted to His faithful people through the regeneration of the life-giving bath, and through the pouring out of the Holy Spirit, he understands that God should not be served languidly. Even

3 2 Cor. 6.18; cf. also. Jer. 31.9.

4 Ps. 53.8.

5 Jer. 48.10.

though we daily give God whatever honor or gift we can, we never pay Him all we owe.

For, when can a man pay all he owes, who so evidently has been redeemed by that free gift of the pain which another, as his representative, suffered in his place?—unless, perhaps, for the love of his Redeemer he receives a similar sentence of death or condemnation? Only some souls, the very brave, can do this. But, let us at least do the one thing we can—daily offer to our Christ sacrificial gifts of esteem. Thus, if the merits accruing from their virtues may commend others, at least those acts of devotion which spring from our willing service will prepare a place of favor for us.

(4) Above all, then, let us free our hearts from contact with evil, that we may be better able to nourish the fruits of justice. For, he who wishes to show full compliance with the commandments of heaven ought to renounce worldly deeds completely. Just as truly as a man never gives a good service if he gives it unwillingly, so neither does a man concerned with other things take really good care of the goods entrusted to him.

'I will freely sacrifice to thee.' Not without reason did the Prophet use this phrase to commend himself to God. He was aware that many give their service by compulsion, with reluctance in their hearts; and that they promise one thing with their mouths, but arrange something else in the depths of their hearts.

'I will freely sacrifice to thee.' Gifts, though small in themselves, become great from the giver's desire to please. But, those wrenched out by compulsion often consume their giver. Thus, a man who has unwillingly prepared a banquet is continually complaining about its cost.

'I will freely sacrifice to thee,' that is, by means of a gift willingly offered. That you may joyfully offer to your Creator, every day, little presents from your tongue, arrange the gift of that praise of Him in sweet-sounding words. Hasten, too, in a spirit of devotion to carry through the service deputed to you. Heed the Prophet's words. 'The free offerings of my mouth, make acceptable, O Lord.'[6]

(5) Therefore, when we assemble here in the church, dearly beloved, above all may faith, fortified by the help of truth, possess the inmost recesses of our hearts. For, God loves a man who is pure, unstained, not prone to lie or given to perjury, not dissembling, not wavering. Here are the indications of perfect lightness:[7] the love of sanctity, or devotion to discipline. This is the presenting of an unspotted victim in one's sacrifices: faithfully to have served the Lord with one's whole soul.

Furthermore, this is a characteristic of our service, that you should always remember the benefits bestowed by our Christ, and that you should attribute to the Author of your Christian liberty whatever progress you make in the practice of your religious faith.

May you, in the midst of your activities, observe the precepts of justice, and serve the one God while honoring the Trinity. May you believe in one faith, one baptism, and may you praise the one refulgent nature of the Father, Son, and Holy Spirit. May you believe that no one of these Persons excels the others or rules by a will divergent from Theirs, but rather that the Father, and the Son, and the Holy Spirit are the possessors of one power, one strength.

In this way will you, as one destined to live forever, overcome the difficulties of the hard and narrow way. And if you make your way through these stages of disciplinary training, and arrange the periods of your life according to this

6 Ps. 118.108.

7 I.e., that we may ascend to God.

pattern of living, you will without any doubt receive in heaven those rewards which have been promised for righteous efforts.

## HOMILY 4

### *Unkept Vows*

(On Ps. 60.9)

(1) Dearly beloved, if a man under obligation for benefits received were faithful to his promise, and if by satisfactory arrangements he showed fidelity to his proclaimed zeal to keep his pledge, never again would anyone feel embarrassment through the disagreeable claiming of a debt. And if the execution soon followed the desire to fulfill a promised obligation, no one would have occasion to call another to task. But, sometimes, the wounded loyalty of friendship does lie prostrate and panting. This comes about because a man sometimes has to complain about delay in repayment, or reprobate his debtor's infidelity. A promised repayment left unfulfilled is a declaration of enmity. It is obviously a quarrelsome matter if one party pays back with reluctance, or the other presses his demand when exasperated by delay.

You have heard the Prophet's words: 'So will I sing a song to thy name, O God, for ever and ever: that I may pay my vows from day to day.' Dearly beloved, the benefits of friendship gain something infinite if a debtor anticipates his creditor by repayment before the date it comes due. Whoever spontaneously repays borrowed money stores it up for himself. For, if he quickly complies with the money-lender's request, in time of need he will get his own plea for anything.

But the man proved unfaithful finds the loaner's door ever shut. Let him knock and beg as often as he pleases; he goes away sad and empty-handed amid reproaches. If therefore, someone stirs up hatred against himself by lying to a man, how much more does he do this if he acts deceitfully to God, and tries to fool the Lord of heavenly majesty by his smooth promise?

(2) We have proposed these considerations, dearly beloved, because, with dangers pressing, some men are prone to make vows in such a way that, when the appointed time comes, they forget they have promised anything to the Lord. This one offers his own self[1] as a victim. That one promises tears of repentance, over and over again. Another is bound by a vow through his love of the churches; still another, by one in honor of the saints. But, it is just as easy to refuse to keep those vows as to make them for those whose intention to fulfill them lasts just as long as their headache. Thus, such a person gradually grows accustomed to take them back after he has begun to lose his fear of death.

And then we wonder why God is sometimes so slow to heed our welling tears, and does not hear the words which spring from our just pains! We wonder why the anxious farmer's care to till his fields does not turn out more fortunate than usual, why multiplied heads of grain do not spring from the fertile sod, why the swollen olives do not bring in their precious gains, why the bountiful harvest of the vineyard yields but little in the full presses!

Let no one blame the earth for this, or the inclemency of the weather; a withered hand does not gather anything, or if it does, it soon loses it. The barns of a shiftless farmer are always empty and idle. From similar reason [of negligence], too, arises the fact that sometimes the art of medi-

1 *Corporis sui*: literally, the victim of his body. Cf. Homily 2 n. 3.

cine does not find the patients it is to heal. It is hard for a physician to manipulate his hand with full fidelity, if the empty promise of the sick man has often left him defrauded of his fee.

(3) See, this man sighs aloud because his son is sick. With his prayers he raps at the doors of the saints day and night. This woman grieving over her husband's illness, or that husband over his wife's, beats a breast resounding to its depths. By her tearful prayers she begs the aid of heavenly pity, and offers herself and her gift to God. But, when the prayers have been granted, we sometimes see that all those promises are suddenly forgotten. One would think that these wretched persons drank a cup of oblivion rather than one of salvation.

Obviously, a happy outcome does not always follow such deceitful vows. When does he who does not pay what he owes receive a beneficial gift? He who by empty words has often mocked the patience of his judge must at some time pay the penalty of his faithlessness. That is why man's prayers fade out upon God's unheeding ears, and tears fail to obtain their request. Those who allure God by promises often vain can scarcely hope to be heard.

(4) Happy are those who have the faithful fulfillment of an agreement as a trait of character, and no tendency to lie. It is clearly better not to promise than to withhold what was pledged. By not promising a man may be branded as stingy, but he is not burdened with the sin of guileful circumvention.

Consult the Acts of the Apostles. You will find that to destroy credence in one's promises conduces to the loss of one's life. For, we read how Ananias and his wife Sapphira, after selling their estate, brought to the Apostles a part of the price for distribution, and kept a part hidden at home.

St. Peter said to them: 'Ananias, wickedness has filled thy heart, that thou shouldst lie to the Holy Spirit, while the estate was in thy control. Thou hast not lied to men, but to God.'[2] Thus, while they were carrying on this deceit, they bought death. While indulging their covetousness, they lost eternal gifts.

See how the Prophet says: 'I will pay my vows to the Lord, in the courts of the house of the Lord.'[3] He who has clearly promised something to the Lord is bound beyond any doubt by a legitimate agreement of debt. He who states that he is going to restore is by that very fact acknowledging a debt. For, your estate is in your possession just so long as it has not been mortgaged to someone else by the effect of a signed deed. Thus, in every agreement, whether friendship prompted it or intention settled it, repayment should not be delayed.

The charm of a proferred gift is lost when the receiver must ask for it over and over again. The man who must reluctantly give what he promised really offered nothing by his promises. We read in the Book of Solomon: 'If thou hast made a vow to thy Lord, thou shalt not delay to pay it: because thy Lord, seeking, will require it from you. And the words which go through thy lips shall be imputed to thee for a sin, unless thou payest thy vow.'[4]

(5) Therefore, dearly beloved, I warn anyone who knows he has vowed a gift to the Lord to fulfill it promptly. If anyone is not certainly able to pay a vow, let him not make it. We are not now exaggerating faults of stinginess, as some may think. Rather, we are talking about fidelity to promises, which we see endangered in some men through the plague of their faithlessness.

---

2 Acts 5.3,4.
3 Ps. 115.18.
4 Deut. 23.21-23.

There are many—and this is something worse—who have held back the price of their freedom. They have brought to the Lord only part of the price, that is, a half-hearted loyalty of religious observance. Listen to the Prophet: 'Vow ye, and pay your presents to your God.'[5] 'Vow ye': by these words he counsels conversion. 'Pay ye': he asks again from them the debt of the holiness they promised.

However, little of religion belongs to the man who, as you see, makes the world his pursuit, and takes more interest in this life than in eternal glory. Then do you prove that you have not fraudulently held back from the Lord any part of your offering, when you cultivate justice in any of its various aspects, cherish integrity, and exemplify the holiness you have promised. But, the man who knows he has lied to the Lord ought to fear the fate of Ananias or his wife.

'Vow ye, and pay your presents to the Lord.' In this passage the Prophet is not tediously treating the subject of generosity, just because he is admonishing us with words suitable for that. Are we, indeed, to be content with unprofitable interpreters who want that sentence to indicate the attitude of one making a demand? Does God ask anything of you because He lacks it? He owns everything; what, then, does He lack?

Because you promise gold in your tribulations, or silver in your sorrows, does God need it for His use? Or does anyone offer precious stones or garments because God has want of them? He seeks gifts from you that you yourself may gleam because of your gold, be resplendent because of your silver, adorned because of your gems, clothed because of your silk. The Lord wants your gifts to result in the ordering of your own soul, which He sees spoiled by the vice of

5 Ps. 75.12.

pride, or wickedness, or avarice, or luxury. 'Vow ye, and pay your presents to the Lord.'

(6) But, perhaps you say: 'God does not need our gifts.' True, He does not need them. But He does require fruit which, because of His redeeming your soul, He ascribes to your acts of mercy. It is right that you bring your body before the altars as a victim uncorrupted and unspoiled, and those services of the voice which we owe to our Maker. But beyond that, this, too, is a sacrifice acceptable to the Lord—your pursuit of goodness and mercy, your cherishing the aspects of justice, your haste to please the Lord always with unblemished faith, your willingly clothing the naked, and feeding the needy, and redeeming the captives, your freeing the imprisoned while mindful of your own redemption.

To all this, perhaps, you reply: 'What shall I do for the poor man, and what am I to leave to my son?' Hear your answer from the Lord: 'He who loves son or daughter more than Me is not worthy of Me.'[6] You see, therefore, that nothing is to be preferred to God. Not even a son should be esteemed more than He. You ask: 'What am I to leave to my son?' Suppose that you have one son, and in your consternation your wife presents you with another. Does not your fatherly love commend each of them to you in one equal degree of inheritance? To make room for the new arrival, do you not pare down the stipulations of your will? We often see that in this way, once the number of heirs has increased, an inheritance apparently about to fall to one suffices for many.

Therefore, if someone has only one heir, let him imagine that Christ has been born to him; and let him so divide his wealth among two or three or more that our Christ does not go away disinherited. If, however, you are very

6 Matt. 10.37.

fortunate in the number of your sons, here is my advice. Admit your Redeemer to a share in your estate. So arrange the division of it that you imagine you have one less son, or that you congratulate yourself for acquiring another, and thus make room for Christ among your dear sons. Why should not those get on earth one allotment of the estate, who in heaven will get the same portion of the promised inheritance?

But, if anyone has deprived the needy and unfortunate of the necessities of life, he has denied an added share to the first-born and best among them all. Listen here to the words of Scripture: 'He that hath mercy on the poor, lendeth to the Lord.'[7]

(7) There are many who think the need of the unfortunate something to be mocked. Consequently, they deceive them by daily promises. This holds true of those vows which we mentioned above, those which become forgotten. What gratification is there in putting off a wretched man if abundant resources are at hand? When you see a man able to do an act of kindness, and putting it off with procrastinated urbanity, you know that only one thing has been lacking there, the good will to act. In regard to this, hear the Psalmist: 'So will I sing a psalm to thy name for ever and ever: that I may pay my vows from day to day.'[8] Did he say from year to year? No, he said from day to day. Therefore, we must labor every day, dearly beloved. A debt to God and a promised gift should not be deferred.

He who has paid his vows daily will owe nothing to his future Judge. Likewise, one who has been enriched by just labor and has offered the fruit of his good works to the Lord from day to day has no reason to put off the reckon-

7 Prov. 19.17.
8 Ps. 60.9.

ing up of his own account. See how Scripture states: 'Whatever you did to one of these least ones, you did it to me.'[9]

Therefore, whether someone has done good or evil, let him be aware that it has a relationship to the majesty of the Lord. Retribution for one or the other is sure to come. Consequently, we should devote ourselves to mercy and almsgiving, for this purpose, that, when the Lord of heaven and earth will come, He may not point out among other defects of our soul the nakedness of the poor, or obtrude upon our gaze the misfortunes of the wretched. Consequently, too, let no one despise the poorly clad, or berate the beggar with harsh words. Among all other offerings, this is a sacrificial gift pleasing to God, this is an array of salutary sacrifices, that you help the wretched in their need; and that, to avoid being branded with infidelity, when you come into possession of what you prayed for, you carry through the fulfillment of your promise.

## HOMILY 5

### *Insolence of the Tongue*

(On Eccli. 28.13-30)

(1) Dearly beloved, among all the vices which harass the life of man on earth, the Prophet bestows special castigation on insolence of the tongue. It is not unprofitable for him to do this. He was necessarily aware that sometimes poisons are concocted by the bitter zeal of the mouth, and hatreds stirred up by the excessive facility of the lips.

Truly indeed, dearly beloved, this is the case. For, a tongue naturally loquacious brings mortals no small diffi-

9 Matt. 25.40 (Douay-Rheims).

culty in living; for example, when it scatters things once well arranged, or casts confusion into agreements reached long ago.

When does a quarrel arise, if the tongue holds itself in check? Or, what place is there for enmity there, where poisonous words cease? For, this is always the business of a malicious tongue: to sow quarrels, stir up hatreds, bring about deaths. That is what Solomon states in this passage: 'The tongue has disquieted many who were at peace; it has destroyed cities and overthrown houses.'[1]

Those who deem nothing stronger than the sword, nothing more violent than poison, are clearly in error. Although those weapons have a peculiar natural effectiveness in producing deaths, they yet yield place in a strife of words. For, there is nothing harmful or malicious whose powers are not less effective if a tongue has been once stirred up and has moved itself into action. The vices of the human being are many, and grave enough, too. But they can accomplish little by their promptings and drives if they are not armed by others' crimes. Cruelty is an example. It does service to wickedness, and with its bloody law of death it guards the gates of hell. Or, what could lying do, if covetousness were idle in sleep? That result itself, death, would occur less often if either the sword would fail or poisons cease.

(2) The tongue is a unique evil. It has welling up in itself so much power to work malice that it needs no help in accomplishing its effects. We must check it, therefore, as the Prophet warns, lest, perhaps, when it has sprung into action, it may wound in its excitement or strike for being goaded. For, it does not ordinarily get away with impunity after vaunting itself in insolent language. Once stirred up

1 Eccli. 28.16,17.

it vomits fire. And while it seeks to harm another, it enkindles internally the whole heart conscious of evil. Hear the Prophet's words: 'In the multitude of words you will not escape sin.'[2]

Rather easily, if it is necessary, can anyone stand up against battle lines armed with steel, and legions equipped with the engines of war. But, who can withstand the shafts which lips imbed in his heart? Without doubt, bodies wounded by the sword get back health quite easily. Else, why should anyone attribute such heavy cruelty to the death of those slain by the sword, since the dangers are sometimes less where greater hatreds spring from the blood? But, whatever shock from outside gets shut up within a man, the cure of that always entails greater difficulty.

It is obviously not hard for a doctor, through the wholesome use of herbs, to cauterize and soothe even swelling sores in the eyes. There is an antidote even for poison with all its power. Even if that which has been drunk is winning out in the depths of the stomach, the drink from the saving cup is sought—with such success that often the perpetrator of the crimes is amazed because through the penetration of the medicine the curse from his mouth has achieved nothing.

But the blow inflicted by the tongue is incurable. The tongue strikes lightly, but it always stirs up deep sighs in the chest through the sorrow it causes. The Prophet no doubt knew how great was the evil of the tongue when he cried out: 'Set a watch, O Lord, before my mouth: and a door about my lips, that my heart may not turn to evil words.'[3] Therefore, if anyone is wise, let him set a guard

2 Prov. 10.19.
3 Ps. 140.3.4.

before his mouth, and let him put the bond of taciturnity upon his lips.

(3) The disagreeable consequences arising from too ready a tongue affect the activities of not one man alone. The first party should indeed take care not to utter anything injurious. The other party ought to take no less trouble to check the words of a frenzied man by a reasonable reply of his own.

Your zeal to preserve peace is great if you meet the bitterness of another's tongue with a soft and soothing reply. Friendly address soon embarrasses men of evil lips. But—and this is something worse—it is easier to find someone all too willing to speak evil or listen to it. Nothing is more cruel or savage than bitter and sharp conversations. The wounds they inflict are as difficult to cure as they are easy to cause. By a thrust of your shield you easily ward off the pointed shafts of steel flying through the air. But the piercing points of words cannot be recalled, or warded off, for they are much swifter than arrows. What fortifications or what bulwark, however well built, can be helpful in a case where the weapon strikes almost before it is in full motion? We cannot enumerate all the weapons with which the tongue is armed in its words. These words can quite easily strike even the secret recesses of the soul. When the ears take in any injury, they transmit it instantly to the depths of the heart, and, if it has once entered there, it does not come out unless by the exit of death. An ailment which, although discovered, is not cast out by any of the beneficial effects of medicine causes continual distress. Wherefore, the speech from the tongue should be cleansed, lest it generate a poison through its facility in words.

(4) Dearly beloved, if we glance at all those pains which

master our bodies, we find them all either curable by the surgeon's knife or tractable to the healing concoction of medicine. Everyone knows how serious are the bites of wolves and how dangerous the poison of serpents. Yet, the juice of herbs or the physicians' skill can easily provide an antidote for these.

But a wound arising from words is unbearable. With difficulty, morevore, can another wound heal a source of pain, once that source of pain has imbedded itself in the heart and secretly pervaded the marrow of the soul. Hear the Prophet uttering: 'Death and life are in the power of the tongue.'[4] Truly, dearly beloved, if you look deeply, and diligently investigate the swelling tumor of an exasperated heart, you will discover that the wounds produced by words cause deaths.

In making a comparison with a malicious tongue, why will anyone hold up to me the concocting of poison? Or why will he cast his accusation on the deadly compounds in the cups? That condition which can be checked only by death exceeds every kind of poison. All malice, indeed, springs from the heart. But, this very malice, even though harmful, can easily be borne if the matter fostered by an evil plan is not carried into open strife. However, either let it keep silence in its grief, or be pondered in the heart until it subsides. A remedy can be applied to a state of evil brooding as long as a sealed mouth holds in the grudges conceived in the heart. But, once it has burst forth from a vibrant tongue, a physician is sought in vain. The sin of words is one without a remedy, because whatever tears injury has stirred up by working its way through the ears cannot be stopped. Hear the Lord's words: 'Make doors and bars to thy mouth, and make a balance to thy words.'[5]

---

4 Prov. 18.21.

5 Cf. Eccli. 28.28,29. St. Valerian would have been clearer if he had quoted the full text.

(5) Perhaps you reply to all this: 'Who can check the lips of his mouth to such an extent as to pass the day in silence? Does not this doctrine put a bridle of taciturnity upon an upright tongue?'

This doctrine would clearly have the man speak, but speak as one who utters noble ideas and devises peaceful measures. Words gain a growing honor if no bitterness of mind worsens the pleasant sounds of the tongue.

We have made these remarks, dearly beloved, because we find many who occasionally mix poison with sweet words in one and the same conversation, and enter into conflicts by feigned persuasions to peace. What can be more unfortunate or dangerous than the case of those men who with all the ardor of their deceitful tongues plot against someone's life? Why do they fail to consider the Prophet's psalm which states: 'May the Lord destroy sinful lips.'[6] Do you perceive under what a curse he lives who is contriving one plan in his heart and placing another on his tongue? Well, indeed, did the Lord of heaven and earth know that evil men thwart the endeavors of the saints by pretended humility. He states through the Evangelist's mouth: 'They come to you in sheep's clothing, but inwardly they are ravening wolves.'[7] Assuredly, it is a tangled evil to mix guileful plans into flatteries. I do not want any gifts amid suspected urbanity. But, who would willingly have sour chitterlings, seasoned with the savor of bitter herbs? Surely, then, he who gives simultaneously a sweet and a salty drink of water can scarcely please anyone. When does the flavor fail to displease if some bitterness gets mixed into the comb of honey? Once the bitterness of gall has infected a man's heart, his very mind, no matter how alert and wise it be, is lacking in complete prudence. Consequently, all the vices of a

6 Ps. 11.4.
7 Matt. 7.15.

crafty mind should be checked. Otherwise, while those vices begin to work something bitter outside, the sweet characteristics in our own selves may begin to cause pain.

(6) Hear the Prophet's voice: 'Set a watch, O Lord, before my mouth.'[8] This is a profitable guard for our mouth: not to let our heart easily turn its attention to any words which base conversation proffers to disturb the pursuits of peace, or which the base acts of some person bring him to utter. No one has regretted keeping silent amid confused utterances. For, as we see, the acts which spring from words often result in crime, and through excessive readiness in aversions hatreds supplant friendships. If a man is either boastful or malevolent in his speech, how can he fail to be disliked? If you want to see an example of this vice, it is abundantly present in some women. Just as they do not hestitate to use foul words, neither do they feel any confusion in listening to what is shameful.

However, we are not mentioning all this to bring anyone to keep his voice always confined inside a closed mouth, and have perpetual silence shut the sound of his tongue behind his contracted lips. Just as it is unpleasant to have the wicked talk too much, so it is harmful to have the good always keep silence. Therefore, when need arises, let us speak out the words of justice. Let ours be a speech well flavored.

(7) But, perhaps you say: 'Sometimes a provoked man cannot refrain from making a reply.'

One should keep completely silent when foul speech is goading his quiet lips into action; and one should speak out when friendly words are promoting the pursuits of peace. Thus, to speak and to keep silent, each is a perfection. The case of each consists in holding to the proper measure of words. Silence is great, and speech is great; but the part

8 Ps. 140.3.

of a wise man is to have control over both. For, excessive silence sometimes is attributed to lack of intelligence, just as an excess of words is often ascribed to madness.

If you care to hear the opinion I have formed on this matter, it is this. I prefer a man to be esteemed dull because of his silence rather than insane because of his loquacity. Therefore, let us speak, but with fear and trembling, aware that we must render an account for every word.[9] Thus we shall take care to have nothing base spring from our hearts, nothing blasphemous fly from our lips, nothing harmful harbored in our thought. The Prophet condemns not only what offends the ears, but also the attitude which some men cherish in their minds. 'With deceitful lips, and with a double heart they have spoken evil things.'[10]

Deliberations, too, then, should be listed among the faults of an insolent tongue. Whatever you speak in your heart you are confessing to the Lord, because God is the Searcher of hearts. Since you cannot hide even your thought from Him, can that which you shout aloud remain hidden from Him or excused? Reffect on this.

In all zeal, therefore, dearly beloved, let us keep our mouths controlled by a proper bar. May our tongue utter nothing unpleasant, may no base speech of ours devise anything harmful, anything deceitful. May our hearts contain nothing guileful, harsh, or idle. For the Lord has said that an account must be given even of idle words.[11] Although a man may fortify his life by faith, rule it by wisdom, and arrange it with purity and sobriety, there is nothing pleasing in him if his tongue alone of all the members in all his body gives offense.

---

9 Matt. 12.36.
10 Ps. 11.3.
11 Matt. 12.36.

## HOMILY 6

### *Idle Words*

(On Matt. 12.22-37)

(1) Dearly beloved, in fulfilling the duties entrusted to us, we have spoken about disciplinary control. As often as we did this, we omitted some lesser matters while treating those more important. Some men may regard these lesser matters as easy. However, if you investigate with greater care, you will find them the occasion of many sins. We should now set our hand to these subjects, and elaborate on them with the aid of the study of medicine. Thus, each vice will reveal the causes of its own infirmity.

Think, if you please, about all the beings which minister to pain or pleasure. You will discover this. Harmful virus has its reign not alone in the fierce dragons, but poisons hide just as truly in the little bodies of the bees.

We have often stated, dearly beloved, that drunkenness and covetousness are sources of vices. From them rushing torrents of sins well forth, and drag along to the depths a great part of the human race. Drunkenness stirs the whirlpool of gluttony, and covetousness enkindles a frenzy for odious thefts. Covetousness is the mother of pride; drunkenness, of impurity. The one is the companion of lying, the other, of ugly deformity. Both impel men to commit murders, to plan deeds of adultery, and to destroy the bases of friendship. After the manner of some depraved business agreement, covetousness suggests a reward for furtive love, and drunkenness provides the occasion.

(2) But, as we have often said, dearly beloved, with a little effort you can check these vices, if you are willing

to cut away the previous sources of the sins. You will not find it difficult to repress the consequence if you oppose and condemn the vices in their source. All the strength of the body to hold together will soon fail if there is no one to give food to a sick stomach. Clearly, therefore, drunkenness and covetousness ought to be attacked before all the other vices; for these two claim a primacy among the rest. Thus, those which trail these two will be in danger of losing their function. The swirling waves of even a deep whirlpool can be easily dried up if the source of the water can be blocked.

Many remarks about these vices we are reviewing, dearly beloved, are still being suggested to our memory. However, since we have at various times satisfied the needs of discipline in opposing them, we think that today a few remarks suffice to call them to your minds. Consequently, we restrain ourselves in regard to many matters apparently contained in our subject, until we shall have explained those persons' crimes which seem so easy to some men.

(3) You have heard the Evangelist stating, dearly beloved, that an account must be given to the Lord for idle words.[1] If you reflect, dearly beloved, on the considerations we have set forth, and on what we said formerly in decrying an uncontrolled tongue, you understand this statement to refer to the insolence of the mouth. Although its words are named idle, they should not be treated lightly. Let no one deem light a fault attacked by so severe a censure from heaven.

Next follow whatever lies rumor spreads, for the fruitless conversations excited by fabricated hearsay are always idle. What conversation is to be deemed idle, if not that which is ignorant of reason and the messenger of falsehood, which

1 Matt. 12.36.

has as its aim either to fabricate ridiculous tales, or to expound dubious ones as if they were certain?

There are men of this type, too. While they thrive on fiction, they do not know how to beware of a lie. Let them listen to the Lord saying: 'The mouth that belieth, killeth the soul.'[2] Also on the list of idle words are those elaborated outcries, composed with senseless effort, carrying many blows—gentle ones, as some think. But those outcries are also armed with fatal stings. Although they excite mirth, enmities often arise.

Dearly beloved, there are many other vices like these. Perhaps they should not be omitted, even if, among all the vices of words, they seem far-fetched. For example, if you call a dark-complexioned man silvery white, you inflict the injury of an idle word. For, if you have told the truth, you have blamed him; if you told something false, you have ridiculed him. When you call a man of tall and venerable stature an infant, are you not doing injury if you suppress the truth and lie in boyish eagerness? If you by your words add something to the human body or subtract it, that is contumely.

(4) But, perhaps you say: 'Those matters are quite trivial, and easily borne.' That is true. For, those words are of that sort—like light feathers which you stick unto someone else's hair, or the prominent ashes or something else of dust-like sheen which you strew on a head lovely with the beauty of early youth. You do not, indeed, burden the head, but you disfigure it. Likewise, someone's hair pulled down in fun does display considerable indignity, even if it causes no pain.

Therefore, dearly beloved, everyone should take care not to injure another by language characteristic of the stage, and not to bring the shame of an injured reputation on a

2 Wisd. 1.11.

brother through the use of actors' language. Excessive wit in the mouth ordinarily stimulates tempers into action, and a conversation barbed with pleasantries brings a quarrel in return. In this way, finally, a small spark begins to emit flames. Sprung from almost nothing, it often starts a great conflagration.

Idle conversation is much promoted by an idle speaker. Wherefore, since we have mentioned words characteristic of the theatre, in accordance with my concern for discipline, I perhaps ought not to keep silent about those matters which captivate curious ears by their idle words, and strike the secret depths of the heart while they flatter by rhythmic blows. These are those vices which we previously mentioned as being compounded with a certain sweetness of honey. This is that business which, as we observed, by a mixture of sweetness produces the sharp pains of wounds.

(5) Here, someone, because of his love of discipline, may think he should ask what those idle words are which inflict injury and are dangerous to those who hear them. It is well that you ask. Otherwise, ignorance of this may endanger your grasp of my sermon.

We frequently find that in the following way the road is made smooth for wantonness, and enticements supplied to acts of adultery. One fellow by his skillful plectrum produces the music of the tingling zither, and another with ready fingers draws forth the alluring sounds of the swelling organ. Those are the attending snares by which the Devil causes, among other wounds, many deaths for men. For, as often as the hearing is soothed by this sweet sound, the gaze is allured to a base crime. Let no one trust these seductive songs, or give further attention to the enticements of a libidinous voice. While they are delighting, they are waxing fierce. While they are flattering, they are killing.

We often observe birds deceived by alluring whistles, and stupid beasts coaxed by a sweet voice into a deadly trap. Similar indeed, dearly beloved, is the case of mortals whose attention is caught by a sweet-sounding song. The different notes of the words and the humming sounds produced without syllables[3] have this effect, that someone either is taken in or takes in someone else.

Dearly beloved, it cannot be explained how dangerous are the snares to which pursuit of the pleasure characteristic of the farces exposes one. If one could peer into the secret corners of the human breast, he would find the hearts of unfortunate men palpitating to every note of the flute. Therefore, if even the charms of humming beguile another to madness, you can easily understand what arises from temptation like these: conversation too familiar and secret between men and women, or their drawing too close together, or the exchange of speech full of quips, or the gluttony brought on by recipes of great variety, or hunger for gold amid an allurement to every sin of prostitution.

(6) Therefore, you should flee that source of sin, the sound of the voice, which has produced bitterness in human hearts by its own sweetness, and by a certain persuading power of its honeylike song has often concocted fatal poisons for sick men. Where that voice is heard, we should raise the shield of faith and stop up our ears, the easier to keep from hearing any of the alluring sound. We should also display disciplinary control to check the curiosity of our eyes and stifle the first movements of a languishing heart. For, that is what the Evangelist teaches: 'If thy eye is an occasion of sin to thee, pluck it out.'[4]

Dearly beloved, do not think that the point of his state-

---

3 *producta sine syllabis verba*. Possibly, the meaning is: the words uttered without rhythm.

4 Matt. 5.29.

ment is this, that the Lord desires to maim a human body, which He made to His own image and raised to a dignity which appears like His own. To pluck out the eyes means this: to cut out what is base in a man and to check foul deeds by amending them, to diminish lust by repressing its temptations, and, for the good of conscience, to cut off hands which are prone to debased covetousness.

He has cut off his hands who has broken the javelins of infidelity in himself and by his just decision has cut the arrows of faithlessness. Something helpful toward salvation is accomplished if the vices fostered by wicked deeds are weakened, and the gaze of evil eyes is, so to speak, pulled out with its roots. If you allow all these vices I have mentioned to reign whole and unharmed, the sting of death soon finds its pleasant repose in them. However, in order to carry out those good deeds more easily, we should heed Christ, who says: 'Give up your possessions and follow Me.'[5]

(7) I am well aware, dearly beloved, that those occupied with the activities of the world find it hard to accept those words. The enjoyment of that worldly life is sweet to them. But, as careful investigation reveals, the world is full of vanity, and, so to speak, clothed with a tenuous, shadowy cover. The world gives service only for a time and all this deceitful pomp of riches which you see is but flattery. Holy David knew that well when he said: 'Turn away my eyes that they may not behold vanity.'[6]

What is that vanity, if not devotion to riches and the pursuit of worldly pleasures? This is confirmed through Solomon, who says: 'Vanity of vanities, and all is vanity.'[7] Therefore, dearly beloved, let no one put his confidence in the vanity of this world. That vanity, as you see, is something

5 Matt. 19.21.
6 Ps. 118.37.
7 Eccle. 1.2.

standing with insecure footing. Devotion to it is short-lived and empty, and its beauty is like smoke in a wind. The comeliness of its countenance is like that which you see when you look on the beauty of that vine which had its early summer blossoms in well-constituted abundance, yet cannot bring forth the actual fruit of the promised grape harvest. While it brings forth too much, it incurs the reproach of perpetual sterility.

(8) A far different beauty, dearly beloved, is that which the time of eternal life promises to us, if only one makes his way as a poor man with regard to sins. He who gathers the fruits of mercy and struggles against the urge to foolish covetousness, he goes as a rich man to Christ. He makes his way with great wealth to heaven who wards off from himself the pomp of short-lived vanity. He who by his zealous practice of religion is lightening his heart once burdened with vices carries with him great resources to Paradise. Finally, he has escaped all the penury of begging who has daily planted in his heart the commandments of our Christ, and with watchful faith has filled the barns of his soul with seeds heavenly in their origin.

Wherefore, before all else, check your freedom of that idle speech. Once that freedom has got itself entwined in the pursuit of religious living, it certainly prejudices your holiness when the judgment will come. Among the other vices, unless those of the tongue which we mentioned above are carefully pruned, the best qualities in a man soon lose their value.

# HOMILY 7

## *Mercy*

### (On Matt. 25.31-46)

(1) Dearly beloved, if you look back over all the stages of justice through which the work of religion is carried on, you will not find anyone who gives a gracious service to the Lord and through it fails to win a place of dignity with Him.

But, although these very acts which faith works in us do proceed from human endeavor, they should be ascribed to God.[1] If there are any deeds well done, it is through Him and in Him that they have existence, and are stored up for the future as profitable to individual men.

Wherefore, let no one who is wise think that the benefits of God should be ascribed to his own powers. Otherwise, he will hear that phrase of the Apostle which says: 'What hast thou that thou hast not received? Or if thou hast received it, why dost thou boast as if thou hadst not received it?'[2]

Dearly beloved, we are well aware that, according to the Gospel doctrine which recounts the promises of beatitude, justice has prepared a place for man in heaven. That is, the favor gained by meekness and humility has won the promise of Paradise and the land of promise. Purity of heart has merited to see Christ. Mercy has received a similar reward of retribution. The joy of peace has prepared for many a place among the children of God. The suffering of the saints has gained the crown of victory and the glory of the celestial kingdom because of the merits of their virtue.

But, one and the same power of the Father, Son, and Holy

1 Section 1 of this homily is a strong argument against those who charge St. Valerian with Semi-Pelagianism. Cf. also, Homily 11.

2 1 Cor. 4.7.

Spirit works all these things in us. It gives a perfection to our works of righteousness, and supplies to a good will whatever best aids there are. There is, indeed, one thing, and that very great, which descends from the abode of mercy. In it a mortal man can justly claim glory for himself. It is to feed the poor and to redeem the captives—if, however, neither boastfulness dissipates this glory or unpleasant sadness throws it into disorder.

(2) Behold, you hear the Evangelist saying: 'Come, blessed of my Father, take possession with me of the kingdom prepared for you from the foundation of the world; for I was hungry and you gave me to eat; I was thirsty, and you gave me to drink; naked and you covered me.'[3] Therefore, as you perceive, if it becomes anyone to glory, he should not do it except because of this activity, by which the Lord orders that He Himself be fed and clothed, and that His hunger be satisfied day by day with a little portion of divided bread.

Wherefore, if we desire our glorying not to be vain, let us in the first place redeem the friendship of the highest King by our copious alms. To open the heavenly kingdom to ourselves, let us all turn our attention to showing mercy to the Lord. In this love of Him, we should not regard the tears of the poor lightly or negligently, lest, to our confusion, He who feeds all the world may be seen hungry among those who are begging. Gaze upon the needs of every one of these, and on our Saviour's concern for the wretched. You will understand that our Christ is present wherever you behold an abundance of tears.

You do not have to seek the Lord far away, if you are not a miser. Look, He awaits us right outside with that crowd of His servants. You do not have to cast your glance now here now there, so that you doubt whom to make the chief

3 Matt. 25.34-36.

beneficiary of your pitiful expenditure. Know that our Christ is that man whom you see naked, whom you see as a blind man, whom you meet[4] in a lame man, whom you behold wrapped in rags or covered with dirty garments.

In this clothing, indeed, was He found when sought by the Magi. Dressed like this and lying in the manger was He when He received the gifts they offered from their open treasures. That Gospel phrase has a bearing on these matters which says: 'Lay up for yourselves treasures in heaven where neither rust consumes, nor thieves break in.'[5] These are those treasures which are recorded among our merits stored up in heaven, treasures which nothing adverse spoils. That is the significance of dividing the substance of our resources among the poor.

(3) Wherefore, you first of all, whoever you are who glory in the abundance of your riches, hear my counsel in this matter. If you fear the rust, take my counsel to heart. If you fear a thief, take it all the more to heart. Look, you have an excellent caretaker to preserve your resources for you, and to make them profitable for you forever in eternity. Christ adds to these words: 'Do not lay up to yourselves treasures on earth.'[6]

Dearly beloved, the Lord's advice to a man not to entrust his treasure to the earth is not beside the point. For, as we often see, things stored in the earth get endangered by some blemish. Resources buried too deep get spoiled by the corrosion of the soil. Consequently, I deem it more useful to lend than to hide, and to have greater trust in interest than burial in the earth.

It is a species of folly to keep shut up what can by diversi-

4 Reading *offenderis,* with Sirmond.
5 Matt. 6.20.
6 Matt. 6.19.

fied functioning both profit many men and produce fruit of justice in eternal life. So, I advise that no one should hide his treasure in the earth, that is, let no one think that the dignity of a heavenly soul is to be ascribed to earthly acts.[7] The rust is corroding the treasures of that man who is indulging vanity, and directing his life according to the pomp of this world.

Therefore, dearly beloved, the rust is that worm which alone possesses the recesses of the heart: the worm of envy and of avarice. But the thief is the Devil. Believe this. To lay his plots against good deeds, he flatters with the proferred pomp of the world. To keep a man from sharing in the heavenly kingdom, he puts gold in his hands, silver before his eyes, gems about his neck. In this way he nourishes pride, and by the goad of covetousness enkindles the desires of the flesh. All these things, as Scripture tells,[8] plunge men into destruction.

But, beyond any doubt, he who sends his treasures ahead into heaven lightens [life] here below of many of its pains. Hear what the Lord offers: 'Come, blessed of my Father, take possession with me of the kingdom prepared for you from the foundation of the world. I was hungry and you gave me to eat; I was thirsty and you gave me to drink; naked and you covered me.' After this pronouncement, who would hesitate to migrate from this world with all the attractiveness of his patrimony? Clearly, it is the emptiness of folly, and an error in choosing values, to love the world more than the heavenly kingdom, or to give pleasure to the world more than to Christ. So, if anyone desires to find a place in the heavenly abode, let him not cease to dispense the necessities of life to the indigent.

7 This statement is the opposite of Pelagianism, and even of Semi-Pelagianism.

8 1 Tim. 6.9.

(4) But, perhaps someone may object: 'My resources are slender; they do not allow such great disbursements of payment.' If someone should offer you a very beautiful house for the short possession this life affords, would you not gather money from every source to meet the price of the offer? And if, by chance, your money bag were not heavy enough, would you not make the sum sufficient through borrowed money, until you have your joy in your estate, now increased by this new house?

Look, possession of the kingdom of heaven is now offered to you, and for a very low price. Anyone not accustomed to allege his poverty as a pretext can easily buy this possession.

Let us see what it is that is asked of you as a price: food, drink, and clothing. I do not find anyone unable to make this disbursement every day. If you investigate, perhaps you find that produce is abundant in your barns, and the well-known mellow flavor of your aged wine is a reason to enlarge your cellars. What does it avail you to store all those goods if you do not know how to engage in profitable trade? But you say: 'I am a poor man.' Does this pretext suffice to excuse you to those to whom you set prices marked up because of the bad times? Without reason do you plead the slenderness of your resources. Are you able to possess something to sell, but unable to possess something to give away? Not without purpose was this said: 'Deal thy bread to the hungry.'[9] I think that phrase applies to those inhuman persons who store away their wholesome bread and then let corroding mould consume it. So, break your bread to the hungry man, that he may not perish and shut you out from your share of the heavenly kingdom.

The Scripture adds: 'And despise not the servants of thy

9 Cf. Isa. 58.7. Possibly, Isa. 58.7-12 accompanied Matthew 25.31-46 as the *lectio* which occasioned this sermon.

own seed.'[10] Who are these our servants? Of necessity, all those related to us through the fact of their having been born. Why should no person be excepted from our almsgiving? Why is no selection to be made? Because a thing which is meeting a necessity does not require an order in the disbursement.

Why have you need to ask whether he who makes the request is Christian or Jew, heretic or pagan, Roman or foreigner, free man or slave? When necessity is pressing, you need not discuss the person. Otherwise, in separating out those unworthy of your mercy, you may likewise lose the Son of God. And when can we know in what region of the earth Christ dwells? He who is known to possess everything should be believed to be everywhere.

(5) The Prophet adds to what we quoted above: 'Then shall thy temporary light break forth, and thy vestments will rise up sooner, and justice will go before thee, and the glory of the Lord will surround you. Then shalt thou cry out to the Lord, and the Lord shall hear thee. While thou art still speaking he will say, 'Here I am.'[11] And all this because of a morsel of shared bread. How much more will you get, do you think, if you will give more? Hear the Evangelist's words: 'Blessed are the merciful, for God will have mercy on them.'[12]

There are, indeed, many degrees of mercy, but we should inquire what the chief ones are. The first kind of mercy is, in truth, to extend a helping hand to a fallen man, to show the way of salvation to the wanderer, to visit the sick, perseveringly to console those who are tried by tribulation. Yet, this is the mercy we should especially long for: to feed the hungry, to clothe the naked, to ransom the

---

10 *Ibid.*
11 Isa. 58.8,9.
12 Matt. 5.7.

captive, to make a loan for a time to one who needs it.[13]

Sometimes, we find many other kinds of mercy to which human endeavors are popularly devoted. These do not bring forth the fruits of mercy, but they simulate its compassion. It is about these that James states in his Epistle: 'If a brother or a sister be naked and in want of daily food, and one of you say to them, Go in peace, be warmed and filled, yet you do not give them what is necessary for the body, it profits you nothing.'[14]

Who does not hate such a kind of mercy? In it an idle piety flatters the sick man with elegant language, and fruitless tears are offered to heaven. What does it profit to bewail another man's shipwreck if you take no care of his body which is suffering from exposure? Or what good does it do to torture your soul with grief over another's wound, if you refuse him a health-giving cup? These flattering remarks do not feed the hungry man; those bootless counsels do not clothe another's nakedness. What good does it do to apply soft poultices to an indigent man, if you will not give a bit of food to one on the point of dying from hunger? What kind of mercy is that, in which you desire the man to live, but are unwilling to save him in his need? Clearly, that piety is a cruel one which knows how to grieve over the wretched, but does not know how to help those about to perish.

(6) Dearly beloved, what more do you seek in return for disbursing a bit of divided bread? Even if a share in the heavenly kingdom had not been promised you for it, as sinners you ought to be content with that statement which has brought to mortal men the hope of future salvation and the joy of everlasting security. For if consideration is given to the fruits of your work and the tenderness of heavenly

---

13 Reading *non,* with Sirmond, not *nos.*

14 James 2.15,16.

love, you receive far more than you give. Look, in return for feeding a poor man, the Gospels promise you the kingdom of heaven. Because of your dividing and sharing your bread, or offering hospitable shelter, or clothing the naked, the Lord promises you, through the Prophets, His help when you invoke Him.[15] As the Psalms tell, the justice arising from your mercy is stored up for ever and ever.[16]

If we compare heavenly things with earthly, it is evident that something very valuable is for sale at a rather low price. How great is your alms in proportion to all the things which the Lord has clearly promised to mortal men? Look, we give earthly goods; He, those of heaven. We offer goods which last a while; He, those which endure forever.

Do you wish to know what distance there is between your fortunes and the heavenly gifts? In this comparison of benefits, no equal reckoning is found: to receive everlasting riches, and to give those which are perishable.

Above all, we should take account of those tears brought on by the recent furious and bloody struggle.[17] Then there will be no lack of opportunity for good will to show itself by deeds. For—and this is sadder still—we see so many in anxiety over their own or their dear ones' getting ransomed. A helping hand should be extended to these. But, you say: 'I am a poor man.' We are not urging anyone to give what he does not have. But, let him whose resources are too slender to redeem a captive add at least some little bit to the ransom price. Thus he may seem to comply with the commandment, at least by a little coin.

15 Isa. 58.9.
16 Ps. 111.9.
17 Perhaps a struggle occasioned by the migration of nations, or one with pirates.

# HOMILY 8

## *Mercy*

## (On Matt. 25.31-46)

(1) Dearly beloved, many subjects which spring from a perusal of the Gospels pull the soul in different directions. If we wish to arrange them under one heading or proposition, one subject necessarily hinders another, and the effort to grasp one precludes understanding the other. How can either the speaker's or the hearer's whole manner of thinking escape from being hindered by the confusion of many things?

Therefore, dearly beloved, among the many other subjects for which, according to their values, the gift of blessedness has been conferred (as the Evangelist recounts), we have thought it wise to explain to you the subject of mercy. Mercy must reap the fruit of daily effort. We shall follow through with the other subjects at their proper times, when utility will require. Thus, when each subject stands firmly with its own strong points evident, it does not need the subject matter of another.

Notice that the Lord says: 'Blessed are the merciful, for God will have mercy on them.'[1] I wonder if after this statement anyone will hesitate to expend his own money, since he has seen that profit accrues to the just in return for a kind deed. What does it profit you to keep in a money bag a mass of gold which you have heaped up, when you can every day both do good and gain profit on the money expended?

'Blessed are the merciful, for God will have mercy on them.' Dearly beloved, rejoice, and give without anxiety,

---

1 Matt. 5.7.

and make your contribution without hesitation. Who would not eagerly distribute his resources by a generous disbursement among the poor, when he is aware that he will receive multiplied fruit and redoubled gifts in return? Moreover, observe that the Lord has judged those happy in this life to whom He has promised mercy in the future.

(2) Hear what the Lord says in another place: 'Give to everyone who asks of thee.'[2] Dearly beloved, not without reason does the Lord bid you to give alms to all who ask for them. He was necessarily aware that good men, too, are sometimes hidden among the evil. He mingled the good and the bad together for precisely this reason: He did not want the man worthy of mercy to depart without a gift because an overcautious distribution passes over the unworthy. There is no discernment of the one begging. The need of the poor man is not to be investigated. Profits are being sought for the giver, not for the beggar. It makes no difference to what beggar you give. The Lord is asking, not whether the one begging is worthy, but how much the giver is supplying.

Listen, here, to the Apostle saying: 'He who sows sparingly will also reap sparingly.'[3] Clearly, as often as we succor the wretched, we give to ourselves. The dispensing of our resources is our gain. For, if you consider again the hope of future reward, whatever is given to the poor is reckoned as a profit. That is what the Prophet states: 'Blessed is he that understandeth concerning the needy and the poor: the Lord will deliver him in the evil day.'[4]

In regard to all these matters, Christ is the guarantor. He says: I shall restore to you a hundredfold.[5] In addition

2 Luke 6.30.
3 2 Cor. 9.6.
4 Ps. 40.1.
5 Cf. Matt. 19.29.

to this, eternal life is promised. The condemnation of the judgment is reserved for impiety and avarice. As the Evangelist says: 'When the Son of Man shall come in his majesty, and all the angels with Him, then He will separate them all one from another, the sheep on his right hand, but the goats on his left; saying to those on his right hand: Come, my sons, take possession with me of the kingdom of heaven. I was hungry and you gave me to eat; I was thirsty and you gave me to drink; I was a stranger, and you took me in; I was naked, and you covered me. He will say to those on his left: Depart from me, accursed ones, into the everlasting fire. I was hungry and you did not give me to eat; I was thirsty, and you gave me no drink.'[6]

Therefore, dearly beloved, let us take thought and care to keep the retribution for impiety from overtaking us. For, just as the Lord is placated by the feeding and clothing of paupers, so is he hurt by contempt of the wretched. So great is His concern for the unhappy that He regards anything which covers or refreshes a needy man as something given to Himself.

(3) Hear Solomon proclaim: 'Son, do a benefit to thy self. Shut up alms in the heart of the poor.'[7] Therefore, whoever wants to consult his own interests should feed the poor without reluctance. If you but attend to others' poverty, you lack no opportunity to gain profit every day. For, Scripture states: 'By alms and faith sins are purged away.'[8]

Look, here a man begs for food with a starved throat. There is one who in his nakedness claims to be in want of even a pitiful garment. Quite cruel and too hard-hearted is the man whom grief does not touch, when either weakness, or nakedness, or poverty is plaguing some part of his body.

6 Matt. 25.31,32,34-36,41-42.
7 Eccli. 29.15.
8 Prov. 15.27.

He who pays no attention to the cause of another's need is clearly taking but little care of his own interests. Your riches do you no good if you do not use their benefits. To be in secret possession of hoarded money is characteristic of miserliness. Are you unaware that he who does not sow reaps no harvest, according to that statement we cited above? 'He who sows sparingly will also reap sparingly.'

Therefore, this is the proportion of the cultivation to be accomplished; the more seeds a man plants in the earth, the greater grows his hope of a future harvest. He who does not plant will with idle hands watch others as they harvest. For, he who has toiled most among the other farmers will store up the most. But, when can it be that he who has added furrow to furrow and filled them with seeds will see his barns empty? What do you gain from brooding over your stored-up wealth, if you reap not profit from it?

Again, we often see a mass of produce grow old and consumed by age. We see wines get so spoiled by the passing of time that they are of no further use to anybody and are thrown out. Sometimes, we understand that before the Lord that wine alone was more profitable which the farmer customarily gives to the needy in order to replace it. But, what avarice reserves, either the excessive heat steals away, or undesirable age consumes, or the abdominable moth spoils. A man stores up for himself only that which he disburses for the sake of mercy. For, that is what the Lord says: 'Lay up for yourselves treasures in heaven, where neither moth consumes, nor thieves break in and steal.'[9]

(4) Therefore, dearly beloved, let us take care to keep the worm of avarice from corrupting our resources. Let us send our wealth ahead to that place where no thief breaks

9 Matt. 6.20.

in and no plotter sets a fire. Let us entrust our riches to the Lord, who says: 'Do not lay up for yourselves treasures on earth.'[10] For, whoever has faithfully dispensed his resources in doing God's work has them hidden away in a corner of heaven, and deposited for safekeeping under a just custodian. Let no one who is wise look back at the trappings of this world. While they satisfy the short-lived whims of men, they make sport of their souls.

There are two kinds of riches: the one kind urges towards death; the other leads to life.

Here are riches of death: to brood like a miser upon another's wealth; to take in money amid the tears of the unfortunate, and stack it up, and count it day by day as something to swell the legacies of this world.

The integral and genuine riches are those by which souls are reedemed and sins purged away. God finds acceptable the riches of that man by whose generosity the poor man is fed, the naked man clothed, the captive ransomed, the imprisoned man freed, and the inheritance of the heavenly kingdom acquired. I do not want those riches which by their growth daily increase the hunger for them, and then, eventually stripped of their attractive beauty, allow their lovers to remain in their hunger.

(5) Finally, let us have recourse to the Scriptures. You will understand that poverty, when compared with riches, has the better lot. In reprobating avarice, the Lord puts a certain man in hell, and has him beg Abraham, our father, to send the beggar Lazarus who has his abode on high. He requests that he bring refreshment to his mouth, and relief to his lips parched with thirst. As the Gospel recounts, he received this reply: 'Son, remember that thou in thy lifetime has received good things, and Lazarus in like manner

10 Matt. 6.19.

evil things; but now here he is comforted whereas thou art tormented.'[11]

You see that changes of fortune are in store for the activities of the good and of the wicked. It is well to anticipate these changes by the practice of mercy. Otherwise, profitless riches will kindle against themselves the flames which avenge crimes.

Consequently, dearly beloved, let us prepare for ourselves a place of favor with the Lord. Let us improve the road of our life by our munificence and generosity. Let us send satisfaction before us to the Lord, and purge away any stain incurred through our affections, while we ponder that statement of the Prophet: 'They that sow in tears shall reap in joy.'[12]

Therefore, if anyone carefully examines his conscience, let him not think that those words should be received into unheeding ears. For, on the coming judgment day you cannot obtain refreshment unless you have either healed your wounds by feeding the poor, or washed them by abundant tears. And you—weep more copiously yourselves, and dispense your resources to those who weep, in order that you may gather the fruits of your mercy while you reap joys along with the others in the future life.

---

11 Luke 16.25.
12 Ps. 125.5.

# HOMILY 9

## *Mercy*

### (On Matt. 25.31-46)

(1) Dearly beloved, whenever we must instruct your charitable selves, in accordance with your desire to live religiously, we think of that account in the Gospel passage which tells of the separation of the good and the bad in the future judgment. If anyone fails to heed that account, he will reap tears. If he takes it to heart, he will gain the richest fruits of joy. The Evangelist states: 'When the Lord shall come in his majesty, and will separate the bad from the good, he will say to those who are on his right hand: Come, take possession with me of the kingdom of heaven. I was hungry and you gave me to eat; I was thirsty and you gave me to drink. And he will say to those who are on his left hand: Depart from me, accursed ones, into the everlasting fire. I was hungry, and you did not give me to eat; I was thirsty and you gave me no drink.'[1]

Therefore, dearly beloved, if any one of you wishes to arrive at a share of that heavenly kingdom, let him first of all extend a helping hand to poverty, and let him not look without concern on other men's tears. For, a judgment of retribution awaits every man, either for his good work or his bad. The Lord has said it: 'What a man sows, that he will also reap.'[2]

Wherefore, dearly beloved, among the other activities by which we carry into practice our desire to live religiously,

1 Matt. 25.31-42. St. Valerian's wording is different from his citation of this passage in the preceding homily, which indicates that he was quoting from memory.

2 Gal. 6.8.

let us not overlook the need of the poor. Otherwise, we may lose what can be gained from the tears of the unfortunate. For, with the Lord, the account of money distributed among the wretched is kept thus: the more a man disburses, just that much more does he store away. In this way, from many seeds come many sprouts, and from many sprouts still more branches. About this, too, hear the Lord's words: 'He who sows sparingly will also reap sparingly.'[3]

Therefore, if, as you see, he who sows sparingly will also reap sparingly, so, too, will he who disburses little receive little. He who sows nothing stores nothing away. Thus it happens that he who stores but little fasts when he does not want to. But, when can it happen that a man who plants no seeds in the ground will see his barns filled with abundant crops? So, if you desire that we should gather crops of joy, let us sow more generously in our tears. 'He who sows sparingly will also reap sparingly.'

(2) We often find that a man who has once given an alms to the hungry thinks that he has completely fulfilled the commandment. Therefore, it will not be enough to have given the food of one day to strengthen limbs weak through hunger. Otherwise, he who is good on one day comes down [to his clients], without good reason, as odious on another. He who thinks that what he once gave to the hungry is sufficient has lost the benefit of his previous mercy.

But, he from whom a poor man never goes away sad sends ahead integral fruits of mercy to the Lord. A doctor must employ continuous medication to prevent another man from groaning in pain, because a sickness which is daily developing requires medicine every day. If anything bloody or obnoxious happens to be in us, we, too, must take care to heal it by abundant alms. For, the wounds you have

---

3 2 Cor. 9.6.

washed only once are not immediately cured. Medicine must be used again and again for a body which has been cut into.

Wherefore, dearly beloved, if we wish no fault of avarice to contaminate the days of our life, let us not close our ears to the pleas of the unfortunate, nor turn our eyes from the nakedness of the wretched. Let no one think he has lost what he has given to the poor. Just as indigence follows upon inhuman conduct, so is wealth gained by the pursuit of kindliness. That is what the Prophet states: 'He that giveth to the poor shall never want; but he who turns away his face, will be in great indigence.'[4]

See, the cry of the hungry man is a challenge in your ears, and the sound of a failing voice from a hungry throat is striking at your door. Why do you not think of that phrase: 'Blessed is he that understandeth concerning the needy and the poor: the Lord will deliver him in the evil day.'[5] The business man who keeps stored away in a sack the money with which he could carry on gainful trading is recognized as being quite a fool.

(3) But, something worse is this. Many vices co-exist with avarice. This man, in order to avoid showing mercy to a poor man, drowns out the voice of those who ask of him by overwhelming them with words. That man, to avoid hearing, pretends that he heard something else. Such a way of living is wretched. In it a man tries to make his ears defective while he is pursuing avarice. Ponder this phrase: 'He that hath mercy on the poor, lendeth to the Lord.'[6]

Why, then, should anyone hesitate to feed the needy, when he sees that in satisfying the poor he is bestowing gifts on our Christ? There are some who make a laughing stock

4 Prov. 28.27.
5 Ps. 40.1.
6 Prov. 19.17.

of those who beg in misery by extending them hope of a kindness ever procrastinated. They are ashamed to make excuses to those begging. So, by making promises they deceive them in their misery.

See, this one says: 'The key is not here. The caretaker is away. As soon as you come back you will get your request.' Are you not aware of this statement of Solomon? 'Say not: Go and come again: tomorrow I will give to thee: when thou canst give at present.'[7] Whence do you know what will happen the next day?

You say: 'As soon as he comes back, you will get your request.' When will your steward, perhaps so often absent at your desire, return for the hungry man? When will your irritating strong-boxes, filled with your stored-up possessions, open up to the one who cries for help? It is while they minister to your desire that they cannot be opened.

You say: 'When you come back, you will get your request.' What if weather severer than usual cuts the naked man like a whip? What if the exit of approaching death receives those limbs which are failing from hunger? Who would not judge that a man was consigned to death by your condemnation, if he sees that your contribution could have saved him? You say: 'When you come back, you will get your request.' With faith in whom does he return, whose every bit of strength has left him? Or with what hope does he come again to a house if he went away from it in shame the day before?

(4) Let us suppose that he does come back to meet the terms of your promise—perhaps to fulfill the condition under which he was to return. Clearly, it would have been fairer to deny the alms right away than to deceive the hungry man by a promise which brought him hope.

---

7 Prov. 3.28.

Give heed to the words of the Lord: 'Deal thy bread to the hungry.' If you wish, dearly beloved, let us investigate with what reward the shared bread is recompensed. Hear the Lord's full statement: 'Deal thy bread to the hungry: when thou shalt see one naked, cover him, and despise not the domestics of thy seed. Then shall thy timely light break forth, and thy garments will quickly arise, and justice will go before thee, and the brightness of God will surround you. Then shalt thou call, and God shall hear: and while thou shalt yet be speaking he shall say, Here I am.'[8]

You see, dearly beloved, in what good stead the dispensing of a slender sum stands us. Because of it the Lord of such great majesty deigns to come at our request. For, He says in another place: 'Whoever gives to one of these little ones a cup of cold water to drink, amen I say to you, his reward will not be lost.'[9]

In this passage, good will is required, not wealth. For, he who in little matters has shown his desire to be merciful has shown his affection for complete devotion in the greatest matters.

Therefore, dearly beloved, in proportion as each one has and is able, let him disburse, give, and expend. Let no one run away from a lame man, let no one pretend he has not heard the deaf man, let no one withdraw his helping hand from the weak man, for all those deeds have a place in the retribution. To clothe the poor man is to cover the nakedness of one's own self. To help a beggar is a great gain. This is what the Lord says: 'Whatever you did for one of these least ones, you did for me.'[10]

That is how great our Lord's care of the wretched is. He regards as offered to himself whatever some tiny dona-

8 Isa. 58.7-9.
9 Matt. 10.42.
10 Matt. 25.40.

tion confers on the poor. Where the trade in wine and produce is brisk, we sometimes observe needy widows whose sex and age have weakened them, who lack the strength to work and earn their living. Wicked, indeed, is that man who is not stirred to mercy by the misfortune of their loneliness, or the weakness of their age.

What is worse, we also often see a group of captives wandering about with bodies scarcely clad. What profit have you from the abundance of your riches, if in your sight one man is cold and another hungry?

(5) Behold, dearly beloved, the time of just retribution is coming, as also the gift of the promised inheritance in heaven. Therefore, let us give and pay out in this world if, as you wish, we are to hold a part of our riches in heaven. Listen to the Lord saying: 'Lay up for yourselves treasures in heaven,'[11] and in another passage: 'Make for yourselves purses that do not grow old.'[12]

Dearly beloved, well indeed has our Christ set the reward of our good work in proportion to the quality of what we give out. Consequently, neither a rich man nor a poor man can excuse himself in regard to giving alms. Thus, He orders this man who has very much to disburse treasures, and that one who exists, as He knows, in the squalor of poverty, to share his bread with the hungry. What barns are so empty that they cannot stand a little withdrawal like that? What fortunes are so wretched that a beggar can cause that much disarrangement?

The man who knows that no contribution beyond his ability has been imposed on him can indeed easily and without difficulty fulfill the commandment. I am, of course, aware that the slenderness of an estate obstructs a good will,

11 Matt. 6.20.
12 Luke 12.33.

with the result that means are unavailable to carry through a splendid plan. But, if we cannot promote projects of greater moment, let us not pass over these which are small and easy. 'Deal bread to the hungry.'

Would anyone fail to heed these words with devotion, even if he is oppressed with poverty, and if he sighs, over-burdened with all the indigence? Otherwise, he is either too much a beggar, or very vain, who in the giving of alms is not content with the dispensation of the bread which is dealt.

But, you object: 'Many possessions gradually dispensed add up to a mass.' That is true. Yet, how great is that in comparison to what the Lord says? 'I shall give you a hundredfold in return, and life everlasting besides.'[13]

However, you who offer a little portion of broken bread with such reluctance, what would you do if you were asked for a weight of gold, or a precious talent of silver, or something unbroken? I do not know if you who sigh so much over so small a matter would ever redeem a captive for a great price.

'He that hath mercy on the poor, lendeth to the Lord.'[14] Wherefore I advise, dearly beloved, that no one should keep back a part of his riches from God. When God gives back the reward for your mercy by His own multiplied mercy to you, in return for your righteous labors, He does not bestow a reward for your good works which is conferred with reluctance. Therefore, let us not hesitate to give, or hide our distribution. For, those who till the earth have always had their chief hope of raising a good crop in this: sowing seed in abundance.

---

13 Matt. 19.29.
14 Prov. 19.17.

## HOMILY 10

### *Parasites*

(1) Dearly beloved, as often as I found it necessary, in accordance with my zeal for discipline, to treat the virtues of good men to the embarrassment of the wicked, I bestowed much praise upon friendships. I did this by placing the pursuit of fraternal union before you while I was praising virtues one by one in accordance with their merits. This pursuit, accompanied by peace and charity, promotes a life of perfect religious living.

But, when I continually and diligently turned my attention to the causes of single events, and adapted the function of my sermon to those honorable pursuits, I discovered much in those very friendships which displeased me. In my praise of good men, I did not want to seem to omit anything pertaining to discipline. So, among the sins of enmity I also dared to find fault with friendship—if those can be called friendships in which some injury, provoked by many wounds, is finding its way into action.

In regard to this matter, some men, to excuse away the odium of this detestable error, perhaps pretend that this is sport. They give the name of fun to cases which deserve punishment. Let no one who has grown accustomed to such insults bear this remark with any attitude he pleases. For my part, I think friendships have escaped from every kind of control in a case where it is not proper for an injured man to show his anger, or for an angered man to be vindicated. Dearly beloved, of two such men I do not know whom to call more unfortunate: the one who lives by deforming someone else, or the one who has prostituted his body to wantonness and handed it over to mockery. In such cases, let no one cry out to me: 'Have patience. That pain which is not being exacted because an injury has been inflicted on the one who is angry does pertain to wantonness.'

Perhaps, however, indulgence should be shown to those whom poverty drags into every sort of insult, and whom unfortunate want compels to subject themselves to these countless blows. While these unfortunate men submit to necessity, they acquiesce to indignities. Let it be granted that the case of their regrettable poverty urges patience upon them. But, what are we to think of those who get their entertainment from this indignity suffered by others? What stage of friendship is that which pain has fettered and injury has irritated? What pleasure of familiarity can accrue to a man who must daily pay his price in suffering?

(2) Dearly beloved, I indeed feel ashamed about the embarrassment of those unfortunate persons whom that hunger, base covetousness, has ensnared. But much more do I sigh over the conduct and way of life of those among whom a blameworthy friendship has killed regret, and a love of familiarity which is bloodthirsty has driven joy away.

I deem those men unfortunate whose stomach is enticing them to continual indignities, and whose appetite, which will never gain them satisfaction from the cups, draws them to endure an injury. Yet, I think those still more unfortunate who stir up fights by a friendly goading, and amid the cups of flowing wine take their satisfaction from others' blood.

Look, this man has prepared a banquet. He has assembled crowds of flatterers by elaborate preparations in which he took a delight. Among them, the appetite of the parasites marches along. It customarily leads them to sell an injury in return for wine, and in return for cups to repair their garments which were torn by many blows. Therefore you see how those men, who find their pleasure in having friendships bloody, carry on their hate-provoking activities.

What is there that an unfortunate man may not get from detestable wantonness? See, a man is made a spectacle before a man! To stir up a bit of mirth foul conversation is asked for, or a disfigured countenance. While this man is eating, his beard gets pulled; while that one is drinking, his chair is pulled out from under him. This fellow eats from wood easily split, that one drinks from a glass which is easily broken. So great is the urge to laugh! Consequently, these unfortunate men think that no banquet should pass without fun; unless they diverted the garments of the guests or the servings in the cups into the foods. How great, do you think, are the miseries to which those deeds add up?

See, whatever loss these guests at the table produced is some insatiable stomach's gain. He who is devoted to pleasures of this kind either diminishes the reward for his efforts by his drinking, or brings it to nothing by getting a whipping.

(3) These censures should be applied above all to those activities which reduce the state of friendship and familiarity to so base a service, just for a little fun. In far better condition is a state of service to a master which consists in a command to stand at readiness, in obedience to an assigned duty. One in service like this has a place where he can laugh among those who recline at table, yet those who await his service do not hold him to any guilt of sin.

Look, someone has arranged the cups in a line equipped with daggers. A contest of words is soon held, and the victory is eagerly awaited. The contest does not end until all the daggers of the cups are moistened with abundant tears.

To wait in eagerness for the fights of one's unhappy friends—that is to defile a banquet rather than to improve it. Can the name of friend be given in truth to those who give services such as captives are forced to give, who eat their meal in the manner of gladiators? Amid all the novel foods and flowing wines, whatever is cheaper or acrid is given to this unlucky fellow, so that it is uncertain whether it would be better to go hungry or thirsty in this abundance of viands.

Clearly, captivity in dark dungeons brings less exposure to ridicule. In them a man endures the hard yoke of domination, yet he gets some solace from the necessity of the situation. He who must unwillingly remain in servitude has nothing to blush about. But I should like to know this, dearly beloved. How does the injury which disfigures someone else give recreation to the man who is looking for it to occur? Perhaps some lovers of this conduct assert that these things are done in fun—just as though there were a lack of reasons why men should refrain from seeking these indignities.

(4) If you so desire, I shall show you some amusements which are not improper. They can easily banish the gloom of a drooping spirit.

Look at the little tots. How enjoyable are those first words they form, when a half-formed word emits the name 'mother,' and the grunt of a syllable deep in the little throat begins the word 'father.' Who lacks fun there, when, in those difficult efforts to speak, the clumsy little tongue tricks the struggling lips and the quivering mouth has indistinctly pronounced the words it drops?

If, however, you have your delight in spectacular displays, you have those of the horses. Sometimes these races are dangerous, but they are always enthralling when the animals speed up their pace at the whips, and sniff the wind or fear it.

Far from small, too, are the pleasures derived from hunting trips, and the contests stirred up by the dogs—contests which involve no dangers or loss. Here is one dog in a race. With rivaling pace it is pressing a long-eared hare. There is another dog. With sensitive nostrils it is following the tracks of a hiding deer.

However, these pursuits should be abandoned in an age in which, through renewal of the ancient error, wantonness is flourishing again. Surely, something else benefits us whom our Christ has encompassed with His laws, whom He has segregated from that folly of superstitious paganism. Nevertheless, we do not lack shows to relieve our weariness. They give sufficient delight to a soul troubled with its cares.

(5) Let us put before our eyes those struggles which the martyrs fought. Let us fasten our attention on the examples of their admirable virtues. Then, as you will observe, the sighs of unfortunate souls soon will give place to growing joy.

To whom will no joy accrue from that conflict in which the just parties gain the victory, in that conflict which the fierce foe arranged by bringing up all his instruments of torture for the persecution of the saints? Who will not smile, who will not be joyful, when he sees the soldier of our Christ exulting in his tortures? When the originator of the persecution blushes, and the torturer through weariness ceases to inflict the blows?

If, perhaps, some one of you finds his pleasure in listening to beautiful songs, let him direct his eager heart to widened interests, and take in the singing of the Prophets' psalms. Let these joyful and divinely inspired psalms ever well forth from our mouths. We thus win the favor of Christ, who wanted us in honoring His name to exult continually because of the hope of salvation which He restored to us. Let this be the exultation of our heart: to rejoice day and night in the Lord.

To exult means this: to keep the commandments of the Lord with our whole soul. He keeps the commandments who guards his life from every infection of vice. He is thus guarding his life who shows fidelity to his neighbors, loves peace, and cultivates friendships. To cultivate friendships means to restrain others' irascibility by one's own habitual moderation, to check others' seething tempers by one's own patience. If in this way you lead a life of self-control and win the approval of our Christ in regard to all these matters which we have mentioned, you will walk without blame among others at the Judgment to come.

## HOMILY 11

### *The Attribution of All Our Good Works to God*

(On 1 Cor. 1.26-31)

(1) Dearly beloved, those[1] are in error who think that the improvements of our lives come from our own effort and that merits for virtues can be stored up without the aid of Almighty God. For, if our being good arises from ourselves alone, why do we find ourselves subject to vices?

1 The Pelagians and the Semi-Pelagians. Cf. above, Homily 7. Almost all of this homily, especially sections 1 and 3, forms an interesting treatise on the necessity of grace for the performance of salutary acts. Cf. Raynaud's remarks in *PL* 52.789-792. St. Valerian clearly states that we need God's help for the performance of all or any good works. Although he does not seem to be professedly engaging in controversy with the Semi-Pelagians, he is here teaching his flock a doctrine which is inconsistent with Semi-Pelagianism, and which in general tenor is very similar to the condemnations of Semi-Pelagianism enacted later at the Council of Orange and confirmed by Pope Boniface II in 529. Cf. Denzinger, *Enchiridion symbolorum*, nos. 176-180.

If everything which can improve or save man comes from ourselves, why are we held fast by the necessity of dying? Clearly, he exceeds all the bounds of sacrilegious superstition who in the case of works of justice takes out the part of God. From God have we received the spirit of wisdom. He controls the whole man, and enkindles the minds of mortal men to every good work. Whatever comes down from that abode of justice is of Him.

Consequently, all[2] the excellences of our efforts should be ascribed to God, in order that He may not annul the gifts of the Holy Spirit. It is a vice of excessive presumption for the soldier alone to wish to gain the palm of victory when the commander, too, is fighting.

You certainly can, if you wish, recognize to whom good and evil deeds should be respectively imputed. The Prophet says in one place: 'Thou hast done well with thy servant, O Lord,'[3] and in another place: 'The fool has said in his heart: there is no God.'[4] Therefore, you see that we ought to attribute our good works to God and evil ones to our human customs. For, just as good deeds are originated through the care of the Lord, so evil ones spring from the Devil as their author.

(2) However, that you may understand that life is a gift of God and that death is under the Devil's power, listen to the Evangelist: 'Come, my children, take possession with me of the kingdom promised to you from the foundation of the world. I was hungry and you gave me to eat.'[5] To the others Christ says: 'Depart from me, accursed ones, into the everlasting fire, because you did not give me to

2 *Omnia . . . laborum insignia*: all the excellences—therefore, even the beginnings of faith should be ascribed to God. St. Valerian here professes doctrine incompatible with Semi-Pelagianism.

3 Ps. 118.65.

4 Ps. 13.1.

5 Matt. 25.34,35,41.

eat.' You see, therefore, that good acts are serviceable for heaven, and evil acts are consigned to the pits of hell.

There is a division of our actions. When we do well, we belong to Christ. When we do evil, we pass over into the power of the Devil. The Lord never abandons a person whose good will is steadfastly devoted to religion. Divine consolations are not wanting where there are deeds of right living. The good deserts us, then, when evil takes place, because without doubt we are deprived of God's help after we occupy ourselves with desires of iniquity.

Therefore, when God our Saviour is assisting us, the Devil's power of domination is certainly absent. But, when the Lord of virtues has withdrawn, the foe easily enters that unoccupied room. Consequently, there is one hope of our salvation: to impute the series of our evil deeds to ourselves, and that of our good ones to the powers of God. He who does not merit the consolations of the divine majesty soon has himself under the Devil's dominating power.

(3) Therefore, we should place our hope in the Lord, that we may be good; when we have become good, we should take pride in the Lord. Listen to the Apostle's words: 'What hast thou that thou hast not received? If thou hast received it, why dost thou boast as if thou hadst not received it?'[6]

This is the perfect way to take that pride in our acts, to take that pride because of the Lord with whom the crown of virtues is stored up for those who conquer. Indeed, a man should take pride in himself when, for the name of the Lord, some voluntary suffering has come his way, but this pride has this fruit if it earns its effect through the help of Christ.[7] For, on this point, the Prophet said: 'Unless the Lord build

6 1 Cor. 4.7.
7 This is another strong statement incompatible with Semi-Pelagianism.

the house, they labor in vain that build it. They watch in vain who keep it.'[8]

You see, therefore, that without the Lord that which is good cannot be built, and that which has been built cannot be guarded. The building of this divine house is the matter of building our life, and our life should be fortified by the help of the divine majesty.

Consequently, we should continually beg our Christ to foster good things in us, and to guard those which have been fostered. And may He so move the seat of our understanding that He does attribute to the power of heavenly glory everything in us which is good.

(4) It is a species of folly for a man under the power of someone else to deem that which he has done to be his own. Look how this fellow now glories in his riches, now sighs in his poverty. If our goods are under our own control, why does not our penury cease at our desire, or our wealth remain? This man is now elated with the vigor of health, now vexed with the pain of sickness. If the health of our life were under the power of man, the beggar would never be in danger, and the sick man would not die.

Let each one think again about the origins of his own life. Let him seek out the Maker of the human race. Who formed the body, who joined its members together, who caused earthly elements to grow for human use? Did not the Lord establish all these matters through His planning wisdom?

Since, therefore, it is not through ourselves that we exist, how is it through ourselves that we possess? It is a species of folly to owe the gift of life itself to another, and attribute to yourself its adornment with virtues. Look! This man is exalted with honor; that man flatters himself over the integrity of his body. This man ascribes his riches to his own

8 Ps. 126.1.

efforts; that man assigns his knowledge of doctrine to his protracted vigils.

We cannot deny that the practice of vigilance adds improvements to religious living. But God is there, where the vigorous desire of a full religious life is present. That is what the Apostle says: 'Do you seek a proof of the Christ who speaks to me?'[9] Where God's help is not sought, human effort is on a pretty weak foundation. Faith is without doubt in danger if it is not strengthened by God's fostering care. Therefore, it is ours to wish good, but Christ's to bring its accomplishment.[10] That is the Apostle's teaching: 'To wish is within my power, but I do not find the strength to accomplish the good.'[11] So, you see that the desiring of a good work ought to come from ourselves, but bringing it to completion lies in the power of God.

But, why should any mortal man attribute the doing of good to his own effort alone, since the Prophet states the following: 'There is none that doth good, no not one'?[12] Does not the Evangelist also teach[13] that there is not anyone good except God alone? Therefore you see that if we sometimes

---

9 2 Cor. 13.3.

10 This statement clearly can mean that we have some part in cooperating with the grace of God. But, if it is taken apart from its context and the doctrine propounded in this entire homily, this statement, like St. Paul's in Rom. 7.18, can be interpreted to be Semi-Pelagianism: We can ourselves begin a good work, but only by God's help can we bring it to completion. The statement taken apart from context, along with others similary taken (listed by Raynaud in *PL* 52.765-770), formed the basis of the charge of Semi-Pelagianism against St. Valerian. Such a procedure endeavors to put the worst of two possible interpretations on an author's words. In *PL* 52.689-692, Sirmond lists similar statements from Sts. John Chrysostom, Jerome, Augustine, and other Fathers which, if taken according to this procedure, would show these Fathers to be Semi-Pelagians.

11 Rom. 7.18.

12 Ps. 13.3.

13 Matt. 19.17.

seem good we are carrying into effect a goodness from God. Listen to the Apostle: 'You are the Temple of God, if indeed the Spirit of God dwells in you.'[14] Clearly, we are a temple of God—but when we are doing good. If a man is a temple of God, then that which we have in the temple is necessarily of God.

(5) But we have spoken the above matters to good men. There is no temple of God where there is a multitude of vices. Where crimes are abundant the Devil is in power.

Clearly, riches with all their display are referred to the one who claims ownership in a large house. We function in the place of an administrator. If a gain is made, it will be referred to the Master. If a loss is sustained, it will be a contribution to the administrator's downfall. For, whatever a servant in a master's power has elaborated is necessarily the master's. The servant receives gratitude for his efforts, but he owes to his master the gain from the task he completed. Money is entrusted to a profitable servant for this purpose, that the gains of a doubled profit may be added to the master's account.

(6) Wherefore, consider men's customary manner of living. Then you will understand that it is for this purpose that money is entrusted to a profitable servant: to have gains of doubled yield added to the master's account. That is what the Evangelist states, in the following passage, about him who brought the gain of doubled[15] money to his master returning from afar: 'Well done, good and faithful servant; because thou hast been faithful over a few things, I will set thee over many; enter into the joy of thy master.'[16]

Thus, the master is praised in the person of his good servant, and the good servant is lauded in the person of

---

14 1 Cor. 3.16.
15 Reading *duplicatae;* cf. *PL* 52.727, note a.
16 Matt. 25.23.

his master. Consequently, we should take care not to ascribe to our own virtues whatever pertains to the glory of a good work. We know that the crown of victory is gained not by boasting, but through faith and the acknowledgment of the Lord's passion. The practice of good works has a relation to these. This is that money to which, as we have said, the benefits of the heavenly kingdom have a relation. This is that business trading, doubled by its yield of just profit. This is that reward due to merits and promised to the blessed in return for their works.

(7) Therefore, let our piety be increased, and also our faith, mercy, and goodness, in order that we may enter into the joy of the Lord our God when He comes to settle the accounts with His servants. We can easily get this if we keep the commandments of heaven till death.

But, to be judged worthy of the reward, we should not work listlessly. Honorable results easily follow upon acts of justice—if, however, base desires do not fill the soul. Those desires easily fade away into the winds if we do not seek after the consolations of God.

Therefore, whoever finds himself placed in this state of living religiously, in which man's salvation consists, should not be elated with the glory of his sanctity. Rather, let him attribute the fruit of his effort to the Lord, who stores up the heavenly gifts for each one in proportion to his merits. Therefore, 'Let him who takes pride, take pride in the Lord.'[17]

Dearly beloved, we should strive with all diligence that our pure faith should recommend our life to the Lord in such a way that human pride may claim nothing for itself, or attribute anything to its own efforts. He who has attrib-

17 1 Cor. 1.31.

uted the fruit of holiness to his own powers has lost all his labor.

## HOMILY 12

### *The Preservation of Peace*

### (On Matt. 5.38-48)

(1) There are, perhaps, some eager with spiteful words to disparage any manifestation of good will. They attribute it to fear or cowardice if a man sometimes withdraws from a fight, or, when exasperated by injuries, has recourse to extreme patience because of his love of peace.

The admonition in the Gospel passage ought to suffice for the refutation of such judgments of a depraved mind. However, we shall pursue proof of these matters in our humble sermon, as far as we can. In accordance with the zeal with which we devote ourselves to charity, we shall promote with suitable desires whatever the fullness of religion requires. We shall do this although I am aware that many, whose love has been thwarted, serve the Old Law so devotedly that they attack with hate any measure which a care to preserve peace suggests.

The very message we are going to convey is proved by many testimonies of Scripture. In this passage the Lord states: 'Love your enemies, do good to those who hate you.'[1] I have no doubt that some deem it quite useless and impossible to return love for enmity, and gratitude for contumely.

Truly, it is difficult, dearly beloved, to keep anger from seething in every part of our body after we have received an insult. Yet it is characteristic of a wise man either to bear

1 Matt. 5.44.

this additional pain patiently or to temper it with soothing applications. But, to overcome hatred by benefits—that is unlimited virtue. For, among men, that one gains the palm of perfect virtue who prepares cups of sweet honey in return for poison.

(2) Thus, the first degree of love is to nourish charitable affection by means of friendship, but to pay back hatred with love is the summit of perfect love. That first degree is ascribed to acts of kindness; this latter is attributed to acts of virtue. To the summit of perfect love we add, besides, that statement of Scripture which says: 'If thy enemy is hungry, give him food; if he is thirsty, give him drink; for by so doing thou wilt heap coals of fire upon his head.'[2]

Therefore—whoever you are, afflicted with an injury which sprang from someone's insolence, and goaded by grief excited by contumely—if you wish to be perfect, check the anger of your spirit by moderation, and through the good of patience keep away from yourslf the grudges which base indignation engenders. Or, surely, if your desire to exact vengeance is so great, show yourself merciful in the case of those who are unaware that the salvation of one's soul depends upon the perfection of love.

Perhaps hatreds are balanced against hatreds, and an injury is paid back to make up for a crime. To provoke a brother to anger is indeed a crime, but for the one provoked to be unremitting is something disgraceful. That is the way the germs of hatred produce their most luxuriant fruits of iniquity and work the punishments of crimes. When the originator of a quarrel is ashamed to make satisfaction to his brother and an injured man to the just man to the extent he demands, one of them seeks revenge in a law court for the injury inflicted.

2 Rom. 12.20.

(3) See, dearly beloved, you have heard the fruits by which the promotion of peace brings joy. Now learn how great are the crimes for which hatreds are blamed. For, the Lord says, as the Evangelist states: 'He who hates his brother is a murderer.'[3] You see the retribution of each party. The latter man incurs the stain of homicide because he hates his brother; the former [who promotes peace] has compensation prepared for him because of a little alms.

Reflect and see with how much honor of peace and quiet friendship surrounds you, and how much favor it shows, if you struggle against enmity by love. 'Love your enemies.' Less by far is the merit if you love one who loves you. For, he who loves another man who does not love back is doing something to improve the other's conduct, but he who loves one who does love back is improving his own behavior. Of two men, the charm of charity necessarily belongs to him who was the first to manifest the affection of love; he who loves back one who already loves him is but returning what is due. There is no new merit where another's service has preceded. When gifts are returned for gifts, or services for services previously given, that is not to be regarded as a matter of perfection.

'If thy enemy is hungry, give him food.'[4] Did He say: 'If thy friend is hungry give him food?' No, give food to your enemy, for your friend himself supplies himself so as not to be hungry. What can your alms accomplish there, where friendship is gratifying to a friend?

(4) But, let us see the difference between him who gives food to a needy friend and him who feeds a hungry enemy. The former pays a debt of gratitude; the latter gives an example of mercy and virtue. It is, in truth, praiseworthy

3 1 John 3.15.
4 Rom. 12.20.

to give food to a needy brother, but something more important to succor an enemy in his need.

'Love your enemies.' Perhaps one smarting under an injury will think those words little consonant with reason. But let this man, whoever he is, look once more to the peace of his own life, and he will understand that to have loved one's enemy is to have won a victory. Unlimited danger hovers over a man when the Devil, that master of strife, has armed for a fight two men who rival each other in their fury. It is his wont to convey bitter remarks, and then carry them back again, in order to stir up hatreds.

However, if provocation is stirring a man to indignation, when does he pass a day without tribulation, or when does his night run its course without wicked thoughts? Suppose that a man always finds it necessary to think about and fear someone he has harmed. Clearly, he will never lead a life free from suspicion.

With the greatest care harsh pains should be assuaged by the soothing medication of words, in order that even hardness of heart may grow milder when softened by the desire of peace. In this connection, I deem those happy who with a set mouth shut in the words on their lips. Mindful of the heavenly precepts, they do not draw forth the insults lurking in another's language. For, hatreds die when an injury is not pondered; anger has no power if the voice of one person is lacking in a quarrel. Consequently, a double victory awaits patience: a man has overcome the impulses of his own temper and restrained the conduct of another.

(5) We know, dearly beloved, that sometimes in a verbal quarrel ears are hurt and hearts emit deep sighs. But, the man who broods upon the words of a contentious adversary injures himself. He who complains that someone's remarks were directed against himself is but staining himself.

The full victory is to keep silent when another shouts, to make no reply when he provokes. Then you get the reward both for your own patience and for your brother's correction, if insult is consigned to oblivion. But, when words follow upon words, fuel is supplied to a fire.

Just as nothing is more disgraceful than to reply to madmen, so nothing is more useful than to keep silent before provoked men. For, enmities grow much if one man defends himself with words, and meanwhile another is challenging what he says. There will be no end to enmities unless we give in to the angered persons for a while.

Perhaps you say: 'There is no blame if you do what the Prophet states: "Set a watch, O Lord, before my mouth, and a door around my lips." '[5] If you do not wish to suffer an injury, tie up the plectrum of your mouth, and stop up your ears to prevent your angered brother's words from reaching you. Or, surely, if they do reach you, let them be an occasion of your silence. Thus, the fury which he conceived will lose its force, if one of you keeps silent and lets the other rave alone.

(6) Hear the Apostle's words: 'Love does no evil to a neighbor.'[6] Do you wish to know what that evil is which shuts out the charm of brotherly love?—hatreds, quarrels, grudges, fights, rivalries. These vices brand the whole course of the present life with disgrace. He who devotes himself to charity is freed from this evil. The ruin which vices bring on has no place in him who spurns hatreds and cherishes his unimpaired affection for charity.

See, the Evangelist adds something to increase love: 'Love thy neighbor as thyself.'[7] Let us see who that neighbor is whom the Evangelist so warmly recommends. The Prophet

5 Ps. 140.3.
6 Rom. 13.10.
7 Matt. 22.39.

did not thus set forth the degree of relationship or the bond of consanguinity in order to exclude foreigners from the benefit of brotherly love. Your neighbor is every man who is united to you by the common bond of Christianity. Your neighbor is he who is not seen to be excluded from communion with the Church. Your neighbor is whoever is neighbor to Christ. Therefore, he who loves his neighbor loves God. And he who thus loves God should venerate the neighbor of His Christ.

The Prophet said in praise of fraternal charity: 'Behold how good and how pleasant it is for brethren to dwell together in unity.'[8] What good is there in the life of men except peace, in which upright pursuits make progress and religious activities are fostered? What is more joyful than all nations serving the one God in peace, and the prayers of all people converging to the praise of the one Lord?

To dwell together in unity is this: to believe in God, and faithfully to remain in the one Son of God. This is the one profitable and joyful union for mortal men: our not dividing, as the heretics do, the Father from the Son, or the Son from the Father, or the Holy Spirit from both, but, rather, our believing that these three names are distributed among the Persons, and that the Persons rejoice in the participation of the one Godhead. Thus it comes to pass that, when there is agreement unto unity, there will be no shattering of charity in the Church.

(7) Therefore, dearly beloved, let us always shun hatreds. But, to be able to shun them, let us above all shun their causes. First, let envy cease; it inflames the tempers of men to every sort of strife. During a quarrel of persons, let no one defame the lineage of another. There is no one free from blame for insolence of language. The growth of

---

8 Ps. 132.1.

grudges through controversy is above all to be guarded against, for irremediable enmity often arises from controversy.

In this connection there is need of patience; you will not practice it without fruit to your own salvation. For, just as the great blame of a grave sin awaits him who injures his brother, so a huge crown of virtue brings protection to you if you refrain from anger over an injury received. If you completely overlook insults and have mercy on others' weaknesses, you have the full spirit of love.

We know that some men find it glorious to await with favoring eyes penalties of body or losses of wretched resources. But let these, if such there are, listen to the Lord: 'Pray for those who calumniate you.'[9] After receiving an insult, many prepare another in return, and in the spirit of the robber they look for a place of revenge. And where is that which the Lord uttered: 'To no man render evil for evil'?[10] Furthermore, to keep anger from appropriating something to itself, He took away even the hope of permission to revenge, when he said: 'Vengence is mine; I will repay, says the Lord.'[11]

Wherefore, let each one forgive his brother from his heart. Let no one harbor a grudge; let no one seek revenge with unrelenting anger. Let your conversation with your enemy be always courteous and faultless. Let detractions cease, and also quarrels. Thus will your enemy be loved by you—if you are not always adding a reason for which he flames up in anger.

---

9 Matt. 5.44.
10 Rom. 12.17.
11 Rom. 12.19.

# HOMILY 13

## *The New Law as the Complement of the Old*

(On Matt. 5.38-48)

(1) Dearly beloved, perhaps some men think that it is to the detriment of great good that the justice of the Law received from the ancients, which its violators deem quit harsh, has been suppressed. They infer this from the Lord's statement in the Gospel: 'Love your enemies, do good to those who hate you, and pray for those who calumniate you.'[1]

Dearly beloved, he who thinks that goodness is not linked to justice has a rather cruel outlook, since Providence has but one and the same plan, namely, to check evil men by goodness, and to protect good men by the obligation which law imposes.

Have recourse, then, to holy David. You will find that one Power is the source of justice and of goodness. David speaks thus in one psalm: 'Thou art good, O Lord; and in thy goodness teach me thy justifications.'[2] So, dearly beloved, let no one deem this description of the Law to be anything else than the mingling of goodness and dutifulness. When dutifulness attends to disciplinary control, she establishes the norms of human acts, and when aroused by evil intentions she restrains daring hearts with severity. In order to know that nothing has been taken away from the Old Law, listen to the Lord: 'I have not come to destroy the Law, but to fulfill.'[3]

(2) Not without reason, dearly beloved, did our Christ want the precepts of the Old and New Testaments to form

1 Matt. 5.44.
2 Ps. 118.68.
3 Matt. 5.17.

one corpus. He was aware that neither one could stand without aid from the other. Truly, this is the case. Where severity exists on the part of the judge, there must always be a tempering through goodness.

Dearly beloved, every cup which aids medicine in bringing hope of human health has a mixture of bitter and sweet ingredients. If some physician, unskilled in his art, cannot mix them properly while he is compounding a remedy, he prepares fatal poison for the sick. If the physician does not know how to mix the acrid juices from the plants with proper proportions of water, the medicine is but something else to increase the pains already within the patient.

Dearly beloved, that is also the case with the Law which governs our Christian duties. It has been composed of bitter and sweet ingredients, that is, the prescriptions of the Old Law and the present one. As it is now composed, its words are unpleasant for sinners, but full of sweetness for the just, to such extent that it promises a heavenly kingdom to the just, but threatens the fire of hell to the sinners. In regard to keeping this Law, if anyone is wise and knows how, by an addition of humility and peace, to preserve the correct proportions in the mixture, he will not thereafter suffer any injury from the stricter Law. For, just as it is easy to mitigate every bitter potion with the sweetness of honey, so it is also easy to temper the bitterness of the Old Law by means of honorable deeds.

(3) Consequently, if any one of you loves justice, let him be devoted to the commandments[4] of both Testaments, and let him observe the new precepts in such a way that he does not overlook the enactments of ancient times. Thus will you fulfill the law of Christ, if you subtract no part of

4 Reading *mandatis,* with La Bigne.

the truth derived from the ancient or the present enactments.

What wise man would deny that the working of justice is the fruit of goodness, when he hears the Prophet say this? 'It is good for me that thou hast humbled me, that I may learn thy justifications.'[5] I have no doubt that there are some, dearly beloved, who in the light of this statement think that that justice can stand as perfect which states: 'Eye for eye, and tooth for tooth.'[6] That justice did indeed reign for a long time among the men of the world, but for this reason, that the Author of goodness had not yet come.

What sort of justice do you think that was which produced that one injury, death? If our Christ had not mingled the oil of mercy into those bloody laws, that is, if He had not truly fulfilled a justice without guile and brought His doctrine of goodness, even till now there clearly would be no end of that penalty.

Therefore, dearly beloved, let us who have been instructed by this information mitigate the bitterness of the Old Law by our pursuit of love, in order that the man who gives an exchange [of good] in return for an injury may not seem to have exceeded the measure of perfect justice.

(4) Look, the Evangelist states: 'Love your enemies.' Perhaps some think it absurd to repay contumely with love. It is not impossible to love an enemy if you think of the benefit to your own interests.

'Love your enemies.' Let no one think that by reason of this commandment he is conferring some benefit on his enemy. He who loves his enemy loves himself. For, the man who has stayed a robber's right hand by giving him the booty of a gift has in reality spared himself. The man who met an armed foe by entreaties, and by some negotiation

5 Ps. 118.71.
6 Lev. 24:20; Matt. 5.38.

has tried to save face for the fighter, has protected his own body. For, to have won the battle by offering a quantity of gold is evidently a part of the victory.

'Love your enemies.' This is to love one's enemies: to make no reply in the face of hatreds, to bear the reception of contumely patiently, to forgive an insult either inflicted by a hand or stirred up by stinging words. That is what the Lord states: 'To him who strikes thee on the right cheek, offer to him also the left.'[7] I know that the word 'offer' is repugnant to some who do not know how to avoid quarrels, and how to ward off the imminent retaliations of torture by means of moderation.

(5) However, what patience bestows on one contestant, if the other alone insanely raves, is something indefinitely great. Just as the one who fights back stirs up doubled blows against himself, so does he who restrains his hand when another is striking win the gain from a greater struggle.

'Do good to those that hurt you.' The first degree is that we have mentioned, that you love your enemy. The second degree is that you do him good. In the first degree, affection is inculcated; in the second degree, a work of mercy is asked for. For, it is one thing to love an enemy, and another to help him. The favor of your love avails your enemy little if you suffer him whom you say that you love to go hungry.

Hear Paul's statement: 'If thy enemy is hungry, give him food; if he is thirsty, give him drink; for by doing so thou wilt heap coals of fire upon his head.'[8] Here, as far as I see, mercy is acting as a servant for a kind of cruelty. Therefore, why does not he who is waiting for the time to work the vengeance which he promised be free from care and spend his money on his enemies? He who hesitates to

7 Matt. 5.39.
8 Rom. 12.20.

be merciful without doubt fails to know the way to vent his anger. It is clearly beyond expected happiness to have saved one's enemy and by it to have avenged an injury.

In this passage the text continues: 'Pray for those who calumniate you.' No doubt, the Lord is here admonishing us about experiencing a feigned sentiment. He knew that a love consisting in words, and an expenditure of payment, even though it is generous, often becomes irksome. In this way, therefore, you show that you willingly made your alms your avenger, if by suppliant prayer you commend to the heavenly Physician the wounds which your enemy inflicted, and by copious tears you beg help for his salvation.

'Love your enemies.' If we are commanded to love our enemies, in what state do you think that man is, who without provocation of insult pursues a brother with vicious attacks? I think that it is about this man that the Apostle says: 'He who hates his brother is a murderer.'[9] Truly, he who persecutes an innocent man in hatred does act as if he had killed a man.

(6) However, let us see who those are whom St. John deemed worthy of damnation because of fraternal hatred. They are, I think, those of whom the Prophet said: 'Their heart has been struck with envy.'[10] They are those who start fights against themselves, and burn their houses with a fire of their own making. The flame of conflagration is kept shut inside their own heart. For, here, where there is no quarrel with another party, there is not anything which ought to be blamed upon somebody else. It is among persons mutually provoked in conflict that almost all cases and hatreds grow bitter. Look at this, if the situation can be imagined: We have an accused man, and no one to accuse

9 1 John 3.15.

10 This statement is not in Scripture. Envy is disparaged in Wisd. 14.24 and in Eccli. 31.16.

him. Consequently, we have a man who ought to be punished, and we find no one who ought to be vindicated.

I deem that man clearly happy whose life remains honorable even under the gaze of another who is scrutinizing it with grim eyes. A man who is sustaining envy from another has his own case in a rather favorable position, for men envy only those better off than themselves. Only those whom better progress has raised to the pinnacles of life are subject to envy.

But I deem those worse than wretched who are disquieted when others gain happiness, and whom anger disturbs by those occult javelins of the heart after they have conceived a base rivalry. Well, indeed, do their own weapons punish them. Envy itself seems to me to have some power of discernment, since it strikes back at the heart of its own author, and with its bloodthirsty spite consumes that abode of a bad conscience.

(7) First of all, therefore, we should disparage envy. Once conceived in the mind, it works painful results. When our eyes happen upon the splendor of another's happiness, let the zeal of emulation take hold of us, not that of envy, according to the Apostle's advice: 'Strive after the better gifts.'[11]

Clearly, he who without envy strives to match another man's goods takes nothing away from true friendship. He who strives after the better gifts because of another man's example does him no injury.

Therefore, if anyone is wise, let him imitate the fruits of justice, devote himself to the practice of continence, and acquire the charm of humility. Let him in emulous love so run with the good men that he may obtain the better gifts, looking often on the Apostle's words: 'So run as to obtain.'[12]

11 1 Cor. 12.31.
12 1 Cor. 9.24.

Therefore, if anyone is stirred by another's glory, let him run after the good men, and let him strive to obtain. I even allow him to precede them, provided only that he is struggling without envy in his soul. That is truly a practice of unspotted virtue: to conquer a better man without injury to him.

Assuredly, let us yield place to the proud, but only to conquer ourselves by humility. Let not the gain which accrues from the warfare of secularistic living provoke us to emulation. Let the attractive pomp of their riches remain to those who have the care of their descendants so much in mind, despite the fact that he who cultivates mercy gains far more and stores it up for himself.

However, there is no safer course than to store away a portion of one's resources in the mouths of the poor. That is what Scripture tells us. The Lord says: 'He who sows sparingly will also reap sparingly.'[13] You defraud yourself of whatever you hold back. Therefore, dearly beloved, let us dispense much, that we may gather the multiplied fruits of mercy.

The money kept in a bag gains nothing. If it is put out in trade, a little later it comes back quadrupled. Whatever you give to the poor you do without doubt put out at interest. This interest will yield you its returns later on when the labors of every man will be evaluated and multiplied honor conferred. Retribution for their work will come to all men, both those whom their religious faith adorns and those whom their generosity commends. That is what the Evangelist states: 'Blessed are the peacemakers, for they shall be called children of God.'[14]

Consequently, dearly beloved, let us have a care, first, of peace, and second, of mercy. Let our hearts suggest nothing

---

13 2 Cor. 9.6.
14 Matt. 5.9.

false to our lips, and let our mouths utter nothing ambiguous. We should be mindful of that statement which tells us: 'Do not do to another what thou wouldst not want done to thee by another.'[15] This is what we have spoken about, that perfect love which makes up the affection of integral love.

Therefore, if you obediently observe what the fullness of the Law requires, it will come about that the severity of the Old Law will have no power over you.

## HOMILY 14

### *Humility*

### (On James 4.6)

(1) Dearly beloved, to bestow public praise on the merits of virtues whenever there is need always entails some detriment to something else. For, when one praises what is better, he is disapproving what is worse. Without doubt, a fool thinks that he is attracting some notice if he departs from a court of good men with praise for being wise.

But, what are we to do? We can neither set forth good things in orderly fashion without inveighing against the bad, nor deplore the bad without mentioning the good. Therefore, if anyone feels he receives an insult through our work of preaching, surely he will be forgiving. The bettter thing is that evils should flee, conscious of their shame—if it be only for this, that praiseworthy matters come to notice.

Hence it is that the two subjects come to one: humility and pride. The nature of things makes it impossible to explain one of them without shame to the other, since the

15 Tob. 4.16.

one is embarrassed over its own deeds, the other over another's. Therefore we must tell you how much usefulness humility carries with it, that you may know how much unhappiness goes with pride. We should explain how great are the hatreds brought forth by pride, that you may learn how much love the charm of humility attracts. Thus, each of you can more easily know what he ought either to correct or to choose in his own case.

The dominance of pride should not be deplored in such a way that the charm of humility is passed over. Nor should humility get so much preference that nothing is said about the vices of pride. What good is it to know the cause of an illness if you do not know the remedy? What does it profit to know the aid good health furnishes if there is no care to check apathy?

(2) Hear Scripture on these matters: 'God gives grace to the humble, but resists the proud.'[1] Learn now, dearly beloved, what retribution each party gets, and you will understand what you ought to love and what to hate. See, the one man is invited to grace in proportion to his love of humility, and the other is consigned to punishment in proportion to his sin of pride. Therefore, if the swelling of pride is taking place in anyone, let him repress it, lest he draw the arms of heavenly justice against himself. He who must strive against a higher power hardly lives without danger to his life. Therefore, we should bend our soul toward all humility, that we may have an opportunity of gaining grace with the Lord.

You can understand how grave the fault of swelling pride is, and how necessary it is that it be checked by so much care of God. Well indeed does humility remain ever unharmed, for one who has no reason to fight cannot be de-

1 James 4.6.

feated. But pride is exposed both to hatreds and to dangers. One who inflicts an insult can hardly escape a fight. But we easily keep every need of incurring this danger away from ourselves if we fight against the vices of pride by humility. 'God gives grace to the humble, but resists the proud.'

(3) Dearly beloved, if you diligently investigate all the sins by which we have begun to displease God from the beginning of the world, you will discover that pride was the source of all vices. You will also easily understand how humility won heavenly esteem and pride incurred divine displeasure. The lot of the Devil has made it clear that man is in danger through pride. When established on high the Devil despised the lowly; driven from his angelic dignity because of the sin of his presumptuous attitude, he received the sentence of damnation proper to a tyrant.

Hence you see that he who indulges pride plays the role of pride. If arrogance dominates a man, what is left for him save the sentence of damnation? If you wish, let us compare evil things with good, and worse with better. Then you will understand how great is the hatred under which a man labors day by day because of the vice of pride. We need not go far to seek the person. Take the status of a freeman, and you will immediately recognize the spirit of a proud man. What, I ask, is the life of those who have hatreds every day? Clearly, he who moves about puffed up with pride never passes a day without his own or another's sin, because, whether he be among his superiors or inferiors, he is always despised and feared. Pride is a vice of cheapness and an indication of ignobility; nobility of soul does not know how to be puffed up. Where manners are impolite, pride always grows along with power, but where splendor of life exists, there is also the charm of gentle humility.

(4) I call that humility true and holy which is motivated by the love of religion and of God, not extorted by fear of another who dominates. We are making mention of that humility which is joined to charity, which is not wrested from one because of the prestige of another's high position, but is nourished by the law of living. When pride is nourished by its own abundance, and haughtiness grows with power, let no one think that the customs of nature should be ascribed to vices alone. When, therefore, would medicine suffice for sick bodies, if wounds, too, were born along with a man? Pride is nourished when this man deems himself wiser in words, and that one judges himself better in ancestry; while this fellow is unwilling to be removed from his position, and that one thinks it possible that he is being despised.

Thus, we all see that, when we compare persons, hatreds grow because of the vice of pride—for example, while this fellow dangles a mass of gold and silver before the eyes of his flatterers, and that one sets up in opposition the bounds of his honor; while this one vaunts his abundant resources, and that one his readiness in conversations; while this one desires to be sought because of his ability to counsel, and that one wants to be greeted because of his banquets.

The vices which spring from pride can scarcely be counted. If a man could overcome or guard against them, he would not get caught in any snare which the Devil sets to bring on damnation. Look, one man, in order to seem always clean [in his attire], orders an excuse to be conveyed to his greeters; another feigns sickness, that he may be saluted daily; another, to find an opportunity of laying charges, pretends to be solicitous about everybody, not because he really desires the absent one, but in order to call him guilty of neglect of duty. He asks what door the greeter sought in the morning hours, that he might reckon up why the vast display of friends failed to come. Thus, while the man who does come does not get admitted to perform his greeting, he who remains away gets blamed. Thus, while the door remains shut for the man who comes, an insult is prepared for the one who stays away. I do not wish to narrate those contemptuous snubbings he gives to men when he goes out, with his proud thoughts long nursed in his heart, and when he sets up arrangements for his places and services. Thus, when he gives kisses, he exposes his own bosom [to be kissed]. No speech is pleasing to him, and there is no affection in conversation. He turns his eyes away from some, and scorns others by his manner of address. He loves[2] one man in order to show himself angered at another. I ask, what hope of living well is there there, where one man under the guise of friendship is gaining domination, and the other while growing too obsequious is falling into slavery?

(5) But let us see what kind of a character this proud man is when, perhaps, he takes his seat with his fellow citizens in a law court, certain to give an opinion.

I easily imagine the contests springing from the explosions of words, when one man urges leniency and the other feigns that he favors justice—not so much to preserve his integrity, but to wait to see which way some person of superior rank inclines. He pretends to have a different opinion in order to disagree with the contention of the first. He deems nothing right in the deliberations except what he alone has thought up. He thinks nothing just except that of which he has convinced himself. He is eager to monopolize the speaking, and to be the only one praised by all. What is worse, there will be someone to favor him in this respect. For, pride

2 Reading *alterum amat, ut alteri se ostendat iratum.*

soon opens the way of flattery, when either the proud man seeks favor or his flatterer fears to give offense.

The pride which he shows at banquets is not small, either, when his place is prepared higher than the couch; in fact, his couch is elevated so much that he seems to be hanging down rather than reclining.

This is how pride acquiesces to insult, that it itself may not seem to suffer an insult. Someone is sought to give him a helping hand as he rises, someone to care for his shoulders, someone to prop up his side. No one can make excuse to me that this is not the vice of tyrannical domination. For, the service one man renders to another, if it is not that given solely to help a weak man, is clearly slavery. In this connection I praise that poverty which a man endures who relinquishes his own excellence while doing service to the customs of others.

But, why do we lay such a weighty charge of pride only upon the rich, when we often see men in great penury who soil themselves by a similar unfortunate attitude? Solomon, so full of wisdom, says about them: 'Three sorts my soul hateth. . . . A poor man that is proud,'[3] and the other words which follow. He who retains no awareness of what his resources are does, without doubt, exceed the limits in pride. In great and dignified persons, humility is something highly desirable, but no one marvels at a pauper being humble. For, he who is bent low by the necessity which poverty imposes is humbling himself unwillingly. Humility is something pleasing in a poor man and glorious in a rich one. Humility is something charming among enemies, but pride is odious even among friends.

(6) In contrast, dearly beloved, let us inquire what the good qualities of humility are. Humility is always pleasant

3 Cf. Eccli. 25.3,4. The balance of the quotation is: 'a rich man that is a liar; and old man that is a fool and doting.'

and ready to serve, welcome in friendships, hated in the midst of insults. It is not puffed up by prosperity, or altered in adversity. It does not enslave or extort. It is the first to greet in courtesy, and slow to take a seat. It does not tarry in order to be led along by a herd of flatterers, nor seek to be fawned upon with greetings. It does not seek the attentions of praise nor favor of language. It hates crowds of applauders, because a good conscience does not get praised without a feeling of shame.

No one needs the words of flatterers except him who knows himself to be unworthy of praise. He who is worthy gets praised in more modest fashion through the devotion of his friends. But, he who is under a feeling of unworthiness thinks that his acts are being scrutinized if he goes away without praise.

Humility is hedged about with goodness. Just as it knows not how to injure, it seeks nothing from invective. In a quarrel a humble man would rather remain silent than win, and in law courts he grows willing to seem unskillful rather than be deemed impudent. He is not hasty in speech, or always quick to reply.

But, the speech of the proud is accelerated and facile, full of scorn and packed with insults. It is never uttered without a wound, never hurled without pain. Its blow is incurable and its stain indelible. However, the remedy of satisfaction follows where this fault of language has been at work.

(7) Dearly beloved, in order not to lose the grace promised in the gift of our reward, we should love this humility to seek it, and choose it, and hold it fast. Heed the Evangelist's words: 'He who humbles himself shall be exalted and he who exalts himself shall be humbled.'[4]

4 Luke 14.11; 18.14.

The exaltation is a condemnation which moves into action the power of the future judgment in the case of the arrogant and proud. Consequently, we should so bend our inclinations as to suppress every mark of pride and let the pursuit of grudges die out. Thus, a man will make progress from a more humble station until he arrives at the higher ones, is rewarded with fitting honor, and gains the grace of heavenly power.

## HOMILY 15

### *The Excellence of Martyrdom*

(1) Dearly beloved, I feel great confidence in speaking to you whenever there is need to recall the praises of martyrdom to your memory, because of our love of the blessed martyr.[1] Vivid faith, stirred by his profitable sufferings, has brought those praises forth, even though language is insufficient to praise as warmly as marytrdoms warrant. But, when will cultured man's service avail to bring out every-

1 Apparently, some martyr whose relics were at Cimiez; we do not have any positive identification. Possibly, he was the youthful St. Pontius, who suffered under the Emperor Valerian about 258. The Abbey of St. Pontius at Cimiez dates back to very early times, and this saint is the center of many traditions at Cimiez and Nice (cf. *DACL* 12.1, col. 1174, *s.v.* Nice-Cimiez). His feast is celebrated on May 14. According to a legendary account printed in *Acta Sanctorum* 3 for May, Pope Pontianus instructed Pontius as a boy in the Christian faith. When Pontius' father died, he gave his inheritance to the poor. He converted the Emperor Philip and his son to Christianity. After the emperor's assassination, Pontius fled to Cimiez, where he was arrested, condemned as a Christian, and exposed to the beasts. When they would not attack him, he was beheaded. Although this account carries a claim of giving the reports of contemporaries, the Bollandists show that it was written no earlier than the sixth century and is historically valueless. Cf. A. Butler, *The Lives of the Saints* 5, rev. H. Thurston, S. J., and N. Leeson (London 1936) 173.

thing which power from heaven has wrought in preparation for the conflict? Assuredly, we do what we can by bestowing the favor of our words on just merits, especially since no one can fail to notice the deeds performed in that struggle which every year renews for us the examples of virtues.

You have heard the Psalmist's words: 'Precious in the sight of the Lord is the death of his saints.'[2] What can be more precious than that death which knows not how to yield to hostile weapons in the raging fight? That soul which does not let itself be deceived into compliance with wicked laws clearly carries off the greatest palm of victory.

This is truly a sign of outstanding virtue: to be more inclined to death than to life in time of persecution. However, this prepares a place of eternal life, a place recommended by the pain of the cross suffered in the voluntary confession of our Christ. As the Lord says: 'He who loves his life, loses it; and he who hates his life, will find it in life everlasting.'[3]

If the occasion should come, what wise man would not contemn the gains of this life and hasten eagerly to martyrdom, since he sees that giving up his present life is part of the gaining of life? Why does not a devout man run to a task so precious, and boldly throw himself into the hands of the wicked? The gift of a heavenly reward awaits him, according to the Lord's words in that description of beautitude: 'Blessed are they who suffer persecution for justice' sake, for theirs is the kingdom of heaven.'[4]

(2) You see how great are the fruits which faith tried by human tortures has produced! And how exalted is that victory gained by the contempt of the body! Who could

2 Ps. 115.15.
3 John 12.25.
4 Matt. 5.10.

doubt about the reward we have mentioned when he observes that, lo, the devotions of all men converge in loving the saints? and that men come from every direction, far and near, to celebrate the annual festival? We easily understand what a place is prepared in the heavenly abode for those whose memory is celebrated by such great and devout attentions.

Therefore, let us fasten our thoughts on the glory which is stored up for us. Let us prefer the heavenly goods to the earthly ones, to be able to obtain those promised benefits of eternal life. Let no one delude himself by his pursuit of this world; he sees it fade away day by day as time passes away and age comes on. If we compare present goods to the eternal, those which we possess merely for a time become quite clearly rather cheap and useless.

Next, meditate on the grace of that inheritance due to us. Then you will be aware that the riches of this world fail to give satisfaction. You will judge nothing to be more ignoble than gold, nothing more despicable than the splendor of silver. In comparison with Paradise, even a rather precious gem is like to glass. The respective worth of the light of this life and of the future world can be indicated by the moon standing in the heavens while the morning sunlight pours itself into the eyes of men. The illumination of the moonlight pleases us just so long as it offers its service in the darksome night by the set laws of nature. But the glow of its nocturnal illumination, even if it gives some satisfaction, is obscured by the brilliance of the rising sun.

(3) This alone commends the spans of the present life: our doing the deeds which are not liable to accusation in the future judgment, and which cannot be proved defective if a charge is brought. But, that no soul may suffer before God in the future from the odium of injustice, we should by all

means heed that psalm which states: 'They that sow in tears shall reap in joy.'[5]

This is to sow in tears and reap in joy: to condemn past deeds of one's life by one's own judgment, and to subject a lascivious soul to just punishment. Joy quickly follows sorrow[6] if by satisfaction you anticipate the severity of the judge, and by steady chastisement reduce the defects of the crime you committed. But, lest you be deemed one who has stored up only a little grace by this, help the afflicted and grief-stricken, and better your case by your generous distribution to the poor. For, the Lord speaks thus: 'Blessed are the merciful, for God shall show mercy to them. Blessed are they who mourn, for they shall be comforted.'[7]

Therefore, dearly beloved, if any one of you diligently seeks the consolation of Christ, let him reduce another's sorrow by alms. Let him devoutly commend his own tears to this patron in whose honor we have assembled. Let him get himself into this saint's frequent prayers of intercession; he can thus obtain more easily whatever the saint suggests to the Lord in his favor. We should always have recourse to the friends of God, and serve our neighbors, and pray unceasingly to obtain the favor of holy intercession. What place will be left for forgiveness from the just Judge, if you do not know how to implore the friends of the King?

(4) Glance next at the orderly arrangements of worldly discipline. Then you will understand what concern you ought to have about devotions to the saints. Beyond doubt, unless one previously wins the good will of him who guards the secrets of the praetor's house, one will not easily attain to friendship with that higher power. Similarly, one should

5 Ps. 125.5.

6 Reading *tristitiam laetitia,* not *tristitia laetitiam,* which seem impossible in the context.

7 Matt. 5.7,5.

seek the intercessory services of the patrons to whom alone has been granted knowledge of how to soften the onsets of the angry God, and to temper His rage.

Therefore, in a large house the second rank after the owner is that of his friends. Through them alone is available free opportunity to make suggestions to the owner, and to obtain an easy access. Hence, we should cultivate the memory of the saints with unusual veneration, that they may open the door of salvation and cause the desires which arise from our servitude to come to the notice of the Lord. A great part of security consists in having, during adversity, an intercessory power in the King's house. The odium of a crime somehow decreases when the one accused begins to share in the friendship of the royal family. Similarly, a man passes his life without danger if he has someone to excuse his negligence as a sinner before the Lord.

There is no one who has no need of an intercessory power more powerful than himself—even in his greatest security. For, although their tested faith sanctifies some in this number of secure persons, they still have need of someone to commend their very faith to the Lord by his suppliant intercession. You will not find anyone so strong that he does not need the help of one stronger. Just as military fighting is carried on well under the shield, so is any project carried on safely for the witnesses when it is under a patron. Although some penalty is imminent in a case, if there is an intercessor an insult covered by the laws is forgiven. But, what limit could be put upon death, if there should be no one to intercede suppliantly and help the defendant when the judge is striking him with his sentence.

(5) Dearly beloved, if we should reflect how much the virtue of our martyr fellow citizen has brought us, neither the activity of our tongue nor the service of our mouth would

ever cease from praising God. Look at the devotions of those who drink the waters of pilgrimage, and seek with thirst the distant springs, and you see how much grace their possession of this water brings them. Now, no one can estimate how much profit accrues to our own possessions if that which is so eagerly sought elsewhere becomes present in our own holding.

Look! the Lord of virtues has granted you a living fountain from which to draw every day—a fountain unfailing, not brackish, not bitter. If anyone wants to drink of it, he will always thirst for justice, and he will never depart from the law of the heavenly commandments.

Therefore, dearly beloved, if we wish to have that share in the heavenly abode which the Lord promised to victors, let us first of all imitate in our confession the holy martyr's faith, and let us by virtue follow his path, and in our love of the Lord, let us have no hesitation to expose our own breasts to the lictor's bloody hands.

In a raging fight, a crown of victory soon covers the volunteer soldier. But, in the meantime, while such rewards are accruing to the blessed, and are being conferred because of the merits of the happy ones, let us resist the opposing forces in what has a bearing on the salvation of our souls. You do not lack an opportunity to win a victory every day, if you are willing to resist the desires of the flesh.

Look about, and see the criminal conflicts ranging all around you. See, too, how extensive the drawn-up battle line of vices is. Here, pride, and there, envy, attack our faith. Now, drunkenness suggests matter for impurity; then, covetousness enkindles the soul to every sort of falsehood, which devotes itself, among other vices, to sowing quarrels, encouraging disagreements, fostering grudges.

Hence, it is against those legions that we must fight with

spiritual arms. We must hold our place in the battle line day and night, until the vices either withdraw or bend and flee towards repentence. Then, when they are overcome, we can enter even that conflict which seeks the greatest palm of martyrdom. Who would not be willing to fight, or who would not strive to win in that conflict where a man gains instruction not merely from preceding meritorious endeavors, but also from the present examples of virtues?

## HOMILY 16

### *The Excellence of Martyrdom*

(1) Dearly beloved, example is a teacher; therefore, knowledge of such an outstanding victory was quite necessary for this world in order to promote the honoring of virtues. Without doubt, the world would still lie in darksome fetters if it were not illumined by the shining examples of the saints. It would be struggling for obscure and uncertain objectives if the crown of martyrdom, shedding its light throughout the world, were not confounding the unbelieving minds of men.

For this, thanks should be returned to God, who has armed the souls of men with such endurance, and has not looked without concern on the labors of their great work. Hence, when He was telling His lovers about the necessity of fighting, He was preparing a reward of just retribution for the victors. Thus the Evangelist says: 'Blessed are they who suffer persecution for justice' sake, for theirs is the kingdom of heaven.'[1]

Therefore, if any wise man is struggling toward the

1 Matt. 5.10.

heights through his devotion to religion, let him learn first of all where the crown of virtues comes from. We need not seek far for one whom we can imitate. Look, here before our eyes is one who daily stimulates us by his salutary examples, and with fatherly affection invites us to share his sanctity. Hence, if you wish, you grasp with ease aids worthy of the kingdom of heaven. For you have someone whom you can follow every day, and whom you ought to imitate.

Look about, dearly beloved, at other regions and the devotions of love toward the saints which we see flourishing quite extensively through the traffic of pilgrims. Then you will understand how much the Lord has given us, how much loving solicitude He has exercised upon us. He who has looked on the other nations with concern for their salvation has moistened your region, too, with the blood of martyrdom.

Investigate, and you will find out how eagerly nearly all the world seeks the intercession of sanctity. Consequently, by their emulous prayers and frequent acts of homage men continually pursue the merits of virtues so great. Hence, you easily recognize what care we in turn should have of the offices to honor the martyrs, since you see the outlying nations coming together here through the love in their devout minds, and seeking comfort from the holy martyr, as [each one's] case requires.

You do have something about which to manifest special joy. From a spring of your own flows whatever is drunk elsewhere with religious devotion; in your own midst springs up whatever is ministered to thirsting souls afar.

Learn from all this, dearly beloved, to love God, who through His heavenly command daily commends Himself by the shedding of His blood. Recognize how much patience bestows on the lovers of our Christ, and how much the sadness endured in time of persecution contributes to our acts of religion.

(2) Look, as Scripture teaches, the possession of the heavenly kingdom awaits the victor. Clearly, how worth while it is to endure the executioner for one whose suffering is gaining a reward! Therefore, if occasion comes, what wise man in his right senses will not seek so virtuous a work, and boldly expose himself to the foes? If so precious a gift of remuneration awaits a man, why should he not gaze on the flames without concern? Why should he fear the torturer's claws? To give occasion for such profitable tortures is a mark of perfected faith, especially since you gain instruction from such great examples of the virtues of those who preceded you.

You can indeed easily understand what profit each heroic man gets from winning the victory in a persecution when you see every day that throughout all the shrines of the saints, the condemnation of a spiritual court is hurled against the wickedness of diabolical presumption. Dearly beloved, the matter is not one to be taken lightly. For, we often observe that in the exorcism of an unclean spirit human bodies are harassed, and, after the names of the saints have been invoked, the activities of these bodies give testimony about the author of their crimes.

When would reading alone suffice to convince incredulous minds? When would the ancient knowledge convey an integral belief of the truth to the human powers of perception? Or when would a mind condescend to the belief of matters so momentous if, when past events are narrated, nothing beyond the hearing could be expected?

Therefore, quite unfortunate and estranged from Christ is that man whose judgments are still beset by the error of disbelief, although he sees that the merits of the saints rest upon such great signs.[2] For, this unfortunate[3] man looks back at this,[4] that we often see some invisible spirit singing psalms through the person of someone else, and uttering the language of his troubled confession through another's mouth. And when the flame is operating in this case, no injury appears; the one who is being tortured is different from the one uttering the praise.

(3) That is why the Lord puts such great power into operation through His saints. He wants to confound, by the weight of His own condemnation, those acts of diabolical wickedness which are perpetrated through wounding blows and invisible tears. He also wants to disapprove and check the attractions to sin which lie hidden in the authority of some torturer. What wise man, aware that he must face those attractions, would not immediately deplore whatever infidelity he finds in himself? Mindful of his conditions, would he not through his unceasing sense of duty very properly honor the memory of the saints? Clearly, he can easily understand what place those men have with the Lord, or in what honor we should hold them, to whom, as he sees, a favorable judgment has been awarded because of consideration of their martyrs' palms.

Therefore, dearly beloved, the examples of these saints should be followed, and their faith pursued, and their virtue imitated. It is not difficult for anyone to accomplish all this. If you think about the crown that is promised as a reward, you will find it easy to overcome every injury of the persecution. Behold, the Lord says: 'To him who perseveres I will give a crown of victory.'[5]

2 *virtutibus*, deeds showing power, miracles; cf. Souter *s.v.*

3 He is rationalizing his disbelief in Christianity.

4 Reading *hoc*. If *hos* is the correct reading, a gesture may have indicated that the men to whom the speaker was referring were not the saints, but those through whom the diabolical wonders were being performed.

5 Apoc. 2.26.

Therefore, if the occasion thus comes, let no one flee from the noise of the chains and the torturing thongs, still untouched but ready for the use of the wicked in the darksome dungeons. Without doubt, all that apparatus of death fades away if only the determination to fight grows strong. Wherefore, all hope of gaining the victory lies in faith and determination. For, if determination attends faith, faith will never abandon determination. It can hardly be that he who has accepted the injury of suffering willingly should feel the pain of the body.

Assuredly, that you may more easily advance with security in the battle line, you should keep the deeds of the saints always before your eyes. For, in the greatest battles the fighter does not lack solace if he keeps the examples of the bravest men in mind. Reflect that the Lord says: 'Take up your cross and follow me.'[6]

Perhaps those words do not apply to all, because a pampered body shrinks from the onset of pain. Let him who is in despair over the fragility of his body flee to the arms of justice, which is assigned to a voluntary service. But, he whom determination has armed for the fight easily overcomes the onset of the attacking foe. Neither does he whom the strength of souls fortifies fear the sword of the bloody lictor.

(4) However, if all those measures seem too laborious to anyone, dearly beloved, let him undertake easier ones. As the Evangelist says, there is one way which leads to life, and that a hard one.[7] Yet, if we investigate, we find many ways which lead to glory. Look, impurity is always lurking near, pride is domineering, avarice is always in ferment; against those vices we should fight through our devotion to disciplinary control. All the glory of heavenly virtue follows

6 Matt. 16.24.
7 Matt. 7.14.

upon it. Lessen your pride, and you will immediately get a crown of graces. Check your avarice, and without doubt you will be able to win a victory over all your other passions.

Wherefore, first of all conquer the desires of the flesh, and you will not find it difficult to overcome the tortures of the executioner. You know how great are the evils to which envy is subject. When it is exercising itself on others, it is wounding itself. You understand how much the soul is endangered by the fire of covetousness. You know how effective looks are to excite desire, how quick are glances of the eyes, how base is drunkenness, and how dangerous are the arrows of words. They neither hit their target without causing pain, nor get pulled out without leaving weakness.

We should prepare ourselves to carry on the fight of the Cross against all these vices. You will win a reward as many times in a day as you overcome the impulses of your heart.

(5) Dearly beloved, there are also many other things which frequently impose on us the necessity of this fight. If you conquer and overcome them, you will be a victor getting no small palm by your honorable efforts. Just as a man's wounds are as great as his vices, so are his rewards as great as his battles. He gets as many crowns as he wins victories. He who walks with his soul purified and his vices checked never passes a day without some little triumph. See, the Lord says: 'Take up your cross, and follow me.'[8]

I am well aware that the crown of martyrdom is due only to a few. The Lord Himself says: 'Many are called but few are chosen.'[9] But, while those benefits accrue to the happy few, we should stir up our own faith in regard to the matters we have treated above. Thus, when need arises, the attack of the foe will find us ready by means of a counter-attack of religious living.

---

8 Matt. 16.24.
9 Matt. 20.16.

Great virtue undergoes a test in little things. Thus, before the inexperienced soldier enters battle, he tries his strength against a mutilated tree, and by training he parries the wounding blows of a hand raised against him. Now his foot is raised, now he rivals the winds by the great speed of his horses. Eventually, he makes so much progress in this training that it is almost less effort for him to conquer the enemy than to exercise his strength.

Therefore, dearly beloved, we should train ourselves in advance by similar exercises, and by our exertions we should train our soul which will encounter more difficult struggles. Virtue of which a promise is given in small matters is more easily practiced in the great ones. Thus, when we are accustoming ourselves to overcome in little things, we are learning how to bear the greater.

## HOMILY 17

### *The Excellence of Martyrdom*

(1) Dearly beloved, careful farmers assert that soil which is crude and has never been plowed into furrows is not immediately responsive to good seeds. Unless it is softened by hoeing and continual cultivation, it does not properly nourish a seed planted in the furrow. The owner can with security expect the fruits of his little farm only then, when the older sod has ceased to be sour. If in his farming he suddenly abandons his practice of plowing, the earth will soon grow untidy again and resume its old appearance. For, this makes the difference between good and evil: that diligence overcomes nature, negligence brings things back to nature.

It is according to this rule of living, dearly beloved, that the cultivation of the Christian religion either increases or wanes. In this work, that man does not sigh with any less concern who finds it necessary to soften the hardness of his human heart by continual chastisement, and, by the rather frequent use of his faith, to work on his affections so beset with vices. Without any doubt, among the negligent the pursuit of their religious profession is endangered, too—especially if a bitter mind is receiving the seeds of the words from heaven, and inclinations to indocility cannot nourish fruits of justice. Just as fields are wont to grow untidy with thorns when the cultivation ceases, so is any vice of nature renewed when the cultivation of religion is neglected.

(2) Dearly beloved, it can be granted that for those nations to whom the faith of Christ has become known only through word, it is perhaps difficult to set down the way of salvation by means of proper language. There are some who say that examples of admirable deeds never were committed to them for their imitation. Perhaps these men can find some sort of excuse, even if it is vain. The Prophet refutes their plea with his words: 'Their sound hath gone forth into all the earth; and their words unto the ends of the world.'[1]

But, dearly beloved, to what degree can we excuse ourselves in reply to these words, if the Lord finds any negligence or infidelity in us? Our embracing the Christian name arose from deeds of valor. Through the presence of such a great martyr, a proof of the Christian religion is given daily, not alone to our ears but also to our eyes.

Who is this martyr in whose presence we are? Necessarily, he who was the first to fight here that fight of renowned power, and to show by what arrangements we can obtain possession of the heavenly kingdom. He daily teaches us by

---

1 Ps. 18.5.

his examples what we should do, and he inquires what progress we are making. Let no one doubt that his own acts fall under the solicitude of this martyr, who, as he sees, is joined to him in an affinity of relationship.

(3) Hence we should, first of all, take part in the frequent devotions shown to this patron, in order that he may stand ready for us as our own intercessor with the Lord, and commend our life to Him through the good will which springs from his esteem. When a man is placed in any necessity, there is nothing he cannot get if a friend of the highest commander begs for him unceasingly.

Dearly beloved, consider the zeal of those who thirstingly seek the waters from springs of pilgrimage; that is, who in their practice of religion eagerly travel over wide regions of the earth to seek the holy and venerable relics of the martyrs, and by their own devotions carry out practices warranted by the meritorious deeds of virtue performed everywhere on earth. Then you will understand in what honor we should hold him who as victor in that battle of the heavenly warfare has sprinkled the territory of this city with his blood.

We have seen pieces of cloth[2] from his mangled body distributed here and there through diverse and distant regions, and precious reminders of his wounds carried throughout the world. Consequently, those who had entrusted to them only these souvenirs of martyrdom have a devout care of the saints no less than ours. Therefore, the Lord of majesty has generously granted to us this protection which faith brings to others.

2 This rendering interprets *plagas* to be from *plaga,-ae,* a net, and, therefore, a curtain, a piece of cloth, a napkin. Cf. Souter, *s.v.* Possibly, however, the word is from *plaga,-ae,* a region, a district, a section,—here used to mean portions. Then the rendering should be: We have seen portions of his divided body distributed.

Consequently, we need not go far to seek him whom we should follow. We have right here a teacher of endurance, examples of rewards, a pattern of virtues, evidences of his merits. So, let us mould our souls to all endurance, in case occasion should arise. Mindful of this yearly festival, let us follow also for his examples him whom we venerate for his merits.

(4) You see the marks of honor on his breast. You cover them, like a work of God, with precious silk, and you heap yellow gold on his heavenly countenance. Learn what is the splendor of his wounds, and the crown for his tears. Learn what it means to have endured the executioner, and how much it is worth to have overcome the torturer; or in what exultation that victory issues which is gained through torments. The Prophet says: 'They that sow in tears shall reap in joy.'[3]

Instructed by these facts, what wise man would not judge the enjoyment of this temporal life something to be despised in comparison with martyrdom? Moreover, if you look again at these devotions which are paid to the saints every day, you will acknowledge that in time of persecution it is better to perish than to live. But, why do we say perish, when the Prophet says: 'The just man will live with life forever'?[4]

Therefore, dearly beloved, let us shed our tears every day and supplicate this teacher of virtues to teach us to be devout to these profitable wounds. May he show us how to expose our breast in this warfare, and sustain every onset of injury. It is not hard to enter a fight where you see that a victory has already been won. That which is taught by example quickly lodges in our minds.

But, there is something rather unfortunate. Because of

3 Ps. 125.5.
4 Ezech. 18.9.

the vanity of this world it is hard for anyone to arrive at heavenly goods. The delicate care of the body does not gain the promised kingdom. Neither will he who has not fought in a legitimate contest easily arrive at the crown of virtues. Hence, he who sets out to arrive at the goal of victory must prepare his body for every injury. The opportunity of gaining the glory consists in this, that he who wants to please Christ should first learn how to displease the world.

(5 Hear the Lord's words in this connection: 'He who loves his life, loses it; and he who hates his life in this world, keeps it unto life everlasting.'[5] There are many kinds of suffering which by the rule of living will commend a mortal man to our God. Even if the crown of martyrdom is not in them, there is, nevertheless, no small palm of virtues.

Indeed, dearly beloved, because this crown which we mentioned is stored up for the victors, let us in the meantime fight back against the sins which encircle us, in any way we can. Wherefore, let him to whom the first glory, martyrdom, is not granted, strive at least to be among all the bravest men who win the rewards for upright and religious living.

You are not unaware of how great are the shipwrecks of which the mind is in danger. See, the desire of your eyes is continually rapping on our doors, and exciting the hearts of men with the attractions of wealth. On this side a man's impulses, and on that side his glances are alluring him to every crime. Therefore, you do not lack an opportunity of conquering, if you do not cease to fight, and if, as though you were in the battle line, you fight back against the foe's weapons every minute.

(6) Indeed, to fight with success against these weapons we need this instruction from the Gospel: 'If thy eye is

5 John 12.25.

an occasion of sin to thee, pluck it out!'[6] To pluck out one's eye is this: to correct one's vices, to extinguish the desires of the flesh, and to check lasciviousness of life by pursuing disciplinary control.

Look, the field is ready for you. You are being tempted by the allurements of impurity, and, as customarily happens, you are being deceived by appearance and ornamentation. If you wish to overcome all that, you must fight by practicing chastity.

Let the purity of Thecla be before your mind. She guarded it amid the flames and the raging beasts. To such an extent did she despise the trappings of this world that, although engaged, she desired so much to preserve her chastity that she considered the bridal chamber unimportant. By struggling she nourished in its integrity that virginity which she professed, and by conquering she preserved it.

Anger often provokes us into a fight, as does also the fury of our impulses. We are goaded on by injuries, and harassed by insults. Learn with what zeal we should overcome all those difficulties. Let us arm our souls unto patience, and, in regard to these matters, may this passage of the Gospel teach us that which we cannot get by our speech: 'If someone strike thee on the right cheek, turn to him the other also.'[7]

As you see, to have acquiesced to an injury is to have won a victory. Clearly, he wins no small crown of victory who, although injured, can hold himself in peace, according to the words of the precept just quoted. Sometimes, our eyes suggest something our soul does not need. Often, too, the tongue itself betrays its errors, and breaks into language revealing things base and foul. Here, this plan of virtue should

6 Matt. 5.29.
7 Matt. 5.39.

be employed: words of love should be circumscribed by a proper practice of silence. In a verbal quarrel, moderation in speaking is the height of virtue. Hear the Prophet's words about this: 'Set a watch, O Lord, before my mouth, that my heart may not incline to evil words.'[8]

Wherefore, avarice should be overcome, anger repressed, impurity restrained, and the mouth bridled by an encircling bond. By these steps do we make progress toward Paradise, and by the merits from these virtues do we arrive at fellowship with the saints.

## HOMILY 18

### *The Martyrdom of the Mother and Her Seven Sons*

(On 2 Mac. 7.1-42)

(1) Dearly beloved, our yearning for eternal life is fired with great hope if from time to time we recall the deeds of individual martyrs. As often as the mother of the Machabees occurs to our memory, our soul bestirs itself with a joy somehow far greater to love God and win His favor. By the encouragement she gave, she on one day put the crown of martyrdom on seven sons. She was just as strong in faith as she was fruitful in offspring.

In her case there are as many proofs of her virtues as she had sons![1] For, on one day she gave to the almighty God as many martyrs as she had gained sons on separate occasions of motherhood. Blessed is she among mothers, and more

8 Ps. 140.3.

1 *pignora*. The Christians of this period frequently called their children 'pledges' entrusted to them by God. Cf. Souter, *s.v.*

fortunate still in her very bereavement! Her faith brought her this great blessing: to migrate on one day with all her offspring to the glory of the heavenly kingdom.

Turn your attention from her to that passage in the Gospel which tells that we should prefer neither parents nor children to Christ.[2] Let it be, perhaps, with some a glorious thing, to be explained with salutary examples, that they have offered one son as a victim to God. This mother has exceeded all the power and wishes of souls—so much so that in the grief of her fierce sufferings she did not let the affections of her motherly love keep back even one of her sons.

Furthermore, notice through how many degrees of virtue her precious faith grew. It is enough to acquiesce once. Yet, because of her love of the Lord, through her willing bereavement she did violence to her motherly love seven times. She was well aware of what she was about, since she knew that all her offspring was taking its place in that eternity of life, according to the Scriptural statement: 'He who loves his life will lose it; and he who hates his life, keeps it unto life everlasting.'[3]

(2) From reading the Old Testament we learn that our father Abraham offered his only son Isaac as a sacrificial victim to be immolated to God. All the world is well aware that this was a memorable proof of his faith. And, although no blood moistened the altar, there nevertheless was a victory in his prompt will. For, in the sight of the Lord, to will and to do are one. As we read, the angel called to Abraham: 'Abraham, Abraham, lay not thy hand upon the boy: it suffices that I know that thou lovest the Lord thy God.'[4]

2 Matt. 10.37.
3 John 12.25.
4 Gen. 22.11,12.

If, therefore, our father Abraham offered one son in sacrifice and pleased God, how much more has this mother pleased Him! At one time she immolated seven sons to God, with prayers of approving desire. Then she offered herself as the eighth victim. As a result, did not she, who had been the teacher of so many brave men by encouraging them towards heavenly glory, become also herself an example of outstanding virtue?

If you wish, dearly beloved, let us recall the details of that conflict one by one. Thus, parents may learn how to love their children, and children how to obey their parents. All of them should put the most value upon the love of our Christ, who prepares a crown of life resplendent with heavenly beauty for those who struggle in a legitimate contest and win. Thus, the Lord states: 'To him who overcomes I shall give the crown of life.'[5]

See, dearly beloved, how much the belief in this accomplished deed teaches us! A contest for the sake of the ancestral laws is arranged between the representatives of the Almighty God and those of the Devil. Many, yes innumerable, instruments of torture are at hand. It is when armed by them that the author of iniquity is accustomed to employ his poisonous wickedness. But, although this hostile anger hurls all its hissing fury against the representatives of justice, they show no trembling in the conflict. Consequently, on this occasion the deviser of crimes and foe of the good uses a deeper plan to dismay their courage. He moves the weapons of his iniquity against them one by one, and by his customary, threatening language arranges a single combat. He thinks that in adversity this group of brothers, once divided into sections, can easily be frightened; and

5 The phrases of this quotation can be gathered from James 1.12; Apoc. 2.10; 3.21.

that, if the pain consumes each brother as he is called up alone for examination by torture, the whole group of them will be overcome with little trouble.

(3) Hence, the eldest is led forth first. The noisy activities of iniquity and all its death-dealing apparatus are around him on every side. Far from light is the treatment of the persecutor, who thinks that if he can blot out this leader of their sworn virtue, the whole struggle can be finished off. But his all too clever plans with their enforcing cruelty failed him. Moreover, the disgrace in which a foe is vanquished is greater in proportion to the number of his satellites doing him service against one just adversary. It is a striking indication of cowardice if one man carries off the palm of victory in a struggle against his enemy's compact groups.

When the proud fury of this foe has received this wound in spite of all the kinds of torture he was employing, this executioner runs with his bloodstained hands to the brothers one by one. To excite the fear of death, he carries to each one of them his brother's blood. Thus he tests the effectiveness of these proofs of his cruelty to excite fear of death. But, even while he is trying to create an opportunity of victory over one of them, he acknowledges himself already conquered by another. The faith of them all remains unshaken, and also their resolution, strengthened by the tortures of their brothers.

The second brother steps up for the conflict. A short while later, the third one follows. These are crowned, and the fourth comes on. This horrible death does not scare away the fifth, or the sixth. In them all is one faith, one virtue, one common determination. Consequently, you would think and believe them all to be one, although the injury is harming them as individuals one by one. This is how all the brothers in the group, encouraged by their share in a common victory, observed their ancestral laws, and simultaneously won the distinctions of their multiplied virtue.

(4) Therefore, the mother runs about amid many rows of corpses. She is amazed, anxious with cares, stricken with fear and trembling. But, let this fact deceive no one. She trembles indeed, but it is about the victorious outcome, not over the death of her sons. At each investigation she is anxious lest his faith may slip away from any one of the sons, lest human frailty may segregate one from the saintly group. For, in spite of the threats of the enemy she keeps close to each son, continually encouraging him not to will anything different than his brother.

They, indeed, suffer singly, but she suffers with every single one of them, and with every one she endures torture in her soul. Therefore, she carries off the palm of her own virtue in loving Almighty God. But, if you look at the single pangs which her motherly concern endured, you see that she gained the lot of martyrdom with all her sons.

Now look! After all those palms have been won, they come to the one whose tender age gave the enemy hope of gaining a victory. He who had previously seen that the cross-questioning of his threatening words had availed so little in the case of those brave men thought that youthful minds should be given milk, the language of coaxing persuasion. So he makes his approach by every manner of guileful urging. He judges this youth worthy of riches and honor, and thinks that the mother should be coaxed by the freeing of her one son. But, that soul already wholly directed toward heaven does not readily accept this counsel from a worldly party. Amid the mother's encouragements, the soul of the intrepid boy is fired the more toward the summit of virtue.

(5) O new and admirable example of virtue! A mother rejoices in her own bereavement, and her love gains profit

from the same source which brought it loss. After she has sent ahead even this son whom she loved so tenderly, she herself enters the way of this glorious death. Pained for a short while by innumerable tortures, she followed her sons in triumph. Despising this short-lived light, she extended her grasp toward heavenly and eternal goods.

Therefore, dearly beloved, if any mother has loving anxiety for the children of her womb, let her imitate the numerous and brave examples this mother has left. If anyone has gazed on her with eagerness to emulate her, without any doubt he makes his way gifted with the honor of far greater glory. Hence, let any mother whatever judge her children worthy of this honor.. After the exhortation about which you have just learned, let her instruct them, that they may learn to observe the prescriptions of the heavenly laws.

Furthermore, let those who serve our Christ imitate the struggles of those brave men. Proof that she loves her sons is given by that mother who has banished the error on which this world relies, and from the fruit of her womb she has given a victim to God, and offered willingly herself and those dear ones whom she was every day to immolate.

In order to obtain the rewards of that heavenly virtue more easily, we should spurn the gifts and honors of this world. They deceive human eyes with their alluring vanity. But this is clearly a sacrifice acceptable to the Lord: to prefer the honor of heaven and to begin to despise the world.

# HOMILY 19

## *The Termination of Lent: A Sermon for Easter Sunday*

(1) Dearly beloved, if we investigate the reason for this present solemnity[1] which gives us hope of eternal salvation through the decree of our future resurrection, it is not improper for us to spend all these days in joy, and thus to temper our recent pursuit of an austerer life. But, in this matter, I sometimes find myself displeased at the crowd of merry-makers for the following reason. Many a person thinks he may now licitly do anything which he had put under that disciplinary control during the time of, Lent.

No one doubts that your preceding devotions only issue in disorder if you do not know how to preserve what you so evidently gained for the purification of your soul by your difficult fasts and vigils. He who is heedless of spiritual duties and gives in to his bodily desires swiftly destroys everything he has acquired. Wherefore it is important to hold fast to that way of religious discipline, even amid the pleasures we mentioned. Without any doubt, that discipline brings a man of good will into favor with the Lord. If we know how to observe toward Him the proper reverence which His laws demand, hell would go without prey, and the penalty of everlasting death would fall on no one.

Therefore, dearly beloved, we should strive with all effort not to indulge in excessive relaxation and spoil our awareness that our body has been purified. We should not be content to keep religiously only those days which our observance of fasting annually brings upon us. Even this observance is evidently distasteful to some because of their excessive

1 That of Easter.

sleeping and insatiable appetite. While making their way toward the day of the Holy Pasch under the urgings of their strong desire, they complain about the observance of vigils, the benefits of continence, the meager meals and the abundant fasts. They do this as if the long-desired festival made licit what the days of Lent forbid, and as if the termination of the fast gave freedom to sin.

(2) Consequently, let no one think that all things are licit for him just because he sees that the time of stricter living has passed. Careless relaxation ordinarily works deception into every state of upright living. A man sees that the appointed termination of the fast has come; let him not infer that some drunkenness is now permitted. Someone sees that with the arrival of this feast the constant vigils have been suspended; let him not think that men's souls have now been directed to somnolence. The servant who waits for holidays merely in order to sleep is not a profitable one.

After a farmer has broken up the earth by his long toil, he must employ still more care. He must keep watch to prevent some presumptuous beast or lurking bird from contemptuously eating the seeds he has planted in the furrows. Next, in his spare time he must dig an ample ditch for water. Otherwise, some sudden storm may kill or wash away his budding sprouts. He must uproot weeds and soften the parched sod by plying his hoe, and then, on those otherwise workless days which farmers seize, he must, by building an encircling fence, keep out any chance destructive animal.

So great is the desire to support life, and the care to be far-sighted, and the diligence to maintain cultivation, that it little befits anyone to be idle even then when the ear and the perfect blossoms are already promising harvests to the farmer. For, even full-grown crops often get hindered by growing thorns; and plants right on the point of maturing frequently get choked by some foreign growth. We must understand that in this way things grow well through the farmer's diligence, but even the greatest perish through his negligence.

(3) Perhaps you object: 'Everybody excuses the heedlessness of a festival.' Without any doubt, the man who at any time surrenders his life to heedlessness is exposed to all dangers. It is never well to give free rein to horses that have been idle. So, too, a luxuriant growth springs out of the earth under the heavy rains which follow the rigor of winter. Likewise, we often observe that sea-going vessels suffer shipwreck when near to port, through some sudden force while the oars are idle.

In the light of these examples, dearly beloved brethren, let us so arrange our life that we banish first of all that extravagance of banquets. In this way we can also cause passing desires of the flesh to leave us.

I am not, because of all this, speaking as if we should refrain extensively from food, or abstain completely from the cups. Even if our bodies have been fashioned for the cross, they should neverthless be sustained. This alone is what displeases me during these days: insatiable appetite, and those purposeless gorgings of the stomach; or a banquet with profuse drunkenness and scoffing all night long.

If someone drinks in excess of his natural thirst, he clearly exceeds the limit of discipline. What remains unwelcome to men who incur not only the vice of drunkenness, but also the impairment of their faculties? Who would bear with those evils of excessive wine-bibbing where the tendency is not so much to drink as to get drunk? Who willingly gazes on the appearance of that dining room in which everything is filthy with the odor of spoiling wine? For, where the wine unmixed with water flows in too much abundance, the entire banquet necessarily takes on an appearance which is frightful with base squalor; and whatever was poured into the full water jug evidently goes to waste.

(4) Therefore, let him who finds his pleasure in drunkenness see what will happen. Let him wisely turn his attention on what we shall say. Then he will without difficulty recognize the cause of his own misfortune.

If you pour too much oil into a vessel, the swirling liquid from the olive harvest wells up to the open brim, and with soiling effects the vessel spills out the excess. Also, as we often see, goatskin containers are spoiled by having too much wine to put in them. Because of the agitated liquids, the potter's wine casks develop cracks. Clearly, death would have nothing offered to it if wretched men knew how to avoid the causes of perishing. He who loads additional burden upon infirm bodies is preparing a road of weakness. Thus, a man burdened by the weight of an excessive pack undertakes and continues a journey with doubtful hope of success.

Therefore, dearly beloved, I give this admonition. If anyone is making arrangements to be pleasing to our Christ, let him first of all check the desires of his appetite. Appetite, abetted by drunkenness, is wont to be a mistress who inflicts injuries. From this source some men get nakedness, beggary, and needy poverty. As Solomon says: 'Every drunkard shall be clothed with rags.'[2]

In contrast, may those fruits of continence endure in those good men who during the days of Lent think it good to serve the Lord continually with devout affection. Otherwise, when we perhaps have surrendered ourselves into the possession of negligence, we may seem to have devoted our pursuit

2 Prov. 23.21.

of an upright life merely to that season, not to our moral improvement.

What does it profit if you display your goodness to the Lord for forty days, and on one day offend Him by a frenzy of wicked cruelty? What good does it do to preserve one's esteem of chastity for many periods of time, if afterwards, under temptation to unchastity, you let yourself be drawn into a base sin? What benefit is there in cheating covetousness for a time if, after garnering such great fruits of mercy from your generous hand, you take delight from other men's losses and tears? Whatever grace a man has acquired by his good works through many years obviously perishes if he is depraved for one hour by deviation to base living.

(5) Wherefore, here is the procedure of preserving disciplinary control: foster your integrity, love chastity, promote peace, check, under the fear of discipline, everything which ministers to iniquity. Thus, a person of lesser quality will not act proudly to a superior, nor will poverty receive scorn when persons are compared.

Just as it is something great to serve one's betters, so is it something profitable and glorious to show reverence to a humbler person. A man endowed with dignity is exalted to the same extent that he is humbled. The Lord's words are: 'Whoever exalts himself shall be humbled and whoever humbles himself shall be exalted.'[3] Thus above all else we should choose the path of humility. It is not beset with grudges, and it always gains much love. The Apostle says: 'God gives grace to the humble, but resists the proud.'[4]

Wherefore, in the case of iniquitous conduct such as we have described, let anyone take thought to hesitate[5] because

3 Matt. 23.11.
4 James 4.6.
5 Reading *dubitare,* with Sirmond.

of the penalty of the future Judgment, when he sees that the punishment of heavenly anger is being threatened against himself. But, if anyone forestalls the anger of heaven by his humility, he will without difficulty find a place to possess forever in heaven. Through the functioning of his pride, the Devil was expelled from that place and received a sentence of everlasting damnation. Therefore, let us practice humility, sobriety, continence, and purity. Let us strive to hold fast to our pursuit of sanctity, that our life may not be shaken with losses to our soul, and never sigh before the Lord because it has been given up to His animosity.

## HOMILY 20

### *Covetousness*

(On 1 Tim. 6.3-10)

(1) Dearly beloved, the physicians who effect cures state that different beneficial medicines are suitable for different aches, and that definite remedies provide their own proper benefits for definite illnesses. Hence they teach that swellings ought to be checked by the knife or softened by a preparation of medicine; that hidden diseases are explored better by means of potions; that cold areas of the body profit from warm remedies, and areas too hot are relieved by cooling measures.

But, in the work of our religious education, I think the case is different. If you review that Epistle written to Timothy you will discover that many illnesses can be cured by the effect of one remedy, or by the cutting off of one wound.

The holy Apostle Paul clearly explained what that wound

is in which so many diseases unite and work their deadly effects. His words are: 'Covetousness is the root of all evils, and some in their eagerness to get rich have strayed from the faith and involved themselves in many troubles.'[1]

Therefore, dearly beloved, we should treat of this: What work and labor should be used to cut down such a great forest of sins? But, first, you ought to recognize one thing as the cause of all the vices which come together from every direction. You should diligently investigate the origin of these single vices, their outcomes, and what deformity or pain they have. For, the greatest hope of recovering one's health lies in knowing the source of one's weakness.

(2) 'Covetousness is the root of all evils.' Truly, dearly beloved, if we look again at the single vices to which men in their present state have prostituted their lives through their desire to possess, there is no one of the evils which covetousness does not conceive, or bring to birth, or feed, or nourish. From this tinder, as we see, spring the flames which cause hatreds. From this source criminal fights arise, and groups engage in fraternal strife, and friendly agreements are broken.

Therefore, let no one lay the blame of his own trouble on any of his own weaknesses. For, although all the vices stand in their own names, they nevertheless lean also on other sins. That is why we see pride concocted from the swollen excess of vanity, and why even every thoroughly humble man is troubled by an infection of arrogance. If by some chance you suddenly glance at him among his equals, you judge him to be someone different from what he was. When he is elated by some remarks, you see him walk with an expanding appearance, his head raised toward the sky. Weighty words from his tongue are opening a road

1 1 Tim. 6.10.

long closed by the benefit which his poverty had conferred upon him. He utters the words from his haughty mouth with so much force that when he wants to speak he will not listen to anyone else. These faults are serious by their own nature; evidently, they get their animation from the allurements of covetousness. In time, the ostentation of riches ceases, and then you do not so easily find one who labors under the hatefulness of pride.

(3) 'Covetousness is the root of all evils.' Let us run through the vices one by one, if this seems good. Then you will learn how great are the evils which sprout from the vice of covetousness.

Look, in many an instance a neighborhood is armed for strife. Why, unless for this, that this man is perhaps planning to expand beyond his own property lines, and preempt someone else's field? Why does he not put that statement before his eyes: 'Pass not beyond the ancient bounds which your fathers have set.'[2]

See, in this neighborhood there occurs first a quarrel about property. While each party is stirring his own covetousness by words, he is enkindling the impulse to fight. Out of the quarrel grows an accusation—and would that this alone were enough for covetousness! That fact is more serious, that, while no one wants to suffer the loss of dropping the malicious charge he has inaugurated, everyone is on the verge of battle. The slaves are being armed, the neighbors are being incited, and one man's breast is exposed for the sake of another man's gain. The hired anger is stirred up by wine, and blood poured out becomes the price which brings possession. Later, a court is opened for the legal processes, and even while the opportunity of gaining revenge is being sought, murder is repeated.

2 Prov. 22.28; cf. Deut. 19.14.

Also, we often see battle lines drawn up because of covetousness, while this man wants to seem richer or that one blushes to be poorer. While they vie with each other, the community of property arising from their being neighboring owners is endangered. One of them is seeking to be the first to invade, and planning to gain possession with immunity. Thus, while one man's covetousness is planning an acquisition, another man's estate is growing insecure.

(4) Why do such men fail to think of this Scriptural statement: 'Thou fool, this night will thy soul be demanded of thee; these things that thou hast provided, whose will they be?'[3] Truly, nothing is more foolish than to seek goods of doubtful value or to acquire those which will perish. For, of what avail to a man are resources which are gathered solely to perish? When you die, the field your avarice acquired surely remains behind. So does your augmented estate. Even it has been passed on to another's ownership, it endures as a testimony of its criminal acquisition. In this connection we should always remember that statement of the Prophet: 'Woe to him who joins farm to farm.'[4]

But, you object: 'I read, "The parents should save up for the children." '[5] From this very statement you can learn what your paternal concern profits you. See, the trappings of your riches pass to another, and the odium of making the invasion[6] remains with you. The splendor of your resources is in the possession of another, and the penalty migrates along with yourself. It is a species of folly to produce gain for others, and prepare torture for one's self. That is what

3 Luke 12.20.
4 Isa. 5.8.
5 2 Cor. 12.14.
6 Conjecturing as the correct reading *pervasionis invidia,* which occurs below in section 6 (*PL* 52.754B) and fits the context, while *persuasionis invidia* does not.

the Apostle tells us: 'Those who seek to become rich fall into temptation and a snare of the devil.'[7]

(5) But, not merely after a long time is the powerful severity in that heavenly statement applied. Somehow, an increase of vices gradually follows and works a revenge for past deeds.

Here, for example, a man of parricidal attitude either threatens his father's life, or awaits his mother's death. Suppose that the thought of the inheritance due to him perhaps keeps him from the crime. That is true. But, although he is a legitimate heir, it is not without the vice of covetousness that he is fostering his desires of succession. He would wish to be the only heir if he could. At one time, he is thinking about his father's death; at another, sighing about his brother's life. All this is not free from a grave sin of filial disloyalty. For, whoever feeds his soul with expectation of a parent's death comes into his inheritance by the crime of parricide.

Here, too, under the instigation of covetousness hatreds are nourished among the fellow heirs. The corpse is not yet carried out, and already the true meaning of the will has been destroyed by an interpretation of law. One man is disputing about the father's signature; another is in despair over the person of a brother. One man affirms[8] that the will is not confirmed by witnesses; another gives as a reason that the will is not consonant with the times.

Thus, the farm is at stake while the cases are argued. What was acquired through the avarice of the parents is lost through the covetousness of the sons. Hear the words of Scripture: 'Thou shalt not covet thy neighbor's posses-

7 1 Tim. 6.9.

8 Here *astruo* does seem to mean 'affirm' despite the doubt cast by Harper's *Latin Dictionary* (1907), *s.v.*

sion.'[9] It is impossible to enumerate all the ways in which covetousness grows fierce. Look, when a will is brought out, immediately there is thought of falsehood. Someone asks: 'Who heard the mute man speaking? What heir knew the dead man while he was making his dispositions?' What is worse, it is not hard for someone to find persons who are associated in his crime or bribed for a price. This unfortunate fellow imitates the signature of another's hand. Thus, covetousness, by a pen often exercised in copying, often produces a document which the testator did not draw up.

(6) 'Covetousness is the root of all evils.' To strengthen his fraud, one man arms his falsehood by perjury, and another sometimes opposes someone else's lawsuits with a corrupted heart. Thus, through the vice of covetousness alone an estate is both gained and rent apart. Where is esteem for what Scripture says: 'A false witness shall not be unpunished'?[10]

To what do we think should be ascribed the fact that even innocent persons are summoned and charged among those whom we sometimes hear participated in crimes? For in an investigation suspicion often arises; when the guilt of theft resides in one man, the odium of making the invasion[11] passes to another. In this way, while an increase of resources is sought, goods rightly acquired are torn apart. The upshot is often a progression from covetousness to falsehood to poverty.

'Covetousness is the root of all evils.' What is the source of this, that we often see armed legions drawn up against each other? What else is it but this, that one party wants

9 Exod. 20.17.
10 Prov. 19.5.
11 Cf. note 6, above.

to seize the possessions of another, or the other is guarding those he has seized? The result is that sometimes a strife arises about the power of command and a fight in the contest for primacy. All these matters would remain in peace if covetousness to command were not removing another man from that office.

(7) 'Avarice is the root of all evils.' Let us inquire: What is responsible for this vice, that a man's life is entrusted to a thin floor of planks, that the uncertainties of the sea are incurred when the results are so doubtful? When a storm arises and the shout of the sailors blames the sea, is not covetousness the cause? When a corpse from a shipwreck is dashed against the sharp rocks, and its water-swollen limbs are tossed on unknown shores by the swells of the sea, does not this add to the reproach of covetousness? Clearly, the sailor would never have entrusted himself to sailing if covetousness for business had not stirred up his desire to travel.

A man voyages over the heaving waves with the desire to quadruple his money. Gold is carried along, that falsehood and perjury combined may be carried back. Trading is never done without fraud when something is bought rather deeply for the sole purpose of retailing it more dearly. In all this, even if the crossing is tranquil and successful, according to men's desires, it is not without a shipwreck when between the buyer and seller someone gains or someone suffers because of unjust weights or measures. Why do these men fail to think about this phrase of Scripture? 'Just as you will have measured, it will be measured out to you.'[12]

(8) Dearly beloved, we blush to speak about those deeds which are carried out under the drive of impurity. Indulgence in this vice springs from covetousness.

Conjugal fidelity often becomes esteemed as something

12 Matt. 7.2.

cheap in comparison with money; virginity long unsullied, prostituted because of a small weight of gold, has given up its own firm promise of integrity. Covetousness is so great with some persons that chastity is put up for sale and finds a price for its own depravity. Thus money is eagerly weighed out for the corruption of a body, just as if something worthy were being purchased. Clearly unfortunate is that man who has more interest in covetousness than in his chastity. To have thrown away one's integrity is to have consigned to loss the grace of the promised inheritance.

See how diverse beneath one species of sin is the activity of covetousness. This man has given money to buy an act of corrupting. The woman has lost her chastity to get the money. As often as sin is committed, nothing is done without covetousness. If you remove your array of jewels, you will suffer no shipwreck of defilment to your body. In brief, let the desire of gold cease. Then, conjugal fidelity does not perish, and virginal integrity does not blush.

(9) 'Avarice is the root of all evils.' One man is accused of treason; another, reproached as the informer of another's crime. Who would doubt that a bribing weight of offered money crept into his inner heart? Clearly, nothing is so enclosed that it does not open up before gold and silver; nothing has been hidden which has not been discovered if money led the way. With danger is a confidence entrusted to the knowledge of those who are under the sway of covetousness. Their integrity indeed would hold the whole secret fast if money did not have an entrance, like a traitress in someone else's house.

'Covetousness is the root of all evil.' Look, our Lord and Saviour underwent the consummation of His voluntary Passion because of another's vice of covetousness. We read that the condemnation of our Redeemer was procured by thirty pieces of silver. Just as you saw that covetousness led to His betrayal, so ought you to recognize that His betrayal led to His condemnation.

The One betrayed was indeed led to the torture, but the betrayer ran to a halter. Behold what fruit covetousness produces! The money which brought His condemnation was stored away for his burial, that is, it was destined for his funeral. Futhermore, understand in what state the fault of covetousness is, since the price of perdition came itself under condemnation. The Apostle Peter says: 'Thy money go to destruction with thee.'[13]

Let there be, perhaps, someone of the foolish and avaricious persons who feels happy over this statement, and who prefers what he hears, that his money is going to migrate along with himself. For our part, we do not subtract anything from his desires. Your money will indeed go with you, not, as you think, to array your body, but to be evidence of your falsehood.

However, this matter does not pertain to those whom mercy accompanies. One judicial process awaits those whose generous disbursements in expending their money on the poor have commended them to the Lord, and another awaits those whose resources stored up through crime are their accusers. That money counts toward their torment, while for the others it brings a kingdom. Thus the Lord speaks: 'Come my children, take possession with me of the kingdom prepared for you from the foundation of the world. I was hungry, and you gave me to eat; I was thirsty and you gave me to drink; naked and you covered me.'[14]

(10) Wherefore, dearly beloved, let each of you be content with that financial state which procures the grace of

13 Acts 8.20.
14 Matt. 11.34-36.

salvation for you, not that which brings on a cause of damnation. Consequently, let us in the first place check covetousness if we wish to overcome the delusion of all vices.

Let no one seek after someone else's possessions; then, no one need suffer the odium of enmity. Let no one rush into what is held in common with another; then, there is no struggle about an invasion. Let each one be content with his own possessions; then, there is no complaint about appropriated ones.

Despise gold; then, the contemplated homicide fades away to nothing. If a covetous eye is restrained, parricidal hatreds are not sown. There is no reason for an heir to blush if he approaches his own moderate portion with content. Let no one seek an increase of his money; then, no one will fall under the guilt of treason. If you do not pursue money, you will suffer no shipwreck in a storm. And when you leisurely take care of the inner portions of your little farm, you will be free from personal anxiety as you gaze on others' danger.

Dearly beloved, to avoid those vices by single measures is perhaps hard, and it is toilsome to meet at once so many foes attacking by different paths. Hence, we should search for some simplification of the warfare. We should seek the leader of the fight, that our struggle can be with him who inflicted the injury. Without doubt, you can conquer legions drawn up in arms if you can get hold of their sovereign. And he who has overcome the originator of a fight has finished off the whole cause of the war.

Let us, therefore, draw up a line of virtues against the serried legions of vices. But, above all, with help from our faith let us fight against that legion which is the head of the war, that is, against covetousness. With that mother of vices captured, it will not be difficult to win the victory over the afore-mentioned disgrace which they cause.

## APPENDIX

### *St. Valerian's Letter to the Monks,*[1] *on the Virtues and Order of the Apostolic Doctrine*

Although I am meanwhile absent from you in body, as it has been written,[2] but present in spirit and thought, I now take up the burden which your good wishes have put upon me. It is not, I think, a small portion of my duty and love that I give in return for your love. I am confident that you, too, act in the spirit and not in the flesh, according to the Apostle: 'They who are carnal cannot please God. You, however, are not carnal but spiritual, if indeed the Spirit of God dwells in you.'[3]

Indeed, I am not following a road unknown to spiritual men if I express my solicitude for your edification through the language of epistolary communications. I have ready at hand that eminent example, St. Paul, whom we desire to follow even if we are unable to imitate him fully. In a comparison with him we indeed find ourselves his equal in nothing. Nevertheless, you should equal the obedience of those men whom he teaches.

That his doctrine may be set forth in the established order, may you desire with the Romans[4] that your faith should be

1 Although we have no solid evidence as to what monks this letter was addressed, they may well have been those of Lerins. The monks of that monastery were very influential in southern Gaul at this period, and it is not unlikely that St. Valerian was once a monk there himself. The writer of this Letter wove something apropos from book after book of the New Testament, so that his letter is a tapestry of allusions. It is worthy of note that the quotations fall into an order which is about the same as the order of Epistles in our Bibles today.

2 1 Cor. 5.3; Col. 2.5.

3 Rom. 8.8,9.

4 Rom. 1.8.

proclaimed all over the world; with the Corinthians[5] may you, as men corrected by means of a second healing, in unbroken peace and unaffected love, greet one another with a holy kiss, as it is written.[6]

With the Galatians,[7] rejecting the observance of months and seasons and days, and repudiating the world and following God, understand that you are sons, not of the slave girl, but of the free woman.

Remaining steadfast in the word of truth, with the Ephesians[8] you should recognize one Lord, one faith, one God the Father of all, who is above all, and throughout all, and in us all.

With the Philippians,[9] being blameless and guileless, doing all things without murmuring and without questioning, may you shine like stars in the midst of a depraved people.

With the Colossians,[10] may you teach one another by psalms, hymns, and spiritual songs while the word of Christ dwells in you abundantly.

With the Thessalonians,[11] strive to do the will of God, while abstaining from impurity, praying without ceasing, testing all things, holding fast those which are good. Next, follow the order of the precept with all diligence, so that, if any man will not work, neither let him eat.[12] For, He is the bread that has come down from heaven,[13] and no one ought to consume it unless he does the works by which He is pleased.

Timothy should be your model. After long use of water,

5 2 Cor. 6.6.
6 1 Cor. 16.20; 2 Cor. 13.12.
7 Gal. 4.10,30,31.
8 Eph. 1.13; 4.5,6.
9 Phil. 2.14,15.
10 Col. 3.16.
11 1 Thess. 4.1,3; 5.17-21.
12 2 Thess. 3.10.
13 John 6.51,59.

he was instructed to use also a little wine to support his stomach,[14] not to overburden it. Even if a man is instructed by double admonitions, unless he keeps sober he will not be able to fulfill his ministry.[15]

The example of Titus[16] should mould your character, in this, that you ought to be not merely sober but also continent, because all things are clean for the clean, but for the defiled and unbelieving nothing is clean.

To sum up: This entire conclusion of the Apostolic doctrine through a mystical number has fulfilled the greatest purification of cleansed body, because nothing is so near to God as the fact that a man is not corrupted.

Next, let us pay a little more attention to what follows. A certain fugitive returns as a servant to his former master, and his state is changed by his conversion.[17] Begotten while the Apostle was in prison,[18] from a useless servant he became a useful one, and not only a brother but one most dear. He surpassed the attainment of his contemporaries in the peak of spiritual development. He earned not merely the bond of becoming named, but also affectionate love. For, through the condescension of the Lord, unsullied chastity nourished by sobriety is developed to this, that what the moderate use of wine cured in the case of Timothy, what abstinence and continence purged out in the case of Titus, that was to grow to a very indulgent freedom in the case of Onesimus.

The learned should carry out all these instructions, and the unlearned should acknowledge them, because, as it is written, ignorance is death,[19] and faith without works is

---

14 1 Tim. 5.23.
15 2 Tim. 4.5.
16 Tit. 1.8,15.
17 Philem. 1-25.
18 Philem. 10.
19 1 Cor. 14.38.

dead.[20] A twofold course of showing observance is incumbent upon you: Care to know, and care to carry into practice with effort. For, it is a sin not only to fail to carry out the deeds commanded in God's revelations, but also to remain ignorant of them.

Finally, taking the Hebrews for an example of consummate perfection, I inculcate contempt of present goods for the love of heavenly rewards. I do this that, if someone perhaps imposes the burden of persecution upon you, or seizes all your possessions, you also may receive, with no less affection toward imitation, that noble and unusual testimonial which Paul uttered from his venerable mouth, in his outstanding praise of those Hebrews. He said with feeling: 'For you both have had compassion on those in prison and have joyfully accepted the plundering of your own goods.'[21]

20 James 2.26.
21 Heb. 10.34.

# *INDEX*

# *INDEX*

www.ingramcontent.com/pod-product-compliance
Lightning Source LLC
Chambersburg PA
CBHW032022290426
44110CB00012B/632
* 9 7 8 0 8 1 3 2 1 3 8 9 7 *